SPEAK, BIRD, SPEAK AGAIN

SPEAK, BIRD, SPEAK AGAIN

PALESTINIAN ARAB FOLKTALES

Ibrahim Muhawi and Sharif Kanaana

University of California Press · Berkeley · Los Angeles · London

University of California Press
Berkeley and Los Angeles, California

University of California Press, Ltd.
London, England

Library of Congress Cataloging-in-Publication Data

Speak, bird, speak again.

Bibliography: p.
Includes index.
1. Tales—Palestine. 2. Palestinian Arabs—Folklore. 3. Folklore literature, Arabic—Palestine—Translations into English. 4. Folk literature, English—Translations from Arabic. I. Muhawi, Ibrahim, 1937– . II. Kanaana, Sharif.
GR285.S64 1988 398.2'095694 88-4832
ISBN 0-520-05863-1 (alk. paper)
ISBN 0-520-06292-2 (pbk. : alk. paper)

Printed in the United States of America
2 3 4 5 6 7 8 9

The paper used in this publication meets the minimum requirements of American National Standard for Information Sciences—Permanence of Paper for Printed Library Materials, ANSI Z39.48-1984. ♾

The Publishers wish to express their gratitude to Joan Palevsky for her most generous contribution to the publication of this book.

Contents

Sexual Awakening and Courtship

The Quest for the Spouse

Group II · *Family*

Brides and Bridegrooms

Husbands and Wives

Family Life

Group III · *Society*

Group IV · *Environment*

Group V · *Universe*

Foreword

It was with great pleasure that I watched a joint collaborative effort between a man of letters and a social scientist come to fruition. The marvelous results of this partnership lie in the pages ahead. Not only are there forty-five splendid Palestinian Arab folktales to be savored, but we are also offered a rare combination of ethnographic and literary glosses on details that afford a unique glimpse into the subtle nuances of Palestinian Arab culture. This unusual collection of folktales is destined to be a classic and will surely serve as a model for future researchers in folk narrative.

For the benefit of those readers unfamiliar with the history of folktale collection and publication, let me explain why *Speak, Bird, Speak Again: Palestinian Arab Folktales* represents a significant departure from nearly all previous anthologies or samplers of folktales. When the Grimm brothers collected fairy tales, or *Märchen,* from peasant informants in the first decades of the nineteenth century, they did so in part for nationalistic and romantic reasons: they wanted to salvage what they regarded as survivals of an ancient Teutonic heritage, to demonstrate that this culture was the equal of classical (Greek and Roman) as well as prestigious modern (French) cultures. The publication of *Kinder- und Hausmärchen* in 1812 and 1815 sparked a host of similar collections of fairy tales from other countries by scholars imbued with the same combination of nationalism and romanticism. By the end of the nineteenth century, numerous folklore societies and periodicals had been initiated to further the collection and analysis of all types of traditional peasant art, music, and oral literature.

Unfortunately, despite the laudable stated aims of these pioneering collectors to preserve unaltered the precious folkloristic art forms of the local peasantry, all too often they actually rewrote or otherwise manipulated the materials so assiduously gathered. One reason for this intrusiveness was the longstanding elitist notion that literate culture was infinitely superior to illiterate culture. Thus the oral tales were made to conform to the higher canons of taste found in written literature, and oral style was replaced by literary convention. The Grimms, for example, began to combine different versions of the "same" folktale, producing composite texts which they presented as authentic—despite the fact that no raconteur had ever told them in that form.

The Grimms and their imitators were trying to create a patrimony for purposes of national pride (long before Germany was to become a nation in the modern sense), and tampering with oral tradition suited their goals. Texts that are rewritten, censored, simplified for children, or otherwise modified may well be enjoyed by readers conditioned to the accepted literary stylistics of so-called high culture. Such texts, however, are of negligible scientific value. If one wishes to understand peasant values and thought patterns, one needs contact with peasant folktales, not the prettified, sugar-coated derivatives reworked by dilettantes.

Sad to say, the vast majority of nineteenth- and even twentieth-century folktale collections fail to meet the minimum criteria of scientific inquiry. The tales are typically presented with no cultural context or discussion of their meaning (we do not even know if their tellers were male or female), and rarely is a concerted attempt made to compare a particular corpus of tales with other versions of the same tale types. Let the reader think back on folktale anthologies he or she may have read, as either a child or an adult. How many of these standard collections of folktales contained any scholarly apparatus linking the content of particular tales to the cultures from which they came? Appallingly, these criticisms apply even to collections of folktales published by reputable folklorists. The highly regarded *Folktales of the World* series, published by the University of Chicago Press, for example, includes volumes of bona fide folktales from many countries, but the tales are accompanied by only minimal comparative annotation. The reader may be informed that a given folktale is identifiable as an instance of an international tale type (as defined by the Aarne-Thompson typology, available since 1910), but little or no information is given on how the tales reflect, let us say, German, Greek, or Irish culture as a whole. This criticism applies as well to most folktale anthologies published in other countries.

Another reason for the inadequacy of nineteenth-century folktale collections, especially those representing countries outside Europe, is that the collectors were typically not from the place where the tales were told. English, French, German, and other European colonialist administrators, missionaries, and travelers recorded stories they found quaint or amusing. Either informants self-censored the tales to protect their image or else the collectors, who were not necessarily fully fluent in the native languages, simply omitted details they deemed obscene (by their own cultures' standards) or elements that were not altogether clear to them. Thus most nineteenth-century collections of tales from India or the Middle East contain only the blandest tales, sometimes in severely abridged or abstract form, with no hint of even the slightest bawdy or risqué motifs. Although folklorists today are not ungrateful for these early versions of folktales, they cannot condone the lack of honesty in the reporting of them. What remains badly needed are collections of folktales made by fieldworkers whose roots are in the region and who speak the native language of the taletellers.

In the present volume we have two scholars with the requisite expertise. Ibrahim Muhawi was born in 1937 in Ramallah, Palestine (nine miles north of Jerusalem). After completing high school at the Friends Boys' School in Ramallah, he went to the United States where, in 1959, he earned a B.S. in electrical engineering at Heald Engineering College in San Francisco. Then came a dramatic shift of intellectual gears, with a B.A. (magna cum laude) in English from California State University at Hayward (1964), followed quickly by an M.A. (1966) and a Ph.D. (1969), both also in English, from the University of California, Davis. After teaching English at Brock University in St. Catharines, Ontario, Canada (1969–1975), and at the University of Jordan in Amman (1975–1977), Muhawi joined the English department at Birzeit University in the West Bank, where he served as department chairman from 1978 to 1980. It was there that he met the coauthor of this book.

Sharif Kanaana was born in ʿArrābe in the Galilee, Palestine, in 1935, and he too received his higher education in the United States. Following a 1965 B.A. in psychology and economics from Yankton College in South Dakota, he transferred to the University of Hawaii where he was awarded an M.A. (1968) and doctorate (1975) in anthropology. After teaching anthropology at the University of Wisconsin–Oshkosh for four years (1972–1975), he became chairman (1975–1980) of the sociology department at Birzeit University, and from 1980 to 1984 he was affiliated with An-Najah National University, West Bank, as dean of the Faculty of Arts (1980–1982) and acting president of the university (1982–1984). In 1984 he became the director of the Birzeit University Research and Documentation Center.

In 1978, when Muhawi was teaching modern poetry, Shakespeare, and composition courses at Birzeit University, he was reintroduced to a rich tradition of Palestinian folklore through the pages of a locally published journal, *Heritage and Society* (Al-turāth wa-al-mujtamaʿ). Although he had grown up with this tradition, his formal education first in engineering and later in English literature had not led him to seriously consider it as an object of study. Now, however, he began to remember his childhood when he would seek out and avidly listen to the tales of the best raconteurs in the town of Ramallah.

During this time, Sam Pickering of the University of Connecticut, a former Fulbright Scholar at the University of Jordan and a colleague of Muhawi, assumed the editorship of *Children's Literature*. He wrote to Muhawi asking for illustrations of Palestinian traditions. Muhawi approached Sharif Kanaana, whom he knew as an advisory editor of *Heritage and Society* and as author of several papers on Palestinian folklore that had appeared in that journal. He discovered that Kanaana had already collected a substantial sampling of Palestinian folktales, and when he heard the oral renditions on tape he was spellbound by their esthetic quality and expressive power. The two scholars decided to pool their talents and collect, from throughout Palestine, as many types of tales from as wide a range of raconteurs as possible.

Collecting the tales proved to be only the first step. Transcribing and translating the tales took many, many hours of arduous, meticulous work. Then, to make the tales intelligible to readers unfamiliar with Palestinian society, Muhawi and Kanaana elected to prepare a comprehensive yet succinct cultural overview with special emphasis on family dynamics. The ethnographic portrait provided in the introductory essay is a remarkable achievement, and it certainly facilitates a better understanding of the tales that follow. The relationships and tensions between generations, siblings, in-laws, and males and females are lucidly delineated. The anthropological influence is also felt in the very organization and sequential order of the tales, which move from the concerns of childhood through the life cycle to the intricate details of marriage arrangement and beyond. The anthropological bias, however, is always balanced by attention to literary topics; the poetics of opening and closing formulas, for example, are discussed in depth, and careful comparative annotations relate these tales to other Arabic folktales as well as to the international folktale scholarship in general.

This extraordinary combination of anthropological and literary expertise has achieved a set of exquisite folktales, translated accurately, sensitively, and lovingly, together with a dazzling array of ethnographic and folkloristic notes providing a landmark entrée into Palestinian Arab ethos and worldview. I am not sure either of the coauthors could have written this volume alone. It is precisely because such close attention was paid to the concerns of the humanist and the social scientist alike that this collection of folktales is so special.

This collection is important for yet another, political reason. These tales belong to a people, the Palestinian Arabs. Whatever one's view is of the establishment of the state of Israel in 1948, it cannot be denied that the event caused considerable dislocation and fragmentation of the Palestinian Arab people. It is somewhat analogous to the colonial powers in earlier times claiming territory which was already occupied. It is perhaps a tragic irony of history that the Jews, who themselves have been forced by bigotry and prejudice to wander from country to country seeking even temporary sanctuary, have through the formation of a "homeland" caused another people to become homeless. Although this complex issue has engendered great emotion on all sides, one fact is beyond dispute: there was once an area of the world called Palestine, where the Arab inhabitants had—and have—a distinctive culture all their own. It is that culture that is preserved so beautifully in the magical stories contained in this volume. In this context, all people, regardless of political persuasion, should be able to appreciate the value of these magnificent folktales: as oral products of the creative spirit of the human mind, they belong not just to the Palestinian Arab community but to all humankind.

Some readers may choose not to refer to the scholarly apparatus, preferring instead to enjoy only the tales themselves, but scholars will surely be grateful for the thoughtful notes and "afterwords" the authors have provided. I have repeatedly heard literary folklorists claim that the fairy tale genre is dead. These misguided academics continue to pore over such purely literary collections as the *Arabian Nights* or the celebrated collections of Perrault and the Grimms, not realizing that the fairy tale is alive and well in the modern world. This collection of Palestinian Arab folktales includes a great many fairy tales (i.e., Aarne-Thompson tale types 300–749), and they provide eloquent testimony that the fairy tale still flourishes. Such tales, I have little doubt, will be told as long as birds sing!

Alan Dundes
Berkeley, California

Acknowledgments

Every book is a collective effort and this one, even more than most, is no exception. The authors are happy to acknowledge the contribution of the following individuals and organizations to the completion of this book.

First and foremost, of course, our thanks are due to the women and men from whom the tales were collected—those for whom we have names as well as those for whom we do not. For initial encouragement to proceed toward publication, we are grateful to Dr. Sam Pickering. For help during the long evenings in the village of Birzeit, where we sat hammering out rhymes and discussing the proper level of formality for the translation, we wish to thank Donna Bothen and Terrance Cox. For his advice on specific matters relating to Palestinian and Arab culture, and for his general concern over the welfare of the project and his unstinting support of it throughout, we wish to thank Dr. Osama Doumani.

Thanks are also due to our colleagues at the University of California, Berkeley, for their invaluable support and encouragement. We are grateful to Dr. Bridget Connelly and Dr. Laurence Michalak for their comments on the first draft of the Introduction. For the generous contribution of her time in discussing certain aspects of the transliteration, we thank Barbara DeMarco. Dr. John R. Miles deserves our deepest gratitude for his unflagging support of the project from the moment he read the first draft of the tales in 1980. And to Professor Alan Dundes, for his enthusiasm about the work, his encouragement during difficult moments, and his guidance in folkloristic matters, we wish to express our most sincere appreciation.

For a very fruitful professional association, we thank also the Center for Middle Eastern Studies at Berkeley and its staff (Dr. Ira Lapidus, Chairman; Dr. Laurence Michalak, Coordinator), as well as Dr. William Hickman, who originally invited Ibrahim Muhawi to become an associate of the Center. In particular, we are grateful to the Center for the postdoctoral fellowship awarded Dr. Muhawi in 1983.

For their financial support, the authors would also like to thank the following organizations: the American Palestine Educational Fund (now the Jerusalem Fund); the Ford Foundation; the American Federation of Ramallah, Palestine; and the Kayali Scholarship Fund.

The authors also wish to express our deep appreciation to the editorial staff of the University of California Press for their excellent and dedicated guidance.

Finally, we wish to single out Jane Muhawi, who, more than any other individual, made a significant contribution to this book. Without her encouragement, editorial skills, and native ear, this book would not be what it is.

Note on Transliteration

The system adopted in this book for transliterating the Palestinian dialect follows the guidelines established by the *Zeitschrift für arabische Linguistik,* articulated in *Handbuch der arabischen Dialekte,* by Fischer and Jastrow, two editors of that journal. Readers are referred to the grammatical discussion in Chapter 10 of that work ("Das syrisch-palästinenische Arabische") and to the examples provided in Section VII immediately following the chapter.

The list of characters used for transliterating the Palestinian dialect phonemically is as follows:

ء	ʾ	خ	x	ش	š	غ	ġ	ن	n
ب	b	د	d	ص	ṣ	ف	f	ه	h
ت	t	ذ	ḏ	ض	ḍ	ق	q	و	w
ث	ṯ	ر	r	ط	ṭ	ك	k	ى	y
ج	j	ز	z	ظ	ẓ	ل	l		
ح	ḥ	س	s	ع	ʿ	م	m		

Short vowels are represented as *a, e, i, o,* and *u,* and long ones as *ā, ē, ī, ō,* and *ū;* diphthongs are rendered *aw* and *ay.*

Because an apostrophe, or hamza, before an initial vowel indicates glottalization, readers should note that the absence of this apostrophe is itself a phonetic marker indicating elision of that word-initial vowel with the final consonant of the preceding word. Furthermore, in the transcription of Tale 10 (Appendix A) only the definite article is hyphenated, whereas in the smaller pieces of discourse included elsewhere in the book hyphenation is used somewhat more extensively.

Key to References

All references to works are keyed to the Bibliography. In the footnotes to the tales, book and article titles are shortened for ease of use. The Folkloristic Analysis following the tales proper utilizes even more abbreviated forms, as explained in the introduction to that section.

The following abbreviations have been used for the names of journals:

JPOS	*Journal of the Palestine Oriental Society,* Jerusalem
PEQ	*Palestine Exploration Quarterly,* London
TM	*Al-turāth wa-al-mujtamaᶜ*, Al-Birah, West Bank
TS	*Al-turāth al-shaᶜbī,* Baghdad

In footnotes, Roman numerals always indicate volume number, whether for a book or a journal article. Arabic numerals *preceding* a colon indicate the issue number of the journal being cited, in references for which this information is essential. Arabic numerals *following* a colon always indicate page references.

Introduction

The Tales

The forty-five tales included in this volume were selected on the basis of their popularity and the excellence of their narration from approximately two hundred tales collected on cassette tapes between 1978 and 1980 in various parts of Palestine—the Galilee (since 1948 part of the state of Israel), the West Bank, and Gaza. The criterion of popularity reflects our intention to present the tales heard most frequently by the majority of the Palestinian people. Both our own life-long familiarity with this material and the opinions of the raconteurs themselves helped us to assess a tale's popularity. We made a point of asking the tellers to narrate the tales heard most often in folktale sessions of the past, and in most cases we selected only those tales for which we had more than one version. In the few cases where variants were not available (e.g., Tale 44), excellence of narration was the determining criterion, as it was in choosing a version (always taken as a whole and without modification) from among the available variants.

In this collection we have included only the type of tale known in the Palestinian dialect as *ḥikāye* or *xurrafiyye*—that is, "folktale" proper. With such terms as *Märchen, wonder tale,* and *fairy tale* all used to designate the kind of narrative under discussion here, the word *folktale* almost defies definition. The Arabic terms, however, provide us with helpful clues. The first, *ḥikāye* (which, correctly translated, means "tale"), is derived from a root that means not only "to narrate" but also "to imitate (artistically)." Hence the designation *ḥikāye* puts the emphasis on the mimetic, or artistic, aspect of narration, whereas *xurrafiyye* (properly translated, "fabula") is derived from a root stressing its "fabulous," or "fictitious," aspect. (The term *xurrafiyye,* we must note, is the more inclusive of the two, for it is also used to refer not only to folktales but to other types of fictional oral narrative as well.)

This "fabulous" element in folktales has doubtless led the community to consider them a form of *kizib* or "fantasy" or "fiction" (literally, "telling lies"). And in fact it was by recourse to such a label as "a tale that is all lies from beginning to end" (as in the last episode of Tale 37) that we most frequently elicited the type of material we sought. The other designation used to obtain them, *ḥikāyāt ʿajāyiz* ("old women's tales"), has major implications for our understanding of this genre, for it clearly indicates that society considers the telling of these tales to be a woman's art form. Of the seventeen tellers included here, only three are men.

In all likelihood there is a direct relationship between the first label ("all lies") and the second ("old wives' tales"). To the extent that the tales are thought to consist of lies, adult men tend to shun them, even though the vast majority of these men were exposed to them repeatedly as children. And to the extent that they are "old wives' tales," folktales are perceived by men as being somehow silly, their telling an activity fit only for women and children. The fabulous element in folktales lends them an air of improbability and unreality. A man who likes to listen to and tell folktales (in other words, an active male carrier) is considered to be a *niswanjī,* or one who prefers the company of women to that of men. In their gatherings (*dīwān*), men prefer to listen to epic stories (*sīra*), like that of Abū Zēd il-Hilālī, which is frequently sung to the accompaniment of the *rabāba* (single-stringed instrument with a flat sound box made of wood and goat skin). They also like to hear tales of Bedouin raids (*ġazw*) and adventure (*muġāmarāt*). These, collectively, are known as *qiṣṣa* (stories). Their content appears more realistic. It is not necessarily thought that the events described in them actually happened, only that they could have happened. The heroes of these stories, especially if they have a historical basis, are thought to have lived just yesterday and their conduct is considered exemplary.

Another major difference between folktales (*ḥikāye*) and stories (*qiṣṣa*) that hinges on the gender of the narrator lies in the manner of delivery. Because most folktale tellers are women, their narration involves little gesticulation or physical movement. The performance aspect of telling tales is minimized, with the tellers relying on their voices and the power of the colloquial language to evoke a response. The tales told in the *dīwān,* in contrast, may involve a considerable amount of physical movement and acting out of the narrative. The distinction is especially apparent in cases where one person tells both types of story. For example, Šāfiʿ, one of our best tellers (see "The Tellers," below), in performing to a male audience in the *dīwān,* would often jump up from his chair and try to act out the narrative, whereas in telling folktales he remained seated and hardly moved at all. Folktales thus offer their tellers a greater potential for linguistic expression than do epic stories. They are told from memory, and their language, though poetic in itself, is still the language of prose and the speaking voice. The tellers are free to give linguistic shape to the tale, to tell it in their own way, even though they cannot change its form. The stories narrated in the *dīwān,* unlike folktales, are frequently in the measured language of poetry, which must be recited rather than spoken, sometimes even with the aid of a printed text.

The Palestinian folktale is a highly developed art form. Its style, though not artificial, follows linguistic and literary conventions that set it apart from other folk narrative genres. It relies on verbal mannerisms and language flourishes not used in ordinary conversation, especially by men. Women were largely responsible for developing this style, and they carry on the tradition. To sound credible, men who tell these tales must adopt the narrative style of women. Šāfiᶜ, for example, was reluctant at first to admit that he knew folktales. He wanted to narrate the tales of romance and adventure preferred by men at the *dīwān.* We therefore had to tape several hours of these romantic tales before he consented to tell folktales. The art of the narrators consists in their ability to use creatively the narrative style received from tradition. Folktale style matures with age, and it is not surprising that the majority of tellers represented here were over sixty years of age when the tales were recorded (a fact also perhaps indicating that the Palestinian folktale tradition is dying out; more on this below). The cultural significance of old women's dominant role in folktale narration is not to be underestimated. As we shall see, women in their maturity are at the apogee of their authority in the society.

Folktales, moreover, are told in a special setting that distinguishes them not only from the stories recited in the men's *dīwān* but also from other types of folk narrative current in the society. Among these are tales illustrating proverbs (*maṯal*), describing a rare event (*nahfe, nādre*), or recreating a past occurrence (*sālfe*); animal fables (*ḥikāyet ḥayawān*); jinn tales (*ḥikāyet jān*), saints' legends (*ḥikāyet wilī*); myths (*usṭūra*); and memorates (*muġāmara*). A good illustration of the last category occurs at the end of Tale 42, where the men are sitting around on their side of the tent exchanging stories. These forms of narrative do not require a special setting for their telling. They are occasional and come up by chance in the course of ordinary conversation, when someone might say, "This reminds me of . . . ," and then proceed to tell the appropriate story. The narration over, normal conversation resumes. These stories are rarely told for their own sake, as folktales are, but are usually used to illustrate a point, offer subtle recommendation concerning behavior, or volunteer a different perspective on a subject.

The settings in which the folktales presented here were recorded generally resembled the authentic folktale settings of the past, except for the presence of the tape recorder. The tales were all recorded at the homes of the tellers in the presence of a small audience, usually consisting of the collector and members of the teller's family. Occasionally children would be present, influencing thereby the course of the narration. Other than providing appreciative responses and asking the occasional question about unfamiliar words or expressions, the collector played a largely neutral role. Once a session began, tellers usually volunteered tales of their own accord. At the end of each telling, the collector thanked the teller, saying, "God save your tongue!" Although it was not difficult to locate tellers, it was not always easy to get the material we were seeking (as in the case of Šāfiᶜ).

In the past, folktales were told for entertainment, usually after supper during winter evenings, when work in the fields was at a minimum and people were indoors with time on their hands. During the summer there were likely to be other forms of entertainment or subjects for conversation, such as weddings and festive occasions, and folktales were not told. The most common setting for taletelling was the small family gathering, consisting of two or three mothers from a single extended family and their children, combined perhaps with a neighbor or two and their children. Although men were occasionally present at these sessions, they preferred to spend their time in the company of other men at the *dīwān*. Large gatherings and formal visits are not appropriate settings for the telling of tales, which requires a relaxed and spontaneous atmosphere, free from the constraints imposed by the rules of hospitality.

Telling these folktales, then, is a social activity, part of a culture that puts heavy emphasis on the oral tradition and verbal ability and where conversation is valued for its own sake. People do not go visiting expressly to hear folktales, but rather because they enjoy each other's company and like to sit around in the evening chatting (*sahra*). They go where conversation is good, and the evenings entertaining. (The house of Šāfiᶜ is popular because both he and his wife are good conversationalists and storytellers.) At these small, intimate, family gatherings people casually drift into telling folktales. Someone might say, "Tell us a tale!" and if the mood is right a session begins. Usually the oldest woman present is deferred to. If she knows a tale and wishes to tell it, she will proceed with an opening formula such as "Testify there is no god but God!" When she finishes, she pronounces a closing formula, and someone else will take a turn. (Not all the tales in this collection, it should be noted, begin with an opening formula or end with a closing one. The closer a recording session came to duplicating an actual folktale setting, the more likely the tellers were to pronounce the formulas.)

The opening formula creates an air of expectation as the session unfolds. A casual evening's visit turns into an esthetic occasion for the duration of the telling. The atmosphere is aided by the dim light of an oil lamp or a kerosene lantern and by the attitude of the audience, who huddle around a clay brazier (*kānūn*) warming their hands over the embers. In modern times the experience of a folktale session would be equivalent to going to the cinema. The introductory formula ushers the audience into a space radically different from the space outside. Darkness, light, and shadow help shape the experience, as does the modulation in the teller's voice. Once begun, the tale is narrated straight through to the end. Long interruptions are not appreciated, nor would it be permissible for someone else to start another tale. The continuity of narrative time is essential, allowing the element of fantasy in the tales to take over the listeners' imaginations and help them break from ordinary experience. The audience are encouraged to suspend their disbelief until the closing formula brings them back to the world of everyday reality.

For such a setting, a special style and narrative attitude are necessary. The style imitates the speech patterns of ordinary conversation (we recall the root meaning of *ḥikāye,* "tale," as "to speak"), and the narrative attitude reflects beliefs about magic and the supernatural that Palestinian society attributes more readily to women than to men. For men in general, not only is the fictional world of the tales something of a lie, but the manner of speech required to bring it into being sounds artificial as well. Folktale style depends on a variety of devices to put the action into the realm of fiction, whereas the story style preferred by men tends to emphasize historicity. The fact that the most common opening formula (*waḥdū l-lāh,* "Testify that God is One!") is a kind of invocation to dispel the influence of jinn and ghouls would seem to indicate that the telling of folktales is a magical process involving the aid of powers whose influence must be neutralized before the narrative even begins. It would, for example, be totally inappropriate for someone to interrupt an ordinary conversation with an opening formula and then proceed to tell a folktale. The gap between the domains of life and fiction must remain absolute.

Among other devices of style that help to maintain this distance—and which audiences expect in a successful narration—are the frequent threefold repetitions, a passive manner of delivery, and a reliance on verbal mannerisms and flourishes that are more characteristic of women's speech than of men's. Threefold repetition (which is certainly not unique to the Palestinian folktale) lends an air of unreality to the events, as though an action were not valid until ritualistically repeated three times. Three is a magic number in many cultures, and in the tales its power works at the level not only of action but also of sentence structure. The most frequent syntactic pattern in all the tales is the parallel sentence with three verbs ("She reached out her hand, took the ring, and bolted the door again"), reflecting the paratactic pattern of narration in the tale as a whole. Absence of gesture removes visual stimulus, throwing listeners back on the expressive power of language. Finally, the verbal flourishes and mannerisms derived from women's speech give the tales their particular character and are to be found in every tale without exception, even in those narrated by men. Those encountered most frequently in this volume include exclamatory interjections of all sorts (e.g., "Far be it from the listeners!"—*bᶜīd ᶜan is-sāmᶜīn*—when a socially odious subject is mentioned) and the forms of address used by women among each other ("O you whose face has been smeared with soot!"—*yā mšaḥḥara*).

Thus we see that the tale creates a time and space set apart from the rest of life in which events and transformations, because they have no equivalent in experience, can be understood only by the imagination and not by rational thought. The narrative attitude appropriate to folktales must somehow present the possibility of magical transformation as though it were an ordinary event, yet still allow the narrator to remain skeptical. Tellers frequently interject remarks such as "If the tale is to be trusted!" (an alienating device in the Brechtian sense) to remind listeners that the tale is, after all, a fiction. In this manner the narrative attitude identifies the elements of a possible fictional world but distances it from experience. For example, because merely to mention the jinn in narrative time (that is, while the tale is being told) could bring them into being, the narrator must avoid this possibility by invoking the name of Allah. This in fact is another verbal mannerism of women: mention of the jinn (who occur frequently in the tales) is immediately followed by the formula, "In the name of Allah, the Compassionate, the Merciful!"

Although the folktales told in the type of setting just described are not specifically children's tales, the presence of children in the audience is essential to the whole activity. One would never find grown men and women telling folktales just to one another. Of course, adults, including the men, enjoy the tales and are usually on hand during a session, but it is the presence of children that shapes the event, affecting the manner of delivery and helping to create a sense of anticipation during which anything can happen. The tales in any case appeal to the children, who, more easily than the adults, can imagine the jinn, ghouls, and other supernatural beings that abound in them. These are frightening creatures, which mothers frequently use in warning ("You'd better behave, or the ghoul will devour you!"). The presence of the adults at these sessions, especially the mothers, is therefore reassuring to the children, and the whole process helps to socialize and imbue them with the values of the culture.

Folktale sessions do not go on for long hours into the night, partly because the fellahin go to bed early but also because a natural rhythm, or span of attention, exists beyond which telling and listening become tedious. The length of a session is determined by the audience and the mood. If adults outnumber the children, the tales are likely to be more serious; with more children, shorter and more humorous stories are likely to be told. If people feel bored, or if there is an interruption from the outside, the session will come to an end. At any rate it rarely lasts longer than the time it would take to narrate four or five tales. Spontaneity is essential.

The Palestinian folktale is part of the Arabic folk narrative tradition. The tales are told in the Palestinian dialect, with its two major divisions of *fallāḥi* (village speech) and *madanī* (city speech). Most of the tales included here were narrated by villagers only because tellers were more available in the villages, where the tendency to preserve folk traditions is today much greater than in the cities. In times past, however, the folktale tradition was as popular in cities as in villages, perhaps even more so since city dwellers had more leisure time compared with peasants, who were tied to the cycle of the seasons. City dwellers tend to be more polished in their use of language than villagers, and they are less likely to hold the variety of folk beliefs exhibited by village tellers.

The tradition, as we have noted, is carried on mostly by older women in a household setting, but it is not unusual for girls and prepubescent boys to tell tales to one another or to their younger brothers and sisters for practice or pleasure. When going visiting, for example, parents will sometimes tempt their younger children to stay at home with promises of tales from their older brothers and sisters. Once puberty is reached, however, the boys will stop telling the tales; they now want to be regarded as men, who consider the telling of folktales a womanly, household activity, one intimately connected with the rearing of children. Before radio and television, folktales were the main form of entertainment for the young during the evenings. They were universally popular throughout the country, and there are very few Palestinians over the age of forty who have not heard them on at least one occasion. Their preservation up to the present day attests to this popularity.

Tellers have little room to improvise. Their function, as the audience understands it, is to give the tale its due by narrating it with all the stylistic devices and verbal flourishes at their command, but they may not change any of the details. Despite this expectation on the part of the audience, however, variation does arise (and necessarily so, for without variation the folktale traditions of the world would have ossified and died out long ago). Narrative details, or folk motifs, can fit into more than one plot context, and it would be surprising if different motifs were not woven into the same tale. The important consideration here, however, is not how variation comes into being—a thorny theoretical question in any case—but what the attitudes of tellers and audience toward that variation are. If a teller should narrate a tale with details different from the ones the audience knows, she will never claim originality but will always say she is telling it the way she remembers it. Or she might say she knows two versions of the tale and has decided to tell one rather than the other. Both explanations are acceptable to the audience. In this manner, once a new motif enters a tale it becomes a part of it, particularly for those hearing it for the first time.

The folktale tradition we have been describing falls within the context of the extended family and forms part of the social life of a settled and flourishing peasant community. With the recent displacement of the Palestinian people, the social and geographic bases for the tradition have been severely disrupted. Certainly, the frequency of taletelling sessions has declined markedly, and with the people's continued dispersal the chances that the tradition will survive are dim. Modern, educated Palestinian parents are more likely to read than tell tales to their children, and the tales they do read are frequently European ones translated into Modern Standard Arabic. Because, as we have said, the colloquial language is itself an essential aspect of the experience of the tale, the children of today are not hearing the same tales their parents did.

Yet in spite of the odds against it, the tradition still survives. Grandmothers in the villages and refugee camps still tell the tales to the children, and young people interested in the tradition do become active carriers. One of the tellers included in this volume is a twenty-two-year-old woman from the West Bank (Tale 31).

The Tellers

There is nothing unusual about the seventeen tellers from whom the tales were collected. They do not think of themselves primarily as taletellers, nor do they feel they have a special ability. They are all householders, the great majority (fourteen) being housewives who can neither read nor write. Only two of them live in a city (Gaza and Jerusalem); the others have lived in villages all their lives. To introduce readers to the life circumstances of the tellers, we have chosen to focus on those among them who have given us the largest number of tales. Knowledge of their circumstances will help us understand the tales they have told.

Fāṭme (Tales 1, 9, 11, 23, 24, 26, 36, 38, 43), fifty-five years old when these tales were collected, is a housewife who lives in the village of ʿArrābe in the Galilee, next door to her father's family. Married to her (patrilateral parallel) first cousin, she has never lived more than twenty yards from the house of her birth. She has given birth to twenty live children, eleven of whom have survived. A passive carrier of the tradition, she does not normally tell tales, nor is she known in the village as a teller. When she did consent to tell some tales, she was apologetic because she could not remember details quickly enough. Not being literate or a regular teller, she was not entirely comfortable using the flourishes that enhance the style of the tales. She apologized frequently when using them, saying that was the way she had heard them from her mother. Nevertheless, she is a good conversationalist and, in spite of all her apologies, told the tales well.

The presence of the collector's children, who were hearing these tales for the first time, was a great help in drawing the material from her. She would not have told the tales straight into the cassette machine, or to an audience composed only of adults. The children made her feel it was not a serious matter, and, not surprisingly, most of the tales she related are those that could be considered "children's tales." Enjoying the telling, she laughed along with the children at the funny spots; the relaxed mood no doubt colored her choice of material, for her tales are among the most humorous in the entire corpus. (A good teller in a natural taletelling situation, it must be noted, would normally not break the spell of narration so frequently, commenting on the action and laughing with the audience. She would give the tale its due by telling it as it should be told, leaving the rest to the audience.)

Šāfiʿ, in contrast, is an active carrier of the tradition, that is, one of four or five in any village community who show an intense personal interest in preserving and transmitting the practice. Because he has a good memory, his repertoire is large, and he is always seeking to increase it. He differs from most other active carriers in being male and in having learned to read simple texts. He therefore has access to the material from the Arabic oral tradition available in print, such as the epic story (*sīra*) of Abū Zēd il-Hilālī and tales from the *Thousand and One Nights,* which have left an indelible mark on his work. Indeed, he at times had recited parts of the epic stories, performing them to an audience of friends at his home in ʿArrābe (Galilee).

These few facts tell us a great deal about his tales (5, 8, 10, 15, 25, 44), which most resemble the type of adventure tale available in print. At age sixty-five, he is a mature teller. His sense of plotting and double-plotting is superb, and his narrative style is highly polished. The actions in his tales evolve logically, and the transitions are natural; there is none of the clumsiness in delivery or forgetfulness of detail that collectors sometimes encounter. Having been a shepherd and a plowman all his life, he has direct knowledge of the land and its contours and of the details of the husbandman's daily life. The material culture of the Palestinian peasant is open to our gaze in his tales, as are human virtues and vices. Being an experienced teller, he was able to pace himself, filling approximately one side of a sixty-minute cassette for each of his tales.

His wife, Almāza (Tales 14, 18, 37), is also an active carrier of the tradition. She has told stories all her life, enjoys telling them, and prides herself on knowing many. Unlike Fāṭme, who has heard tales from only one source (her mother), Almāza has heard them from a wide variety of sources. She was in her late fifties when her tales were collected.

At age sixty-five, Im Nabīl (Tales 17, 19, 28, 30, 39) lived with her son in the village of Turmusʿayya (district of Ramallah) when we collected her tales. Like most of the other tellers, she could not read or write, but she knew many tales—long ones, short ones, humorous ones, tales of adventure, and "tales for children." In some respects she is the archetypal old woman, the repository of old wives' tales. Because she had not told the tales in a long time, her narration was not always fluent; she halted frequently, recalling details. Nevertheless, her delivery was authoritative, and she knew exactly the type of tale the collector was seeking. Of the eight she volunteered, five were selected for inclusion.

Finally, a word about Im Darwīš, who is responsible for two of the best tales in the collection (Tales 21, 45). She was about sixty-five when we recorded her. The daughter of the village chief of Dēr Ḥannā, she is married to the son of the village chief of ʿArrābe (both villages in the Upper Galilee). Although she can neither read nor write, unlike most of the other tellers she is not directly connected with agriculture. Both her tales weave prose and poetry in an organic manner, relying on a good memory for poetry and the ability to use it effectively in the structure of the tale. Tales like "Šōqak Bōqak" (Tale 21), a sophisticated romance, are rarely ever told by peasant tellers in a village milieu. Her mother, who was originally from the city of Haifa, had taught her both tales.

The Tales and the Culture

Having selected the forty-five tales to be included in this volume on the bases discussed earlier, we then had to arrange them so as to give the reader the most meaningful perspective. In many collections, tales are presented at random, without regard to form or content. We rejected this arrangement because it does not demonstrate an organic connection between the tales and the culture that gives rise to them. Other arrangements are based on the form of each tale—that is, on its Aarne-Thompson type number (for which, see Appendix C)—but this approach too was rejected on the same grounds. The best arrangement, we thought, is one that not only relates the tales to the context but also helps them cohere one to another. On considering the tales as a whole, we observed that they fit into a pattern reflecting an individual's life cycle from childhood to old age. We therefore decided to divide them according to this pattern into five thematic groups—individuals, family, society, environment, and universe—some of which are further divided into subgroups. These categories are useful only to the extent that they help us understand the tales; the discussion in the afterword to each group will make clear why certain tales were grouped together.

Our decision to adopt this scheme is based on our desire to ground the tales in the culture from which they arise. It would be wrong to start out with the assumption that the tales merely reflect the culture, or that the culture constitutes the subject matter of the tales, for then their interest would be strictly regional, limited to the cultural area from which they came. Rather, the forms of these tales, which are derivable directly from the Arabic and Semitic traditions in folk narrative, are related also to the Indo-European tradition, with which they share recognizable plot patterns (as identified by Aarne-Thompson type numbers). Certainly, the form of each tale is part of its content. If, for example, we consider "Sackcloth" (Tale 14) on the basis of plot alone, we see that it is in essence the story of Cinderella (and indeed, both tales have the same Aarne-Thompson type number). To the extent that "Sackcloth" embodies a courtship ritual in which an eager male pursues an elusive female, the content (and meaning) of both tales is similar. Yet when we examine "Sackcloth" more carefully, it becomes apparent that much of its content is derivable from Palestinian (and Arab) culture. Therefore, knowledge of at least that part of the culture embodied in the folktales will enrich our study of them; without it, analysis would suffer from a certain degree of abstraction. The culture and the art form are not reducible to, or deducible from, each other. The tales do not simply mirror the culture; rather, and more accurately, they present a portrait of it. It would surely be of interest to readers of these folktales to observe how thoroughly that portion of their form which is common with other traditions has been adapted by local tellers to express indigenous realities. Then we will be better able not only to understand the tales as cultural documents but also to appreciate them as works of art.

In the footnotes accompanying each tale and in some of the afterwords following each group, we will explore further specific aspects of this relationship between the tales and the culture. Our concern here is to present the general features of Palestinian culture that inform the tales—that is, the common assumptions that hold narrators, audience, and material together. The tales assume a stable social order, which no doubt characterized Palestinian society for hundreds of years before the advent of the British Mandate in the early 1920s; the current situation for most Palestinians, however, is one of diaspora and exile, requiring adaptation and cultural change. This is not to say that the cultural assumptions informing the tales and those prevailing in modern Palestinian society have been severed. Ideals of behavior that have developed through the institutions of the culture over countless generations do not simply vanish overnight. Even though the majority of Palestinians no longer live in extended families, for example, the standards of behavior characteristic of this ancient institution are still current in their social milieu. Indeed, the very survival of the tales as a tradition with a recognizable narrative structure, a coherent moral universe, and a set of assumptions immediately understandable to audience and narrator alike confirms the cultural continuity of Palestinian social life.

The Palestinian folktale, as we have seen, is primarily a woman's art form, and certain stylistic features give the tales their particular character. Yet Western readers will be struck as much by the tone of the tales—the narrative voice that speaks through them—as by their style, for the tales empower the women who narrate them to traverse, in their speech, the bounds of social convention. This speech is direct, earthy, even scatological, but without awkwardness or self-consciousness. The narrators are keen observers of the society around them, particularly those features of the social structure that touch directly on their lives. Because the tale-tellers are older women who have gone through the cycle of life, they are free of blame and at the same time endowed with the experience and wisdom necessary to see through hypocrisy and contradiction.

The "household" context of the tales, moreover, is that of the extended family, and our understanding would not be complete without some knowledge of the structure of this institution, within which women have traditionally spent their whole lives. As in the case of Fāṭme, older village women who have spent their lives with contact limited almost completely to the social unit that is the extended family are not uncommon. A Palestinian proverb says, "The household of the father is a playground, and that of the husband is an education" (*bēt il-ʾahil talhiye, u-bēt il-jōz tarbiye*). Whatever the truth of the proverb, the fact remains that a woman always belongs in one household or the other.

Folktales, like other forms of narrative, thrive on conflict and its resolution, not only as a theme but for plot structure as well. As we shall see, the tellers do not have to invent situations of conflict, for they are common in the social milieu, just as the colloquial language, with all its expressive potential, is in the linguistic environment. The majority of conflicts embodied in the tales have their basis in the structure of society—and necessarily so, if the tales are to be accepted as presenting a portrait of that society. The organizing or orienting principle in Palestinian life is the kinship system, which defines both social position and roles and modes of interaction. Out of this stable, conservative ground arise figures in the tales whose desires put them in conflict with the established order as represented by the dictates of the kinship system, and who in the long run must learn to harmonize their separate wills with the will of the collectivity. Much can be learned about conflict and harmony simply from contemplating the definition of the Palestinian family, which is extended, patrilineal, patrilateral, polygynous, endogamous, and patrilocal. (Unless otherwise indicated, all future reference to the "extended family" will be to the Palestinian version.) We consider the elements of this definition as structural patterns that generate the types of behavior encountered in the tales. By looking more closely at these elements, then, we can learn something about the grammar of that behavior.

The extended Palestinian family has traditionally had three or more generations living in close proximity as one economic unit, sharing all income and expenses, with ultimate authority lying in the hands of the patriarch who heads it. It is patrilineal because descent is traced through the father, patrilateral because only the relatives on the father's side are considered relatives in the formal system of relationship, and patrilocal because the wife leaves her own family to live with that of her husband. The criterion of endogamy permits a male to marry his (patrilateral parallel) first cousin, while that of polygyny allows him, under certain conditions, to marry more than one wife.

Patrilineality and patrilaterality define social identity for the patriarch's descendants, providing them with a ready-made basis for interacting with others, both inside the family and outside. The patrilineal bond is the foundation on which the whole system is built. Individuals are rarely ever referred to by their first names: married men with children are referred to as "Father of So-and-So" (Abū Flān), women as "Mother of So-and-So" (Imm i-Flān). Three of our tales have titles derived from this naming system (Tales 27, 33, 45). According to Palestinian practice, a full name need consist of no more than a person's name followed by the first name of his or her father. The oldest son will usually name his firstborn son after his own father, thereby confirming for the grandfather the continuity of his line during his lifetime. Indeed, even before they are married or have children, Palestinian men may still be referred to as "Father of (name of his own father)" in anticipation of their having sons. From this practice we conclude that the ideological basis of the system lies in this father/son bond. With social identity being by definition masculine, the female is simply defined out of it. If "self" is ipso facto male, then the female becomes the Other—the outsider or stranger. Thus, for the female, conflict is inherent in the structure of the system. We shall explore female Otherness in relation to several aspects of the extended family, but first let us focus on conflictual situations arising out of the general characteristics given above.

Polygyny serves as a good example of the dialogue we are establishing between the tales and the culture. It is one thing to state simply and objectively that the society is polygynous and completely different to observe how polygyny is treated in the tales, where its direct or implied occurrence (Tales 3, 5, 6, 7, 9, 20, 28, 30, 35, 44) is greatly out of proportion to its incidence in the society. This frequency, we feel, serves an educational function, especially if we keep in mind that children are listening every time these tales are told. In none of the tales is polygyny presented in a good light. More than any other institution or practice, it represents the power of men over women, setting females in competition for the affections of the male. In the tales, as in life, it is disruptive of family unity and harmony; the only case of cooperation occurs when the wives unite against the introduction of yet another wife into the family (Tale 30). The institution is abhorrent to women and denigrated in the culture. A proverb says, "A household with one wife is a source of pride, one with two is a laughingstock, and one with three—uncover yourself and defecate!" (*bēt waḥade faxra, bēt tintēn suxra, bēt talāte—šammir w-ixrā*). Fights between (or among) co-wives will, more often than not, spill out into the surrounding community, thereby causing shame and embarrassment and violating one of the most cherished of family values, that of keeping its secrets *mastūra,* or to itself (literally, "hidden," "behind a screen").

In a polygynous situation the stage is set for conflict the moment a man decides to marry his second wife (Tales 20, 30). If he has children by his first wife, they will raise strong objections out of respect for their mother and in defense of their inheritance. The struggle between the co-wives continues throughout the formation and growth of the family, down to—and sometimes as a direct cause of—the family's ultimate breakup. If the age difference between the co-wives is extreme, the older may save face and retain her self-respect by sponsoring the younger one, guiding her as a mother would. Publicly she might say she does not need sex, that she now has sons to look after her. If, however, the age gap is not so great, struggle is inevitable. As we see frequently in the tales, the women fight and conspire against one another, each trying to win the affection of her husband in different ways. They compete in all things, especially in producing male children. The one with more sons increases her prestige in the family and her husband's affection for her. (Note the title of Tale 3: "Precious One and Worn-out One.") If both have children, the conflict is transmitted to the offspring (Tales 5, 6). Each woman with her children forms a subunit within the family; the mothers socialize their children to hate the other group, and each woman uses her own children to manipulate the father and thereby gain advantage for them and for her (Tales 5, 28). The husband himself may stoke the fire of conflict between his wives and their respective offspring, too, by showing preference for one set over the other.

Nevertheless, polygyny serves a useful function in the society. From the perspective of a social system that perpetuates itself through the patriarchal extended family (and leaving economic considerations aside), the purpose of marriage is to produce offspring, especially sons. A childless marriage, then, contradicts its very reason for being. Under these circumstances, polygyny enables a man to combine his personal desire to keep his first wife, whom he may love, with his duty to the family to produce children. It can best be understood in relation to the cultural view of marriage as *sutra* (protection) for the woman; it is economically and socially more advantageous for a woman to be married than divorced (though cases where divorce has been beneficial to the woman are not unknown), even if that means putting up with a co-wife. Polygyny is not practiced by Christian Palestinians, and for Muslims it is regulated entirely by Islamic law (*šarīʿa*), which restricts to four the number of wives a man may have and defines his duties and obligations to them, fair and equal treatment being of foremost importance.

Also helpful to the understanding of polygyny is the feature of endogamy, another characteristic of the Palestinian extended family. A man's first duty in choosing a wife is to his patrilateral parallel first cousin (or, more accurately, it is the duty of the family to reserve their daughters for these cousins). In the majority of cases where polygyny is an issue, the man marries his cousin first, and when he has no children by her he marries another woman (Tale 6). Only in one case (Tale 30) is sexual pleasure presented (and even there through symbol) as a motivation for polygyny. In all the tales where polygyny occurs, the men love their first wives and are loath to part with them, and the first wives are always vindicated against the others.

Endogamy (Tales 6, 16, 21, 25) may be seen as a necessary adjunct of the social system defined by the patriarchal extended family because it combines the two major poles of relationship in the society—descent (*ḥasab*) and affinality (*nasab*)—under one roof. It serves the purposes of the family well because it guarantees husbands for the daughters and wives for the sons. Presumably, it forms the ideal marriage because it exercises a positive pull toward family harmony. When a man marries his first cousin, he is not bringing a stranger (cf. Tale 6) into the house; she will therefore, it is thought, share her husband's economic interest. Because both derive their identity from the same patrilineal source, it will not be easy for him to divorce her. Even when they are not related by blood, husbands and wives address each other as "cousin" (*ibin ʿammī* and *bint ʿammī*, or "son of my father's brother" and "daughter of my father's brother") and each other's parents as *ʿammī* (uncle) and *mart ʿammī* (uncle's wife).

Occasionally, however, endogamy is disruptive of family unity. When, for example, one of two brothers living together in the same family has a son, and the other a daughter, these offspring are expected to marry. But if for some reason either set of parents obstructs the marriage, conflict is bound to ensue. If they do not marry, then something is considered to be wrong with one of them (Tale 21). In this respect, as with polygyny, the tales provide a critique of the culture, because they do not automatically reflect the prevailing view that first-cousin marriage is best. In Tale 21 a young man passes over seven of his first cousins, all of whom prove nasty and vindictive when he marries a "stranger." And in Tale 25 two sets of marriages are compared, one in which a maligned wife is actually faithful to her husband, the other in which three cousins in a row, though protesting their faithfulness, turn out to be licentious and unfaithful to their shared husband.

The two issues discussed thus far, polygyny and endogamy, are fundamentally related to the third feature of the Palestinian extended family, patrilocality. A woman may marry outside her family, but her in-laws will always consider her a stranger because she does not belong to the patrilineal network of relationships that define social identity for them: she is not one of them. Thus, given a choice, a woman will always prefer to stay as close to her paternal family as possible (we shall see why in our discussion of brother/sister relationships below). For unlike endogamy, which does not require but merely favors first-cousin marriage, patrilocality leaves the newlyweds no choice: the bride *must* move into the household of her husband. This requirement, as can be immediately perceived, has major implications for our understanding of women and their behavior in the tales. At no time in her life is a woman considered to live in her own space. When she is single, she lives in the household of her father; after marriage, in that of her husband. In the tales patrilocality is taken for granted and is not questioned like polygyny, although in one fantasy (Tale 44) the husband, who has just married the king's daughter, lives with her in a palace given to them by her father.

Not only in kinship and space is the woman turned into the Other, but in other important areas of social behavior as well, such as the related subjects of family economy and the structure of family authority. Both of these spheres will be discussed in detail later; here we will focus on the woman's place in the structure of the family itself. The backbone of the family is a set of brothers who have grown up together and by adulthood have found their own places within the family. In the early stages of the family's formation, and before the brothers are married, they share a common goal—namely, the unity and solidarity of the family, which they recognize as the basis for their economic existence and social identity. As a unit, it also becomes their shelter and their source of strength (*ʿizwe*) against the outside world. Wives are brought into the family as attachments to the brothers. If they are not first cousins, they come into an alien environment in which they are considered strangers. Their role is therefore assumed to be divisive, aimed at splitting the family up so they can form their own separate families. Thus a married woman, too, becomes the Other, for she pulls the man away from the orbit of the family as son and brother and into her own orbit as husband. Because she is perceived as a threat, her coming into the family is generally viewed with apprehension. We have several examples of this syndrome in the tales, the most outstanding being Tales 2 ("The Woman Who Married Her Son") and 7 ("The Orphans' Cow"). The conflict in these tales, in which a wife is victimized by her mother-in-law, is generated from the contradictory role a wife is supposed to play in the network of relationships within the family. The tales in these cases draw their material directly from life.

Just because, by virtue of their gender, women do not form part of the kin group does not, however, mean that they have no power in Palestinian society. On the contrary, the power of the Other is at least equal to that of "self"; the difference is merely one of perspective. That power may express itself in various ways, the telling of tales being one of them. Women also have the power of their sexuality (see below), as we see in nearly all the tales (e.g., Tales 2, 5, 12, 14, 15, 17, 18, 21, 25, 35). Indeed, the tales themselves show us the power women have over men and each other: most of the tales have grammatically feminine titles, many of which are women's names (Tales 3, 13, 17, 18, 20, 26, 27, 31, 33, 42, 43), and even those that do not have feminine titles, such as Tales 14 and 43 ("Sackcloth" and "The Rich Man and the Poor Man"), concern women as the major characters. In many tales women instigate action, while the men are often passive (e.g., Tales 1, 15, 27, 29). Furthermore, the exigencies of the patriarchal system require people to prefer sons over daughters. Male children are valued beyond all other values, as a popular proverb confirms: "Pamper your son, and he'll benefit you; pamper your daughter, and she'll bring you shame" (*dallil ibnak binfaʿak; dallil bintak bithīnak*). In the tales the mother's wish is almost always for a daughter (Tales 1, 8, 23). In short, these tales almost always concern, not heroes, but heroines: mothers, daughters, and wives.

Are the women indulging in fantasy here, in wish fulfillment? We think not. No doubt an element of fantasy is involved, as is in all folktales. But if our hypothesis is correct and the tales do present a portrait of the culture, then their treatment of women must contain a large measure of truth, as anyone familiar with Arab society would confirm. Besides, the position of Otherness in which women are cast endows them with objectivity; they observe the society and weave plots for the folktales from the materials of their daily experience. As the proverb quoted earlier says, "The household of the husband is an education." Older women, especially those past child-bearing age, have been through a complete cycle of life in the midst of extended families that could have as many as thirty members ranging from infancy to old age—a very good school indeed. Although we shall return to this subject in our discussion of sexuality, it is relevant here to look at the connection between women's social position and the almost scabrous tone of the tales. When women are past child-bearing age, they are considered asexual and hence beyond the operative social taboos concerning speech and other forms of outwardly acceptable politeness. Omitted from the formal kinship structure, women are left to define their roles in society themselves. They do so through the tales, and in other forms of folklore that in Palestine are traditionally their domain: embroidery, basket weaving, pot making, and verbal arts like wedding songs and laments for the dead. Women provide a large measure of the creative and artistic energy in the society, as these folktales amply demonstrate.

We can better comprehend the social position of the tellers if we consider how authority is managed in the society. Authority devolves upon the individual on the basis of three criteria: sex, age, and position in the family. The greatest authority lies in the male head of the family, who combines all three: he has authority over every member of his family. Women, of course, do not benefit from the criterion of sex, but they do from the other two. By virtue of her position relative to her husband, the wife of the patriarch has authority over all the females in the family. Similarly, the wife of the eldest brother has authority over the wives of the younger brothers, even though some of them may be older than she is. Old age has authority because it commands respect and obedience. Frequently reiterated proverbs help instill this obedience in the minds of the young, such as "He who sees no good in the old will see none in the new" (*ʾillī malōš xēr ib-ʿatīqo, malōš xēr bi-jdīdo*) and "A month older than you, a whole age wiser" (*ʾakbar minnak ib-šaher, ʾaxbar minnak ib-daher*). Therefore, by the time they have become mature tellers, women have acquired not only wisdom and experience in life, but a certain amount of authority as well. This authority is reflected in the tales in the directness of approach, the earthiness of tone, and the concision of narration.

Before we begin our discussion of family structure, a note of caution is perhaps in order. To the extent that the ensuing analysis deals with individuals in terms of the roles they play within the context of the family, it is inspired by the tales. Certainly, the notion of role is more helpful to the study of the folktale than is that of character, which is more appropriate to the analysis of short stories and novels. And indeed, from the perspective of the extended family—the social unit on which our analysis is based—individuals are important only insofar as they fulfill roles (father, mother, son, daughter, husband, wife) that help perpetuate the institution of the family. But because our thesis is that the structural patterns existing in the family generate the types of behavior we encounter in the tales, our approach is not governed entirely by the tales. In other words, we do not, in our examination of family relationships, single out only those that occur in the tales. Rather, we address conflicts in the society that, when translated in terms of the tales, become the existential realities of the heroines and heroes. Furthermore, we do not concern ourselves only with situations that lead to conflict but consider as well those that are conducive to harmony. The reason is simple and compelling: the family occurs in all the tales without exception, either as theme or as background. And because our concern is to explore the relationship between the tales and the culture, we must examine the whole system of family relationships in order to provide the necessary cultural background to the tales. We thus avoid the pitfall of looking at the tales as mere reflectors of the culture but rather see them as esthetic transformations—miniature portraits of an existing social reality.

Assuming for the purposes of the discussion a three-generation extended family, we will explore each set of relationships within it, both vertically (parents in relation to children, and vice versa) and horizontally (in relation to other members of the same set or other sets). In such a family there will be a patriarch (the grandfather), a matriarch (his wife), a set of brothers (their sons), a set of sisters (their daughters), and a set of grandchildren. Because the family is by definition patrilineal, the set of brothers constitutes its backbone, as we saw in our discussion of social identity. The sisters, it is presumed, will marry and move out, but some of them may remain single and live in their father's house the rest of their lives. Because the family is patrilocal, wives are introduced into it as attachments to the sons and share a special category of relationship—namely, that of husband's brother's wife (*silfe;* plural, *salafāt*). Beginning with the father/son relationship, then, we shall examine each relationship in turn, focusing first on its social content and then on its configurations in the tales.

Father/son relationships, although not as numerous in the tales as relationships between mothers and daughters, nevertheless form the basis for action in several (e.g., Tales 5, 6, 30). As we said earlier, this relation constitutes the ideological basis of the family, the cement that bonds it being the cultural value of absolute obedience to the father. Ideally, a son should assert his will as little as possible in the family, and sons are highly praised for loyalty and obedience to the father. Yet the interests of the two generations do not always converge. Conflict can arise, for example, as a result of the father's polygyny, as in Tale 30, or when the son challenges the father's authority (Tale 5), or the father abuses his authority (Tale 3). This last tale also illustrates another type of conflict—that resulting from the father's preference for the sons of one wife over those of another.

Mother/daughter relationships occur frequently in the tales (Tales 1, 7, 13, 15, 18, 23, 27, 28, 35) and form the basis for the action in at least four (Tales 1, 18, 23, 27). Even though technically they belong to different families (the mother remains part of her father's extended family), mother and daughter have no cause for conflict; rather, their interests are mutual and they share a bond of trust (Tales 1, 15, 28). Argument over inheritance—a major cause of conflict among male members of the family—does not touch them because they do not usually inherit. Despite the obvious emphasis on having male offspring, women appreciate their daughters as much as they do their sons, and childless mothers in the tales wish for daughters far more frequently than they do for sons (Tales 1, 8, 13, 23). Common sayings confirm this appreciation—for example, "Girls are kind" (*il-banāt ḥanāyin*) and "Daughters will help you [literally, 'you will find them'] in your old age; they will take pity on you" (*il-banāt bit-lāqīhin ib-kabarak, bi-šfaqū ʿalēk*). Whereas a son is duty bound to take care of his mother, a daughter will do so out of kindness (Tale 1). A son may neglect his mother for his wife or side against her in cases of conflict between the two, but a married daughter, because she lives in her husband's household, never faces that situation. And although she is not supposed to, because the household technically belongs to her husband, a married daughter will frequently send her own daughter with food for her mother, particularly if the older woman has been neglected by her sons or brothers.

Mothers are also expected to be kind to their daughters and make a special effort to keep in touch with them, as we see clearly in Tale 27. They play a major role in their daughters' marriages as well (Tale 23). Moreover, because mother and daughter fulfill many family functions together, they form a natural unit within the family. One of the most important of these functions involves locating a bride for the son (brother), as in Tale 21, and providing him with a critique (*bunuqdūhā*) of the intended's deportment and character. If she is from a different village and they have not seen her before, they might even give her some simple tests, such as threading a needle (to test eyesight) and cracking a nut with her teeth—as we see in an exaggerated form in Tale 12. By and large, the tales accurately reflect the mother/daughter relationship as it is in life.

It would be difficult to conjecture the extent to which the mother/son relationship as portrayed in the tales reflects the actual situation. Certainly this relationship is depicted throughout the tales as extremely complex. In Tale 2 a mother kills her daughter-in-law and pretends to be her son's wife, and in Tale 4 a son sends his mother to certain death because she wants to marry at an advanced age. In Tale 22 a son tears his mother to pieces, along with the children she had borne to a giant. Obviously these things do not go on in real life; the tales must therefore reflect the emotional complexity of the relationship rather than its social content. Although there are psychological and mythological explanations for this complexity—a favorite theme in all literature—we will explore it in terms of the parameters already established. Despite the closeness that should characterize the relationship, the contradictory criteria for authority do cause contention. A son, particularly the eldest son, is second in command to his father and can therefore wield power based on both his gender and his position in the family. The mother, in contrast, commands respect and obedience by virtue of her age and her position as mother. As long as the son is young and under her protection, no problems arise. But as he approaches manhood and is pulling away from the sphere of his mother to that of his father (Tale 21), the potential for conflict increases. A son must start asserting his authority early in order to establish himself as a man, and a mother who impedes this process is bound to cause problems. Furthermore, a son in some respects plays the role of husband to his own mother, because he must guard her honor. Her sexuality, then, especially if she acts on it as in the tales cited above, is a certain source of conflict.

Other aspects of motherhood are also significant in the tales, such as the role of the stepmother (Tales 7, 9, 28) and the significance of the process of adoption by a ghouleh, or feminine ghoul (Tales 10, 22); these aspects will be discussed in the footnotes and afterwords to the tales.

The father/daughter relationship is extremely important in the structure of the family, because it is the father (or more accurately, the patriarch) who gives his daughter in marriage, thereby establishing a relationship of *nasab* (in-laws) with another family. She remains a member of her father's family for the rest of her life and does not take her husband's name even after marriage. The father and his sons thus remain responsible for the daughter throughout her life, whether she remains single and lives under their roof or marries and moves out. The tales (5, 7, 9, 12, 13, 14, 22, 28, 34, 44) present this relationship as one of great complexity, which does not necessarily reflect the way it is managed in life. Neither by virtue of her gender, age, or position in the family is the daughter endowed with any authority. Some of the tales (5, 12, 15, 22, 44) confirm the image of a carefree daughter able to manipulate her father into acceding to her wishes, even those that go against social convention, as in Tale

12. In Tale 14 the father interprets his relationship to his daughter as one of ownership—he wants to give her away in marriage, but to himself. Although this desire, like some of those discussed in the mother/son relationship, is susceptible to psychoanalytic and other types of explanation, the root cause of the conflict in the first part of the tale stems from the father's overstepping the bounds of authority that should regulate his behavior toward his daughter.

Natural brothers from the same mother generally maintain a harmonious relationship; they have grown up together, and by the time they are adults they have found their rightful places in the family (Tale 15). Because they share gender and position in the family, the criterion of age becomes all important in regulating their mutual relationships. As a result, the youngest brother must submit to the authority of his older brothers, who have priority over him in every respect (Tale 8). They get married before him and dispose of the collective property of the family according to their own needs. By the time the father dies and the extended family begins to break up, the older brothers have children of their own and have allocated to themselves enough of that collective property to be well established. Thus, when the family property is formally divided the younger brother may not obtain his fair share, and he must struggle on his own—although his older brothers may help him out as a favor.

In light of our thesis that the Palestinian folktale is a woman's art form, it is interesting to note that conflict over inheritance among natural brothers is not an explicit theme in these tales, even though in the society stories concerning unfair division of property are remembered for generations. Perhaps this is because conflict over the father's inheritance, which is one of the major causes of strife among natural brothers, is an exclusively male concern. Nevertheless, instances of conflict among half-brothers abound in these tales (e.g., Tales 3, 5, 6, 7), here because of polygyny, the father preferring the sons of one wife over those of the other. The situation at the opening of Tale 5, where the king treats the son of one wife gently while abusing the son of the other, is a dramatic representation of what actually does take place. In life, people understand such treatment; the tales, however, which always vindicate the youngest son against his older brothers, show it to be an injustice.

The relationship among sisters is accurately reflected in the tales (10, 12, 20), though of course not down to the smallest detail. Until they are married, sisters live together in one household, each having established her place and relationship to the rest of the family. The most sensitive question among them, and indeed, the major issue in the lives of all Palestinian women, is that of marriage. Thus, all three of the tales cited show conflict among sisters as being caused by jealousy. In Tale 10, the strife arises from jealousy over the youngest sister's marriage to the son of the king; in Tale 12 likewise, the older sisters are jealous of the youngest one, who has a secret lover; and in Tale 20 the improvident older sisters end up punishing the younger one. The tales derive from their folk narrative form—and in this respect they do not accurately reflect the culture—a high degree of violence inflicted by sisters on one another. People do, however, recognize that jealousy and envy are potent motivating forces toward evil, and they attribute the power of the evil eye to these forces.

Between brother and sister the relationship is warm and harmonious. It is certainly the relationship most idealized in the tales (7, 9, 10, 31, 42, and even 8). Generally, the sister's attitude toward her brother is one of love and respect, and his to her is one of lifelong concern and protectiveness. An older sister may exercise a nourishing and maternal role toward her brother (Tales 7, 31), particularly if the mother is dead (Tale 9); whether younger or older, she willingly serves him and his family, moving into his house if she remains unmarried after the parents die. Such a relationship is important because her brother remains her protector (*sanad, ᶜizwe*) for the rest of her life. As we noted earlier, a bride's position in the extended family of her husband is one of relative weakness at first, but if she comes into her new situation with a strong and supportive set of brothers behind her, she can in fact enjoy a certain sense of power. A bride with no brothers is pitied; she is considered to be "cut off" (*maqṭūᶜa*), with no one to stand up for her in time of need.

Despite the potential for harmony between brother and sister, however, conflict is possible in several areas. The most important of these concerns the issue of sexual honor, as we see clearly in Tale 42, where the sister must run away from her brothers in order to save her life. Sexual honor is also addressed in Tale 8, although obliquely, as we explain in the footnotes. A brother is bound to protect his sister's sexual honor, and she in turn can ruin her own reputation and that of her family through indiscreet behavior. Another possible area of conflict involves inheritance. Although entitled by Islamic law (*šarīᶜa*) to half what a man inherits, women usually forgo this right in favor of their brothers. If she marries, the sister will share in her husband's wealth—or poverty (Tale 43); and if she remains single, her father or brothers will provide for her. A sister, however, can pose a threat to her brothers by demanding her share of the inheritance, thereby, if she is married, transferring family property to others who may be enemies. (Although it is not attested in the tales, the issue of inheritance is socially very significant, for it constitutes yet another way—economics—in which women are turned into the Other.) A third source of conflict might lie in a hostile relationship between a sister and her brother's wife, as in Tale 31; yet regardless of how much tension exists between the two women, a sister will never break her relationship with her brother, even if he wrongs her (Tales 8, 31, 42).

Because the wives of brothers (*salafāt*) may come from different extended families, and possibly from divergent social backgrounds, their mutual relationships form a potentially great source of conflict, both for themselves and for those around them. In this respect the relationship resembles that of co-wives; and indeed, the two sets are structurally similar. Because Levirate marriage is practiced in Palestine, *salafāt* can become co-wives. Furthermore, because marriage to a man is also marriage into a family, all the brothers' wives come into the same family from the outside, and each must find her own place in it, competing for the favor and attention of all her in-laws. A clever woman (*malᶜūne*) who gets along well with her husband's family (*dār ᶜamhā*—literally, "her uncle's household"), like the heroine of Tale 15, is much admired in the society.

The causes for jealousy and hostility among *salafāt* are many. Work distribution becomes a source of friction when one of the wives is perceived to be doing less than her fair share. Even a pregnant woman who is close to term may be criticized for not doing enough; and after the birth, her sisters-in-law are watching for her to resume her duties. If after forty days she has not yet started working her full load, she will definitely hear about it. Her husband could add fuel to the conflict by taking his wife's side against her *salafāt*. The only example we have in the tales of this kind of relationship combines it with a sister relationship—that is, two sisters are married to two brothers, a combination that does occur in actuality (Tale 43). In this tale the transformation of social reality into fiction and its adaptation to the pattern of a widely known folktale can be clearly seen (cf. Tale 28). Again recalling our observation that the Palestinian folktale is a woman's art form, we note that here the protagonists are not male, as is typical in other traditions, but female, with maleness retained only in the title. Moreover, this tale collapses two sets of conflicting situations into one. By marrying two sisters to two brothers, it not only puts them in conflict in their roles as *salafāt* but also forces them to compare their respective situations. And by making one husband rich and the other poor, it exacerbates their jealousy and conflict as sisters. Thus the tale puts the sisters into a situation where they are as closely related as possible but the potential for conflict is at a maximum level.

The conflict-ridden relationship between a mother-in-law (*ḥamā*) and her son's wife (*kinne*) is of course proverbial, and the Palestinian context is no exception. Tale 34, for example, presents the husband as a ghoul and his mother and sister as ghoulehs, none of whom possess any redeeming features whatsoever. As we have seen, until she has acquired a daughter-in-law a woman in Palestinian society has no adults over whom she can exercise authority. Daughters-in-law (*kanāyin*), who may be in conflict with each other as *salafāt,* always unite against the mother-in-law when the occasion calls for it. The image we have of the mother-in-law in the tales, however, although usually negative, is not entirely that of an oppressive tyrant. In Tale 2, for example, the harm the mother inflicts on her son's wife is obviously due to sexual jealousy, whereas in Tale 7 the mother and the sister fear that the wife will replace them in the son's affections. And Tale 21 shows us a completely different facet of this relationship as the bride, whom her husband has shunned out of fear, conspires with his mother to bring him back home.

In contrast to the mother-in-law's presumed hostility, the father-in-law's attitude toward his son's wife is expected to be warm and protective. It would not be unusual in a domestic quarrel for the wife to appeal to her father-in-law ("uncle") against his own son. From the father-in-law's perspective, unlike that of his wife and daughters, the son's wife is not divisive; rather, by providing the family with children, she contributes materially to its growth and therefore its strength. In Tale 21, the king blesses his daughter-in-law's efforts to bring his son back home. He should treat her as if she were his own daughter, for he is responsible to the head of her family in case of conflict involving her. If a woman is unhappy with her husband's treatment of her, her family complains not to her husband but to his father. Indeed, the tales present pictures of some complexity in this relationship between the patriarch and his son's wife. Tale 32, for example, would be totally obscure if divorced from this social context. The father in that tale perceives his first daughter-in-law as a jinni, presumably because she has enchanted his son and keeps him all to herself and away from his filial obligations; the attention the father and his wife lavish on the obedient second daughter-in-law, in contrast, is meant to exemplify the harmony that can prevail when a son's wife subserves her will to theirs.

The relationship between the bride's father and her husband is a critical factor in two tales (12, 44), and it assumes secondary importance in a third (Tale 22). In some respects Tale 12 is the counterpart of Tale 32, for now we have the son-in-law enchanting the daughter and taking her away from her father. Here also, the tale would remain somewhat obscure if we did not take this relationship into account. The father's forgetfulness in bringing his favorite daughter the bird she had asked for indicates his unwillingness to part with her. Hence the husband in this tale, like the wife in Tale 32, is given the shape of a magical and utterly remote creature. In Tale 44, the king has a daughter but no sons; his interest in a son-in-law, then, represents interest in a son to make his heir. Finally, the second half of Tale 22 also takes for its theme the relationship between father and son-in-law; there, the king ostracizes his daughter for marrying against his will. In life, such an action could lead to a permanent rupture, but in the tale the father is ultimately reconciled with his daughter and accepts his son-in-law as his own.

We now turn to the relationship between husband and wife. From our discussion thus far it should be clear why this is the most prominent relationship in the tales: it occurs as a theme in nearly all of them and provides the basis for the plot in several (Tales 24–27). Marriage is a threshold event in a woman's life; not only does she form a lifelong bond, but she moves out of her father's house as well. This journey to the husband's household constitutes the plot of several tales, including 7, 12, 13, 14, and, most notably, 18. For the male too, marriage, although not so traumatic, is nevertheless an important event, bringing great responsibilities, some of which he may not yet be ready, or willing, to shoulder (Tale 21). Because marriage creates an alliance between two extended families, it complicates the system of relationships in the society. It is generally acknowledged that the relationship of *nasab* (in-laws) is never an easy one; indeed, it could be fraught with problems throughout, from the early stages of familiarity through, perhaps, the husband's taking another wife later. Marriages are usually arranged between socially equal members of extended families, who at the same time are likely to be adversaries competing with each other for power and influence in the society.

The tales explore various facets of married life, from the first stirrings of desire to the building of a family and the birth of children. With regard to the awakening of sexuality (the third group of tales in Group I, and elsewhere), the cultural sensitivity about this subject is accurately reflected, being dealt with indirectly, usually through symbol (a bird in Tales 10, 11, 12). Yet at the same time the tales adopt an imaginative reality that would not be tolerated in the culture. In fact, what gives some of these tales their particular character is the way this reality is used to present the woman's viewpoint. Specifically, in several tales (10, 11, 12, 13, 15, 17, 23) it is the woman who either expresses an interest in acquiring a husband or goes out and actively pursues one. In life, in stark contrast, a woman must show no public interest in the subject of sex, lest she compromise her honor. Even when the subject is her own marriage, a modest woman would not say yes should her father consult her wishes in the matter; most likely she would leave it to her father to make the decision. Yet in some tales, as we have seen (Tales 12, 22), the girls decide themselves, and against the wishes of their parents.

The marriage relationship is not necessarily a harmonious one, especially when the couple remains within the confines of the extended family. As we have said, the wife comes from the outside into an already formed unit whose members share not only a common descent but also a way of doing things. They have established a life together over many years, and until the wife learns to conform to their ways she is subject to criticism, perhaps even ridicule. Her in-laws do not necessarily accept that she comes from a different background and so may do things differently; more likely they will simply consider her way wrong. With the husband under strong pressure to remain loyal to the family, he may, even against his will, find himself in a situation of conflict with his wife, as in Tales 18, 29, and 32. In Tale 29 the man chooses—to his peril—to believe a ghouleh who claims to be his aunt rather than listen to his wife. A striking theme common to several of the tales (24, 25, 35, 42) is that of the calumniated wife. Tale 24, in which a suspicious husband wrongfully punishes his wife, clearly serves a didactic purpose, for it addresses a specific abuse in domestic relationships. Tale 25, too, deals with male suspicion and jealousy of a wife who proves to be in the right. And in Tale 26 the wife insists on living with her husband on her own terms—and wins.

Finally, we turn to the relationship between the sister and the brother's wife. This is one of the most important of women's relationships, and the one with the greatest potential for growth. Initially, the sister feels great joy at the prospect of her brother's marriage, which she expresses publicly by dancing at his wedding and singing songs of praise for his wife. And in fact, as we mentioned earlier, the sister plays an important role in the selection of her brother's wife. Together with her mother, she searches for a girl with whom they can get along, since they will be living together in one household possibly for life. Thus the sister provides her brother with a critique of the girl's character and appearance—at which juncture the potential for conflict is already strong, for the sister might find fault with a potential bride who nevertheless marries the brother. In the close-knit social milieu of the family the sister's negative judgments cannot long remain a secret, and so already at the start the new bride must overcome the sister's antipathy in order to please her husband.

Assuming, however, that harmony reigns at the beginning, nevertheless the conflicting interests of wives and sisters are bound to give rise to hostilities and friction. The wife sees the sister as a junior mother-in-law, and so she lumps them together as a common enemy. This conflict, which springs out of the brother's lifelong obligation to his sister, is clearly exemplified in Tale 31, where the wife accuses the sister of being a ghouleh. It may also explain the paternal aunt's portrayal as a ghouleh, both in this collection (Tales 6, 29) and throughout the tradition. Here again, the conflict between brother's wife and sister in the tales may arise from the conflicting loyalties both of them expect from the brother in real life. Even though the family has actually gained a new member in the daughter-in-law, the sister (and her mother) still feel that they have lost a brother (and a son). The sister may think she is losing not only influence over her brother but also his affections as a result of this "stranger" coming into the household. Whereas the struggle between mother and daughter-in-law frequently breaks out into the open, that with the sister is more likely to remain muted. The wife in turn fears, and not unreasonably given the structure of the extended family, that her husband will be more of a brother to his sister and a son to his mother than a husband to her.

Another possible source of friction here (which does not occur in this collection) is resentment over inheritance. Sisters, at least before they marry, spend much of their lives working in the house, assisting the wives in housework and childrearing. Yet the sisters do not inherit, whereas the wives at least benefit from the fact that their sons inherit. If a sister marries into a family poorer than her own, she is bound to feel that her brother's wife has somehow disinherited her.

With age, however, especially after the sister marries and becomes occupied with the affairs of her own conjugal family, raising her own children, and coping with her husband's sister, the hostility between her and her brother's wife lessens. As we said, the sister has a vested interest in maintaining a harmonious relationship with her brother and his children, and very often this harmony eventually includes the wife, who herself no longer feels threatened by the sister's presence in the house.

The Tales and Authority in the Society

Thus far we have discovered that the tales are themselves empowering and constitute a form of authority for the old women who narrate them. The narrative style and method used draw their authenticity from the rules and conventions handed down by the Palestinian tradition in folk narrative. Similarly, the individual tellers, who already enjoy social authority through their special position as old women, derive moral authority from the tradition, which serves to validate the act of narrating the tales to the young, thereby providing them with heroic models for behavior. Furthermore, we discovered that the social structure itself, which provides material for basic plot situations, also provides the models for the authority that regulates individual behavior in the tales.

Authority, we said, is also invested in gender (male over female) and in age (older over younger). We now turn our attention to these categories, particularly in relation to the tales. Because authority regulates behavior, knowing how it works helps us understand the meaning of action in the tales. Reinforcing the working of authority is a system of rewards and punishments based on deeply held cultural values, such as respect for tradition and old age and obedience to parental authority. Age commands respect and should command obedience. A man, for example, might feel offended if he is taken to be younger than he actually is. Children are taught from a very early age to kiss the hands of their parents, uncles and aunts, and grandparents. Even grown men do so as a sign of obedience and respect. To the extent that behavior follows the rules, it is rewarded—mothers are always asking for divine blessing for their children (Tale 4). Obedience to one's father, even in situations where he is unfair or cruel, is considered honorable behavior. In most of the tales the action embraces a cycle of conflict and resolution that revolves around these themes. Conflict arises when a person in authority abuses his or her power (as in Tale 3), or when an individual wishes to go against the dictates of the family (as in Tales 4 and 22). Resolution consists of the return of the domestic situation to a new harmony, entailing necessary adjustments on the part of the individual. The social order always remains intact.

The question of authority is also relevant to the individual's relationship to society, and hence to the meaning of heroism in the tales. The extended family deals with the outside world as a corporate unit; because it is ultimately responsible for the behavior of its members, it supports them materially, shelters them, and comes to their aid in case of conflict. In return, the family must be able to count on the loyalty of individual members, for only then is its viability as a unit that can incur and fulfill social and legal obligations guaranteed. If, let us say, the head of one family were to promise his granddaughter's hand to the head of another family, he must be able to count not only on her approval but also on that of her father, his son, even if the younger man was not consulted ahead of time. Similarly, the head of the family receiving the offer must be able to count on all those concerned to accept it. Therefore, the family exhibits a proprietary interest in its members, viewing them not as independent agents but as resources. In the tales, because the social order always remains intact, the ethic of authority is constantly confirmed; yet at the same time there is an unquestionable focus on the individual. One aspect of heroism thus consists in individuals undertaking or initiating action on their own, an emphasis that we see reflected in nearly all the tales.

Heroic action in the tales also concerns the idea of identity in the society. Again, from the perspective of the extended family, identity is collective. Through respect for tradition and deference to age, individuals are socialized from childhood to harmonize their will with that of the family. They are encouraged to perceive themselves as others see them and to validate their experience in terms of the approval of others. Standing out, doing things differently, or disobeying authority bring punishments ranging from the physical to the psychological, such as the show of displeasure, reproach, public censure, or social ostracism—as in Tales 10 and 35, where the calumniated wives are placed in the "house of desertion" (*bēt il-hijrān*). Therefore, heroic action—that is, action in accordance with individual will—necessarily entails a capacity for isolation and separation of self from the collective identity. In the tales, this capacity is reflected in the prevalence of the journey motif (Tales 5, 6, 7, 8, 9, 12, 13, 14, 16, 17, 18, 23, 28, 35, 42, 44), with separation generally being followed by some form of reunion after a new balance is established. Significantly, the journey is often undertaken by a woman, as in the archetypal (in this regard) Tale 13.

With reference to sexuality, the third determinant of authority, the relationship between the tales and the culture is extremely complex. On the one hand, the tales reflect prevailing moral standards; yet on the other, they also articulate attitudes and explore relationships and practices that are in almost total contradiction to social norms. The attitude of frankness we find in many of the tales may be attributed to the fact that their narrators are older women who are liberated from the social constraints governing verbal expression of taboo subjects like sex. The best example we have of this freedom occurs in a variant of Tale 1, as told by Im Nabīl. When she came to the part about the man defecating in the cooking pot and the pot closing on him, Im Nabīl laughed; then, still laughing, she said that the pot chopped off the man's "equipment" (*ʿidde*). In Tale 33 there is a reference to the child's "little pecker." Such examples are to be found throughout the tradition. In ordinary conversation, however, especially in mixed company, women would almost never bring up the subject of sex, particularly if they are still unmarried.

We noted earlier that the extended family as an institution maintains a proprietary relationship toward its individual members. This relationship manifests itself in a system of social controls based on family structure and on a highly developed sense of shame (*ʿēb*) that is inculcated in the individual from a very early age. And of all the forms of behavior that the family seeks to control, the sexuality of its women, which has the greatest potential for incurring shame, is by far the most important. The sexual urge is recognized to be a powerful drive that by its very nature threatens family unity because, as a private and individual matter, it is not susceptible to control or direction from the authority figure. At the same time, sexuality constitutes a vitally important resource that, if handled properly according to the traditions of the society, can advance the goals and interests of the family in relation to the outside world. If mishandled, however—if, for example, family members, especially females, allow themselves the freedom of acting on their individual needs or desires—it can be a most dangerous resource.

Female sexuality is precious for several important reasons. First, it is the source of reproduction. Palestinian families value children highly, as the tales often show, the prevailing attitude being that the more children the better, as long as a reasonable sexual balance obtains (e.g., three males to two females). Second, women's sexuality, through marriage, involves the actual winning or losing of individuals, a most important economic resource in an agrarian society based on manual labor, in which women as well as men play an important part in the production of food. And third, marriage commits a family to a relationship of *nasab* (in-laws), through which it can make allies or enemies and compete for power in the society. The value of sexuality in the Palestinian context of endogamous family relations, in which first cousins can marry, is clear, for it allows the family to grow larger and more powerful without having to resort to an outside relationship. Furthermore, because the Palestinian extended family is also polygynous, an excess of daughters, even though they are less favored than sons, is not necessarily viewed as an evil, as long as there are enough cousins to marry them—provided, of course, that no two sisters end up as co-wives, since that is forbidden by Muslim religious law (*šarīʿa*).

By viewing sexuality from the perspective of the extended family we can put into meaningful focus one of the most important themes in Palestinian and Arab culture—and in the tales as well (e.g., Tale 28)—namely, the question of sexual honor. It is important to note that in a sexual relationship the man is generally considered to take, or gain, something, whereas the woman gives away, or loses, something. Undoubtedly, the issue of female honor (which is actually the honor of the male) also involves psychological, religious, and perhaps even spiritual considerations, but these do not negate the notion of possession if a man feels that what he holds most sacred has been violated because his sister has given herself illicitly to a man. The wife in Tale 44 helps her husband escape her father's wrath because she, having been together with him sexually, was now "beholden" to him—that is, she had surrendered to him part of her identity.

Because female sexuality is such a valued possession of the family, it is guarded with utmost care. The family that fails to protect this most precious of assets incurs great shame, because the stakes are high, as in Tale 22, where the hero's revenge on his mother for marrying behind his back is quite terrible. Protecting female sexuality (that is, male honor) is the most important value in Arab society, on which the family's sense of honor, its integrity, and its self-respect all hinge. If a female were a willing participant in an illicit relationship, she would be considered a great offender, a traitor to the honor of the family (Tale 25), and her punishment could be severe indeed, including (until recently) the possibility of death. Illicit sex is considered as serious a crime as murder and carries, along with the revenge feud, the greatest potential for violence in the society.

Because sexuality is so important and so closely connected with the family's honor and reputation, families do restrict, channel, and control the sexual activity of their members. It is on the foundation of the power of sexuality that the Arab practice of sexual segregation rests. Although this practice is perhaps not as pronounced in the Christian as in the Muslim community, nevertheless gender governs social relations from childhood to old age in both communities. Generally, individuals are given no chance to abuse sexuality by engaging in it outside prescribed channels, and all possible temptations that might lead to sexual activity are removed through segregation. Indeed, a girl need not actually establish a sexual relationship for her reputation to be ruined; just falling in love—by which she transgresses the barriers of separation—if it becomes publicly known, is enough. Because people consider that even an innocent love relationship could be the pathway to sex, it is a definite threat to the family's honor.

The separation of the sexes starts early. Boys grow up in the men's world, and girls in the women's. Although they are allowed to play together when young, as they grow older and the potential for sexual contact increases, the barrier of separation is made stronger, particularly if marriage is a possibility. For example, first cousins living in the same house, who may be intended for each other, will stop talking together and will avoid each other on every possible occasion; thus their relationship will take on a sexual definition. Regardless of whether the pair are cousins or not, however, the stronger the possibility of a sexual relationship (i.e., marriage) between them, the more intense is the isolation imposed on them by society and the separation they feel individually. If a girl hears that a certain family is interested in her for their son, she will start to feel bashful in front of him and his family and will probably try to avoid contact with them altogether. As we have indicated, for a girl merely to show interest in any matter relating to sexuality is dangerous to her reputation. Hence the safest course for her is to act as if she does not want it (as Sackcloth does at the end of Tale 14), even on her wedding night—or perhaps particularly then, for a display of aversion would prove her innocence and modesty.

After marriage husband and wife must behave discreetly, showing no affection in public. Indeed, public show of affection is permitted only in situations where there is no likelihood of a sexual connection. Thus men will hug and kiss each other on the cheek after a prolonged absence, and women will do likewise, but the men will not kiss the women, or vice versa. Teenage males hold hands unself-consciously, and may come into much closer physical contact in public than would be acceptable in Europe and North America. Women, at least until menopause, are supposed to be more circumspect in their behavior at all times; thereafter, however, they are given wide leeway.

It is not because sex is considered evil that behavior in sexual matters is so strictly circumscribed by society. Quite the contrary; Palestinian and Arab society is not prudish. Any society that loves children so much cannot possibly denigrate the activity that leads to their birth. Rather, it is restricted because it is viewed as the force with the greatest potential for disrupting family unity and harmony. Beauty and sexual desire can drive people out of their wits, making them feel as if possessed by the jinn—as at the beginning of Tale 30. They say of a beautiful woman, *bitjannin,* "she will drive one mad." Women in the tales frequently appear in the guise of jinn (Tales 17, 30, 32, 37). In the final analysis, the separation of the sexes, the pretense in front of the young that sex does not exist, and the value placed on sexuality as a signature of family honor all merely confirm its supreme importance. Sexuality, in short, is affirmed through constant denial.

Denial is not, however, the prevailing ethic in many of the tales here; rather, we find women's sexuality and their emotional needs largely affirmed. Indeed, women play a much more active role with regard to their sexuality in the tales than in real life. For example, they actively choose their mates at least as frequently as the men do, whereas in the society they play a passive role, being chosen by the family of their potential mates and then having merely to accept the decision their guardians make on the subject. Rarely does a woman ever negate this decision, especially if her father or the head of her family has already given his word. The image we see in such tales as 13 and 35, where the woman is stranded in a tree, looking as beautiful as the moon but waiting for a man to rescue her, is counterpoised by the figure of the vizier's daughter in Tale 15, by Gazelle in Tale 17, or even by the cricket in Tale 23—all of whom actively search out their mates. Even where the woman awaits rescue by the man in the tales, it is she who accepts the offer of marriage and not her family. This pattern in the tales concerning mate choice is so consistently at odds with the facts of social life that we must finally conclude that a deeply felt emotional need is being articulated.

Another aspect of sexuality in the tales that society plays down is the affirmation of a romantic attitude toward love, which would lead to a questioning of some basic social assumptions. As we have seen, premarital contact of any sort is considered detrimental to a woman's reputation, making it difficult for her to find a husband. Yet frequently in the tales (12, 14, 16, 18, 21), this contact constitutes the very basis on which the marriage relationship is formed. Concomitant with the aura of romance, we find also an attitude of permissiveness and playfulness, which stands in sharp contrast to accepted social practice. The appearance of a nightly lover (Tale 12), for example, would be absolutely forbidden, yet in the tale the father himself summons the lover to his daughter. And (obviously) the dalliance of pursuit in such tales as 15 and 17 would be out of the question in real life.

No doubt, the basic situation in many of these tales is dictated by the tale type, as for example the father's express desire to marry his own daughter (Tale 14) in many Arabic variants of the Cinderella type. The same thing may be said of the symbols and the fantasy through which many of these tales convey their meaning. Indeed, social context helps illuminate the very significance of these elements in the tales. Presented in a form that might rely less on literary displacement and more on verisimilitude, the events that take place in the tales would jar the prevailing sensibility of the society. The fact that the nightly lover in Tale 12 comes in the form of a magic bird or that the sexual playfulness in Tale 15 takes place in a mysterious underground cavern removes the action from the realm of the plausible without diminishing its meaning. Nor does it detract from the tales' value as a form of wish fulfillment or from their esthetic purpose in presenting possibilities not permitted in real life. We said earlier that men generally do not concern themselves with these tales. Our discussion here will have made that aversion a little clearer, particularly since some of the mores of which men are the guardians, such as the strictures safeguarding women's honor, are consistently challenged in the tales.

As we remarked earlier, heroines predominate over heroes in the tales, and in the corpus as a whole we discover that the men's portraits are usually restricted to their social roles as sons, brothers, fathers, and authority figures, whereas the women's are more complex. On one end of the scale we have images of women as magical beings who can be enchanting and ethereal like the jinn, or bestial and destructive like ghoulehs; and on the other, the tales also embody a wide range of social relationships involving women. Thus we have situations in which women act in relationships as daughters, sisters, cousins, brides, wives, co-wives, mothers, mothers-in-law, daughters-in-law, aunts, grandmothers, widows, old wives acting as go-betweens, and foster mothers. The reason for this accent on women is twofold. First—and most obviously—the majority of tellers are women, and folktales constitute their genre par excellence. And second, the Palestinian patrilocal social arrangement does not bring men into as complex a set of relationships as it does women. Men, for example, have no relationship equivalent to that of co-wives, certainly one of the most prominent relationships in the tales; nor is there one equivalent to that of *salafāt* (husbands' brothers' wives).

Leaving aside the opposite poles of jinn and ghouls (which will be discussed extensively in the footnotes), we note that the image of women presented in the tales conforms to no stereotype. We have, for example, faithful wives, unfaithful ones (though the former predominate by far), and calumniated ones. Passive women are rare in the tales (Tales 32, 35); rather, women generally constitute the active element. Whether in preparing herself for marriage (Tale 11), in pursuing a husband (Tales 11, 12, 13, 14, 15, 21, 23), in helping him out of a crisis (Tale 37), in avoiding danger (Tale 29), in defending her children (Tale 38), or in claiming her right to be taken seriously (Tale 26), a woman initiates the action. As a sister, she is protective of her brother (Tales 7, 9, 31), although toward her sisters she tends to be jealous and envious (Tales 10, 12, 43). As a daughter she can be manipulative of her father (Tales 5, 15), and as a wife, of her husband (Tale 7). She can also be harsh, especially to her co-wives (Tales 20, 30). As a stepmother she may be very cruel (Tales 7, 9, 28), but as a foster mother she is very kind, even when outwardly portrayed as a ghouleh. In fact, the image of the fearful ghouleh who at the same time shows only kindness to her own children and to her adopted son, the hero, is as complex as any we are likely to find for women in folk literature. For, despite her terrifying appearance and her superhuman power, the ghouleh is still a nourishing female, as symbolized by her huge breasts, which, because they dangle over her shoulders, allow the young hero to approach her from behind and receive nourishment from her before having to face her directly (Tales 10, 22). In contrast to the figure of the ghouleh, who outwardly inspires fear but is gentle on the inside, stands the figure of the jinni, whose exterior is enchantingly beautiful, but whose reality could be something else entirely (Tale 30). This complex image of women in these tales simply has no parallel in the portrayal of men.

Food in Society and the Tales

In a peasant society that relies on labor-intensive agriculture on limited land, and in which the size of an individual household could be thirty or more, food is the most important material resource at the family's disposal. The cultivation, consumption, storage, sale, and distribution of food are the family's primary concerns and take up the greatest portion of its time. It is therefore not surprising that food assumes such an important role in the tales, and not merely as nourishment but as a motivator for the action in some and a source of metaphor and symbol in others. The titles of four tales refer to foods: "Jummēz," a type of fig (12); "Jbēne," cheese (13); "Chick Eggs" (28); and "Pomegranate Seeds" (35). In Tale 12 the name of the food is also that of the hero, and in 13 and 35 it is that of the heroine—and in all three the symbolic association of food imagery with sexuality is fairly clear. Food is the basic motivator of action in all the "Environment" tales in Group IV, and it figures prominently in several others as well (e.g., Tales 1, 9, 14, 15, 27, 29, 34, 36, 45). In its symbolic aspect food has magical properties, being used, for example, to make a woman conceive, as in Tales 6 and 28. The symbolic figures of ghouls and ghoulehs have as their most outstanding characteristic an insatiable appetite. As metaphor, food in the tales designates a state of well-being and satisfaction, especially when available in abundance, as in Tales 29, 43, and 44. It is also used as a sign of love (Tales 14, 15).

In using food and the processes associated with it—from growing and storing it to eating and then defecating—to generate metaphor and symbol, the tales accurately reflect cultural attitude and practice. Although consumed collectively, food, like all other material goods belonging to the family, is considered the property of the patriarch, and his permission must be sought before it is given away. The patriarch's authority in this respect extends even to mother's milk, which belongs not to her but to her husband. Thus she may not nurse another woman's baby without his permission. (Actually, the concern here may be less over the loss of the milk than over the fact that milk siblings, who will likely be first cousins, are forbidden by religious law from marrying each other.)

The distribution of food is the responsibility of the patriarch's wife, and it represents her authority in the family. If the family is small, its members eat together, but if large, she divides the food among them. The proper message of that division, which children are taught from a very early age, is fairness to all. Sometimes, however, food is distributed not according to need but according to position in the family hierarchy. The family, for example, may wish to honor its head by serving him food prepared separately and with better ingredients than those used for the rest of the family. If the food is prepared in the same way for all, the patriarch is usually given first preference and served the best pieces of meat. Certain situations, of course, call for special treatment without attracting attention. Invalids are served rich meat broths to help them recover (Tale 22), even though the rest of the family may not taste meat more than three or four times a year. Newlyweds are also favored, as exemplified in the wedding feasts at the ends of many tales. On their wedding night the groom's mother brings the couple dinner, appropriately called the "mouthful of happiness" (*luqmit is-saʿāde*); she will also bring them a good breakfast the next morning. They may receive this special treatment for a few days, but if it goes on too long the other members of the family will begin to complain. A pregnant woman who craves a particular food can also reasonably expect her craving to be satisfied (Tale 2). It is up to her mother-in-law to see to her desires, and although this is not done openly, no one minds much if the women are found out. After giving birth, too, a mother may be served meat dishes for several days (Tale 24), if the family can afford it; and if the newborn is a boy, the mother may be favored more openly and for a longer period of time.

The very importance of food production in the family economy and the emphasis placed on fair distribution make it an ideal tool for showing favor. Although not necessarily scarce, food was not always plentiful, as we see in Tale 29, where the family crosses the river into Trans-Jordan in search of food. Two contradictory forces are at work here: the love (and need) of Palestinian fellahin for large families on the one hand, and the limited productivity of land parcels that were becoming smaller with each succeeding generation on the other. Clearly, then, the extended-family ethic of equal treatment is based not only on the utilitarian imperative of keeping the family together but also on objective conditions of near scarcity. Favoritism in food distribution is thus not an act that could be easily overlooked, and its occurrence beyond the relatively few permissible occasions outlined above can lead to envy, jealousy, and conflict. Those who conspire in this favoritism are considered traitors to the collective interests of the family and thieves who allocate to themselves a resource that rightfully belongs to all.

Those singled out for favor through food appreciate its value as a sign of love. The giving and sharing of food are associated with the expression of love in all its forms. Mothers use food to establish special relationships with their children; young men bring sweets when visiting their intended brides; and newlyweds use food on the first night of marriage to help break the ice. In the tales, as in life, the rituals of love are always accompanied by rituals of food (e.g., Tales 10, 14, 15). There is in fact a whole corpus of tales and jokes concerning the theme of illicit love in which the affair is always discovered as a result of missing food. (Indeed, when food starts to disappear from a house, an affair is always suspected.) A common expression people use when faced with a confusing situation, "Is this the cat or the meat?," has its origin in one such tale, in which the husband brings home two kilograms of meat and asks the wife to prepare it. The meat, however, disappears; she claims that the cat ate it, whereupon he, taking hold of the cat and weighing it, discovers it weighs two kilograms. Turning to his wife, he asks, "If this is the cat, where's the meat? And if this is the meat, where's the cat?"

Food is also important outside the confines of the extended family. Two of the most basic values of Arab culture, hospitality and generosity, are expressed through the giving or sharing of food. Hospitality is shown to all guests (Tale 41), who were traditionally welcome for three days with no questions asked. In the tales, even the hostile ghoulehs show hospitality to the aspiring young hero. Even today a poor family might slaughter its best lamb or go into debt in order to show hospitality to a visitor. The guesthouse (*maḍāfe*), where strangers were received, was a feature of Palestinian villages and towns well into the period of the British Mandate. The ideal form of generosity is to give food to someone who cannot be expected to reciprocate, such as a beggar or a poor family—and to ensure that reciprocation is not even attempted, those who wish to exercise the purest form of generosity will give anonymously, usually during major religious festivals.

Food is also used to give other messages, entailing less noble motives. In competing for prestige, a family may take advantage of the numerous ceremonial occasions that present themselves to prepare huge feasts, offering much more food than their guests can possibly eat. They thus seek not reciprocation, but a general recognition of their generosity on the part of the community, and comparison with other prominent families. Such splurging and shows of wealth are even more striking when the competition is for power. By offering an individual or family a big feast, the host puts them under the social obligation of having to reciprocate. If they do not, they incur a social debt; but if they do, the competition could continue with the exchange of even bigger feasts.

All major stages in the life of an individual or a family, whether in joy or in mourning, are celebrated with the sharing of food. Among these occasions are the birth of a son (Tale 18), his circumcision or first communion, his marriage (several of our tales end with a wedding feast), the raising of a roof on a house, or the death of a family member. On this last occasion food is also given as alms to the poor on behalf of the soul of the deceased (Tale 45). Other occasions include dinner invitations for the sake of establishing a relationship of friendship between two families, for exploring the possibilities of *nasab* (in-laws), and for sealing a reconciliation (*ṣulḥa*) between two warring families. The sharing of food, in short, is a regular and very important feature of Palestinian social life, forming an important link in the bonds that give the society its coherence and its distinctive character. This importance is accurately reflected in the tales, although the emphasis there, by the genre's nature, is more on romantic than social relationships.

Religion and the Supernatural

Whereas food provides the tales with a social ethic reflected in action and imagery and based on the interactions of human beings both among themselves and with the physical environment, the supernatural imbues them with an entirely "other" apprehension of reality based on the beliefs and superstitions of the folk. Thus action in the tales, as we have explained, has its basis in Palestinian social reality, but management of this action is never free of supernatural influence, as dictated by the genre. Sometimes the supernatural takes specific shape in the form of jinn, ghouls, giants, or other supernatural beings (e.g., Tales 5, 6, 8, 16, 17, 18, 19, 22, 29, 30, 32, 34, 35, 36, 37, 40); at other times it remains an abstract force, such as chance or predestination (e.g., Tales 13, 14, 28, 32, 42, 43, 44, 45). In some tales the supernatural helps the action along, whereas in others it presents obstacles to be overcome so that the desired result, such as the completion of a quest or the ridding of an evil influence from the community, may be achieved.

The pattern of action in most of the tales has as its dominant motif the journey. In a few (e.g., Tales 2, 7, 12, 34), the journey motivates the action only when the authority figure (father or husband) decides to leave;

in the rest, however, the journey itself constitutes the major action. In this latter case, the journey motif serves the tale's purposes well, for it accommodates the occurrence of marvelous or magical events. The tellers usually open and close the tale in the home or village environment familiar to the audience, but in between they send their heroines and heroes on journeys in which they travel to strange places, encounter supernatural beings, or both. One location popular with Palestinian tellers is under the ground (Tales 15, 16, 20, 30, 32, 36, 42, 43). This place may be a duplicate of the world above, as in Tale 43; a well in which ghouls (Tale 20) or jinn (Tale 36) dwell, or into which human beings have been thrown for punishment (Tales 7, 30); or a generalized cavern in which treasure may be found (Tale 44) or unusual events take place (Tale 15). If the location of the action is not under the ground, it could be in a tower (Tale 18), at the top of a mountain (Tale 12), in a cavern under the sea (Tale 25), in a cave remote from civilization (Tale 28), on an island (Tale 45), or in a mysterious country beyond the seas (Tale 5).

By weaving the super-real into the fabric of the real, folk narrative asserts the primacy of the imagination, creating a dialectical relationship between the supernatural and the physical. It also closes the door on facile or one-dimensional interpretations, lending the action a timeless quality by placing it neither fully in the real nor in the realm only of the supernatural. Of course, the jinn, ghouls, and other supernatural beings who inhabit these tales are derived from the general Arabic folk tradition; there is, however, a specifically Middle Eastern dimension to belief about the supernatural as well, which must be addressed.

Village peasants in Palestine do not distinguish between official religion and its teachings on the one hand and the beliefs and superstitions of folk religion on the other. Naturally, then, no sharp distinction exists between the domain of the supernatural and that of everyday life, or between the realms of the spiritual and the material. All these categories shift back and forth and merge into each other. For example, when she cannot be seen but can make her presence felt, a ghouleh resembles a supernatural being; yet she may also appear as an animal, a human being, or a combination of both (Tale 19). Likewise, the soul of a dead person may be heard, imagined, and felt; but it can also materialize and stand next to, talk to, or even touch someone. A religious or holy person may be very real—a relative perhaps, with whom one shares food and engages in conversation—but that person is also thought to have the ability to disappear and then reappear a few minutes later in another town or village. Because we have restricted this collection to folktales and excluded saints' legends, there are no examples of this ability on the part of holy men to move magically from one place to another; nevertheless, the magic journey is a major motif in all the tales.

This concretization of the spiritual applies to all the domains of the supernatural, including the divine. On occasion God is heard talking, or He may be addressed directly. At the moment of childbirth, for example, the "gates of heaven" (*bwāb is-samā*) are supposed to open, and if someone were to make a request at this time, God would respond. Another such auspicious moment occurs at midnight on the twenty-seventh of Ramaḍān, at the onset of the new moon. On this night, which is known as the "night of destiny" (*lēlt il-qader*), people stay up late, and some have reported seeing a door in "heaven" open and a strong light emanate from it. God is imagined as a physical being who could be seen if it were not for the brilliance of the light shining from the "gates of heaven." In the imaginary world of the tales, the very beginning seems to be such an auspicious moment. In several tales (1, 8, 13, 40) a childless woman asks for a baby, and God fulfills her request. It seems to follow, then, that the distinction drawn in the West between the sacred and the profane—between religion and life—is not operative in the Palestinian peasant's world.

Villagers do, however, find one major distinction very meaningful: that between good and evil, each of which has forces or powers that pull in its direction. These forces range along a continuum from the immediate and tangible to the more abstract and intangible. No clear line separates a good man or woman, a pious one, a virtuous one, and a holy one. The virtuous man (*rajul ṣāliḥ*) and the holy man (*wilī*) are both physical beings who also have spiritual powers. The holy man can make himself invisible, and he can communicate with the souls of the dead, with spirits, ghosts, and angels. These virtuous people occur most dramatically in the last three tales, where a heroine (Tale 43) and heroes (Tales 44, 45) are assisted by supernatural powers in bringing about material blessings for themselves and their families.

The evil forces, too, range along a continuum from the physical to the supernatural. An evil person, such as an envious man who may possess the power of the evil eye, is not totally disconnected from the abstract forces of evil. It is no accident that in the tales women's sexuality outside the prescribed channels is often (Tales 2, 4, 8, 22) associated with ghoulishness or other evil forces. And in the animal kingdom, the hyena and the monkey have a special significance. Although a real animal, the hyena is traditionally linked with supernatural forces, its effect on human beings being considered similar to that of possession by the jinn. The same holds true for the monkey (*qird*, or *saʿdān*). When the word *saʿdān* comes up in conversation, people usually invoke divine protection by repeating the *basmala* ("In the name of Allah, the Compassionate, the Merciful!"), as they would at the mention of a ghost, ghoul, or devil. Likewise, whenever the jinn are introduced in the tales—and they occur frequently—the teller usually invokes the name of Allah. Along the continuum after the hyena and the monkey we find a range of evil spirits, including ghosts (*ašbāḥ*), demons (*ʿafarīt*), the *qarīne* (female childbed demon), and the jinn.

The forces of good and evil are believed to work against each other continuously in the life of the individual, on both the material and the spiritual level. Allah may grant a couple a baby, for instance, but the *qarīne* is always ready to harm or kill it (Tale 33). These evil spirits must always be defended against; if one is sensed in the environment, the best protection is the invocation of the name of Allah or the name of the cross. Moreover, although evil forces will disappear the moment the good forces are called upon or mentioned, invocation of the devil will not cause an angel to run away. The good forces are thought to be more powerful than the evil ones, but not powerful enough to eliminate them. The two forces must coexist, and the best the good powers can do is to limit the influence of evil.

Both sets of forces have some measure of control over human behavior, and in a sense they collaborate; if people are not behaving righteously and acting according to the dictates of morality or religion, the good forces may withdraw their protective influence and allow an evil force to bring harm. Conversely, evil beings do not necessarily embody pure, unmitigated evil, because they can bring good to human beings. In such tales as 10 and 22, for example, ghouls and ghoulehs assist the young protagonists on their quests. Similarly the jinn, who according to the Qurʾān are creatures of fire, are capable of goodness. Some are even thought to be Muslims, for people see them standing and praying, just like human beings. But some are certainly evil: if one of these were to possess a human being, it could bring about that person's death. The jinn nature, however, is capricious, as we may observe in Tales 30 and 32, and the same jinni can cause harm or do good.

Given this interpenetration of the supernatural and the physical, of the spiritual and the mundane, life on earth becomes the stage on which the meting out of rewards and punishments is performed. The supernatural need not intervene in human affairs in a miraculous way for it to be believable; the moment-to-moment events of daily life are one's rewards and punishments. All material and nonmaterial blessings are gifts from Allah. Of course, rewards and punishments, like the forces that give rise to them, range along a continuum from the immediate and tangible, such as a good harvest, healthy livestock, or the birth of a son, all the way to entering heaven in a second life. Punishment can also range from, for instance, the death of a child to entering hell in the afterlife. Thus heaven and hell are tangible in a sense: people see them as real states of being comparable to ordinary experience, but much more intense. They know what these places look and feel like and can imagine them in every detail. Paradise (*il-janne*) is a garden with rivers, trees, milk, honey, beautiful women, and wine—in short, all the good things in life, including those that are forbidden during earthly existence. And in hell (*jhannam*) there is nothing but fire and big, powerful, bad angels who allow no one to get out.

Of course men and women, being subject to the punishments and rewards meted out by the forces of good and evil, can hide nothing. The angels, the jinn, the devil, and God—all have a way of knowing everything that one thinks or does. And regardless of content, neither thought nor action can be neutral. Everything has consequences, either rewards or punishments. Thus only two angels (Raqīb and ʿAtīd) are necessary to keep account of a person's actions. One sits on the right shoulder recording the good deeds, and the other on the left recording the bad. On the Day of Judgment the two books in which these angels have recorded an individual's life are weighed: if the one on the right is heavier, heaven is the reward; otherwise, hell. Here again, the angels Raqīb and ʿAtīd are almost tangible. People feel their presence and sometimes even talk to them. At the end of prayer, a Muslim will turn the head first to the right and then to the left, greeting the angel on each shoulder by saying, "Peace to you!" (*as-salāmu ʿalēkum*).

Despite the influence of supernatural forces, human beings can do nothing that is not predestined. Each person's fortune is written on the forehead at the moment of birth, and life is an unfolding in time of the plan already drawn by destiny, which is the instrument of God. Belief in predestination does not necessarily entail abandonment of individual effort or lack of responsibility for one's actions. A clear logic impels toward taking initiative: even though from the perspective of the Divine the future is known, from a human perspective it is unknowable. And because it is unknowable, it remains mysterious and full of promise—it can be acted upon. All actions have commensurate consequences, and by performing good deeds (*ḥasanāt*) individuals help their destinies in this life and improve their chances in the life to come.

But by the same token, because the future is unknowable, consequences are unforeseeable. One can know them only after they have taken place, and so it is useless to worry about the future. Having acted, one awaits the results, which one has no choice but to accept. Herein lies the true meaning of belief in fate and predestination. It is not that individual will is abandoned, but rather that one's fate is accepted. People thus use the doctrine of predestination to justify and help resign themselves to what happens, especially in the case of misfortunes. "There is no strength or power save in Allah," says the heroine of Tale 42 after she falls into the well. The fruits of action, whether bitter or sweet, must be accepted, for they cannot be changed. Nor would it be useful to blame oneself or feel sad or guilty when misfortune strikes, because what comes is only the unfolding of what has already been decreed, regardless of one's personal feelings about it. Belief in predestination thus helps people cope with the present and eliminates worry about the future.

Using the ideas we have thus far explored, we can begin to develop a theory of action in the tales. Our last observation about action was that final judgment concerning its ontological status must remain tentative, since the tales, through their use of the journey motif in the basic plot structure, locate action neither fully in the domain of the supernatural nor in that of the physical. The parameters of our discussion will be the major topics discussed thus far—namely, the concretization of the nonmaterial; the interpenetration of the physical and the supernatural; the distinction between good and evil, and the balance of forces between them; the notion of rewards and punishments as aspects of daily life; and the doctrine of predestination. Certainly these ideas are not discrete and separable; taken together, they form a unitary whole constituting the entire moral outlook of the community. If, as we claim, the tales present a portrait of that community, action in them can only reflect this outlook.

Of course, by "action" we do not necessarily mean only physical activity. Through the process of concretization, or reification, of the nonmaterial—a very important process operative not merely in these tales but in all folk narrative—a thought or wish becomes an action the moment it is put into words. And in fact, that is precisely how many tales are begun: a lack is articulated, the fulfillment of which then becomes the central action of the tale. Language thus becomes a silent "actor" in the drama of the tales, giving narrative form to the unspoken attitudes, feelings, and dreams of the community, and awareness of the power of language on the part of the tellers is evident throughout. We recall that the root meaning of the Arabic word *ḥikāye,* or "folktale," is "that which is spoken," and we have already alluded to the use of opening, closing, and protective formulas, distancing devices, and invocations. Language, particularly in verse form, has power over the nonhuman world in the tales—both the physical, such as animals and rocks, and the supernatural, including the jinn, ghouls, and divine power. By repeating a certain incantation, the heroine of Tale 35 exorcises the demon who had been haunting her, and Jbēne (Tale 13), by repeating her lament, enlists the sympathy of both animate and inanimate nature. The power of language is also manifest in formula tales, a representative sample of which is included in Group IV (Tales 38–41). Here language aids not only in the memorization of the tale but in plot management as well. Tale 41 in particular, through the use of a rhymed formula, evokes the unity and interconnectedness of human beings with nature. It is as if the end rhyme, which unifies the tale, also unites human with nonhuman nature. Other potent linguistic processes in these tales are onomatopoeia, puns, and naming, which may operate singly or in combination. Thus Tale 1 derives its name as well as its central action from a linguistic imitation of the sound of a rolling cooking pot (see Tale 1, fn. 1), and the resolution of Tale 45 relies on the use of the hero's name as a pun. Naming is itself an important confirmation of the power of language, for by giving something a name it can become a material reality—the "water of life" (Tale 5), the "robe of anger" (Tale 5), the "fart" that becomes a person (Tale 43), the name that the heroine of Tale 26 adopts ("Mistress of All and Flower of the House"), and so on.

Ambiguity concerning the ultimate status of action is a critical feature of all folktales. On the one hand, Palestinian tellers do resort to narrative distancing devices to put the action in the realm of fiction. On the other hand, by concretizing the supernatural they manage the opposite effect, locating fictional entities in the domain of the real. The out-of-the-ordinary locations in which tellers like to place the action are, as we have pointed out, essential aspects of plot in nearly all the tales. These places cannot, of course, be reached by mere human effort: the protagonists, on their way to retrieve some magical object vital to narrative continuity, must seek assistance from supernatural beings. The ghouls and jinn who populate these tales, however, do not act merely as donor figures. They also assume fully human roles as fathers (Tale 20), husbands (Tale 16), lovers (Tale 12), daughters (Tale 8), sons (Tale 40), wives (Tales 17, 30, 32, 37), sisters (Tale 8), mothers-in-law (Tale 34), aunts (Tale 29), and mothers (Tale 18). These supernatural beings are not only creatures of the imagination but also part of people's experience in life. In presenting them, Palestinian tellers, who can rely on the audience's belief in their reality, do not have to use distancing devices to help suspend disbelief. And it is precisely this absence of distancing devices in connection with these creatures that gives the tales their special character, adding to the ambiguity in the action and thereby making the task of interpretation more difficult.

Action is of course organically connected with the hero and plot in the tales. As we have seen, the Palestinian folk do not conceive of this world in terms of unmitigated good or evil. By humanizing supernatural creatures, the tales remove them from susceptibility to facile moral judgment. In Tale 22, for example, the ghouleh is kinder to the hero than is his own mother, and in Tale 12 the magic bird is more trusting of his wife than she is of him. It is therefore more appropriately the balance of forces proper, rather than an assortment of capricious supernatural beings, that controls rewards and punishments in this world. The plot is set into motion when this balance is disturbed. The agents of this balance are the heroines and heroes, who, much like the supernatural creatures with their human dimension, themselves have a superhuman dimension. Whether in fulfillment of individual desire or in serving the community, they undertake difficult journeys and seemingly impossible tasks. Because every action in life has its consequences, the events of plot—of their journey, of their deeds—are narrative manifestations of this balance of forces. Resolution is not achieved until all the forces that have been set into motion are neutralized and a new balance is achieved. If a wish is articulated, it must be fulfilled; if a vow is made, all its conditions must be fulfilled. By thus removing an absolute scale for judging action, the tales, despite their reliance on the paraphernalia of the supernatural, throw the onus of responsibility on human beings. In their very essence, the tales affirm a human reality.

The concept of plot in the tales is an artistic imitation of the unfolding of fate. Or, viewed the other way around, belief in predestination implies that the plot of human, and therefore individual, destiny has been planned from the very beginning. In life, human beings tread a delicate balance between the powers of good and evil. The future is predetermined, yet it is unknowable. And because fate is sealed, causality is eliminated. Chance thus becomes an essential aspect of plot in the tales precisely because this plan for the universe exists—even though human beings do not know what it is. Every event has a meaning in relation to the unfolding story of the world. Taking this thought a bit further, we can say that only chance is meaningful in the tales because, in the absence of causation, heroes and heroines have no interiority. There is no space in their world for reflection. They do not know, nor can they evaluate, the meaning of their actions. They *are* their actions, as the names of some of the tales make so clear (e.g., Tales 1, 2, 3, 31, 32, 42, 43).

So far in our discussion we have distinguished between the specific contribution of the culture and that of the genre itself, with its concomitant plot requirements for any particular tale type. From that perspective, we considered briefly the documentary aspect of the tales—that is, their relation to the social context. Now, as we study plot structure and the meaning of action, we observe a congruence of the traditional, predominantly Islamic Palestinian worldview and the significance of action in the tales. The equation we make between the concept of plot in art and the doctrine of predestination in life may be verified from the metaphor alluded to earlier, "It is written on the forehead," that is used to express the notion of a preexisting order. Life from birth to death is like a story authored by God, who breathes life into the soul at conception and sends the angel of death at the end. All folktale readers are familiar with the tale that begins with the prediction of how a newborn will die, a prophecy that is fulfilled regardless of the parents' efforts to frustrate the inevitable. For obvious reasons, this folktale is very popular in the Arab world, for it articulates one of the most profound and cherished attitudes the people hold about the meaning of life. Human beings are God's slaves (*ʿabīd;* sing., *ʿabid*), and they can no more attempt to change their fate than can folk heroes and heroines alter the laws of folk narrative (see especially the tales included here in Group V). Those individuals who succeed most fully in embracing their destiny unquestioningly are, then, the heroines and heroes of our tales.

THE TALES

Notes on Presentation and Translation

Following the scheme articulated in the Introduction, the tales are divided into groups, each of which is followed by an afterword. This commentary follows rather than precedes the selections in order not to interfere with the reader's individual response to the tales. Likewise, we hope that the enjoyment of a first reading will not be interrupted by the footnotes. Notes have been provided to explain or explore many of the terms and concepts found in the tales. Extensive cross-referencing should allow readers to pursue particular topics, and the Footnote Index provides even more comprehensive surveys.

A translation must sound natural in the target language while still remaining faithful to the original. In translating these tales, several basic issues had to be considered. The first is the language of the original, which is the Palestinian dialect. In rendering colloquial Arabic into English, the translator must decide on the linguistic level, or tone, that best conveys the spirit of the original. A too-formal translation distorts that spirit, and a heavily colloquial one is equally deleterious.

In addition to purely linguistic considerations, there are also stylistic ones. Many stylistic features of oral performance cannot be duplicated in print without destroying the fluency of the narrative. Among these, for example, are comments reflecting the teller's own viewpoint (included in parentheses) in the midst of speech uttered by one of the characters. Literary oral narrative, when translated for print into another language, obviously undergoes in reality a process of double translation: the first is from one language to another, and the second is from one medium into another.

Fortunately, linguistic practice in English is helpful to the translator in both cases. The division in English between formal and informal language is not quite as important as it is in Arabic, where standard speech is used mostly on formal occasions and in writing. Thus, the solution to both problems (linguistic level and stylistic propriety) lies in steering a middle course between standard and informal speech, avoiding intrusive colloquialisms on the one hand and expressly "literary" diction on the other. The translation, in short, must sound good to native ears when read out loud.

In every case the translation follows the original very closely, attempting where possible to duplicate its narrative rhythm and its grammatical structure. The philosophy of translation articulated here assumes that the tellers must tell their own tales, with as few interpretive intrusions as possible. No liberties are taken with the text by adding invented material or by censoring scatological references through euphemistic substitution or excision. Necessary departures from the literal intent of the text are either included in square brackets in the body of the tale or footnoted—or both.

Although the translations remain faithful to the literal meaning of the originals, they are not word-for-word translations. All dialogue in the tales, for example, is introduced in the originals by the word *qāl,* "to say." *Qāl* is translated in a variety of ways (as "said," "spoke," "answered," "replied," "called"), depending on the context. We feel that following the text too literally here will yield a turgid translation that is not faithful to the original either in letter or in spirit. In rhythms, gestures, and intonations oral narration holds the attention of the listener; the verbal text, seen on the printed page, does not by itself (so to speak) tell the whole story.

Group I

INDIVIDUALS

Children and Parents

1. *Ṭunjur, Ṭunjur*[1]

TELLER: Testify that God is One!
AUDIENCE: There is no god but God.[2]

There was once a woman who could not get pregnant and have children. Once upon a day she had an urge; she wanted babies. "O Lord!" she cried out, "Why of all women am I like this? Would that I could get pregnant and have a baby, and may Allah grant me a girl even if she is only a cooking pot!"[3] One day she became pregnant. A day came and a day went, and behold![4] she was ready to deliver. She went into labor and delivered, giving birth to a cooking pot. What was the poor woman to do? She washed it, cleaning it well, put the lid on it, and placed it on the shelf.

One day the pot started to talk. "Mother," she said, "take me down from this shelf!"

"Alas, daughter!" replied the mother, "Where am I going to put you?"

1. The name of the tale is an onomatopoeic derivation for the sound of a rolling cooking pot (*ṭunjara*). The feminine ending of this word helps to establish the equation of "pot" with "girl." In the translation the neuter "it" is used when the pot is perceived as an object.

2. This opening formula, —*waḥdū l-lāh!* —*lā ʾilāha ʾillā l-lāh!* is the most common way of beginning a folktale in the Palestinian tradition.

3. "Why of all women am I like this?" is a common way for a woman to express self-pity. Considering the value placed on children in Palestinian society, it is understandable why the woman should feel as if her inability to bear children is a punishment from Allah. Cf. Tale 8, n. 1; Tale 40, n. 2.

"May Allah grant me a girl . . ." The Arabic for "grant" is *yiṭʿam* (literally, "feed"). Palestinian village folk believe that divine will, through the agency of the angel Gabriel, causes conception. Granqvist (*Birth:* 34) quotes the saying, "If He will feed me with sons, He does not mistake where my mouth is, and if He shuts me out He does not trouble Himself about me."

4. "Behold!" is the closest English equivalent to *willā,* which is one of several devices used by our tellers for interrupting the flow of narrative to express surprise or to alert the listeners that something out of the ordinary is about to occur. Some narrators use the term more frequently than others, and we have not translated it in every instance, sometimes relying instead on the context to carry the emotion. Cf. Tale 5, n. 8; also see n. 9, below.

"What do you care?" said the daughter. "Just bring me down, and I will make you rich for generations to come."

The mother brought her down. "Now put my lid on," said the pot, "and leave me outside the door." Putting the lid on, the mother took her outside the door.

The pot started to roll, singing as she went, "Ṭunjur, ṭunjur, clink, clink, O my mama!" She rolled until she came to a place where people usually gather. In a while people were passing by. A man came and found the pot all settled in its place. "Eh!" he exclaimed, "who has put this pot in the middle of the path? I'll be damned! What a beautiful pot! It's probably made of silver." He looked it over well. "Hey, people!" he called, "Whose pot is this? Who put it here?" No one claimed it. "By Allah," he said, "I'm going to take it home with me."

On his way home he went by the honey vendor. He had the pot filled with honey and brought it home to his wife. "Look, wife," he said, "how beautiful is this pot!" The whole family was greatly pleased with it.

In two or three days they had guests, and they wanted to offer them some honey.[5] The woman of the house brought the pot down from the shelf. Push and pull on the lid, but the pot would not open! She called her husband over. Pull and push, but open it he could not. His guests pitched in. Lifting the pot and dropping it, the man tried to break it open with hammer and chisel. He tried everything, but it was no use. They sent for the blacksmith, and he tried and tried, to no avail. What was the man to do? "Damn your owners!" he cursed the pot,[6] "Did you think you were going to make us wealthy?" And, taking it up, he threw it out the window.

When they turned their back and could no longer see it, she started to roll, saying as she went:

"Ṭunjur, ṭunjur, O my mama,
In my mouth I brought the honey.
Clink, clink, O my mama,
In my mouth I brought the honey."[7]

5. Honey was, and still is, a rare and expensive food and is thus worthy of such a precious pot, as are the meat and jewelry placed in the pot later. The custom of offering sweets to guests is still observed, although the practice of offering jam or honey alone is no longer current (see Grant, *People:* 86–87).

6. *Yilʿan abū ṣḥābik*—literally, "Damn the father of your owners!" This curse is not as weighty in the original as the translation makes it sound.

7. The Arabic for "honey" here is *naḥḥa,* baby talk for anything sweet. In the refrains that follow, similarly, the words for "meat" (*maʿmaʿ*) and "treasure" (*daḥḥa*) are also baby

"Bring me up the stairs!" she said to her mother when she reached home.

"Yee!" exclaimed the mother,[8] "I thought you had disappeared, that someone had taken you."

"Pick me up!" said the daughter.

Picking her up, my little darlings, the mother took the lid off and found the pot full of honey. Oh! How pleased she was!

"Empty me!" said the pot.

The mother emptied the honey into a jar, and put the pot back on the shelf.

"Mother," said the daughter the next day, "take me down!"

The mother brought her down from the shelf.

"Mother, put me outside the door!"

The mother placed her outside the door, and she started rolling—ṭunjur, ṭunjur, clink, clink—until she reached a place where people were gathered, and then she stopped. A man passing by found her.

"Eh!" he thought, "What kind of a pot is this?" He looked it over. How beautiful he found it! "To whom does this belong?" he asked. "Hey, people! Who are the owners of this pot?" He waited, but no one said, "It's mine." Then he said, "By Allah, I'm going to take it."

He took it, and on his way home stopped by the butcher and had it filled with meat. Bringing it home to his wife, he said, "Look, wife, how beatiful is this pot I've found! By Allah, I found it so pleasing I bought meat and filled it and brought it home."

"Yee!" they all cheered, "How lucky we are! What a beautiful pot!" They put it away.

Toward evening they wanted to cook the meat. Push and pull on the pot, it would not open! What was the woman to do? She called her husband over and her children. Lift, drop, strike—no use. They took it to the blacksmith, but with no result. The husband became angry. "God damn your owners!" he cursed it. "What in the world are you?" And he threw it as far as his arm would reach.

As soon as he turned his back, she started rolling, and singing:

---

talk. Interestingly, the word for "feces" in the final refrain, *kaᶜkaᶜ*, is very close to its English equivalent. Cf. Tale 4, n. 8.

8. The exclamation "Yee!" is used by women in a variety of contexts to express surprise, admiration, or pleasure.

"Ṭunjur, ṭunjur, O my mama,
In my mouth I brought the meat.
Ṭunjur, ṭunjur, O my mama,
In my mouth I brought the meat."

She kept repeating that till she reached home.

"Lift me up!" she said to her mother. The mother lifted her up, took the meat, washed the pot, and put it away on the shelf.

"Bring me out of the house!" said the daughter the next day. The mother brought her out, and she said, "Ṭunjur, ṭunjur, clink, clink" as she was rolling until she reached a spot close by the king's house, where she came to a stop. In the morning, it is said, the son of the king was on his way out, and behold! there was the pot settled in its place.[9]

"Eh! What's this? Whose pot is it?" No one answered. "By Allah," he said, "I'm going to take it." He took it inside and called his wife over. "Wife," he said, "take this pot! I brought it home for you. It's the most beautiful pot!"

The wife took the pot. "Yee! How beautiful it is! By Allah, I'm going to put my jewelry in it." Taking the pot with her, she gathered all her jewelry, even that which she was wearing, and put it in the pot. She also brought all their gold and money and stuffed them in the pot till it was full to the brim, then she covered it and put it away in the wardrobe.

Two or three days went by, and it was time for the wedding of her brother.[10] She put on her velvet dress and brought the pot out so that she could wear her jewelry. Push and pull, but the pot would not open. She called to her husband, and he could not open it either. All the people who were there tried to open it, lifting and dropping. They took it to the blacksmith, and he tried but could not open it. The husband felt defeated. "God damn your owners!" he cursed it, "What use are you to us?" Taking it up, he threw it out the window. Of course he was not all that anxious to let it go, so he went to catch it from the side of the house. No sooner did he turn around than she started to run:

"Ṭunjur, ṭunjur, O my mama,
In my mouth I brought the treasure.

9. The teller here uses two devices ("it is said" and "behold!") to distance herself from the action. Possibly she felt that the coincidence of the king's son going out at that particular moment was too unlikely. See n. 4, above.

10. For a sister, the wedding of a brother is one of the happiest occasions.

Ṭunjur, ṭunjur, O my mama,
In my mouth I brought the treasure."

"Lift me up!" she said to her mother when she reached home. Lifting her up, the mother removed the lid.

"Yee! May your reputation be blackened!" she cried out.[11] "Wherever did you get this? What in the world is it?" The mother was now rich. She became very, very happy.

"It's enough now," she said to her daughter, taking away the treasure. "You shouldn't go out any more. People will recognize you."

"No, no!" begged the daughter, "Let me go out just one last time."

The next day, my darlings, she went out, saying "Ṭunjur, ṭunjur, O my mama." The man who found her the first time saw her again.

"Eh! What in the world is this thing?" he exclaimed. "It must have some magic in it, since it's always tricking people. God damn its owners! By Allah the Great, I'm going to sit and shit in it." He went ahead, my darlings, and shat right in it. Closing the lid on him,[12] she rolled along:

"Ṭunjur, ṭunjur, O my mama
In my mouth I brought the caca.
Ṭunjur, ṭunjur, O my mama,
In my mouth I brought the caca."

"Lift me up!" she said to her mother when she reached home. The mother lifted her up.

"You naughty thing, you!" said the mother. "I told you not to go out again, that people would recognize you. Don't you think it's enough now?"

The mother then washed the pot with soap, put perfume on it, and placed it on the shelf.

This is my story, I've told it, and in your hands I leave it.[13]

11. *Ya mšaḥḥara*—literally, "O you who has smeared herself with soot!" A woman blackens her face as a sign of mourning when someone dear dies. Hence, metaphorically, when a woman does something she is not supposed to do, her honor dies and her reputation becomes black. See Tale 13, n. 8; Tale 41, n. 5. This expression, however, need not always carry connotations of ominous wrongdoing; it is frequently used, as in the present context, as a form of mild reproach.

12. In the version of this tale supplied by Im Nabīl (see Introduction, "The Tellers"), after the man defecates into the pot, she emasculates him.

13. One of several closing formulas used by Palestinian tellers. Our translation here de-

2. *The Woman Who Married Her Son*

Once upon a time there was a woman. She went out to gather wood, and gave birth to a daughter. She wrapped the baby in a rag, tossed her under a tree, and went on her way. The birds came, built a nest around the baby, and fed her.

The girl grew up. One day she was sitting in a tree next to a pool. How beautiful she was! (Praise the creator of beauty, and the Creator is more beautiful than all!) Her face was like the moon.[1] The son of the sultan came to the pool to water his mare, but the mare drew back, startled. He dismounted to find out what the matter was, and he saw the girl in the tree, lighting up the whole place with her beauty. He took her with him, drew up a marriage contract, and married her.

When the time for pilgrimage came, the son of the sultan decided to go on the hajj. "Take care of my wife until I return from the hajj," he said to his mother.

Now the mother was very jealous of her daughter-in-law, and as soon as her son departed she threw his wife out of the house. Going over to the neighbors' house, the wife lived with them, working as a servant. The mother dug a grave in the palace garden and buried a sheep in it. She then dyed her hair black and put on makeup to make herself look young and pretty. She lived in the palace, acting as if she were her son's wife.

When he came back from the hajj, the son was taken in by his mother's disguise and thought her his wife. He asked her about his mother, and she said, "Your mother died, and she is buried in the palace garden."

After she slept with her son, the mother became pregnant and started

---

parts somewhat from the original—"This is my tale, I've told it, and to you I've thrown it" (*hāy iḥkāytī ḥakēthā, u-ʿalēku ramēthā*). The notion of "throwing" is used by analogy with the passing of the handkerchief in folk dancing (see Tale 14, n. 8). If the teller names someone to whom she "throws" the tale, then it would be that person's turn to tell the next one.

1. The full moon is implied. It is the most common image used to represent female beauty. When attempting to draw the attention of a beautiful girl on the street, a young man may call out, "ʾĒš yā qamar?" (roughly, "What's happening, O moon?"). Two important components of the image, brightness (fairness of skin) and roundness (of face), convey the popular conception of beauty in Palestinian and Arab culture. In popular expression it might be said that the roundness of a beautiful girl's face resembles that of the moon (*ʿalēhā dōrit hal-wijeh miṯl il-qamar*), or that her face shines like the moon (*wijeh-hā biẓwī miṯl il-qamar*). See Footnote Index, s.v. "Beauty."

to crave things. "My good man," she said to her son, "bring me a bunch of sour grapes from our neighbor's vine!"[2] The son sent one of the women servants to ask for the grapes. When the servant knocked on the neighbor's door, the wife of the sultan's son opened it.

"O mistress of our mistress," said the servant, "you whose palace is next to ours, give me a bunch of sour grapes to satisfy the craving on our side!"

"My mother gave birth to me in the wilderness," answered the wife, "and over me birds have built their nests. The sultan's son has taken his mother to wife, and now wants to satisfy her craving at my expense! Come down, O scissors, and cut out her tongue, lest she betray my secret!" The scissors came down and cut out the servant's tongue. She went home mumbling so badly no one could understand what she was saying.

The son of the sultan then sent one of his men servants to fetch the bunch of sour grapes. The servant went, knocked on the door, and said, "O mistress of our mistress, you whose palace is next to ours, give me a bunch of sour grapes to satisfy the craving on our side!"

"My mother gave birth to me in the wilderness," answered the wife of the sultan's son, "and over me birds have built their nests. The sultan's son has taken his mother to wife, and now wants to satisfy her craving at my expense! Come down, O scissors, and cut out his tongue, lest he betray my secret!" The scissors came down and cut out his tongue.

Finally the son of the sultan himself went and knocked on the door. "O mistress of our mistress," he said, "you whose palace is next to ours, give me a bunch of sour grapes to satisfy the craving on our side!"

"My mother gave birth to me in the wilderness, and over me birds have built their nests. The king's son has taken his mother to wife, and now wants to satisfy her craving at my expense! Come down, O scissors, and cut out his tongue. But I can't find it in myself to let it happen!" The scissors came down and hovered around him, but did not cut out his tongue.

The sultan's son understood. He went and dug up the grave in the garden, and behold! there was a sheep in it. When he was certain that his wife was actually his mother, he sent for the crier. "Let him who loves

2. Pregnant women are assumed to crave sour grapes, much as in Western society they are assumed to crave pickles. See Tale 32, n. 6; Tale 43, nn. 4, 5.

the Prophet," the call went out, "bring a bundle of wood and a burning coal!"

The son of the sultan then lit the fire.[3]

Hail, hail! Finished is our tale.[4]

3. *Precious One and Worn-out One*

Once there was a man who was married to two women, one of whom he called "Precious One" and the other "Worn-out One." Precious One had two sons, and Worn-out One had only one.[1]

They had an animal pen from which one sheep was stolen every night. "Sons," said the father, "every night one of you must stay up to watch the sheep and find out who's been stealing them."

"I'm the son of Precious One," said the eldest.[2] "I'll keep watch tonight." In the evening he went to keep watch by the sheep pen. He stayed awake till ten o'clock, then he fell asleep. A ghoul came and stole a ewe, and the boy did not know about it. When he woke up in the morning, he counted the sheep and found one ewe missing.

"I see that one of the sheep is missing," said the father.

"I want to keep watch by the sheep," the second son of Precious One said. His watch was like that of his brother, the ghoul stealing another ewe. The next morning he said to his father, "I too didn't see anything come into the sheep pen."

"Now we'll make the son of Worn-out One keep watch," said the father.

3. The teller's narrative style tends toward greater brevity as the tale proceeds. Hence there is no need for her to say that the fire was intended for the mother. She may also have omitted that detail out of delicacy.

4. This is a common closing formula, used mostly by urban storytellers and heard at the end not only of Palestinian but also of Syrian and Egyptian folktales. Our teller is an eighty-two-year-old woman from Rafīdya, which is part of Nablus, one of the largest Palestinian cities. The translation attempts to duplicate the rhyming quality of the original: *tūta, tūta; xilṣit il-ḥaddūta*. The expression translated as "hail"—*tūta*—is composed of two nonsense syllables, repeated twice and used as a device to rhyme with *ḥaddūta*, "tale."

1. The number of sons each wife has given birth to explains why each has earned her respective title.

2. Aside from being the eldest, the son of Precious One derives his right to be first from the preferred status of his mother.

"I want three kilograms of roasted watermelon seeds," the son of Worn-out One said to them. They brought him the seeds, and he stayed awake until the ghoul came.[3] The son of Worn-out One saw the ghoul as he entered the sheep pen, and kept himself well-hidden in a corner until the ghoul took a ewe and left. The boy followed, staying behind him until the ghoul reached the mouth of a well with a huge rock blocking it.[4] When he wanted to go in, the ghoul would move the rock aside and drop into the well. The youth heaped stones into a cairn, and put a stake in the middle of it to identify the well. Then, returning to the sheep pen, he fell asleep.

The father came to check on him in the morning. "What did you see, son?" he asked.

"I've discovered who's been stealing our sheep," answered the boy. "Call my brothers together, and let's go to his place. I'll show you where it is." The brothers were called, and they all set out with their father until they reached the mouth of the ghoul's well.

"Let's each give a hand," said the son of Worn-out One, "and with a little effort we can move this rock."

"What!" exclaimed the father, "Are you crazy?"

"Just help me turn this rock over, you and your sons," said the boy, "and see what happens!"[5]

When they moved the rock, they found it covering a dark and deep well whose bottom could not be seen. He who looked down into it became afraid.

"Which one of you is going to go down into this well?" the father asked the sons of Precious One. Neither of them was willing.

"I'll go down!" volunteered the son of Worn-out One. [When he got down to the bottom of the well] he discovered three girls, each of them like the full moon. But the youngest was the most beautiful.

3. Watermelon seeds, along with other types of seeds and nuts, are eaten at social gatherings, and cracking them is a means of passing the time. See Tale 8, n. 4, and cf. the opening of Tale 8.

4. Wells figure prominently in this corpus (cf. Tales 7, 20, 30, 36, 42). Abandoned wells are an important feature of the Palestinian countryside (see Grant, *People:* 21), which explains why human beings can, as they do in all but one of the tales enumerated above, be placed inside wells, or even live in them, without coming into contact with water. Wells are also thought to be the abode of supernatural beings. Cf. Tale 20, n. 2; see Tale 36, n. 3.

5. The son of Worn-out One is the underdog on two counts: he is the youngest and the son of the less favored woman. The teller, in setting him apart from the others, emphasizes his isolation.

"Are you human or jinn?" the girls asked.

"Human."

"And what made you come down here?" they asked, and he told them his story. Then he asked, "Are you human or jinn?"

"We're human, by Allah," they replied, "and we were kidnapped from our homes by the ghoul."

"When does this ghoul come back?" he asked, and they said, "In a little while."

"I want to hide," he said, and the eldest answered, "You've got no place but the recess in the wall."[6]

Going to hide into the recess, the youth found a sword above his head.

"I want to kill the ghoul with this sword," said the boy.

"Don't strike until you see that his eyes are red," she cautioned. "That's the only way you can be sure he's asleep. If you see him acting any other way, be careful not to strike. He'll be awake, and alert to the slightest movement. Every night he sleeps in one of our laps, and tonight it's the turn of the youngest. Take care not to strike the girl!"[7]

"I smell a human!" announced the ghoul when he came home.

"It's you who brought the smell in your wake!" the girls answered. "How could a human being possibly get in here?"

The ghoul went to sleep in the lap of the youngest one. Looking at him carefully, the boy saw that his eyes were red and realized he was asleep. Immediately, he drew the sword and struck him a blow in the neck.

"Strike again!" urged the ghoul.

6. *Qōs il-ḥawāyij* means literally "the arch for the bedding." Bedding, when not in use, was stacked inside these arches, a curtain hiding it from public view. It is interesting to note that the teller imagines the ghoul's house at the bottom of the well to resemble a typical old-style Palestinian house (see Schmidt and Kahle, *Volkserzählungen* II: pls. 33, 34). See Tale 14, n. 4; Tale 15, n. 5; Tale 16, n. 3; Tale 26, n. 8; Grant, *People:* 75–76.

7. Ghouls play an important role in this corpus, occurring in this and sixteen other tales (6, 8, 10, 12, 16, 18, 19, 20, 22, 28, 29, 31, 33, 34, 35, 40). In Palestinian and Arabic folklore they are not simply evil spirits who rob graves and feed on the flesh of the dead (the typical English dictionary definition); the image of the ghoul, as we shall see, is much more complex. See Tale 3, n. 4; and Footnote Index, s.v. "Ghouls and Jinn."

This tale presents two particular characteristics of ghouls: lack of intelligence (similar to the "Stupid Ogre" in Western folklore), manifested in this case as credulity, and the turning red of their eyes during sleep. For a thorough discussion of Palestinian folk belief and practice concerning supernatural beings, see Canaan, "Dämonenglaube."

"My mother didn't teach me how," replied the lad.[8]

He then called up to his father, "I've killed the ghoul! Let a rope down so we can all get out!" When the rope was lowered, the young man said to the girls, "You go up first." He first let the eldest up, then the middle one. Before he let her up, the youngest, who had two identical bracelets, took off one of them and gave it to him.

The moment he laid eyes on her, the father was bewitched by her beauty. He lowered the rope to bring his son up, but when the boy was near the mouth of the well the father cut the rope.

[Landing at the bottom of the well, the son of Worn-out One] searched about and found a cave. He wandered around inside until he came to the end of it, where he found a door. Opening it, he stepped outside, and behold! he was back on the surface of the earth. He walked till he reached the city, where he heard that his father was preparing to marry the youngest of the three girls, but that she was refusing to marry him until he could match her bracelet. Now, the father had been going from one goldsmith to another, but none of them could match the bracelet. Chancing to meet his father at one of the jewelers in town, the boy said, "I'll make another bracelet just like the one you have. Bring me three kilograms of roasted watermelon seeds to crack so I can stay up a couple of nights and make it. Come back and take it in two days."

"Fine," said the father.

In two days the father came back. "Here it is," said the boy, "I've finished it," and he gave his father the bracelet the girl had given him in the well. Taking the bracelet, the father went to see the girl.

"You must show me the one who made it for you," the girl said.

The father brought the boy, and as soon as she saw him, the girl recognized him.

"Bring me a sword from our house!" the young man commanded.

She brought him a sword, and he killed his father and married the girl.

The bird has flown, and a good evening to all.[9]

8. A ghoul must be killed with one blow, without hesitation or ambivalence, because the second blow will revive him. Killing with one blow is also the mark of a hero.

9. The closing formula *ṭār iṭ-ṭēr u-titmassū bil-xēr,* used frequently by village tellers, is based on the rhyming pair *ṭēr* and *xēr.* See Tale 13, n. 11.

4. *Šwēš, Šwēš!* [1]

Once upon a time there was a man. His mother was always calling down curses upon his head. He strung a hammock for her and put her in it, saying to his wives,[2] "Rock my mother in this hammock, and take very good care of her."

His wives organized themselves so that one of them was always rocking her while another was doing the work. His mother spent all her time in the hammock, and his wives were always rocking her.

One day a traveling salesman came by.[3] "What's going on here?" he asked. "Why is this woman always being rocked in the hammock?"

"Brother," answered the man, "she's always calling down curses upon my head."

"Is she your mother?"

"Yes, my mother."

"What do you want, old woman?" asked the salesman. "Do you want a husband?"

"Heh! Heh! Heh!" she chuckled.[4]

"Your mother wants a husband," said the salesman to the son. "I asked her, and she started to chuckle."

"Fine," said the son to the salesman.

"Mother," he said to her, "I'm going to find you a husband."

"May Allah bless you!" she said.[5] For the first time in his life she called down blessings upon his head.

1. The name of the tale is the diminutive form of the common expression *Šway, šway,* "Not so fast!"

2. As noted in the Introduction, the frequency of reference to polygyny (cf. also Tales 5, 6, 7, 20, 30, 35) is out of all proportion to its actual occurrence in the culture.

The situation prevailing at the beginning of the tale, where the two wives serve the mother, reflects fairly accurately the expectations (if not the actual practice) prevalent in the culture, which holds motherhood in very high esteem. They say that "paradise is under the feet of the mothers" (*il-janne taḥt aqdām il-ʾummahāt*).

3. Traveling salesmen occur fairly frequently in the tales (cf. Tales 10, 12, 26, 34, 42). They brought with them not only household goods, such as cloth and glassware, but also much lore, especially in folk medicine. Considered jacks-of-all-trades, they often gave advice on taboo subjects as well. They say of a woman who badly wants marriage, for instance, that she is "after that which the salesman talked about" (*bidhā mn illī ʾaḥkā ʿanno l-bayyāʿ*).

4. Sexuality is an especially taboo subject in Palestinian culture. In showing discontent with everything, the mother uses the culturally approved code to communicate her message.

5. *Alla yirḍā ʿalēk*—literally, "May Allah be pleased with you."

He gave her nice clothes to wear, put earrings in her ears (she was blind), and said, "*Yalla!*[6] Come with me! I'm going to find you a husband."

He carried her over to the lair of the hyena.[7] Setting her down, he said, "Sit here a while! Your husband will be arriving soon."

The hyena came and approached her, but she drew away from him, saying, "*Šwēš, šwēš!* Not so fast! Not so fast! Water has been spilled on the new clothes, and the cat has eaten the candy. Not so fast, lest you break the seed!"[8]

"Hmmm!" thought the hyena. "This woman's blind and can't see me."

(She's in even worse shape than I am!)[9]

Every time the hyena approached her, the woman said, "Water has been spilled on the new clothes, and the cat has eaten the candy. Not so fast! Not so fast! Lest you break the seed."

Her son sat opposite, watching, until the hyena devoured his mother. Then he left.[10]

6. "Let's go!" from *yā Allah* (O Allah!), is a very common expression in Mashreq Arab culture. The name of Allah is invoked at the beginning of a journey to make it a propitious one.

7. The hyena—an appropriate creature in this context—is ascribed characteristics bordering on the supernatural. It is thought to be a very ugly creature that does not attack its victims directly. Rather, it rubs against them and urinates and, by its eerie sound and the smell of its urine, entrances them and lures them to its lair, where it devours them. At the end of the tale the hyena approaches the old woman several times, but she is already entranced. The son sees the mother's sexuality as a form of possession resembling the magic power of the ugly hyena. Linguistic evidence corroborates this view. They say *bitẓabbaᶜ* ("he's behaving like a hyena") of an ugly old man who attempts to behave seductively, and indeed, the actions of the hyena—at least in the old woman's eyes—are seductive. See Grant, *People:* 18; Hanauer, *Folklore:* 270–273; Sirḥān, *Mawsūᶜat* V:47; and Granqvist, *Problems:* 116–118.

8. In this formulaic expression, the words for "water" (*mbū*), "new clothes" (*daḥḥa*), and candy (*maḥḥa*) are all derived from baby talk (see Tale 1, n. 7). The last two are a rhyming pair; the part of the expression about breaking the seed is obscure.

9. This interjection by the teller, who was nearly blind and over seventy years of age when we collected the tale, identifies her with the woman in the tale, which possibly explains why the woman's blindness—a significant narrative detail—is introduced so casually.

10. The woman in this tale would be considered to have achieved what all women are supposed to dream about: loving and obedient sons and grandchildren, and dutiful daughters-in-law. Not only is she loved and cared for, but she can now be complete mistress of her household. On the complexity of the mother/son relationship, see Introduction, "The Tales and the Culture."

5. *The Golden Pail*

TELLER: Testify that God is One!
AUDIENCE: There is no god but God.

There was in remote times a king who had two wives, a new one who was precious to him and whom he loved, and an old one whom he did not care for. The old one had one son, while the new one had two.[1]

"Wait till your father has assembled the Council of State," said the new wife to her eldest son one day. "Then go up to him, kiss his hand, and ask him to give you the kingdom."[2]

Waiting till morning, when all the ministers and dignitaries of state were meeting with his father, the son went up, wished the assembly a good morning, came up to his father, and kissed his hand.[3]

"What do you want, son?" asked the king.

"Father," said the boy, "I want the kingdom in your lifetime, not after your death."

"Go work as hard as I did and suffer the same hardships," answered the father. "Then come back, and I'll give you the kingdom."

The boy went back to his mother, who asked, "What did he say to you?"

"He said such and such," the boy answered.

She then sent her other son, who went up the next day, wished all a good morning, came up to his father, kissed his hand, and waited.

"What do you want, son?" asked the father.

"I want the kingdom in your lifetime, not after your death," answered the boy.

"Go work as hard as I did," the father said. "Suffer the same hardships. Then come back and I'll give you the kingdom."

The boy turned around and went straight back. He and his brother had not achieved anything.

Meanwhile, the old wife found out what was going on. Calling her son over, she said to him, "Clever Ḥasan,[4] go up to your father, kiss his

1. On the number of children and a wife's status, see Tale 3, nn. 1, 2.

2. "Council of State"—*dīwān*—is anglicized as "divan." "Go up to him" (*ʾiṭlaʿ ʿindo*): the language here, as in many other tales, reflects the place of kings and notables, which is always pictured to be "up."

3. It is common practice among Palestinians to kiss the hand of an elder, especially the father, as a sign of obedience and respect. The gesture consists of taking the older person's right hand in one or both hands, kissing the back of it, then bringing it up to one's forehead.

4. "The Golden Pail" belongs to a cycle of adventure tales in which the hero's name is

hand, and ask him for the kingdom." The boy went up and, finding the divan already full of people, wished everyone a good day and came up to his father. He kissed his father's hand and waited.

"What do you want, boy?" snapped the father.

"Father," answered the boy, "I want the kingdom in your lifetime, not after your death."

Taking hold of him, the father gave him a beating and dismissed him. When he came back to his mother, she said, "What's the matter with you?" He answered, "Such and such happened."

"Go back up and ask him again," she said.

The boy went up again, and again his father beat him and threw him out. When he came back down, his mother asked, "What happened to you?" He answered, "Such and such he did to me. He beat me."

"Go back another time," she said, and he went up for the third time.

This time the king shot up out of his seat, wanting to kill the boy. He wanted to take hold of him and throw him down the stairs. The ministers and lords of state also jumped up. "What! O Ruler of the Age!" they said. "Just say to him the same words you said to his brothers, and he'll go away. Do you think that this one is going to come and take the kingdom?" They calmed the king down, until finally he said to his son, "Go work as hard as I did and suffer as I suffered. Then come back and I'll give you the kingdom."

Turning around, the boy went straight to his mother.

"What happened, son?" she asked.

"Such and such he said to me," answered the son. "And if it weren't for the ministers, he would have thrown me down the stairs."

The following day his mother prepared provisions for a journey and took her son to the outskirts of town, you might say down around the house of Faraj,[5] beyond all the other houses, where there was a slab of stone. Standing on it, she called out, "O Ballān!" and, behold! a horse appeared. It was a jinn horse. She put the food provisions and a waterskin in the saddlebags and said to her son, "Mount!" "Ballān," she said to the horse, "take care of your rider. Farewell!" Then she went home.

---

always either Clever Ḥasan or Clever Mḥammad. Other such tales in this collection include 17 (see n. 5) and 18 (n. 9).

5. Faraj is a member of the storyteller's own community whose house fits the description in the tale. Tellers will often either identify directly with the hero or heroine or locate the action in their own village and the surrounding environment. See n. 14, below. Cf. Tale 18, n. 12; Tale 30, n. 11; see also Footnote Index, s.v. "Geography," "Narrative Devices."

Turning to the west, the horse started moving. They traveled for a day, two, three, four, ten, a month (Allah knows how long!),[6] until they arrived at the seashore. They had been traveling along the shore awhile, when lo! there was a feather. And how it sparkled all by itself! Finding it beautiful, the lad wanted to dismount and pick it up. "By Allah," he said to the horse, "I want to get down and take it up."

What was the horse's response? "By Allah," he said, "you're going to be sorry if you take it, and sorry if you don't."

"If I'm going to be sorry either way," replied the boy, "by Allah, I'm going to get down and bring it with me." Dismounting, he picked up the feather and put it in his pocket. He then got back on the horse, and they traveled and traveled until they arrived in a city.

Where does a stranger go? To the khan.[7] Straight to the caravansary they went, where the boy rented a room for himself and his horse, and stayed.

That night, as it happened, the king of that place let it be known that it was forbidden for people to light their homes. He wanted to find out who was obedient and who was not. Now, the youth knew of this order, and did not dare light his room. Toward the end of the night, you might say, he pulled the feather out of his pocket and stuck it into the wall. If the teller is not lying,[8] that feather lit up the whole room.

Just about then the king, in disguise, was conducting a tour of inspection in the city with his minister, to see who was obeying his order and who was not. They went around the entire city, and found it all dark. When they passed by the inn, however, they found one of the rooms lit.

"Councillor," ordered the king, "manage this for me!"

6. The teller's reluctance to be specific about time reflects not only a cultural but also a religious attitude, since the future is imponderable and in the hands of Allah.

7. The khan (*xān*) was a public inn where caravans used to stop for the night. Grant (*People:* 209) describes the one at al-Bīre: "Their khan is typical of a country caravanserai. Thousands of people pass it: messengers going up and down the country, village priests or teachers going to Jerusalem to get their monthly pay, sellers and buyers, caravans of wheat, . . . tourists, pilgrims, missionaries, . . . camping outfits, mounted Turkish soldiers sent to some village to bring in an offender or to collect taxes."

8. *ʿAlā ḍimt ir-rāwī*—literally, "Upon the word, or responsibility, of the teller." Despite the magical elements in this and many other of the tales, the tendency in narration is toward realism. Thus narrators frequently disavow the literal truth of what they are relating by distancing themselves from the action through such devices. In this case the teller employs two in succession, here and in the preceding sentence ("you might say"). See n. 13, below. Cf. Tale 1, n. 4; also see Footnote Index, s.v. "Narrative Devices."

"The owner, O Ruler of the Age," replied the vizier, "manages his own property."

"Put a mark on this place!" ordered the king, and the vizier marked it.

In the morning the king sent after the young man, and he came.

"Didn't you know the king had ordered a blackout last night?"

"Yes, Your Majesty, I did."

"Well then, why did you put a light on in your room?"

"My lord, I didn't light my room."

"But I saw it with my own eyes. So did the vizier."

"Your Majesty, I didn't light any lamps."

"What! Are you calling me a liar? Executioner!"

"Your Majesty, please, wait a moment. I tell you I didn't burn a light in my room, but on the path I found a feather that glows by itself. I hung it up, and it lit the room."

"What kind of feather is this, that can light up a whole room?"

"A bird feather, your Majesty."

"Bring it over, and let me see if you're telling the truth!"

The lad went and brought the feather. When the king saw it, he fell completely in love with it.

"How strange, O Ruler of the Age!" exclaimed the vizier. "Could it be that you're so completely taken with a feather? What if you were to see the bird from which this feather came? What would you do?"

"And who's going to bring this bird?" asked the king.

"He who brought the feather," answered the vizier, "can also bring the bird."

"Young man!"

"Yes."

"You must bring me the bird from which this feather came. You have two days and a third, and if you don't bring it, I'll have your head."

"Please, O Ruler of the Age!" the lad begged. "Where can I bring it from? And how am I ever going to find it? This is a feather I found by the seashore while riding my horse. How should I know the bird to whom it belongs?"

Now the boy went home crying. To whom? To the horse, who, since he was from the jinn, knew what was going on.

"This one is easy," he said.

"What do you mean, it's easy?"

"I tell you," returned the horse, "this is not a difficult task. Go back to the king, and say, 'O King! I want a cage made of silver and gold from the vizier's treasury, and it must be decorated such that no two figures are the same. Otherwise, the task will never be done.'" The horse had understood that the whole idea had come from the vizier.

Returning to the king, the young man said, "O Ruler of the Age! I must have a cage made of silver and gold from the vizier's own treasury; otherwise, what you requested will never be accomplished." By Allah, having said that, the youth turned around and left.

The king sent for the vizier, and he came. The king said to him, "You will have a cage made of silver and gold from your own treasury, and no two decorations on it can be the same. Otherwise, I'll have your head!"

What was the vizier to do? He went and gathered what he had about the house in money and gold, and had the goldsmith make the cage ordered by the king. The lad then came and picked it up.

"Mount!" said Ballān, and he mounted. The horse flew with him, and kept flying until he landed at the place where he knew the bird would come.

"Do you see that tree?" the horse asked.

"Yes."

"Go climb it, and hang the cage in it. Open its door, and wait. When the bird comes to roost for the night, she'll see the cage and will be delighted by it. 'By Allah,' she'll say to herself, 'this cage is suitable to none but me for spending the night.' Meanwhile, wait till she's right in the center of the cage, then come from behind, close the door on her, and bring her down."

The lad took the cage and hung it in the tree, leaving the door open. Toward sunset, the bird came to roost in the tree. "By Allah," she said when she saw the cage, "this cage is suitable to none but me for spending the night." She went in it to see if there was enough room for her, and our friend (he was not asleep!) quickly shut the door on her and brought the cage down. Returning to the horse, he mounted, and they flew until the horse had brought him back.

Taking the cage and the bird with him in the morning, the youth went to see the king. "Here, O Ruler of the Age," he said, "is the bird that's the owner of the feather you admired!"

Well, brothers, the moment the king laid eyes on the bird, he went out of his mind over her. The vizier was there, and wanted to take revenge on the boy. He wished to send him on a task that would be his end.[9]

"Truly, O Ruler of the Age," he broke in, "you've gone crazy over this bird. What would you do if you were to see its owner?"

"And who will bring her?" asked the king.

"He who brought the feather and the bird will bring the owner," responded the vizier.

The king summoned the youth, and he came.

"Young man!" said the king.

"Yes, O Ruler of the Age!"

"You must bring me the owner of this bird. You have two days and a third, and if you don't bring her, I'll have your head."

"Please have mercy, O Ruler of the Age!" begged the boy. "This was a bird flying in the wilderness. She isn't owned by anyone, and even if she does have an owner, how am I to find her?"

The boy went home to the horse, crying. "What's the matter?" asked the horse, and he answered, "Such and such is the problem."

"Didn't I tell you you'd be sorry if you took that feather and sorry if you didn't?" the horse reminded him. "In any case this is an easy one. Go back to the king and say to him, 'O Ruler of the Age, I must have a boat seven decks high, made of silver and gold from the treasury of the vizier. Otherwise, your request will never be fulfilled.'"

The lad returned to the king and asked for the boat. Sending after the vizier, the king said, "You will have a boat seven decks high made of silver and gold from your own treasury, with no two figures in its decoration the same. Quite a sight this boat will be, eh, my vizier?"

Where was the vizier to go, and what was he to do? He gathered a bit of this and sold a bit of that, putting money in one account and taking it out of another, until the boat was made. When it was finished, the king sent for the boy.

The horse spoke with the boy, teaching him what to do. "Now board this boat," he said, "and sail until you reach the port, where there will be a city. Anchor the boat there and call out, 'Hey people! Free showing!'

9. The vizier, whose office resembled that of lord chancellor, is a stock villain, frequently portrayed as a devious and conniving creature, jealous of any favors his master might bestow on outsiders and willing to go to any length to protect his privileged position. Cf. Tale 44, n. 15; and the behavior of the vizier in Tale 45.

You'll wait the whole day, but the king's daughter won't show up. The second day she'll hear about your boat and will come. But when she does come, how will you recognize her? When she approaches from the distance, you'll see two servantgirls guarding her, one on each side. As she gets closer, she will have the people of the city cleared out of her path. That's how you'll recognize that she's the daughter of the king. At that moment, stop people from coming on the boat. Say to them, 'O uncles,[10] I'm not charging you admission and yet you're damaging the boat. You can't come on to this boat except one at a time!' Wait until she comes aboard and becomes absorbed in looking at the decorations on this deck or that, then weigh anchor, start moving, and bring her with you." The horse taught him what to do.

The youth boarded his ship and sailed until he reached the port. He dropped anchor on the edge of town and started calling out, "Free showing!" And what do you think happened, my dears? Here was this boat, decorated in silver and gold with no two designs alike. People came running to see it.

The first day no one fitting the horse's description showed up. The second day, however, one of the servantgirls happened to be on her way to the oven to bake bread. She had just placed her loaves in the oven and sat down when she saw people rushing over to take a look at the boat. Leaving her loaves, she went along and became absorbed. When she returned, she found the bread burned. She took it to her mistress, who commenced beating her.

"Please, mistress, have patience! Wait and let me tell you what happened."

"Yes. Tell me."

"There is a boat in the harbor," related the slavegirl, "and each of its decorations is different from the others. People have been looking at it free for the past two days."

The king's daughter put on the robe of anger and sat around the house, scowling.[11] When her father came in, he asked, "What's the matter, dear daughter? Who has angered you? Did someone say something to you?"

10. See Tale 14, n. 7; Tale 35, n. 5.

11. The "robe of anger" here is metaphorical. Dark colors, especially black, are worn as a sign of mourning, and colorful clothes are worn on happy occasions, such as public feasts and holidays, but no specific garment in Palestinian folk costume would indicate a state of mind like anger.

"Of course I'm angry," she retorted. "There's a gold-and-silver boat in town, people have been seeing it free, and you don't even tell me to go have a look!"

"Well, daughter," returned the father, "is it that serious? Why don't you go ahead and have a look."

She went, my dears, and dressed for going out, taking a lot of care with her appearance. You should have seen the king's daughter then! With her two servants by her side, she came, and when people saw her coming they scattered out of her path.

The youth recognized her. "O uncles!" he announced. "You can't be on this boat except one at a time. You're tearing it apart, and I'm not even charging you admission."

When the king's daughter arrived, she wanted to go on board with her servantgirls, but he said to them, "One at a time." Of course, no one can go before the king's daughter, so into the boat she went and started looking around. The lad waited until she was engrossed, then weighed anchor and started for home. By the time she was aware of herself again, they were halfway across the sea.

"Please! Young man!" she pleaded.

"Don't waste your breath!"

"O so and so! O son of the people!"[12]

"It's no use," he answered.

Removing a ring from her finger, she dropped it into the water. Meanwhile, he sailed and sailed until he reached the city, where he moored his boat and took the girl straight to the king.

"O Ruler of the Age," he said, "this is the owner of the bird."

Eh! The king, when he saw her, went out of his mind over her. Taking her with him, he led her into a palace. It was her own palace, which he had given to her, but no sooner did she enter than she bolted the door behind her. He wanted to go in and visit with her, but she would not open for him.

"Not for you," she declared, "or even someone above you, will I open this door. I swear by my father's head, and by Him who gave my father

12. *Yā bn in-nās* is a hortative expression frequently used when people are being asked to be reasonable. The implication here is that the person so addressed is the son (or, later in the tale, daughter) of good or worthy people with whom one can reach an understanding. Note the emphasis on lineage, as discussed in the Introduction ("The Tales and the Culture"). Cf. Tale 14, n. 2; Tale 44, n. 15.

the power over other people's heads, I won't open unless my ring were to come back from the bottom of the sea!"

"What!" exclaimed the king. "Who could bring your ring back from the bottom of the sea?"

"O Ruler of the Age," the vizier jumped in, "he who brought the bird and brought her can also bring the ring."

Sending after the youth, the king said to him, "You must bring the ring back from the bottom of the sea."

"O Ruler of the Age," the boy asked, "how can I possibly recover a ring that has fallen into the sea?"

"You have two days and a third," the king insisted. "Otherwise, I'll cut off your head."[13]

The boy went home to the horse, in tears.

"What's the matter?"

"I must bring back the ring she has thrown into the sea."

"Didn't I tell you you'd be sorry if you took that feather, and sorry if you didn't?" the horse asked. "In any case, this one is easy. Go speak to the king. Say to him, 'I must have a boat full of flour from the treasury of the vizier. Otherwise, what you want will never come to pass.'"

The lad returned to the king, who sent after the minister and said, "You will have a boat made, and will fill it with flour."

The minister had the boat made, and filled it with flour. They sent for the boy, and the horse gave him instructions. He said, "Sail this boat until you reach the place where she tossed her ring overboard. There, halt and drop anchor, and throw all the flour you're carrying into the water. All the fish in the area will come to eat until they're full. The head fish will then come up and ask, 'Who has done us this favor? We'd like to reward him.' Ask for the ring, and they will fetch it for you."

The lad boarded the boat, and headed for the place where the king's daughter had dropped her ring and stopped. He threw the flour overboard, and when the fish had eaten their fill, their chief appeared. "Who was it that did us this favor?" he asked. "We'd like to reward him."

"By Allah, it was I," answered the lad.

"What would you like?"

13. *Willā baqtaʿ rās l-ibʿīd*—literally, "Or I'll cut off the head of the distant one!" Here the teller switches from the second person to the third, as if to say to the audience, "May this not happen to you!" or "May it be distant from you!" Such distancing devices are used to ward off possible harm. See n. 8, above; Tale 34, n. 5.

"A ring fell from my hand."

Going back down and searching for it, the head fish found the ring in the mouth of another fish. He brought it up and gave it to the lad, who turned around and set sail for home. When he arrived he went to see the king.

"Open up!" said the king to the girl. "Here's your ring! Take it back!"

Reaching out her hand, she took the ring and bolted the door again.

"O so and so!" the king called out. "O daughter of the people!"

"By Allah," she answered, "I'm not opening this door unless I get my horse."

"And who will bring your horse?"

"O Ruler of the Age," the vizier said, "he who brought her and brought the ring from the depths of the sea can also bring the horse."

The king sent for the young man, and when he came, said to him, "You must bring her horse, wherever he is, or else I'll cut off your head."

"Please, O Ruler of the Age!" he begged. "How can I go back to her country? Her father will kill me. And where am I to find her horse?"

"I don't know," the king answered.

The boy went home to the horse. Tears had filled his eyes.

"What's the matter?"

"They want me to bring her horse."

"Didn't I tell you you'd be sorry if you took it, and sorry if you didn't? Anyway, this is an easy one. Go back to the king and say, 'I want a gold-and-silver bridle from the treasury of the vizier. Otherwise, the task will never be done.'"

Returning to the king, the youth made his request. The king summoned the minister, and said, "You must provide him with a bridle made of silver and gold."

Selling nearly everything he owned, the minister had the bridle made. They sent after the boy, and he came and took the bridle with him back to the horse. After the lad put the bridle on him, the horse told him to mount, and he flew with the boy till he crossed the sea and came to the country of the girl's father, where he landed in hilly territory.[14] The boy dismounted.

"Do you see that mountain?" asked the horse.

14. Despite the magic flight, the horse lands in territory very much resembling the region of Upper Galilee around the village of ʿArrābe, where the tale was collected. See n. 5, above; cf. Tale 17, n. 7; Tale 26, n. 11; Tale 36, n. 2; Tale 44, n. 11.

"Yes."

"Over there, by the side of that mountain, there's a cave, and in the depths of the cave is the horse you want. He's bigger and stronger than me, and I can't let him see me. If he sees me, he'll kill me. Take this bridle with you. When you approach him, he'll neigh so loud the earth will shake, but don't be afraid. Come up to him fearlessly, put the bridle on his head, the bit in his mouth, tighten his cinch, remove his hobble, mount him, and ride him straight back.[15] You'll find me back at the inn. Don't worry about me!"

The boy went and did as the horse had instructed him. He mounted the girl's horse, and it flew with him until they reached the city, where he headed straight to the king.

"O Ruler of the Age," he announced, "here's her horse! I've brought it." Giving him the horse, the youth returned to his room.

The king led the horse with him, and said to the girl, "Open up! Here's your horse! It has come."

Seeing her horse, the girl brought out a sword, opened the door, mounted him, and set to slashing him until she had chopped him into three or four pieces. Then, going back into the palace, she locked the door.

"O so and so! O daughter of worthy people!" the king pleaded.

"By Allah, I won't open," came the reply, "until my horse has been made to stand up as he was before."

"Eh!" exclaimed the king, "who's going to revive your horse?"

"O Ruler of the Age," the vizier broke in, "Do you think it's such a big thing? He who brought the bird and the girl, and brought the ring from the depths of the sea, can also bring the horse back to life."

The king sent after the lad and said, "You must bring the horse back to life, just as he was before."

"Please have mercy, O Ruler of the Age!" the boy entreated. "The living creatures you've asked for, I've brought. But reviving the dead! Is it possible that anyone can bring dead creatures back to life except their Maker?"

"You have two days and a third to raise this horse from the dead," the king said. "Otherwise, I'll cut off your head!"

The boy went home to the horse, his eyes full of tears.

15. In providing this detailed description of equestrian equipment, the teller, Šāfiᶜ, who is a farmer, demonstrates direct knowledge of the subject and adds a touch of realism by incorporating details from his daily life.

"What's the matter?" asked the horse, and the boy answered, "Such and such is the problem."

"All right," the horse reassured him. "This is an easy one. Go back to the king and say, 'O Ruler of the Age! I want a pail made of silver and gold from the treasury of the vizier. Otherwise, this thing will never come to pass.'"

The king summoned the vizier. "You must have a pail of silver and gold made for him."

If his wife had any jewelry left, the minister did not spare it. He sold every last thing he had to make the gold-and-silver pail, which he delivered to the young man, who brought it to the horse.

"Go get me five piasters worth of rope from the shop," said the horse.[16] The boy went and got the rope. "Tie the handle of the pail with the rope," said the horse, "and dangle it from my neck." The boy tied the pail and dangled it from the horse's neck. "Mount!" said the horse. He mounted, and the horse flew with him. "Soon we'll be landing on the sea of life," said the horse in flight. "I'll have to dip my head in the water to fill the pail. When I bring my head out again, I'll be drunk. You must be careful to stay awake so you can splash some of the water on my face and revive me. Otherwise I might fall into the sea, and it'll be the end of both of us."

"Don't worry," said the lad.

The horse flew until he reached the sea of life, then landed, filled the pail with water, and pulled his head out. But the boy's attention had wandered, and he forgot to splash him. The horse reeled from side to side, and he was about to fall when some of the water from the pail splashed on his face and he revived. "See what you've done!" the horse chided him. "You've almost cost us both our lives." And he flew back. Where? Straight to the inn.

"Go bring me a few empty bottles," said the horse when they landed at the khan. The lad went and brought them. The horse then filled them with water from the pail, saying, "Take these and put them away now. They'll be needed later. Then carry this pail over to the cut-up horse. Bring the severed joints together and splash them with the water, and

16. The units of currency used in the tales vary. The names of Ottoman coins are sometimes used, as are units of Palestinian currency under the British Mandate and units of Jordanian currency. The piaster, a hundred of which equaled one Palestinian pound (*lēra*), was the basic unit of currency in the Mandate. It is also the basic unit of Jordanian currency, one hundred equaling a dinar.

they'll stick. Open his mouth and pour some of the water into it, and he'll rise up, neighing as he did before."

The youth went, stuck the horse's joints together, and poured some of the water down his mouth. The horse jumped up, neighing as he used to.

"Open your door!" said the king to the girl. "Your horse is like it was before!"

"I swear by my father's head," she answered, "and by Him who gave him power over people's necks, I won't open, and you won't see me, until you've burned at the stake the boy who brought my horse and my bird!"

"My dear girl," exclaimed the king, "what's his fault except to be doing us favors?"

"I don't know," came the response.

Now the minister saw his opportunity. "O Ruler of the Age!" he jumped in. "Are you afraid for him? Why should you care about him at all?"

The king sent the crier into town to announce that everyone must bring a load of wood and some burning coals.[17] The boy was summoned and informed of his fate, and he went crying to the horse. The wood was piled, and the boy was brought and put on top. They were ready to light the fire.

The horse had meanwhile gotten hold of the boy and said to him, "Take off your clothes and rub yourself with the water from the pail until your body is all wet. Then go up to the top of the pile, stand in the middle of the fire, and tell them to throw more wood into it. Don't be afraid!"

The lad did as the horse had advised him, mounting to the top of the woodpile. They started the fire, and the flames engulfed him till he was no longer visible. Turning the logs over, the lad called out to the king, "Bring, O King, bring more wood and add to the fire! This is the reward for good deeds! Bring more wood!"

17. Grant (*People:* 149) says of town criers: "Often of an evening one will hear the crier publishing something of general concern to the villagers. . . . The tribal elders decide upon some matter for general observance and the crier makes it known. For instance, when an especially dry season was on, the village crier was heard proclaiming that no woman should draw more than one jar of water from the springs at a time. . . . At another time it was forbidden the people to harvest the olives until a certain date. Lost articles are advertised by the criers, and those lounging about in the evening are kept in touch with business news, as the voice penetrates all quarters of the village."

The king then asked the boy to come down from the fire. He did, and behold! he was completely unharmed.

"Where are you from, my lad?" asked the king.

"I'm from such and such a city," answered the young man. "I'm the son of King So and So."

The king rushed up to the boy, hugged him, and started kissing him. "You're the son of my brother," he exclaimed, "and I'm doing *this* to you!" Taking hold of the vizier, he pushed him into the fire. Then, dear brothers, he gave the lad the girl for a bride. He also gave him the horse, the bird, the boat, the pail, and everything else, and they rode out together. They were on their way to the king who was the father of the boy.

This king was sitting at home, and what did he see but a troop of horsemen approaching from afar. Thinking he was being attacked, he alerted his army, and they got themselves ready and mounted their horses. The king sent a scout to discover what was going on. The scout rode out, and found it was the king's own brother, come to pay him a visit. When the king heard this news, how happy he was! He went out to meet his brother in person, and found his own son with him.

When they had gone inside, the king's brother related to him the story of his son and what had happened to him. At that moment, in the presence of his brother, the king stepped down and handed his kingdom over to his son, who accepted it from his father and was content.

This is my tale I've told it, and in your hands I leave it.

Afterword

The five tales brought together here are concerned with the different aspects of the relationship between parents and children, touching on the theme of individual freedom, which will recur in many of the tales that follow. The first tale focuses on the relationship between mother and daughter, the second and fourth on that between mother and son, and the third and fifth on that between father and son.

The opening episode of the first tale, itself a recurring motif in the corpus, demonstrates the importance of having children (a major theme in the culture), and subsequent events in the tale demonstrate the economic value children have for the family. It is significant that the woman in "Ṭunjur, Ṭunjur," as in nearly all the other tales in which a similar wish is made, should ask for a daughter rather than a son. But in addition to the emotional bonds that hold mother and daughter together, an economic motive is operating in the tale as well. The mother's initial wish is not only for a daughter but also for a source of income, and her willingness to let her daughter out of the house is conditioned by her poverty. The daughter, for her part, does not want to remain "on the shelf," which is considered the proper place for a woman—well scrubbed and beautiful, but out of sight. She wants to go out and see the world.

Yet this urge for freedom is fraught with danger to the family honor. A kind of inevitable logic is evident in all the tales: whenever a girl is allowed out of the house or left on her own, trouble follows. This point emerges clearly from the fifth tale in the group (and from following tales as well), where the father's indulgence of the princess's whims leads to her abduction by the hero. In "Ṭunjur, Ṭunjur," in contrast, the theme of individual freedom is intertwined with that of economic necessity. Ṭunjur's adventures, which by the standards of the community are morally ambiguous, are forgiven by her mother; the daughter would not have been able to get away so easily if there had been any males in the family. Perhaps because of these constraints on the freedom of women, the daughters in both tales must rely on a ruse to achieve their aim of getting out of the house.

The second and fourth tales present a different aspect of the child/parent conflict; the focus here is on sexual jealousy, a taboo subject in the family circle. In the second tale, "The Woman Who Married Her Son," the conflict arises from the son's need to switch roles—he must cease to be his mother's son and establish himself as his wife's husband and the head of his family. In the situation of the patrilocal extended family, when a son marries, both mother and daughter-in-law have difficulties. The mother's possessiveness in the tale, her need to keep her son under her control, drives her to throw the wife out of the house so that she can be both mother and wife to her own son. In the fourth tale, in contrast, the mother wishes to break free of her role, which confines her to being a passive recipient of her son's attention. In addition to being a mother, she also wants to marry again and become a wife.

The third and fifth tales are concerned with the relationship of fathers and sons. Both illustrate the son's struggle to achieve independence by challenging the authority of the father. In the third tale, "Precious One and Worn-out One," the father is shown as being a deceitful tyrant who resents the son's courage and independence and attempts to compete with him sexually. By overcoming the father, the son succeeds in demonstrating his maturity and achieving independence. Similarly, in the fifth tale, "The Golden Pail," the son proves himself worthy of inheriting his father's kingdom by meeting his uncle's challenge. Here the co-wives also compete, wishing their respective children to inherit the throne. In particular, it is the rejected co-wife who urges her son to challenge the father and who provides him with the means to achieve success, thereby vindicating her position in the family. In a polygynous situation, the struggle over inheritance starts very early in the marriage; indeed, often the main worry of a first wife and her children is to prevent the father from marrying again because of concern over inheritance. Although the stake in the last tale is the entire kingdom, the struggle over a family's small piece of land could be just as intense.

Siblings

6. *Half-a-Halfling*

TELLER: Allah has spoken and His word is a blessing!
AUDIENCE: Blessings abound, Allah willing![1]

Once upon a time there was a man who was married to two women. One of them was his first cousin and the other was a stranger, and neither of them could get pregnant.[2]

"I'm going to visit the sheikh,"[3] he said to himself one day, "and maybe for the sake of Allah he'll give me some medicine to make these women conceive." He went to the sheikh and said, "I want you to give me a medicine that'll make my wives get pregnant."

"Go to such and such a mountain," the sheikh advised, "and there you'll find a ghoul. Say to him, 'I want two pomegranates to feed my wives so they can get pregnant,' and see what he says to you."[4]

The man went forth, and came upon the ghoul. He approached him

1. See Tale 16, n. 1, for a literal translation and a discussion of this opening formula. *Inšālla* (Allah willing!) is one of the most commonly heard expressions in the Arab world, representing, among both Christians and Muslims, an all-pervading belief in the will of God. For a story of what befell a man who refused to say *inšālla,* see Schmidt and Kahle, *Volkserzählungen* II:42.

2. Presumably the man married his cousin first, and when she could not get pregnant he married the stranger. Many proverbs and folk sayings illustrate the desirability of endogamy, such as "A first cousin with [nothing more than] a cloak, and as for the stranger—damn his father!" (*ibn il-ʿam w-il-ʿabā, w-il-ġarīb yilʿan ʾabāh*). A first cousin is in fact entitled to his cousin even when she has been promised to someone else: "A first cousin can bring a bride down from the mare [even if she's on her way to marry someone else]" (*ibn il-ʿam biṭayyiḥ ʿan il-faras*). For a discussion of endogamy, see Introduction.

3. The sheikh was a practitioner of holistic folk medicine. Among Palestinian peasants, no clear distinction is drawn between exorcism, the use of charms, folk psychotherapy, and folk medicine, although only a religious person is trusted to provide care. See Tale 22, n. 7.

4. For a discussion of the ghoul figure, see Tale 3, n. 7. Ghouls, as we have said, play a complex role in the tales; here, they are helpful figures. Although their unkempt appearance gives the impression of neglect and wildness, their favor can be won by giving them the comforts of civilization, such as shaving their beards and trimming their hair, particularly the eyebrows. See nn. 7, 11, 12, 13, below; and Footnote Index, s.v. "Ghouls and Jinn."

Pomegranates are a symbol of fertility; see Tale 35, n. 1.

immediately, shaved his beard, trimmed his eyebrows, and said, "Peace to you!"[5]

"And to you, peace!" replied the ghoul. "Had not your salaam come before your request, I would've munched your bones so loud my brother who lives on the next mountain would've heard it.[6] What do you want?"

The man told him what he wanted, and the ghoul said, "Go to the next mountain over there, and you'll find my elder brother. Ask him, and he'll tell you what to do."

The man went to the next mountain over and found the ghoul. He did with him as he had done with his brother. Then he said, "Peace to you!"

"And to you, peace!" replied the ghoul. "Had not your salaam come before your request, I would've munched your bones so loud my sister who lives on the next mountain would've heard it. What can I do for you?" The man told him what he wanted, and the ghoul said, "Go to my sister on the next mountain over there, and she'll tell you what to do."

The man did as he was told, and found the ghouleh grinding wheat, her breasts thrown over her shoulders.[7] He came forward and sucked on her right breast, then on her left. After he did this, he put a handful of her flour in his mouth.

"You've sucked at my right breast," declared the ghouleh, "and now you're dearer to me than my son Ismāᶜīn. You've sucked at my left breast, and now you're dearer than my son Naṣṣār. And now that you've eaten my flour, you're dearer than my own children. What can I do for you?"

"I want two pomegranates to feed my wives so they can have children," he answered.

"Go to that orchard over there," she said. "You'll find a ghoul sleeping, using one ear for a mattress and the other for a blanket. Pick two pomegranates and run away as fast as you can."

Having done as he was told, the man took the two pomegranates and started on his way home.

As he was traveling, he became hungry. "I'm going to eat part of my

5. "Peace to you!"—*salāmu ᶜalēkum*—is one of the most important expressions in Arab culture. Not to be so greeted when encountering a stranger is considered a hostile gesture, whereas an enemy who utters it can neutralize an already existing hostility.

6. *Lōla salāmak sabaq kalāmak, kān xallēt . . . tismaᶜ qarṭ iᶜẓāmak.* Variants of this formula occur in similar situations in Tales 10 and 22.

7. For further details on ghoulish behavior, see nn. 4, above; 11, 12, 13, below; and Tale 22, n. 9. Human behavior and institutions are generalized in the tales to include even ghouls. Cf. Tale 8, n. 9. It is said that a boy who suckles from a woman will always call her

cousin's pomegranate," he thought to himself. "She's my cousin and won't get angry if I offer her only half a pomegranate."

When he reached home, he gave his other wife the whole pomegranate and his cousin the half. They became pregnant at the same time. The stranger gave birth to twin boys, and he called one Ḥasan and the other Ḥusēn. His cousin gave birth to half a human being, and they called him Half-a-Halfling.

The boys grew up. One day they told their father they wanted to go hunting. Ḥasan and Ḥusēn said they each wanted a mare and a gun, and the father consented and granted them their wish. Half-a-Halfling said he wanted a lame and mangy she-goat and a wooden poker.[8] He got what he had asked for, and the boys all set out together to hunt. Ḥasan and Ḥusēn fired their shotguns, but they did not hit anything. Half-a-Halfling, meanwhile, would lie in wait on the ground until the deer came near, then he would hit and break their legs.

"Give us the deer you've hunted," said Ḥasan and Ḥusēn, "so we can take them home and say we killed them."

"All right," he replied, "but on one condition only. I'll heat my brand, and brand each of you on the backside."

They agreed, and he branded both of them.[9] They took the deer and gave them to their mother, who cooked them and threw away the bones at the doorstep of Half-a-Halfling's mother. She started to cry. When Half-a-Halfling saw her crying, he asked, "Why are you crying?"

"Look!" she answered. "Your brothers Ḥasan and Ḥusēn were able to hunt deer, but not you."

"What!" he cried. "Do you think they killed the deer? You'd better go and see my brand on their behinds." His mother went, and she could see the brand.

The following day they went hunting again. The sun set while they were still away from town. They came to another town and found no one there except a ghouleh chasing a rooster.[10]

---

yammā, or "mother"; Islamic law (*šarīʿa*) considers him her son and forbids his marriage to milk-siblings.

8. The wooden poker, or *muqḥār,* is an implement for clearing and stacking the ashes in the outdoor oven known as the *ṭābūn*. For more on the *ṭābūn,* see Tale 26, n. 1; for an extensive description, see Kanaana, "Al-Ṭābūn." See also Sirḥān, *Mawsūʿat* IV : 343.

9. This act of branding would be considered the ultimate humiliation, for, in effect, the two brothers have been feminized.

10. "Chasing a rooster" is another characteristic of a ghouleh's behavior; see Tale 8,

"Welcome to my nephews!" she said when she saw them.[11] Tying their horses and the she-goat in front of the house, she invited them in, and made dinner and fed them.

"What do your horses eat?" she asked.

"They eat hulled barley and pure milk," they answered. She brought feed for the horses. Then she asked Half-a-Halfling, "What does your she-goat eat?"

"Bran left over from sifting," he answered, "and water left over from kneading."

She put food in front of the she-goat and laid out bedding for the brothers to sleep on. Ḥasan and Ḥusēn went to sleep on the floor, but Half-a-Halfling said, "I can't sleep on the floor." Seeing a reed basket hanging from the ceiling, he said, "I'll sleep in this basket. But first you must give me a waterskin and a handful of fava beans for munching." He pierced the waterskin and hung it above his head and let it drip on him, as he sat in the basket munching the fava beans.

In a while the ghouleh, thinking they were asleep, started jumping around and singing, "O my teeth get sharper and sharper, for Ḥasan and Ḥusēn his brother!" Now, Half-a-Halfling was awake, and he heard her.

"How am I going to sleep?" he said. "And how am I going to sleep, when my belly has no food in it to keep?"

"What do you want to eat?" asked the ghouleh, and he answered, "I want a stuffed rooster so I can eat it and go to sleep."

She prepared the rooster for him, and he ate it and climbed back into the basket. Again the ghouleh started prancing around, singing, "O my teeth get sharper and sharper, for Ḥasan and Ḥusēn his brother!"

Half-a-Halfling jumped up and said, "How am I going to sleep? And how am I going to sleep, when my belly has no food in it to keep?"

"What do you want to eat?" she asked, and he answered, "I want a lamb, stuffed and roasted to a turn."[12]

By the time she finished preparing the lamb, the sun had risen.

"We want water so we can wash," the boys said. When she had gone

---

n. 7. The boys would not necessarily have been able to recognize the figure they encounter as a ghouleh because of her presumed ability to take any shape; cf., e.g., the situation in Tales 19 and 33.

11. The ghouleh always pretends to be the paternal aunt of the hero, perhaps because it is the closest relation she can have with him without being his mother.

12. As in the European tradition, a ghoul (or ogre) is thought to prefer human flesh; he would therefore rather fatten and eat the boy than eat the lamb. See Tale 15, n. 5.

out to fetch the water, Half-a-Halfling said to his brothers, "You'd better get up! This woman is a ghouleh." They got up, mounted their animals, and ran away. When she came back and found them gone, she called out, "O milk, thicken! thicken! and tie up their joints so they can't move." The horses came immediately to a stop and would not budge. They got down and mounted behind their brother on the lame she-goat, and he prodded the animal with the poker, calling out, "O flint, spark and spark! O bran, fly and fly!" The she-goat flew with them and brought them home, while the ghouleh caught up with the horses and gobbled them up.

The father was very pleased with Half-a-Halfling, who was able to save his brothers from the clutches of the ghouleh.

"And what would you say," the boy asked, "if I were to bring the ghouleh herself right here?"

"We'd confess you're cleverer than both your brothers if you could do that," replied the parents.

Half-a-Halfling went and bought a donkey, and loaded it with a huge box filled with halvah. "Here's the halvah! Here's the halvah!" he cried out when he reached the ghouleh's house. She came out and asked how much it was. He answered, you might say, "A piaster for a quarter of a kilo."

She ate one quarter, then two and three, but she was still hungry.[13]

"What do you say to getting into the box," he suggested, "and eating as much as you want. We'll figure out what you owe me later." She agreed and got into the box. He closed the lid on her, securing it with a rope, and started moving. She was too busy eating to notice. When he approached their town, he called out, "Light the fire and let the flames rise! I've brought the ghouleh herself. And let him who loves the Prophet bring a load of wood and a burning coal!"

"What're you saying?" asked the ghouleh.

"I was saying," he answered, "spread the silk and put the silk away! I've brought you the princess, daughter of the prince."

When the fire was big enough, they threw the box in it and rid themselves of the ghouleh and her evil.

The bird has flown, and a good evening to all!

13. Insatiable appetite is a major characteristic of ghouls. Cf. Tale 8, where the ghouleh devours the whole town.

7. *The Orphans' Cow*

TELLER: Testify that God is One!
AUDIENCE: There is no god but He!

There was once a man who was married to a certain woman. The wife died, leaving behind a son and a daughter. The man said, "This cow is for the boy and the girl."

One day the man married again. His wife became pregnant, gave birth, and had a boy. She became pregnant again, gave birth, and had a girl. She fed her children only the best food, and the others nothing but bran.

The orphans used to roam with their cow in the countryside every day. When they were well out of town, they would say to her, "Open, O our cow!" The cow would open the space between her horns, meat and rice would come out of it, and the children would eat their fill. When they were fed bran at home, they would boil with anger.

When the children played together in the evening, the woman noticed that her children were sallow, while the orphans were like red apples. She said to her son, "Tomorrow you'll go out to the countryside with them and find out what they eat!" He said, "All right."

The next day he went roving with them. Early in the morning the children fed their pieces of bread to the cow. And what? Were they going to suffer from hunger all day? "Listen!" they said to their brother. "Do you promise not to tell our mother and father?"

"No. I won't say anything," he answered.

"Good," they said. "Open, O our cow! We want to eat."

The cow opened between her horns, the three of them ate till they were full, and then the cow closed her horns again.

"Hanh!" snapped the mother when they came home. "What did you eat out there?"

"What did we eat?" he answered. "We ate the dry bread you gave us." He refused to tell. Not believing him, the woman then said to her daughter, "You go out with them in the morning, and whatever you see them eat, you must tell me."

The following morning, the girl went roaming the countryside with the orphans. "Do you promise not to tell?" they asked her, and she replied, "No, I won't tell." They said, "Open, O our cow! We want to eat." The cow opened between her horns, and what rice and meat there was! They ate until they had their fill; but the girl was putting one bite in her mouth and hiding the next in the front of her dress. When she came home, she said, "Mother, see! Here's what they eat! Their cow does such and such."[1]

The woman brought some straw and boiled it until the water turned yellow, yellow. Then she bathed in this water, laid out her bed, and put her head down and went to sleep.[2]

"What's the matter with your mother, children?" asked the father when he came home.[3] The children said she was ill.

"Don't talk to me!" she said. "I'm not well."

"Woman, what's the problem? I'll take you to the doctor, just tell me what you need!"

"I was told no prescription would cure me, except that you slaughter for me the orphans' cow."

"O no, woman!" he said. "The children are having such a good time with her," and so on and so forth.

"Nothing else is possible," she answered. "I won't get well until you slaughter the orphans' cow for me."

So he caught the cow and slaughtered her, and they ate her, while the orphans wept and lamented.

Angry, they ran away, the sister with her brother. They walked and walked until a shepherd met them. The girl was the older, and the boy the younger.

"Sister, I'm thirsty," said the boy. "I want to drink."

"Uncle," she asked the shepherd, "do you happen to know where there's water for us to drink?"

"Listen, daughter," he replied. "You'll come upon two springs. Drink from the lower one, but the other one—don't drink from it! A gazelle has pissed in it, and whoever drinks from it now will turn into a gazelle."

1. For a discussion of mother/daughter relationships, see Introduction, "The Tales and the Culture." It is commonly believed that women are incapable of keeping secrets.

2. The feigned illness here reflects a culturally approved pattern that permits a woman to gain her ends through subterfuge, by manipulating her husband or her son. Cf. Tale 22 (see n. 5) and the behavior of the fourth wife in Tale 30.

3. ". . . children?" (*yābā*)—literally, "O father!" In Palestinian society the father addresses his children as *yābā* ("O father!") and the mother addresses them as *yammā* ("O mother!"), and the children in turn address their parents using the same words. This custom is so powerful that Palestinian-American parents often use it in addressing their American-born children in English. The practice applies to all other kinship terms as well. Thus pater-

"Thank you," said the girl.

They reached the springs, and quenched their thirst from the lower one.

"By Allah," insisted the brother. "I must drink from the other spring too, just to see what will happen."

"O brother, brother, please!"

He would not listen to her, and drank from the upper spring.[4] When he drank, he turned into a gazelle. The girl led him away, her tears flowing into her mouth. She arrived by the walls of a palace and sat down. A servantgirl looked out and saw her.

"Sir," said the servant to her master, "down by the palace wall there's one so beautiful she'll take your mind away."

"Go call her for me!" he said. She went and called over to her, "Girl, come up and see my master," and the girl replied, "I have a gazelle with me." The king said to his servants, "Take the gazelle and tether him down below, and have her come up here!"

"No," said the girl. "This gazelle—wherever I stay, he stays with me."

"Very well," said the king. "Let him come up with her."

She led the gazelle up the stairs with her, and stayed. She stayed a month, perhaps two, Allah knows![5]

"Young woman," the king asked one day, "would you rather have me for a brother or for a husband?"

"No, by Allah [not as a brother]," replied the girl. "Marriage is shelter."[6]

He married her. A day went and a day came, she became pregnant,

---

nal uncles will address their nephews and nieces as *ʿammī* ("O uncle!"), paternal aunts use *ʿamtī* ("O paternal aunt!"), and so on.

4. It is culturally appropriate for a girl to play a motherly role toward her brothers, even if they are a little older. The sister, however, although older, does not have the authority to prevent her brother from drinking at the wrong spring. For a discussion of brother/sister relationships, see Introduction, "The Tales and the Culture."

5. On the general reluctance of Palestinian narrators to be specific about time, see Tale 5, n. 6.

6. "Marriage is shelter"—*il-jīze sutra*. "Shelter" is to be meant both in the material sense and in the moral sense of protecting the girl's reputation. An unmarried girl or woman is always exposed to gossip and evil intent. The social pressure to marry is reinforced by many proverbs and popular sayings. A husband is said to "create a door that protects [the woman] from the dogs" (*xalaq bāb biḥmī min li-klāb*). Even more poignant is this saying: "Marriage is a girl's protection, and burial is the dead man's shelter" (*sutrit il-bint jīzithā, u-sutrit il-miyyit dafno*). The prevailing attitude about marriage may be summarized thus: "Even an old and useless husband is better than no husband at all."

and he set out on the hajj.[7] But before leaving he said to the women of the house, "Take good care of so and so. And this lamb here—when she gives birth, have it slaughtered for her!"

"Yes," they said. But after he left, they whispered, "This one's so beautiful and well behaved, he'll sell us all for her sake when he comes back. What're we going to do with her?" They dropped her into a well, slaughtered her lamb, and ate it themselves, burying its skin under the floor of the house.

Now, the gazelle, whenever they fed him a mouthful of bread, would take it and drop it into the well.

The king returned from the hajj. "Where's my wife?" he asked.

"Allah have mercy on her soul!" they said. "She died. And, by Allah, since she was so dear to us, we've dug a grave for her right under the floor here."

Looking the gazelle over, how thin the king found him! He said, "What use do we have for him now that she's gone? Let's feed him till he fattens up, then slaughter him."

But the gazelle still took the mouthful of bread and went away. The king thought, "By Allah, I've got to follow this gazelle and find out where he takes the food." He followed him, and behold! the gazelle carried the piece of bread in his jaws, went to the mouth of a well, dropped it in, and started calling out:

"O my little sister, O Bdūr![8]
For me they've sharpened the knives
And raised the pots over the fire."

And she answered:

"O my little brother, O Qdūr![9]
My hair's so long it covers me,

7. It is perfectly appropriate for a husband to go on the hajj while his wife is pregnant; in his absence the members of his household will take care of the social duties on the occasion of the birth. See Granqvist, *Birth:* 56–57.

8. The girl's name, Bdūr, is the plural form of *badir* (full moon), which is used very infrequently as a boy's, not a girl's, name. It is more common to liken a girl to the moon than to call her by its name (see Tale 2, n. 1).

9. Qdūr (the plural of *qidre,* "clay pot"; also the plural of *qadar,* "fate" or "destiny") is not used as a boy's name. Cf. Tale 42, n. 12.

The swallowing of the moon refers to a Palestinian folk belief that a lunar eclipse occurs

In my lap sits the son of the king,
And the whale has swallowed me."

Looking into the well, the king asked, "Are you down in this well?"

"Just as you see," she answered.

He had a young man like Mḥammad Mūsā lowered into the well.[10] The man went down and brought her and her child up. Then she told the king what had taken place. "My story is such and such and such," she said, "and so and so. We drank from the springs, this gazelle is my brother, and the women of your house dropped me into the well. This is exactly what has happened to me."

After she was out of the well, the king took her brother and made him drink from the same spring again, and he turned back into this youth that you should come and see.

He then brought together his mother, his sister, and his servantgirl and had it announced that he who loves the sultan must in the morning bring a lapful of wood and a burning coal to, you might say, the town's threshing grounds.[11] He lit a fire and dropped his mother, his sister, and the servant into it, and burned them.

Then he lived happily with his wife, and he made her brother a sultan—and may you wake up to blessings in the morning!

8. *Sumac! You Son of a Whore, Sumac!*

TELLER: Testify that God is One!
AUDIENCE: There is no other god but God.

Once there was a man and his wife, and they had three sons. They also had a flock of sheep. The wife had not given birth to any daughters, and the whole family yearned for a little girl. One day the woman cried out, "O Lord, would you give me a little girl, even if she turns out to be a

---

when a whale swallows the moon. During an eclipse children go outside carrying metal utensils which they beat together while shouting as loud as they can, "O whale, don't swallow our moon!" (*Yā ḥūt, lā tōkil qamarnā*). See Hanauer, *Folklore:* 6, 239–240.

10. Mḥammad Mūsā is the name of someone in the audience.

11. For more on "the town's threshing grounds" (*jrūnt il-balad*), see Tale 38, n. 2.

ghouleh!"[1] Allah fulfilled her wish,[2] and she became pregnant and gave birth to a daughter. The whole family loved her very, very much.[3]

Soon after the birth of the girl, when they made their daily check of their herd, they would find that one sheep was missing. "By Allah," said the boys among themselves, "we're going to keep watch and find out who comes and steals a sheep every night." Taking the watch the first night, the eldest brother stayed awake till midnight, then fell asleep. When he woke up in the morning, he found one sheep missing. The following night the middle brother said he would keep watch. He stayed awake till dawn, then he too fell asleep. When he woke up in the morning, he counted the sheep and found one missing.

"I want to keep watch tonight," said the youngest.

"You're still young and can't stay up all night," his father and brothers said.

"What's the matter with you?" he asked. "Why won't you let me give it a try?" He insisted so much that his father and brothers finally said, "All right, if you want to keep watch, you can stay up late."

In the evening he went and filled his pockets with roasted fava beans.[4] He also placed a thorn bush on either side of him; and, having got hold of a leather bottle, he made a small hole in it, filled it with water, and hung it above his head. Then he sat up to keep watch, munching on the fava beans. If he moved this way or that, a thorn pricked him. And if he started to doze off, the water dripping on his head kept him awake. This way he was able to stay up the whole night. Toward morning he was surprised to see his sister opening the door of the sheep pen. Taking hold of a sheep, she devoured it and wiped her mouth. Then she went back to sleep in her bed.

"Ha! What did you see?" they asked him in the morning.

1. This narrative formula is used throughout the Palestinian tradition in wishing for children. See Tale 1, n. 3; Tale 40, n. 2.

2. *Alla naṭaq ʿa-lsānhā*—literally, "Allah spoke with her tongue." In this folk metaphor Allah is imagined as having made the wish Himself; its fulfillment is thus guaranteed.

3. Although the culture encourages the spoiling of boys, the opposite holds true for girls, because it is assumed that indulging a girl will lead her astray. Cf. Tales 12 (esp. n. 2), and 35 (esp. n. 2); and see Granqvist, *Birth:* 108–109. This attitude is confirmed by many folk expressions, such as "You have to show a girl a red eye" (*il-bint biddak it-farjīhā ʿēn ḥamrā*)—i.e., you must be firm with her; or "A girl should not be given too much freedom [literally, 'eye']" (*il-bint ib-tinʿaṭāš ʿēn*). See Tale 13, n. 3.

4. Roasted fava beans (*Vicia faba*) are used for food as well as to entertain oneself or one's guests. See Tale 3, n. 3; Tale 36, n. 1.

"Listen," he answered. "Our sister is a ghouleh, and we must kill her." Not believing him, they all started to shout at him.

"All right," he retorted. "If you're not going to kill her, I'm going to run away and leave this town to you."

"If you want to run away, that's your business," they answered.

He started on his way out of town, traveling for Allah knows how long, until he came on an old woman living in a shack. She had a small flock of sheep.

"Mother," he asked her, "would you mind letting me stay here with you? I'll take your sheep out to graze, and you'll cook for me, wash my clothes, and take care of me?"[5]

"Why not?" she answered. "I don't have any children of my own, and you'll be like a son to me."

"That will be just fine," he said.

From that day on he took the old woman's sheep out to pasture, coming home in the evening to eat and spend the night. One day, while roaming with the sheep in the rocky countryside, he came upon a lioness giving birth and having a difficult time of it.

"Please help me," she begged him, "and I'll give you two of my cubs."

He came to her aid, and when she gave birth she gave him two of her cubs. He took very good care of them, feeding them milk till they grew big, and he called one Šwāḥ and the other Lwāḥ.[6]

One day the man thought to himself, "It's been ten or fifteen years since I've seen my brothers and my parents. I wonder what's become of them." He went to the old woman. "Mother," he said, "I've been away from my country and my family for a long time, and I'd like to go see what's become of them."

"May Allah make your path easy!" the old woman said.

He mounted his mare and set out. When he arrived at the edge of town, he discovered it was in ruins. His sister had emptied it of people.

5. By using the proper form of address and by circumscribing the situation, tellers always carefully limit the range of inference within any male/female encounter. In this instance, the teller gives other indications besides the form of address ("Mother") that preclude a sexual connection. Cf. Tale 17, n. 11. He specifies, for example, that the woman is old and that she has a flock of sheep but no one to graze them. She can honorably take the young man into her house as a shepherd. Furthermore, a boy on his own is thought to be helpless, needing a mother to cook for him and look after him. Cf. Tale 17, n. 11.

6. The lions' names are plural forms of words meaning "a wooden board." For other situations where wood offers protection from a ghoul or ghouleh, see Tale 34, n. 9; Tale 35, n. 9.

She had devoured her father, her mother, and everyone else. Nothing was left save a one-eyed rooster, and she was chasing it around town.[7] When she saw her brother, she pretended she did not know what was happening.

"Welcome, brother!" she greeted him. "Welcome!"

What was he going to do? She had already spotted him. She spread something for him to sit on, and he came in and sat down. After he had sat down, she went outside where the mare was tethered. Moving this way and that, she gobbled up one of its legs and came back inside.

"Brother!"

"What is it, sister?"

"Your mare," she asked, "is it on four legs or on three?"

Understanding what had happened, he replied, "No, sister [it's not on four]. It's on three."

Going back outside, she moved this way and that, gobbled up the second leg, and came back in.

"Brother," she asked, "is your mare on three or on two legs?"

"It's on two," he answered. "That's the way it is in our country."

She kept going in and out until she had devoured the whole mare. Then she came back in and said, "Brother, did you come riding or walking?"

"No, by Allah, sister," he answered, "I came walking."

"Well, you son of a whore!" she roared.[8] "You're trapped now. What shall I do with you?"

"Please!" he begged her.

"Not a chance!" she answered, and she fell on him, preparing to eat him.

"Just let me do my ablutions and pray before you eat me," he begged.[9]

"But you might run away," she said.

"No," he replied. "I won't. You can fill this pitcher with water and let

7. For an illuminating analysis of the psychoanalytical significance of this image of the one-eyed rooster, see the essay "Wet and Dry, the Evil Eye," by Alan Dundes (*Interpreting:* 93–133, esp. 115–118). Cf. Tale 6, n. 10.

8. A Palestinian woman would not use this crude form of address. The ghouleh's use of it indicates perhaps that the girl's ghoulishness consists of insatiable sexual appetite. Dundes's analysis (see n. 7, above) of the single eye and its phallic implications supports this interpretation.

9. The sister is duty bound to honor the brother's last wish to pray. Here again, human customs and institutions are generalized to include the ghouls. Cf. Tale 6, n. 7; and see Footnote Index, s.v. "Ghouls and Jinn." Like all the ghouls in this collection, as well as ogres in the Indo-European tradition, the ghouleh in this tale is overcome through trickery.

me go up to the roof to cleanse myself. Tie one end of the rope to my hand, and you keep hold of the other end while I'm washing myself."

She tied his wrist, and he took the pitcher and went up to the roof. Finding a large stone there, he untied the rope from his wrist and tied it to the stone.[10] Then, setting the pitcher against the stone so that the water dribbled out of it slowly, he climbed down from the roof and ran away.

Every once in a while she pulled on the rope and, finding it still tied and the water dribbling, put her mind at ease. Eventually, however, she thought he was taking a rather long time, so she called out, but no one answered. Rushing to the roof to find out what he was up to, she found he had escaped. She looked, and behold! Where was he? He was already on the outskirts of town. She came running after him, and almost caught up with him. What was he to do? Looking about, he saw a palm tree and climbed to the top. She ran after him.

"Where're you going to go now?" she asked.

Transforming her hand into a scythe, she said, "Sharpen, O my scythe, sharpen!" and started to chop the tree down. When it was about to fall, the brother suddenly remembered his lions. "O Šwāḥ! O Lwāḥ!" he cried out. "Your dear brother's gone!" And, behold! like the blowing of the wind the two lions came. No sooner did his sister see them than she started to run away, but they followed her, tore her to pieces, and devoured her. The brother could now come down from the tree safely.

As he was resting with the lions beside him, two merchants approached, leading a loaded caravan. When they saw the lions, they admired them and wanted them for themselves.

"Young man!" they called out.

"Yes," he answered, "what can I do for you?"

"How would you like to make a bet with us?" they asked. "If you can guess what merchandise we're carrying, you can take the caravan and its load. But if you can't guess, we'll take these two lions."

"All right," he agreed, "I'm willing."

He started guessing: "nuts, fava beans, lentils, wheat, rice, sugar . . ." It was no use; he could not guess. When he was stumped, with no chance of guessing, the merchants took the lions with them and moved on.

By Allah, they had not led those lions very far away when a drop of

10. An older Palestinian house usually had a stone roller on the roof, which was used to tamp down the dirt-and-clay surface of the roof just before and after a rain to prevent it from leaking.

blood, which had fallen from his sister to the ground when the lions ate her, shouted out, "Sumac! You son of a whore, sumac!"[11]

After the merchants the brother ran. "Wait! Uncles, wait!" he exclaimed. "I can guess what your load is. It's sumac!"

Having guessed, he took his lions back and got the caravan with its load.

This is my tale, I've told it, and in your hands I leave it.

9. *The Green Bird*

Once upon a time there was a man. He had a son and a daughter whose mother had died. They had a neighbor who was a widow, and every day she kept after the children, putting ideas in their heads.

"Tell me," she would say, "doesn't your father intend to get married?"

"No, not yet," they would answer.

"Why, then, don't you say to him," she would urge, "'Father, marry our neighbor.'"[1]

"Father," they would go to him and say, "marry our neighbor."

"Children, you're still too young," he would answer. "If I get married now, your aunt will beat you.[2] When you're older I'll marry again." And to his daughter he would say, "I'll wait until you're old enough to fill the water jug."

The girl would then go to the woman and say, "Such and such says my father." And the neighbor would go fill the water jug [at the spring], bring it to their house, and urge the girl to say to her father, "Father, I'm now old enough. I've filled the water jug. Marry our neighbor."

"I'll marry when you're old enough to knead the dough," the father would say. "When you're old enough to bake the bread. When you're old enough to cook." Whatever chore he mentioned, the neighbor would

11. *Summāq,* the crushed red fruit of a nonpoisonous plant of the cashew family (genus *Rhus*), is used extensively in Palestinian cuisine; the leaves, fruit, and bark are also used in tanning and dyeing. See Crowfoot and Baldensperger, *Cedar:* 94.

1. The children here must be too young to understand what they are doing, otherwise the woman could not have approached the subject of marriage with them.

2. Children, especially if their mother is dead, call their stepmother "aunty" (*xāle*—"maternal aunt"). This polite form of address also reflects the way she is expected to treat them, as if they were her sister's children.

come to the house and do it, and the girl would go back to her father and say, "Father, here! I've done this and that. Marry our neighbor."

Eventually the man did marry the neighbor, and she turned against the children and beat them.

One day her husband said, "Wife, by Allah, we've got a craving for stuffed tripe."[3]

"Bring the tripe," she answered, "and we'll cook it."[4]

He went and got the tripe, and she scrubbed and cleaned it and put it on the fire. Her husband was plowing in the fields. After she had placed the food on the fire, she set to sweeping the floor. She swept a stroke or two and thought to herself that she might as well check and see if the food was ready. She picked up a foot and ate it. Another stroke or two with the broom, and again she said to herself, "Let me poke the food and see if it's ready." She picked up a portion of the tripe and ate it. By the time she realized what she was doing, she had eaten up the whole meal, leaving nothing behind.

"Yee!" she cried out. "The Devil take me![5] What's he going to do to me now? Soon he'll be home from plowing, and what's he going to eat? By Allah, I think he'll kill me. He'll blacken my face. Hey, you! Go call your brother right away."

The girl cried, knowing what the woman was up to.

"What do you want with my brother, aunty?"

"I'm telling you to call your brother. And, by Allah, if you don't call him, I'll kill you right now."

The girl went out, calling:

> "Hey, brother! Come and don't come!
> Come and don't come near!
> For you they've sharpened the knives
> In front of the shop doors."[6]

3. The meal of stuffed tripe (*karš*) includes not only the sheep's intestines but also the head and feet. Most women dread preparing the tripe for cooking, because it requires much work; aside from thoroughly cleansing the inside of the intestines, the hair must be removed from the head and feet by singeing and scraping. The intestines, stuffed with rice and chopped lamb to which spices have been added, are cooked with the head and feet in a rich yogurt sauce.

4. Because *karš* requires so much work, all the women in the family—and sometimes their sisters, too, if they live nearby—participate in preparing it.

5. (*Yā rētnī mšaḥḥara*)—literally, "May I be blackened with soot!" See Tale 1, n. 11.

6. (*Sannūlak is-sakākīn ʿa-bwāb id-dakākīn*). Lamb meat is sold fresh daily, and most

Coming back in, she said, "O aunty! I haven't been able to find him."

"I'm telling you to call him," the woman snapped back. "Quick as a bird! Otherwise, I'm going to slaughter you."

Back out went the girl, and she called:

> "Hey, brother! Come and don't come!
> Come and don't come near!
> For you they've sharpened the knives
> In front of the shop doors."

This last time the woman said, "I'll kill you if you don't bring him." Finally the sister called her brother, and he came.

Taking him inside, the woman locked the door. She slaughtered him, cut him into pieces, and cooked him just as she would cook tripe and in the same pot. The other one sat crying and crying, but the woman said to her, "Consider yourself dead if you speak to your father or anyone else."

The father came home from plowing, hungry.

"Did you cook the tripe, wife?" he asked.

"Yes," she answered.

Setting the pot down, they cut pieces of bread, poured the sauce over it, piled the meat on top, and set to it.

"Come, girl," the father urged his daughter. "Eat!"

"I don't want any," she said.

"How can you not want any?" he asked. "Eat!"

"No, father," she replied. "I'm full. I've just taken some food and eaten."

"Leave her alone!" his wife cut in. "What do you want with her? All day long she's been hanging about and eating."

"All right," said the father. "But where's your brother? Doesn't he want to eat?"

"He just ate and went out to play," answered the wife. "When he comes back, even if it's midnight, I'll give him some food."

From that day on, the man would set out for the fields with his team early in the morning and come home late in the evening, tired. He would ask about the boy, and his wife would say he had just eaten and gone out to play.

---

butchers will not carry more than they can sell in one day. It is still common to see butchers sharpening their knives by their shop doors, preparing to cut meat for waiting customers.

Now the sister, after they had finished their meal, took the bones and dug a hole and buried them at the edge of the garden. And every morning she would sit by the place where she buried the bones and cry and cry until she had no more tears. Then she would go home.

One day there was a wedding at a neighbor's house. Her father, her stepmother, and all the girls [in the neighborhood] put on their best clothes and went to the wedding. "Now that nobody's around," she thought to herself, "I'll dig up the bones and look at them again." She went and dug and (so the story goes) found a marble urn. She dug deeper, unearthed it, and out of it flew a green bird. And what else? The urn was full of gold bracelets, rings, and earrings. There was also a dress, which was something to look at. Putting it on, the girl set out for the wedding wearing all the jewelry. Everyone noticed her, admiring the clothes and the jewelry, but no one recognized her.

In a while, as the wedding procession moved along, a green bird came circling over the head of the bride. He sang:

"I am the green bird
Who graces this gathering!
My stepmother slaughtered me
And my father devoured me
Only my kind sister
(Allah shower mercy on her!)
Gathered up my bones
And saved them in the urn of stone."

"Look! Look!" they all shouted. "There's a bird, and it's speaking!"[7] They forgot about the wedding procession and turned their attention to the bird.[8]

"Speak, bird!" they clamored, "Speak again! How beautiful are your words!"

"I won't say anything more," he replied, "until that woman over there opens her mouth."

His stepmother opened her mouth, and he dropped a handful of nails and needles into it. She swallowed them, and behold! she died.

7. See Tale 10, n. 9; Tale 11, n. 5; Tale 13, n. 11. The green bird in particular occurs in many of the songs sung during wedding celebrations; see Granqvist, *Marriage* II: 36, n. 2.

8. The wedding procession (*zaffe*) is an essential part of the Palestinian wedding ceremony in which relatives and friends of the couple sing and dance in the street in celebration of

"Speak bird!" urged the crowd. "Say more! How beautiful are your words!"

"I won't speak again," he answered, "until that man over there opens his mouth." His father opened his mouth, and the bird dropped a handful of needles and nails into it. He, too, fell dead.

Again the crowd urged the bird. "Speak, bird! How beautiful are your words!"

"I won't say more," he answered, "until that girl over there opens her lap."

His sister opened her lap like this, the bird landed on it, and behold! he turned into a boy again. Her brother had returned as he was before, and they went home and lived together.

This is my tale, I've told it, and in your hands I leave it.

10. *Little Nightingale the Crier*

TELLER: Testify that God is One!
AUDIENCE: There is no god but God.

Once upon a time there were three girls. They were spinners and had nothing but their spinning. Every day they used to spin and go down to the market to sell their product and buy food. One day the town crier announced that it was forbidden to put on a light in the city, because the king wanted to test his subjects—to see who was obedient and who was not.[1] That night the king and his vizier went through the city to check whose lights were on and whose were not.

What were the girls to do? They had nothing but their spinning. Every day one of them would spin, and they would sell her yarn and buy food for all of them to eat. What could they do? They wanted to continue with their spinning, but they dared not put on a light. So the eldest one called out, "O my Lord, my beloved! May the king be passing this way and

---

the marriage. See Granqvist, *Marriage* II:35–137, esp. 55–64 and 79–93. See also Tale 11, n. 4; Tale 14, n. 8; Conder, *Tent Work* II:250–252; and cf. Jaussen, *Naplouse:* 74–84.

1. For the town crier, see Tale 5, n. 17. Kings are presented in the tales as exercising their power in an arbitrary and fear-inspiring fashion. Cf. the behavior of both kings (the hero's father and his uncle) in Tale 5. Emirs, in contrast (see Tale 13, n. 8), who are Bedouin princes, are presented in a more human light.

hear me, and may he wed me to his baker so I can have my fill of bread!" The middle sister prayed, "And may he wed me to his cook so I can have my fill of food!" Then the youngest made her plea, "O my Lord, my beloved! May the king pass this way and hear me! And may he wed me to his son, and I give birth to two boys and a girl. I will call one of the boys ʿAladdīn and the other Bahaddīn, and the girl Šamsiẓẓḥā.[2] If she smiles while it's raining, the sun will shine; and if she cries while the sun's shining, it will rain."

As chance would have it, the king was passing that way, and he heard them.

"Councillor!" ordered the king, "Manage it for me!"

"The owner manages his own property, O Ruler of the Age," replied the vizier.[3] They put a mark on that shack and went home. In the morning the king sent soldiers, who said to the girls, "Come and see the king!" And they came.

"Obedience is yours, Majesty!" they said.

"Come here," said the king. "What's your story?"

"We are three girls, Your Majesty," they replied, "and we have no one to take care of us and nothing to eat. You ordered the lights out, so what could we do? What you heard, we actually said."

"All right," he said. "Let it be as you wish!"

He married the eldest to his baker, the middle one to the cook, and the youngest to his son. Seeing that she had married the king's son, whereas they were the wives of the baker and the cook, her sisters became jealous and wanted to take revenge on her. When she became pregnant the first time and was ready to deliver, they went to the midwife and bribed her.

"Take this little puppy," they said. "Put it under our sister and give us the baby.[4] We'll be waiting for you outside the door of the house. Wrap the baby and hand him over to us, and put the puppy in his place."

The sister had no sooner given birth than the midwife wrapped up the baby, putting the puppy in his place, and handed him over to them. She then went back inside.

2. The names ʿAladdīn (ʿAlāʾ al-Dīn, "The Glory of Religion"), Bahaddīn (Bahāʾ al-Dīn, "The Splendor of Religion"), and Šamsiẓẓḥā (Šams al-Ḍuḥā, "High Morning Sun") occur frequently in the *Thousand and One Nights*.

3. For the sly behavior of the vizier, see Tale 5, n. 9.

4. For relationships among sisters, see Introduction, "The Tales and the Culture"; for customs related to childbirth, see Granqvist, *Birth:* 56–72.

"What did the daughter-in-law of the king's household give birth to?" people asked.[5]

"Yee!" they said,[6] "What did she give birth to? She gave birth to a puppy!"

The king's family, however, brought up the puppy and were proud of it.

Meanwhile, what did the sisters do? Taking the baby, they wrapped him well, put him in a box, and threw it into the river. On the bank of the river was an orchard, in which lived an old man and an old woman. The aged couple went out in the morning and found a box on the water. They picked it up and opened it, and found a baby. Since they had no children, the old man said, "Why don't we bring him up, old lady? He might be useful to us in the future."[7] They adopted him.

Now we go back to the king's daughter-in-law. She became pregnant again, and was ready to deliver. As soon as she was about to give birth, her sisters went to the midwife. "Take this newborn kitten," they said, "and put it under her. And as much money as you want, we'll give you. Just hand the baby over to us."

The same thing happened again. As soon as the sister gave birth, the midwife took the baby, wrapped him in a cloth, and gave him to the sisters, placing the cat by the mother.

"What did the daughter-in-law of the king's household give birth to? What did the daughter-in-law of the king's household give birth to?"

"What did she give birth to?" people whispered. "She gave birth to a cat!"

The two sisters did as before, putting the baby in a box and throwing him into the river. Again the old folks living in the orchard came out and found a box. Picking it up, they opened it and found a boy. They adopted him, and now they had two children.

We go back to the mother. She was pregnant again, and was about to give birth. Her sisters said to the midwife, "Here's money! Take it! Take also this stone, put it next to her, and give us the baby."

5. The way the woman is referred to here, as "daughter-in-law of the king's household" (*kinnit dār il-malik*), reveals her place in the extended family in terms of patrilocality.

6. Here, "Yee!" is an expression of dismay (but cf. Tale 1, n. 8), revealing the importance of public opinion. Arab society, especially in the small villages of Palestine, is highly personal, with anonymity considered a form of death. Later, after the old couple die, the brothers and sister leave the orchard because they do not want to live by themselves.

7. A clear statement of the utilitarian view of children. See Tale 30, n. 7; Tale 40, n. 5.

When the sister gave birth, the midwife came and took the daughter she had had, wrapped her in a cloth, and gave her to them, leaving the stone in her place. The sisters took her, placed her in a box, and dropped her into the river.

"What did the daughter-in-law of the king's household give birth to? What did she give birth to?" people asked.

"What did she give birth to?" came the answer. "She gave birth to a stone!"

The son of the king, meanwhile, thought to himself, "What's going on? One time she gives birth to a dog, another time to a cat, and this time to a stone." He deserted her.[8] The baby girl was also discovered by the old couple, and they brought her up with her brothers.

The boys became young men, and the girl became a young lady. She turned out to be exactly as her mother had wished. If it was raining and she laughed, the sun shone; and if it was sunny and she cried, it started to rain. One day the old man died, leaving them all his possessions. Whatever he had—the orchard and the hut—he gave it to the children.

"What!" said the young people. "Are we going to stay here in this orchard all alone? Let's go somewhere, build ourselves a place, and live in it."

Where did they go? They went to their father's city, bought a piece of land across from his palace, built a palace just like his, and settled in it. There they were, by themselves! They did not know anyone, but as they went back and forth in the town, their aunts recognized them. They realized these were the children they had thrown into the water. What were they to do? They wanted to get rid of them. They found an old crone who was willing to help, and, taking a tray full of trinkets with her, she went to their palace and started crying her wares. Waiting until the brothers had gone out to hunt, the old woman cried her wares by their palace.

The girl was sitting by her window. Her brothers were not around, and, wanting to buy something from the old crone, she started weeping. As her tears fell down, they landed on the henna powder and made it soggy. Looking up, the old crone said, "Yee! What am I going to call down upon your head? Why did you do that, my dear?"

"O grandmother!" answered the girl, "my brothers aren't here, and I cried. I don't know why."

8. The husband, by deserting his wife, ceases to cohabit with her, but he remains responsible for her material welfare. The woman lives separately; she is not, however, divorced, nor is she free to marry again. Cf. Tale 22, n. 21; Tale 35, n. 12.

"Never mind," said the woman.

The girl invited her in, and the old crone came up beside her.

"O, my dearest!" she coaxed. "Here! Take this henna, and whatever else you want—I'll give it to you." Meanwhile, she was looking up and down the palace, inspecting it.

"Yee, by Allah!" she cried out. "Your palace is very beautiful, my dear, and nothing is missing from it except Little Nightingale the Crier."

"Where's Little Nightingale the Crier, grandmother?" asked the girl. "And who's going to bring him?"

"Your brothers will bring him," the old crone replied. "You have two such brothers, Allah bless the Prophet on their behalf! and you ask who's going to bring Little Nightingale!"

The girl sat and wept. Clouds formed, thunder roared, and rain fell. The brothers wondered what might have befallen their sister, and they came home running.

"What's the matter, sister?"

"Nothing's the matter," she replied. "A woman came to see me and said my palace was missing nothing except Little Nightingale the Crier, and I want him."

"And how are we going to get him for you, sister?" they asked.

"I don't know," she answered, "but I want Little Nightingale the Crier to put in our palace."[9]

"Fine," said the eldest brother. "Prepare some provisions for my journey, and I'll go." Removing a ring from his finger, he gave it to his younger brother and said, "Wear this ring, and if it becomes tight on your finger, then I'm in danger and you should follow after me for three days and a third. If the ring doesn't get any tighter, then I'm all right and you shouldn't come for me."

9. Four tales (9, 10, 11, 12) have titles directly connected with birds. In Tales 11 (see n. 5) and 12 (n. 1) the sexual symbolism of the bird is explicit; see also Tale 8, n. 7. In the present context two indications lend credibility to this interpretation. First, in Palestinian and Arabic folk narrative old crones usually serve as go-betweens in illicit relationships. And second, the fact that the brothers run home, anxious about their sister, betrays their concerns about her honor. On the connection between "bird" and "husband," see afterword, below; on the versatility of the bird symbol in the tales, see Tale 13, n. 11; on brothers and husbands, see Granqvist, *Marriage* II: 252–256.

Birds are also significant in other genres of Palestinian folklore, particularly folk songs and proverbs. See Stephan's collection of bird-related proverbs in part 2 (1928) of "Animals in Palestinian Folklore," esp. no. 714—"If your bird shows up, your blessings are on the way" (*in ʾōjah ṭērak, ʾōjah xērak*).

His sister prepared his horse, loading it with provisions, and he departed. He traveled for a while, and in the course of his travels he came upon a ghoul in the wilderness.

"Peace to you, father!" he said.

"And to you, peace!" responded the ghoul. "If your salaam had not come before you'd spoken, I would've torn your flesh to pieces before tackling your bones. What's your story? Where're you going, young master?"

"I'm on my way to fetch Little Nightingale the Crier," he replied.

"In that case," said the ghoul, "go straight ahead. I have a brother who's older than me by a month but wiser by a lifetime. He'll show you the way."

The young man traveled until he reached the second ghoul.

"Peace to you, father!"

"And to you, peace!" answered the ghoul. "If your salaam had not come before you'd spoken, I would've torn your flesh to pieces before tackling your bones. Where're you going, ᶜAladdīn?"

"By Allah," replied the young man, "I'm on my way to fetch Little Nightingale the Crier."

"Son," the ghoul advised, "go straight ahead for a while, and you'll see my sister. If you find her grinding salt and her eyes red, come up to her and eat some of her salt, then suck at her breasts.[10] But if you find her grinding sugar, don't go near her!"

"Fine," said the young man, and moved on. In a while he came upon the ghouleh and found her grinding salt. Her hair was disheveled, and her breasts were hanging down in front of her. Coming forward, he sucked at her right breast.

"Who was it that sucked at my right breast?" she asked. "He's now dearer to me than my son Ismāᶜīn."

He turned and sucked at the left breast.

"Who was it that sucked at my left breast?" she asked. "He's now dearer than my son ᶜAbdir-raḥmān."

Turning to face her, he ate some of what she was grinding.

10. For the ghouleh's red eyes, cf. Tale 33, n. 7; for the ghouleh as a helper, see Tale 20, n. 5.

Salt symbolizes the bond that holds people together. The phrase "They've shared bread and salt" (*bēnhum ᶜēš u-maliḥ*) describes a strong bond, and when someone breaks a trust he is said to have "betrayed the bread and salt" (*yxūn il-ᶜēš w-il-maliḥ*).

"Welcome in Allah's safekeeping!" announced the ghouleh. "And may Allah betray him who betrays this oath! What can I do for you?"

"I want Little Nightingale the Crier," he answered.

"Ah, yes!" responded the ghouleh. "You should know that Little Nightingale the Crier is a bird in such and such an orchard. Better wait till my sons come home. You can't reach him on your own."

Blowing on him, she turned him into a pin, which she stuck in her headband, and sat waiting until her children came. In wind and storm her sons arrived. They were forty, and one of them was lame.[11] Before they had even arrived, they were muttering, "You smell of human, mother!"

"I smell of no human," replied the mother, "nor do I have anything like that around. Sit down and be quiet!" But they kept on chattering and saying, "You smell of human."

"Listen and I'll tell you," she confessed. "He has suckled at my breasts, so he's now my son like all of you. All of you guarantee his safety, and I'll bring him out."

"He's welcome in Allah's safekeeping," they swore, "and may Allah betray him who betrays this oath!"

When the ghouleh brought him out and they had a good look at him, they greeted him, and they all sat down together.

"Do you know what he wants?" asked the ghouleh of her children.

"No," they answered.

"He's your brother," she went on, "and he wants Little Nightingale the Crier. Which of you is going to take him?" One of them said he'd do it in ten days, another said in two, and a third in an hour.

"I'll take him there in the wink of an eye," the lame one jumped in.

"Get moving!" said the ghouleh. "But be careful, ʿAladdīn. There's a cage hanging in a tree, and Little Nightingale comes there to roost for the night. Perching in the tree, he will shout, 'I'm Little Nightingale the Crier! Who dare say, "Here I am!"' He'll say it three times. If you declare yourself, you're lost; but if you don't, you can catch him and bring him with you."

"Very well," he said.

Picking him up, the lame ghoul brought him to Little Nightingale's orchard, where the ghoul let him down and left. The youth went into the orchard, and in flew Little Nightingale the Crier and perched in a tree.

11. The number forty occurs frequently in both Palestinian and Arabic folk narrative. For a discussion of its significance in Palestinian folklore, see Tale 21, n. 7.

"I'm Little Nightingale the Crier!" he declared. "Who dare say, 'Here I am!'" The first time the young man held his tongue, but the second time he shouted back, "Here I am!"

"You!" laughed the bird, and he blew on him, turning him into a stone, and rolled him down the orchard.

Now the ring tightened around ʿAladdīn's brother's finger, and he mounted his horse and came after his brother. As the first brother had done, so did the second. He visited the ghouleh and was taken to the orchard. Before leaving, though, he had given the ring to his sister. When he came into the orchard, the bird flew in: "I'm Little Nightingale the Crier! Who dare say, 'Here I am!'" The first time and the second, he kept quiet, but the third time he shouted back, "Here I am!"

"You!" said the bird, and he blew on him, tossing him down like his brother.

Who was left? The sister. The ring tightened around her finger. What was she to do? "My brothers are lost to me," she said to herself. She wanted to follow them. Saddling the horse, she disguised herself and followed them. She did the same as her brothers, going to the ghouleh.

"Listen!" said the ghouleh. "You'll be lost like your brothers, and all memory of you will be gone forever. But if you can catch him, you'll save your brothers and many other people as well. Take care! Don't talk back to him!"

"No, I won't," said the girl.

When they had brought her to the orchard, she climbed into a tree and sat waiting. In flew the bird: "I'm Little Nightingale the Crier! Who dare say, 'Here I am!' I'm Little Nightingale the Crier . . ." He repeated his call till he nearly burst, but she was waiting for him without making a sound. When he had finished, he went into his cage. Now, she was waiting right behind the cage on the tree. She shut the door on him quickly, locked it, and took the cage in her hand.

"Please!" he begged. "Let me go free! I'll sing for you, I'll do anything."

"Not a chance," she said. "Bring back my brothers!"

"Take a handful of dirt from that molehill," he said, "and sprinkle it on those stones over there, and your brothers will rise."

Lifting some dirt, she threw it over the stones, and her brothers came back to life. She went on sprinkling dirt all over the stones, and a whole creation came back to life. Everyone went back to his family. Carrying the cage with her, she returned to the ghouleh with her brothers. They said good-bye to the ghouleh and went home.

Once they reached home, they hung the cage up inside the palace. The boys would go hunting and then come back and sit in the coffeehouses. Eventually their fame spread in the city. "Whose children are these?" people asked. "Where did they come from?"

One day they met their father at the coffeehouse, but they did not recognize one another. How fond of them he became! He would invite them over and enjoy their company.

"You must come and have dinner with us," said the brothers to him one day. "You've already invited us two or three times, and now you must come and eat with us, O Ruler of the Age!"

"Yes," he said, "why not?"

When they had prepared the dinner, Little Nightingale the Crier said, "Put a dish of carrots with the meal, among the fruits." They served dinner and ate. How delightful it was! They had a great time. After dinner they brought a plate of fruits and served it, along with the dish of carrots.

"Little Nightingale!" they called. "Come and eat!"

"No, by Allah!" he cried out. "Little Nightingale the Crier does not eat carrots, O you stupid people of this city! You bulls and donkeys! In all your life have you ever heard that a daughter-in-law of the king's household would give birth to a dog, a cat, and a stone?"

The king was taken aback. "Say it again, O Crier!" he urged.

"I am Little Nightingale the Crier," answered the bird, "and I don't eat carrots, O you stupid people of this city! In all your life have you ever heard of a daughter-in-law in the king's household giving birth to a dog, a cat, and a stone?"

"What are you saying, O Little Nightingale Crier?" asked the king.

"This is what I am saying," replied the bird. "The daughter-in-law of the king's household did not give birth to a dog, a cat, and a stone. Your children, Bahaddīn and ʿAladdīn and Šamsiẓẓḥā, are the ones who are here with you."

The king sent for the midwife. "Either you tell me the story," he threatened, "or I'll cut off your head."

"Please, O Ruler of the Age!" she begged, "It wasn't my fault. Her sisters bribed me and gave me the puppy, the cat, and the stone to put in place of her children. These here are your children."

The king had the heads of the midwife and the sisters cut off, and it was announced that he who loved the king must bring a load of wood and burning embers. He burned their corpses in the fire and scattered their ashes to the wind.

This is my tale, I've told it, and in your hands I leave it.

Afterword

The tales in this group focus on relationships among siblings in different contexts. Siblings of the same sex generally have relationships characterized by conflict, competition, and jealousy; among cross-sexual siblings, however, relationships of love, tenderness, and mutual cooperation prevail.

In "Half-a-Halfling," the competition between the brothers is acted out against a family background of polygyny and first-cousin marriage. This tale is one of the best loved and most popular in Palestine, perhaps because it dramatizes a situation that can occur in any family—that concerning an underdog younger (or smaller) brother. Here, however, a child who identifies with Half-a-Halfling would not feel too much guilt, for the siblings are only half brothers—they are not from the same womb and have not sucked from the same breast. The use of polygyny as a narrative idiom thus serves to palliate the effects of jealousy and hostility among the brothers. The tale, moreover, has all the elements of a hero fantasy, providing a good role model for children: the hero attains his goal by exercising the virtues of courage, truthfulness, and resourcefulness, and in helping his brothers escape the ghouleh he demonstrates generosity of spirit by rising above the pettiness of sibling rivalry.

The pattern of rivalry among siblings of the same sex in "Little Nightingale the Crier" shows the importance of marriage to a woman. The first concern of the elder sisters is not just for food, but for husbands who can provide food. The teller himself emphasizes their loneliness and isolation before marriage, their struggle for existence, and their hunger. An unmarried woman lacks self-definition, not only because she is without a husband but also because she will have no children. After marriage, however, the sisters change markedly in character—although as we might expect, the elder two sisters' jealousy over the superior marriage of the younger does not manifest itself until after the birth of her first child.

"Sumac! You Son of a Whore, Sumac!" presents us with a rather unusual situation—a hostile brother/sister relationship, based here on the sister's ghoulishness. The sexual interpretation suggested in the footnotes is supported by the context. A girl's honor is her most precious possession, and the only way she can ruin her family is by sexual transgression. Only one socially acceptable reason exists for killing a sister, and that is to regain the family honor by removing the shame of such a transgression. Of course, such situations have always been rare, but when they do occur, this ultimate form of punishment is sanctioned by society. It is said of someone who regains his honor in this way: "So and so is a lion; he took revenge with his own hands" (*flān sabiᶜ, istad ṯāro bʾīdo*). In "Sumac!" the family accepts the shame and is destroyed, but the brother gains everything in the end—his lions as well as the caravan. Nevertheless, the blood bond between brother and sister proves in the long run powerful and indestructible, and finally outweighs the hostility. Even though he has killed her, she is still his sister, and she does not wish to see strangers take something from him. "Blood will never turn into water" (*id-dam biṣirš mayy*), they say; "One drop of blood is better than a thousand friends" (*nuqṭit dam, walā alf ṣāḥib*).

The remaining three tales in this group ("The Orphans' Cow," "The Green Bird," and "Little Nightingale the Crier") show more clearly the nature of the brother/sister bond. In all three the tenderness and love brother and sister feel for each other is selfless. When the brother(s) and sister are left to face the world on their own, they seem to do better at it than husbands and wives, whose relationships inevitably involve some self-interest and therefore conflict. Here, the sisters bring their brothers back to life: a husband, after all, may divorce his wife, but a brother will remain a woman's protector for life, even after he is married and has a family of his own.

"The Green Bird" adds a new dimension to our understanding of the brother/sister relationship. With the father, as usual, under the control of a new wife, the brother and sister are left on their own. The tale thus juxtaposes two sets of relationships. Obviously, the second relationship, that between brother and sister, is superior to the first, for there a power struggle, which seems inescapable when a man marries a stranger, is nonexistent. By presenting the sister as crying over the brother's bones, bringing him back to life through her love, and then living with him, the tale idealizes their relationship, bringing them almost, but not quite, to the point of marriage.

"The Green Bird" provides a meaningful clue concerning the cultural emphasis on first-cousin marriage, a union we encounter throughout the corpus. First-cousin marriage ideally combines both brother/sister and husband/wife relationships. Because a man's first cousin is almost as close to him as his own sister, his relationship with her should be characterized by brotherly tenderness. Yet because she is not a direct blood relative, the relationship can be a sexual one, but without encompassing the conflict the husband would face if he were to marry a stranger.

"The Orphans' Cow" takes the relationship presented in "The Green Bird" a step further. Here the brother and sister are put into situations that serve to increase their affection. Following the death of their mother, they become progressively more isolated and come to rely on each other more and more; indeed, their very survival depends on their mutual love and cooperation. To demonstrate the importance of this connection between brother and sister, "The Orphans' Cow," like "The Green Bird," juxtaposes two relationships: sister/brother and wife/husband. Although the brother cannot be as a husband to his sister, equally important, a husband can never be as a brother to his wife. It is therefore as essential that the sister have her brother by her side as that she have a husband. The transformation of the brother into a gazelle because of his own stubbornness makes the point even more clearly, for it would be much easier for the sister to abandon an animal than a human being. Yet, though transformed, he is still her brother, and when faced with the choice of sacrificing him or marrying, even a king, the sister chooses to keep him by her wherever she goes. This transformation also serves two other related functions: it allows the sister both to marry without offending the brother and to bring him back to human form—with the husband helping to effect the second transformation. The sister has thereby gained a husband without losing her brother, and all three live together in harmony.

"Little Nightingale the Crier" (presented in Arabic in Appendix A) also carries the theme of the ideal relationship between brother and sister, but it adds a new dimension. In this tale the brothers and sister live together happily, free from family constraints and parental authority—an ideal situation. Yet something is missing, and it is not hard to guess what that is, considering the central importance of marriage in a woman's life.

When a girl marries, she is lost to her family, and it is not unusual for them, especially the women, to sing dirgelike songs (*tarāwīd* or *frāqiyyāt*, "songs of parting") when the bridegroom's relatives come to take away their daughter. For the daughter, the move from the house of her father to that of her husband entails a change in sexual and social status. Hence, many brides are too shy, especially of their male relatives, to visit their natal families soon after marriage. Their brothers may worry that their husbands are not treating them decently, and the husbands for their part may fear that their brides are too attached to their natal families. The bride, then, must try to bridge the gap between her two families in order to erase anxieties on both sides. In light of this background, we see why the brothers in the tale did not (or could not) stand up to Little Nightingale's challenge: they are in effect unwilling, or unable, to let go of her.

Looking ahead to Tale 12, we see an explicit equation of bird with husband. It would therefore be reasonable to assume that Little Nightingale represents the same idea, albeit less explicitly. Through the use of symbol, the tale—which, it is important to recall, children will hear—treats the taboo subject of sexuality with utmost delicacy. When the brothers are unable to bring back Little Nightingale, the girl has the perfect excuse of going to save them without compromising her honor. Once she is secure of her mate, as we may conclude from the image of the bird in the cage dangling from her arm, she can revive her brothers. Thus she becomes a model woman, gaining both her brothers and a husband, but without losing her individual identity. And, of course, Little Nightingale is instrumental in bringing about the reunion of the children with their family at the end, thereby completing the circle. Thus Šamsiẓẓḥa, like Bdūr in "The Orphans' Cow," where the choice between husband and brother is presented more explicitly, gains a husband without risking the loss of either her brothers or her honor.

Sexual Awakening and Courtship

11. *The Little Bird*

TELLER: Allah is the only God!
AUDIENCE: There is no god but He!

Once upon a time there was a little bird. She dug in the earth and dug, she dyed her hands with henna.[1] She dug in the earth and dug, she dyed her feet with henna. She looked up to the Lord, and He beautified her eyes with kohl.[2] She went on digging and digging, and found a bolt of silk. "What am I going to do with this?" she asked herself. "By Allah, I'm going to have it made into a dress."

So she went to the seamstress. "Take this," she said, "and make dresses out of it—one for me and the other for you." Coming back later, she said, "Let me see which is better, my dress or yours." She then took them to have a look, put them in her beak, and—frrrr!—away she flew. She hid them in a tree and came back the next day.

She dug and dug in the same place, and found two scarves. "Oh, how beautiful they are!" she cried out. "By Allah, I must take them to the girl who can crochet a fringe on them." So she went to this girl and said, "Do one for me and the other for you." In a while, she came back. "Let me see which is prettier," she said, "yours or mine." Putting the scarves in her beak, she tricked the girl, and—frrrr!—away she flew.[3]

Then, little darlings, she went back and dug once again, and found some cotton. "Oh, how beautiful it is!" she cried out. Going to the mat-

1. Henna (*ḥinnā*) is a vegetable-powder dye (from *Lawsonia inermis*) that stains the body red or auburn. Staining the bride's hands and feet with henna is a formal part of the Palestinian wedding ceremony, usually performed by the women of the bridegroom's family to the accompaniment of singing and dancing. See Granqvist, *Marriage* II: 46–51 ("The Night of the Henna").

2. Kohl (*kuḥul*) is a cosmetic preparation (powdered antimony sulfide) with a bluish tint, used as an eye shadow.

3. Girls prepare their trousseaus from an early age (sometimes as early as ten or eleven), making handkerchiefs, crocheted headdresses, and embroidered dresses, pillow cases, and table cloths.

tress maker, she said, "Would you make me a mattress from this cotton, uncle, and please make another one as payment for yourself." He took the cotton and made a mattress for himself and another for her. "Let me see if you made my mattress exactly like yours," she said when she came back. "Maybe you made yours bigger than mine."

"Take them and see," replied the man.

She took them, put them in her beak, and—frrrr!—away she flew. Folding each of them over, she had four layers, just like a bride's seat. She put on both her silk dresses, one on top of the other, wrapped the scarves around her head, and what did she look like but a bride, sitting in the bridal seat with henna on her hands and feet, kohl in her eyes, and wearing all those clothes.[4]

She sat awhile. Then, my little darlings, came the son of the sultan, who was roaming the neighborhood looking for something. Meanwhile, she was singing:

"I'm wearing my very best!
Ya-la-lal-li
And this is the day of my feast
Ya-la-lal-la."

"Eh!" he thought. "Who is singing like that?" He listened carefully, and behold! it was the little bird singing. Aiming his gun, he fired and shot her. She sang her song:

"What a sharp shooter!
Ya-la-lal-li
What a sharp shooter!
Ya-la-lal-la."

He then plucked her feathers, and she was singing:

"A fine feather-plucker!
Ya-la-lal-li
A fine feather-plucker!
Ya-la-lal-la."

4. The bridal seat (*maṣmade*) is usually an elevated seat, composed of several folded mattresses, where the bride sits after having been led in the wedding procession (*zaffe*) from her father's house to that of the groom with all the female wedding guests singing, dancing, and ululating (*zaġārīt*) around her. The groom usually joins her later in the evening, and the couple sit together in the midst of the dancing and singing. See Tale 9, n. 8; Tale 14, n. 8; Footnote Index, s.v. "Marriage Customs."

Then he cooked her, and still she chirped:

"What a good cook!
Ya-la-lal-li
What a good cook!
Ya-la-lal-la."

Putting her into his mouth, he chewed her until she was soft, then swallowed her. She went down into his stomach. In a while, he got up and shat her. She then sang out:

"Ho! Ho! I saw the prince's hole,
It's red, red, like a burning coal."[5]

This is my tale, I've told it, and in your hands I leave it.

12. *Jummēz Bin Yāzūr, Chief of the Birds*[1]

Once there was a father, a merchant with three daughters. Two were from one mother, while the third was from a different mother. She was the youngest of the three and very beautiful. Her father loved her very much, and had given her the name of Sitt il-Ḥusun.[2]

5. "The Little Bird" is one of the first tales to which Palestinian children are exposed; this version was in fact narrated to children. Although sexual subjects are taboo in polite conversation, Palestinian folk culture in general is accepting of language that concerns other bodily functions, which are a principal source of humor in the tales.

For a discussion of the symbolic use of birds in a sexual context, see Tale 10, n. 9, and the afterword to Group I, "Siblings." The bird is a versatile symbol (Tale 13, n. 11). Whereas in Tales 9, 10, and 12 the bird is associated with male sexuality, in this tale it is used as a symbol of femininity and of the indestructible power associated with femininity. Translated literally, the title of the tale, "*il-ʿaṣfūra z-zġīre,*" is "The Little She-Bird" (cf. Tale 1, n. 1, on the symbolic association of gender in the Arabic language).

1. In Arabic the tale has a rhyming name, "Jummēz bin Yāzūr, šēx iṭ-ṭyūr," consisting of two symbolic references to male sexuality: the bird (see Tale 10, n. 9) and the fruit *jummēz,* a type of fig (*Ficus sycamorus*) that hangs down in bunches more like cherries than figs. The use of fruit and other foods to symbolize sexuality occurs elsewhere in the collection; see Tale 35, n. 1, and cf. the reference to mulberries in Tale 21. Yāzūr is the name of a Palestinian village on the coastal plain not far from Jaffa; *bin Yāzūr* means literally "Son of Yāzūr."

Jummēz is not used as a name in real life. Nor is Sitt il-Ḥusun, which is a generic name meaning "Mistress of Beauty" and the feminine counterpart of Ḥasan, a generic name for a hero; see Tale 5, n. 4.

2. A general pattern is becoming discernible concerning the character types that be-

Wanting to go on the hajj, the father one day asked his daughters what they wished. "Name something I can bring back with me," he said.

"I want a gold bracelet," announced the eldest. "And I want a dress embroidered with the most expensive silk," said the second.[3] "As for me, father," said Sitt il-Ḥusun, "I want Jummēz Bin Yāzūr, Chief of the Birds. And if you don't bring him to me, may your camels collapse in Aqaba and be unable to move!"

The father went, completed the hajj, and returned. On the way back his camels collapsed in Aqaba, and he remembered. "Ah, yes!" he thought. "By Allah, I've forgotten to bring Jummēz Bin Yāzūr, Chief of the Birds."[4] Returning [to Mecca], he wandered around the city asking about Jummēz Bin Yāzūr, Chief of the Birds. Finally he came upon an aged sheikh, who gave him directions to Yāzūr's house. "Go stand by his door," the old man said, "and call out three times, 'Jummēz Bin Yāzūr, Chief of the Birds! My daughter has asked for you.'"

The father walked and walked, until he reached the house described by the sheikh. It was a hot day, and he was thirsty. Seeing a water jar by the door, he reached out his hand to drink, but listen! "Take your hand away!" said the jar. "May it be cut off! You dare to drink from your master's house?"[5] He was afraid, poor man! Stepping back, he shouted out

---

come heroes and heroines. The boys are generally the underdogs—the younger brothers—whereas the girls tend to be their parents' favorites and seem inevitably to get involved in some misadventure of a sexual nature. See Tale 8, n. 3; cf. Tale 35, n. 2.

Here, the father loves the girl not only because of her beauty but also (and more important) because she is the daughter of his second wife (cf. Tale 3, n. 2), a point the teller emphasizes.

3. The dress here (*ṯōb*) is the classic full-length, embroidered Palestinian dress; see Stillman, *Costume,* and Namikawa, *Mon'yō,* for color photographs. MacDonald ("Dress": 55) says that the "outstanding impression of native dress in Palestine, and in particular, women's, was the richness of its diversity." For a comprehensive study of Palestinian folk costume, with abundant color photographs including a catalog of embroidery patterns, see Kanaana et al., *Al-Malābis;* bibliographies in Stillman and Kanaana.

4. Although forgetting to bring something back from the hajj is a narrative cliché (cf. Tale 35), its use here is appropriate to the context. The father loves the daughter very much and wants to fulfill her wishes, yet to do so would mean violating the most sacred mores of the culture concerning women's sexual honor; hence, forgetting is a sort of ambivalence on his part.

5. This whole episode is a satirical comment on a curious practice from Ottoman times, when occasionally Turks living in Arab countries who had no power by virtue of wealth or government position but who still wished to exercise authority over inferiors would set in front of their homes two jars full of water for thirsty passersby; when, however, someone did try to take a drink, the waiting Turk would shout, "Don't drink from that jar, drink from the other one!" The authors are indebted to Professor Lūīs ʿAwaḍ for this information.

three times, "Jummēz Bin Yāzūr, Chief of the Birds! My daughter has asked for you!" and headed straight home.

Three nights after he arrived, look! a bird was beating his wings against Sitt il-Ḥusun's window. She got up and opened it for him, and he came in. Fluttering his wings, he turned into a youth, one of the handsomest of young men. Every night after that he came and stayed with her, and at dawn he would turn back into a bird and fly away, leaving her a purse full of gold under the pillow.

Her sisters found out, and jealousy crept into them.[6] One day her eldest sister came and said, "Ask Jummēz what's most precious to him where he comes from." Now Sitt il-Ḥusun was simple and innocent of heart, and when he came in the evening, she asked, "What does you most harm in your natural environment?"[7]

"Why?" he asked. "What do you want?"

"Because," she answered, "I just want to know." And she kept after him till he told her the thing that did him most harm was glass. If a piece of glass were to cut him, he would never be able to recover.

When she told her sisters, they went behind her back and broke the glass of the window where he came in. That evening when he came to visit her he tried to pass through the window, but the broken glass wounded him. Away he flew, back where he came from.

Sitt il-Ḥusun waited a day then two, a week then two, and when he did not come back, she realized her sisters had tricked her and that Jummēz was now sick. Putting on the disguise of a beggar, she wandered from one place to another in search of him. One day while she was sitting under a tree, two doves landed in the branches and began a conversation.

"You see, sister," said one, "it turns out Jummēz's wife had been wanting to kill him."

"If only there were somebody," replied the other, "(Far be it from my feathers and yours, and my blood and yours!) if there were someone who would slaughter a dove, drain her blood and mix it with the feathers, and then rub it on his legs, he'd get well again."

6. In the tales, jealousy among sisters is usually more vicious than is conflict among brothers, perhaps because it is based on sexual competition. Cf. Tales 10, 20, and 43; see the afterword to Group I, "Siblings."

7. At first glance something seems to be amiss in the telling: the sisters ask what is most precious to Jummēz, and Sitt il-Ḥusun wants to know what does him most harm. The two questions, however, add up to the same thing, for the removal of what is most precious, as the sisters clearly intended, does the most harm. The question nevertheless remains obscure.

Sitt il-Ḥusun rose up. She went and got a dove, slaughtered it, drained its blood, burned its feathers. Mixing them together, she carried the medicine with her and wandered about the city, calling out, "I am the doctor with the cure!"

One day she passed in front of a certain house, and listen! there were girls crying by the window. When they saw her, they called her up, saying their brother was sick and no one had been able to cure him. Sitt il-Ḥusun came in and rubbed the medicine into his wounds, staying up with him day and night for two weeks, until he woke up. When he awoke, he recognized her.

"O Sitt il-Ḥusun!" he cried out. "You did me a great wrong!"

"It wasn't me!" she answered. "My sisters did that to you."

"It's no matter," he responded. "Don't let it worry you."

When his sisters discovered she was his sweetheart and he wanted to marry her, they said, "You can't marry our brother until you've swept and mopped this whole town."[8]

She started to weep, but Jummēz said, "Go to the top of that mountain and cry out, 'O you there, sweep! O you thing there, mop!'" Going to the top of the mountain, she did as he had told her, and indeed, the whole town was swept and mopped.

Seeing that she had accomplished that, the sisters said, "You won't marry our brother until you've brought enough feathers to fill ten mattresses for the wedding." She went crying to Jummēz, but he said, "Don't be afraid. Go up the mountain and repeat three times, 'Jummēz Bin Yāzūr, Chief of the Birds, is dead!'" Going back to the top of the mountain, she called out three times, "Jummēz Bin Yāzūr, Chief of the Birds, is dead!" No sooner had she said it than all the birds gathered and started wailing and lamenting, plucking out their feathers over their chief.[9] Soon there were piles and piles of feathers on the ground.

Gathering the feathers, she took them to Jummēz's sisters, but they said, "You can't marry our brother until you've fetched the straw tray hanging on the wall of the ghouleh's house."[10]

8. For the role of the sisters in "criticizing" the bride, see the section on mother/daughter relationships in the Introduction, "The Tales and the Culture."

9. The birds' lamenting and tearing out of their feathers describes a cultural idiom, namely, the behavior of women during the wake held for brothers, husbands, or sons, when they rend their clothes and tear out their hair. See Tale 25, n. 4.

10. The weaving of colorful straw trays (*ṭbāq;* sing., *ṭabaq*) is a folk craft that is still practiced. The trays are used for many purposes, the most common being associated with

Again she went crying to Jummēz. "Don't cry," he comforted her. "This one's easy! Go to the ghouleh's house, and you'll find meat in front of the horses and barley in front of the lions. Switch the meat and the barley. You'll also find the stone terrace by the ghouleh's house collapsed.[11] Repair it, then go into the house and pull the tray down. But take care! If it scrapes against the wall, the ghouleh will wake up."

So to the ghouleh's house went Sitt il-Ḥusun, to do as Jummēz had told her. But when she went in to take the straw tray, she saw the ghouleh sleeping and shook with fear. As she was pulling the tray down, it scraped against the wall, shaking the whole world and waking up the ghouleh. Snatching the tray, Sitt il-Ḥusun ran with it, the ghouleh following her.

"Retaining wall, catch her!" shrieked the ghouleh.

"For twenty years I've been collapsed, and she repaired me," answered the wall. "I won't do it."

"Horses, catch her!" commanded the ghouleh.

"For twenty years we haven't tasted barley, and she fed us. No!"

"Lions, catch her!"

"For twenty years we haven't tasted meat, and she fed us. No, we won't!"

Thus the ghouleh was not able to catch her, and Sitt il-Ḥusun brought the tray and presented it to Jummēz's sisters. When they were satisfied that she had done all her tasks, they gave their consent to their brother's marriage.

They held wedding celebrations. Sitt il-Ḥusun married Jummēz Bin Yāzūr, Chief of the Birds, and he lifted her up and flew away with her.

The bird has flown, and a good night to all!

---

making bread. They are frequently hung on walls, both to keep them handy and to serve as decoration.

11. Stone terraces or retaining walls (*sanāsil*), built with medium-size stones, are characteristic of the hilly parts of the Palestinian landscape. When they collapse, usually as a result of heavy rain, they must be quickly rebuilt to keep the topsoil in place. Terrace construction, which requires considerable skill, is a rapidly disappearing folk craft.

Obviously, part of the ghouleh's ghoulishness lies not only in her stupidity, since she feeds meat to the horses and barley to the lions, but also in her laziness.

13. *Jbēne*

Once upon a time there was a woman who could not get pregnant and have children. One day, when a cheese vendor passed through, she gathered herself and cried out, "You who ask, your wish be granted![1] May Allah grant me a daughter with a face as white as this piece of cheese!" Allah spoke with her tongue, and she became pregnant and gave birth to a daughter with a face so fair it was like a square of cheese, and she called her Jbēne.[2]

When Jbēne grew up she was very beautiful, and all the girls in the neighborhood became jealous of her.[3] One day her companions came to her and said, "Jbēne, let's go pick *dōm* together."[4]

"Not until you ask my mother," she answered.

So to her mother they went and said, "O Jbēne's mother, for the life of Jbēne, won't you let Jbēne come pick *dōm* with us?"

"It's not my concern," she answered.[5] "Go speak with her father!"

They went to her father and said, "O Jbēne's father, for the life of Jbēne, won't you let Jbēne come pick *dōm* with us?"

"It's not my concern," he answered. "Go speak with her paternal aunt!"

1. "You who ask, your wish be granted!"—*yā ṭālbe, yā ġālbe*—is literally, "O supplicant, O winner!" Cf. Tale 40, n. 2.

For "May Allah grant me," see Tale 1, n. 3; Tale 8, n. 1.

2. Jbēne (diminutive of *jibne,* "cheese") is not used as a name. The cheese referred to here is made from sheep's milk. It is white and comes in slabs (*qrāṣ;* sing., *qurṣ*) of about three inches square by half an inch, with rounded corners, that are stacked in brine. Thus, the mother is asking for a daughter with fair complexion and a round face. See Tale 2, n. 1.

3. With reference to Tale 12, n. 2, and Tale 8, n. 3, we may conclude from the evidence at hand—Jbēne's being an only child, her having been conceived as a result of a craving, and her need to gain the permission of so many people—that she is pampered and that she is about to have an adventure touching on her honor: she is so precious that no one wants to risk the decision to let her go. See n. 5, below.

4. According to Crowfoot and Baldensperger (*Cedar:* 112), *dōm,* or Christ-thorn (*Zizyphus spina-christi*), is a wild tree bearing edible fruit. Tradition has it that Christ's crown of thorns was made from the branches of this tree. Some specimens are centuries old and have attained considerable size.

5. The sense of this response (in Arabic, *bixuṣnīš*) apparently conveys not so much a lack of concern as an unwillingness to claim authority for making the decision (see n. 3, above). Perhaps the order of responsibility given in the tale—the exact opposite of what it would be in life—is meant to foreshadow the evil that befalls Jbēne. Thus, shifting the responsibility for the decision to the person with the least authority (Jbēne's maternal aunt) removes the blame, should something bad occur, from those on whom it should properly fall, namely the parents, particularly the father.

They went to her paternal aunt and said, "O Jbēne's aunt, for the life of Jbēne, won't you let Jbēne come pick *dōm* with us?"

"It's not my concern," she answered. "Go speak with her maternal aunt!"

So to the maternal aunt they went and said, "O Jbēne's aunt, for the life of Jbēne, won't you let Jbēne come pick *dōm* with us?"

"Fine," said the aunt to them. "Let her go with you."

The girls gathered together and went to pick *dōm*. When they reached the *dōm* trees, they asked, "Who's going to climb the tree for us?"

Jbēne was the youngest and the best behaved among them. "I'll climb it," she said.

Climbing the tree, she picked *dōm* and dropped it for them under the tree.

"We'll fill your basket," they said to her.

They filled their baskets with *dōm,* but they filled hers with snails. As the sun was setting, they abandoned her up in the tree and went to their homes. Night fell, and Jbēne could not climb down from the tree.[6]

Her mother went and asked her friends, but they said, "Jbēne didn't come with us."

Later a horseman came by, riding a mare. The mare approached the tree but backed away in fear. Looking up into the tree, the horseman saw the girl. "Come down!" he said, but she would not because she was afraid. "I swear by Allah your safety's guaranteed," he said to her, and only then did the girl heed him. She came down, and he set her behind him on the mare and rode home with her.[7]

6. In another version we collected of this tale, Jbēne's abandonment is more logical. When she comes down and finds her basket full of snails, she decides to go back up the tree and pick enough *dōm* to fill her basket (*jūne*). Her friends, however, claiming it is getting dark, refuse to wait for her.

7. The form, or formula, of this standard and traditional oath—*ʿalēki ʾalla w-amān alla* (literally, "May Allah and His safety be upon you!")—is binding and offers an absolute guarantee of safety. To the basic oath, another rhyming phrase is frequently added—*w-il-xāyin y-xūno ʾalla* ("and may Allah betray him who betrays this oath!"). Phrased differently, the oath would not be considered equally solemn and thus would not carry the same weight. Cf. the oath given in Tale 20, n. 5; Tale 42, n. 7.

The girl taking refuge in a tree and being rescued by a man on a horse is a frequent motif in the Palestinian folktale (in this collection it occurs also in Tales 2, 18, and 35). It is always associated with physical beauty and the arousal of desire. In Tale 35 as well as here, the daughters leave home without the express permission of the mother, and in Tale 18 Lōlabe actually defies her mother in order to leave. In all the tales where the girl takes refuge in a

During the night Jbēne painted herself black all over because she did not want anyone to know who she was. In the morning they thought she was a servant and sent her out to graze the herds of sheep and camels.[8]

Every day after that, while roaming with the herds, Jbēne would cry out:

"O birds that fly
Over mountains high!
Greet my mother and father
And say, 'Jbēne's a shepherdess.
Sheep she grazes, and camels.
And rests in the shade of the vine.'"

Then she would cry, and the birds would cry, and the sheep and camels would stop grazing and cry.

The son of the emir noticed that the animals were going out to pasture and were coming home without having eaten. They were getting thinner day by day. "By Allah," he thought, "I must follow her and find out what the matter is."

He followed the herds until they reached their grazing ground. Jbēne sat down and cried out:

"O birds that fly
Over mountains high!
Greet my mother and father
And say, 'Jbēne's a shepherdess.
Sheep she grazes, and camels.
And rests in the shade of the vine.'"

Then she started crying, and the birds cried. The herds all stopped grazing and stood in their tracks and cried. Everything around her cried, and the son of the emir himself stood up and cried.

In the evening he said to her, "Come here! Confess the truth! Who are you, and what's your story?"

---

tree, she is rescued by a king or an emir who entices her to come down by guaranteeing her safety with an oath, takes her home, and then marries her.

8. This tale seems to be of Bedouin origin: the camel herding by the girls would so indicate, as would the fact that the person in authority is an emir (cf. Tale 10, n. 1).

Jbēne paints herself black by covering herself with soot; see Tale 1, n. 11. This act, which transforms her from white to black (somewhat similar to the king's daughter wearing a sackcloth in Tale 14), may indicate a feeling of shame or guilt in relation to her sexuality. It also makes her look unappealing to the emir, which keeps him from making advances.

"My name's Jbēne," she answered. "This and that and that happened to me." She then removed the soot from her face, and behold! what was she like but the moon?

The son of the emir made her his wife.[9] They arranged festivities and beautiful nights.[10] He married her, and she brought her mother and father to stay with her. I was there, and have just returned.

The bird of this tale has flown, and now for another one![11]

14. *Sackcloth*

TELLER: Testify that God is One!
AUDIENCE: There is no god but God.

Once upon a time there was a king who had no children except an only daughter. One day his wife laid her head down and died, and he went searching for a new wife. They spoke of this woman and that, but none pleased him. No one seemed more beautiful in his eyes, so the story goes, than his own daughter and he had no wish to marry another. When he came into the house, she would call him "father," but he would answer, "Don't call me 'father'! Call me 'cousin.'"[1]

"But father, O worthy man![2] I'm your daughter!"

9. *ʾAmlak ʿalēhā*—literally, "He took possession of her."

10. "They arranged festivities and beautiful nights" (*qāmū ha-l-ifrāḥ w-il-layālī l-imlāḥ*). The wedding festivities are held at the household of the bridegroom (*dār il-ʿarīs*) for seven nights before the actual ceremony. Because most weddings are held in spring or summer, when evenings are most beautiful, communal singing and dancing take place outside, in the courtyard adjacent to the house. See Granqvist, *Marriage* II: 35–41 ("The Evenings of Joy").

11. The closing formula (*ṭār ṭērhā u-ʿalēkum ġērhā*) is a variant of that used in Tale 3 (see n. 9). The imagery and symbolism of the bird in these tales, as we have seen, has varied significance. The bird can be a bride (Tale 11, n. 5), a lover (Tale 12, n. 1), a husband (Tale 10, n. 9), or the spirit of an innocent boy, as in Tale 9. Both the hero and heroine of Tale 18 are transformed into a bird.

Here, in Jbēne's ditty, the birds are messengers, and the tale itself is compared to a bird in the closing formula—the most common type of closing formula in the corpus (cf., the closing formulas of Tales 3, 6, 12, 17, 27, 28, 30, and 31; for a less common variant, see Tale 33, n. 13).

1. "Call me 'cousin.'" See the section on endogamy in the Introduction, "The Tales and the Culture."

2. *Yā bn il-ḥalāl*—literally, "O legitimately begotten son!" The expression *ʾibin ḥalāl* is used generically to mean a good or benevolent man (or woman: *bint ḥalāl*). Cf. Tale 5, n. 12; Tale 44, n. 15.

"It's no use," he insisted. "I've made up my mind."

One day he sent for the cadi and asked him, "A tree that I've cared for, feeding and watering it—is it legally mine, or can someone else claim it?"[3] "No one else can claim it," replied the cadi. "It's rightfully yours." No sooner had the cadi left than the father went out and brought his daughter jewelry and a wedding dress. He was preparing to take her for his wife.

The girl put on the new clothes and the gold, and sat in the house. Her father came home in the evening. When she realized that he was absolutely intent on taking her, she went to a sackcloth maker and said, "Take as much money as you want, but make me a tight-fitting sackcloth that will cover my whole body, except my nostrils, mouth, and eyes. And I want it ready by tomorrow morning."

"Fine," he said. "I'll do it."

[When it was finished] the girl went and brought it home. She put it in a shed in front of the house and locked the door. She then put on the bridal clothes and jewelry [again] and lounged about the house. Her father came home in the evening.

"Father!" she called to him.

"Don't call me 'father'!" he said. "Call me 'cousin.'"

"All right, cousin!" she replied, "But wait until I come back from the outhouse (All respect to the audience!)."[4]

"But you might run away."

"No, I won't," she answered. "But just to make sure, tie a rope to my wrist, and every once in a while pull your end of it and you'll discover I'm still there."

There was a big stone in the lower part of the house,[5] and on her way out she tied her end of the rope to it, together with the bracelets. She then went out to the shed, put on her tight sack, and, invoking the help of Allah, ventured into the night.

Meanwhile, the father tugged at the rope every few moments and,

3. Although the father's initial premise that he owns his daughter is acceptable in the culture, his conclusion that he owns her sexually is totally abhorrent. His use of legalistic language to get around a taboo is interesting. For more on "cadi," an official of the court in the Islamic system of jurisprudence, see Tale 44, n. 5.

4. The description of the king's house makes it sound as modest as that of a Palestinian fellah. Cf. Tale 3, n. 6.

For "(All respect to the audience!)"—*ḥēšā s-sāmʿīn*—see Tale 15, n. 8.

5. For more on "the lower part of the house"—*qāʿ il-bēt*—see Tale 26, n. 8.

hearing the tinkle of the bracelets, would say to himself, "She's still here." [He waited and waited] till the middle of the night, then he said, "By Allah, I've got no choice but to go check on her." When he found the rope tied to the stone, with the bracelets dangling from it, he prepared his horse, disguised himself, mounted, and went out to look for her.

She had already been gone awhile, and by the time he left the house she was well outside the city. He followed after her, searching. When he caught up with her, she saw and recognized him, and clung to the trunk of a tree. Not recognizing her, but thinking she was a man, he asked, "Didn't you see a girl with such and such features pass this way?"

"O uncle, Allah save you!" answered the maiden. "Please leave me to my misery. I can barely see in front of me."

He left her and went away. Seeing him take one path, she took another. [She kept on traveling,] sleeping here and waking up there, till she came to a city. Hunger driving her, she took shelter by the wall of a king's palace.

The king's slavegirl came out with a platter[6] to dump leftover food. Sackcloth fell on the scraps and set to eating. When the slave saw her, she rushed back inside.

"O mistress!" she called out, "There's a weird sight outside—the strangest-looking man, and he's eating the leftovers."

"Go call him in, and let him come here!" commanded the mistress.

"Come in and see my mistress," said the slave. "They want to have a look at you."

"What's the situation with you, uncle?" they asked, when she came inside.[7] "Are you human or jinn?"

"By Allah, uncle," she replied, "I'm human, and the choicest of the race. But Allah has created me the way I am."

"What skill do you have?" they asked. "What can you do?"

6. The metal platter (*sidir*) is available in various sizes, the most common being about one meter in diameter. It is used for communal eating (see n. 10, below). The fact that food is being thrown away at all, and in such quantities, immediately indicates the opulence of the palace.

7. "Uncle" (*yā ʿammī*—literally, "O my paternal uncle") is a respectful form of address to a male stranger. Cf. Tale 35, n. 5; see Footnote Index, s.v. "Forms of Address."

From this point on in the narrative the teller uses masculine pronouns to refer to Sackcloth when she is wearing her disguise and feminine pronouns when she is out of it. For the sake of consistency, and because it is more appropriate for English usage, we use the feminine pronoun throughout.

"By Allah, I don't have any skills in particular," she answered. "I can stay in the kitchen, peeling onions and passing things over when needed."

They put her to work in the kitchen, and soon everyone was saying, "Here comes Sackcloth! There goes Sackcloth!" How happy they were to have Sackcloth around, and she stayed in the kitchen under the protection of the cook.

One day there was a wedding in the city, and the king's household was invited. In the evening they were preparing to go have a look at the spectacle.

"Hey, Sackcloth!" they called out, "Do you want to come with us and have a look at the wedding?"

"No, Allah help me!" she exclaimed. "I can't go look at weddings or anything else like that. You go, and I wish you Godspeed, but I can't go."

The king's household and the slaves went to the wedding, and no one was left at home except Sackcloth. Waiting till they were well on their way, she took off her sackcloth and set out for the festivities, all made up and wearing the wedding dress she had brought with her. All the women were dancing in turn, and when her turn came she took the handkerchiefs and danced and danced till she had had her fill of dancing.[8] She then dropped the handkerchiefs and left, and no one knew where she came from or where she went. Returning home, she put on her sackcloth, squatted alongside the walls of the palace, and went to sleep. When the slaves got back from the celebration, they started badgering her.

"What! Are you sleeping here?" they taunted. "May you never rise! If only you'd come to the wedding, you would've seen this girl who danced and danced, and then left without anybody knowing where she went."

That happened the first night, and the second night the same thing happened again. When the king's wife came home, she went to see her son.

"Dear son," she said, "if only we could get that girl, I'd ask for her

8. The celebration of weddings has given rise to a rich native tradition in folk dance and song (see Stephan, *Song of Songs*). The men celebrate the wedding separately from the women, and each sex has not only its own set of wedding songs and dances but also its own style of performance. The women stand in a circle, singing and clapping while one of them dances in the middle, a colorful handkerchief in each hand. All eyes are on her, and she shows off her dancing ability, her beauty, and her clothes (cf. Tale 11, n. 4). After dancing awhile, she passes the handkerchiefs to another woman, who then takes her turn. Thus the image presented in the tale is of Sackcloth dancing in all her beauty, wearing the wedding garment her father had bought her. See Footnote Index, s.v. "Marriage Customs."

hand—the one who comes to the wedding and leaves without anybody knowing where she comes from or where she goes."[9]

"Let me wear women's clothes, mother," he suggested, "and take me with you [to the women's side]. If anyone should ask, say to them, 'This is my sister's daughter. She's here visiting us, and I brought her with me to see the celebrations.'"

"Fine," she agreed.

Putting women's clothes on him, she took him with them. Sackcloth, meanwhile, gave them enough time to get there, then took off her coat of sackcloth and followed. She went in, danced till she had had her fill, then slipped away. No one recognized her, or knew where she came from or where she went. Returning home, she put on her sackcloth and went to sleep.

The following day the king's son said to the others, "You go to the wedding," and he hid outside the door of the house where the celebration was taking place. Sackcloth came again, went inside and danced, then pulled herself together and slipped away. No sooner had she left than he followed her, keeping a safe distance until she reached home. No sooner did she get there than she went in, put on her coat of sackcloth, and squatted by the palace wall and went to sleep.

"What!" he said to himself, "She dwells in my own house and pretends to be some kind of freak!" He did not say anything to anyone.

The next morning he said to the slaves who bring up his meals, "I don't want any of you to bring my food up today. I want Sackcloth to serve my dinner, and I want him to share it with me."[10]

"O master, for the sake of Allah!" she protested, "I can't do it. I'm so disgusting, how could you want to have dinner with me?"

"You must bring up my dinner so we can eat together," he replied.

The servants prepared dinner, served it onto a platter, and gave it to Sackcloth. She carried it, pretending to limp, until she was halfway up the stairs, then she made as if her foot had slipped and dropped the whole platter.

"Please, master!" she pleaded, "Didn't I tell you I can't carry anything?"

9. On the role of the mother in her son's wedding, see Tale 21, n. 13.

10. Dinner, usually served around two in the afternoon, is the main meal of the day. On the relationship of food to courtship, see Tale 15, n. 3.

"You must keep bringing platters and dropping them," the son of the king insisted, "until you manage to come up here on your own."

With the second platter she came up to the landing at the top of the stairs, slipped, and dropped it.

"This isn't going to get you anywhere," said the son of the king. "Do not for one moment hope to be excused."

With the third platter she limped and limped, leaning here and there, until she reached the top and served him his dinner.

"Come sit here with me," said the prince, closing the door. "Let's eat this dinner together."

"Please, master!" she protested, "Just look at my condition. Surely it will disgust you."

"No. Do sit down! I would like to have dinner with you."

They sat down to eat together, and the prince pulled out a knife and reached for the coat of sackcloth.

"You must take this thing off!" he said. "How long have we been searching, wondering who the girl was that came to the wedding. And all this time you've been living under my own roof!"

He made her remove the sackcloth coat, and called his mother. They sent for the cadi, and wrote up their marriage contract.

"For forty days," the public crier announced, "no one is to eat or drink except at the house of the king."[11]

They held wedding celebrations, and gave her to him for a wife.[12]

And this is my tale, I've told it; and in your hands I leave it.

15. *Šāhīn*

Once there was a king (and there is no kingship except that which belongs to Allah, may He be praised and exalted!) and he had an only daughter. He had no other children, and he was proud of her. One day,

11. For more on the number forty, see Tale 10, n. 11.

12. This tale is the Palestinian equivalent of Cinderella. "Sackcloth" is a literal translation of Abū l-Labābīd, the second word being the plural of *libbād* (sackcloth); the first (literally, "father"), when used in combination with another noun, forms an attributive locution—e.g., *abū šanab,* "he with the mustache." Hence, *Abū l-Lababīd* means "He of the Sackcloths."

as she was lounging about, the daughter of the vizier came to visit her. They sat together, feeling bored.

"We're sitting around here feeling bored," said the daughter of the vizier. "What do you say to going out and having a good time?"

"Yes," said the other.

Sending for the daughters of the ministers and dignitaries of state, the king's daughter gathered them all together, and they went into her father's orchard to take the air, each going her own way.

As the vizier's daughter was sauntering about, she stepped on an iron ring. Taking hold of it, she pulled, and behold! it opened the door to an underground hallway, and she descended into it. The other girls, meanwhile, were distracted, amusing themselves. Going into the hallway, the vizier's daughter came upon a young man with his sleeves rolled up. And what! there were deer, partridges, and rabbits in front of him, and he was busy plucking and skinning.[1]

Before he was aware of it, she had already saluted him. "Peace to you!"

"And to you, peace!" he responded, taken aback. "What do you happen to be, sister, human or jinn?"

"Human," she answered, "and the choicest of the race. What are you doing here?"

"By Allah," he said, "we are forty young men, all brothers. Every day my brothers go out to hunt in the morning and come home toward evening. I stay home and prepare their food."

"That's fine," she chimed in. "You're forty young men, and we're forty young ladies. I'll be your wife, the king's daughter is for your eldest brother, and all the other girls are for all your other brothers." She matched the girls with the men.

Oh! How delighted he was to hear this!

"What's your name?"

"Šāhīn," he answered.

"Welcome, Šāhīn."[2]

He went and fetched a chair, and set it in front of her. She sat next to

1. Šāhīn's masculinity is brought into question right from the start, because he is at home doing the cooking.

2. The values that prevail above ground are reversed once the vizier's daughter crosses the threshold to the world under the ground. Thus, she welcomes Šāhīn ("*ahlan wa-sahlan, Šāhīn!*") even though she is in his house, and she assumes a masculine role for the rest of the tale.

him, and they started chatting. He roasted some meat, gave it to her, and she ate.[3] She kept him busy until the food he was cooking was ready.

"Šāhīn," she said when the food was ready, "you don't happen to have some seeds and nuts in the house, do you?"[4]

"Yes, by Allah, we do."

"Why don't you get us some. It'll help pass away the time."

In their house, the seeds and nuts were stored on a high shelf.[5] He got up, brought a ladder, and climbed up to the shelf. Having filled his handkerchief with seeds and nuts, he was about to come down when she said, "Here, let me take it from you. Hand it over!" Taking the handkerchief from him, she pulled the ladder away and threw it to the ground, leaving him stranded on the shelf.

She then brought out large bowls, prepared a huge platter,[6] piled all the food on it, and headed straight out of there, taking the food with her and closing the door of the tunnel behind her. Putting the food under a tree, she called to the girls, "Come eat, girls!"

"Eh! Where did this come from?" they asked, gathering around.

"Just eat and be quiet," she replied. "What more do you want? Just eat!"

The food was prepared for forty lads, and here were forty lasses. They set to and ate it all. "Go on along now!" commanded the vizier's daughter, "Each one back where she came from. Disperse!" She dispersed them, and they went their way. Waiting until they were all busy, she took the platter back, placing it where it was before and coming back out again. In time the girls all went home.

Now we go back. To whom? To Šāhīn. When his brothers came home in the evening, they could not find him.

"O Šāhīn," they called. "Šāhīn!"

And behold! he answered them from the shelf.

"Hey! What are you doing up there?" asked the eldest brother.

"By Allah, brother," Šāhīn answered, "I set up the ladder after the

3. The phenomenon of feeding a loved one is common among the Palestinians. On love and courtship, see Introduction, "Food in Society and the Tales."

4. On the eating of seeds and nuts to pass time, see Tale 3, n. 3.

5. The *sidde,* an elevated compartment used for storage, is not a shelf as such but part of the actual house structure. See also Tale 26, n. 8.

6. For the platter (*sidir*), see Tale 14, n. 6.

food was ready and came to get some seeds and nuts for passing away the time. The ladder slipped, and I was stranded up here."

"Very well," they said, and set up the ladder for him. When he came down, the eldest brother said, "Now, go bring the food so we can have dinner." Gathering up the game they had hunted that day, they put it all in one place and sat down.

Šāhīn went to fetch the food from the kitchen, but he could not find a single bite.

"Brother," he said, coming back, "the cats must have eaten it."

"All right," said the eldest. "Come, prepare us whatever you can."

Taking the organs of the hunted animals,[7] from this and that he made dinner and they ate. Then they laid their heads down and went to sleep.

The next morning they woke up and set out for the hunt. "Now brother," they mocked him, "be sure to let us go without dinner another evening. Let the cats eat it all!"

"No, brothers," he said. "Don't worry."

No sooner did they leave than he rolled up his sleeves and set to skinning and plucking the gazelles, rabbits, and partridges. On time, the vizier's daughter showed up. Having gone to the king's daughter and gathered all the other girls, she waited till they were amusing themselves with something and then dropped in on him.

"Salaam!"

"And to you, peace!" he answered. "Welcome to the one who took the food and left me stranded on the shelf, making me look ridiculous to my brothers!"

"What you say is true," she responded. "And yet I'm likely to do even more than that to the one I love."

"And as for me," he murmured, "your deeds are sweeter than honey."

Fetching a chair, he set it down for her, and then he brought some seeds and nuts. They sat down to entertain themselves, and she kept him amused until she realized the food was ready.

"Šāhīn," she said, "isn't there a bathroom in your house?"

"Yes, there is," he replied.

"I'm pressed, and must go to the bathroom. Where is it?"

"It's over there," he answered.

7. Hearts, livers, and kidneys are all considered delicacies.

"Well, come and show it to me."

"This is it, here," he said, showing it to her.

She went in and, so the story goes, made as if she did not know how to use it.

"Come and show me how to use this thing," she called.

I don't know what else she said, but he came to show her, you might say, how to sit on the toilet. Taking hold of him, she pushed him inside like this, and he ended up with his head down and his feet up. She closed the door on him and left. Going into the kitchen, she served up the food onto a platter and headed out of there. She put the food under a tree and called to her friends, "Come eat!"

"And where did you get all this?"

"All you have to do is eat," she answered.

They ate and scattered, each going her way. And she stole away and returned the platter.

At the end of the day the brothers came home, and there was no sign of their brother. "Šāhīn, Šāhīn!" they called out. "O Šāhīn!" But no answer came. They searched the shelf, they searched here, and they searched there. But it was no use.

"You know," said the eldest, "I say there's something odd about Šāhīn's behavior. I suspect he has a girlfriend. Anyway, some of you go into the kitchen, find the food, and bring it so we can eat. I'm sure Šāhīn will show up any moment."

Going into the kitchen, they found nothing. "There's no food," they reported. "It's all gone! We're now sure that Šāhīn has a girlfriend, and he gives her all the food. Let's go ahead and fix whatever there is at hand so we can eat."

Having prepared a quick meal, they ate dinner and were content. They prepared for sleep, but one of them (All respect to the listeners!)[8] was pressed and needed to relieve himself. He went to the bathroom, and lo! there was Šāhīn, upside down.

"Hey, brothers!" he shouted. "Here's Šāhīn, and he's fallen into the toilet!"

8. (*ḥēšā s-sāmʿīn*)—literally, "Excepting the listeners!"—is an interjection frequently used to introduce subjects considered unpleasant or socially taboo, such as reference to feces (here; also Tale 14, n. 4), ritual impurity (Tale 18, n. 6), and shoes (Tale 44, n. 2). For a variant, see Tale 29, n. 2.

They rushed over and lifted him out. What a condition he was in! They gave him a bath.

"Tell me," said the eldest, "what's going on?"

"By Allah, brother," replied Šāhīn, "after I cooked dinner I went to relieve myself, and I slipped."

"Very well," returned the eldest. "But the food, where is it?"

"By Allah, as far as I know it's in the kitchen, but how should I know if the cats haven't eaten it?"

"Well, all right!" they said, and went back to sleep.

The next morning, as they were setting out, they mocked him again. "Why don't you leave us without dinner another night?"

"No, brothers!" he said. ["Don't worry."]

Pulling themselves together, they departed. Now, on time, the daughter of the vizier came to see the king's daughter, gathered the others, and they came down to the orchard and spread out. Waiting until they were all caught up with something, she slipped away to him, and listen, brothers! she found him at home.

"Salaam!"

"And to you, peace!" he retorted. "Welcome! On the shelf the first day, and you made away with the food; and the second day you threw me into the toilet and stole the food, blackening my face in front of my brothers!"

"As for me," she said, "I'll do even more than that to the one I love."

"And to me, it's sweeter than honey," he responded, bringing her a chair. She sat down, he brought seeds and nuts, and they passed away the time entertaining themselves. She kept chatting with him, until she knew the food was ready.

"Šāhīn," she said.

"Yes."

"Don't you have some drinks for us to enjoy ourselves? There's meat here, and seeds and nuts. We could eat and have something to drink."

"Yes," he replied, "we do."

"Why don't you bring some out, then?" she urged him.

Bringing a bottle, he set it in front of her. She poured drinks and handed them to him. "This one's to my health," she egged him on, "and this one's also for my sake," until he fell over, as if no one were there. She then went and took some sugar, put it on to boil, and made a preparation for removing body hair.[9] She used it on him to perfection, and, brother, she made him look like the most beautiful of girls. Bringing a woman's dress, she put it on him. Then, bringing a scarf, she wrapped it around his head and laid him down to sleep in bed. She powdered his face, wrapped the scarf well around his head, put the bed covers over him, and left. Then into the kitchen she went, loaded the food, and departed. The girls ate, and the platter was replaced.

When the brothers returned in the evening, they did not find Šāhīn at home.

"O Šāhīn! Šāhīn! Šāhīn!"

No answer. "Let's search the bathroom," they said among themselves. But they did not find him there. They searched the shelf, and still no sign of him.

"Didn't I tell you Šāhīn has a girlfriend?" the eldest declared. "I'd say Šāhīn has a girlfriend and goes out with her. Some of you, go check if the food's still there." They did, and found nothing.

Again they resorted to a quick meal of organ meat. When it was time to sleep, each went to his bed. In his bed, the eldest found our well-contented friend stretched out in it. Back to his brothers he ran. "I told you Šāhīn has a girlfriend, but you didn't believe me. Come take a look! Here's Šāhīn's bride! Come and see! Come and see!"

He called his brothers, and they all came, clamoring, "Šāhīn's bride! Šāhīn's bride!" Removing his scarf, they looked at him carefully. Eh! A man's features are hard to miss. They recognized him. "Eh! This is Šāhīn!" they shouted. Bringing water, they splashed his face till he woke up. Looking himself over, what did he find? They fetched a mirror. He looked at himself, and what a sight he was—all rouged, powdered, and beautified.

"And now," they asked him, "what do you have to say for yourself?"

"By Allah, brother," answered Šāhīn, "listen and I'll tell you the truth. Every day, around noon, a girl with such and such features comes to see me. She says, 'We're forty young ladies. The king's daughter is for your eldest brother, I am yours, and all the other girls are for all your other brothers.' She's the one who's been doing these things to me every day."

9. This preparation (*ʿaqīde*), used in the process of *tiḥfīf*, or removal of undesired body hair, is made of melted sugar and lemon juice, which are boiled to form a thick and sticky substance.

"Is that so?"

"Yes, it is."

"Fine. All of you go to the hunt tomorrow," suggested the eldest, "and I'll stay behind with Šāhīn. I'll take care of her!"

Pulling out his sword (so the story goes), he sat waiting in readiness. By Allah, brothers, in due time she came. She had gathered the girls as usual, and they had come down to the orchard. Waiting until their attention was caught, she slipped away to him. Before he was even aware of her, she had already saluted him.

"Salaam!"

"And to you, peace!" he answered. "The first time on the shelf, and I said all right; the second time in the bathroom, and I said all right; but the third time you put makeup on me and turned me into a bride!"

"And yet I'm likely to do even more than that to the one I love."

No sooner had she said that than up rose the eldest brother and rushed over to her, his sword at the ready.

"Listen," she reasoned with him. "You are forty, and we are forty. The king's daughter is to be your wife, and I, Šāhīn's; and so and so among us is for so and so among you, and so on." She calmed him down.

"Is it true, what you're saying?" he asked.

"Of course it's true," she replied.

"And who can speak for these girls?"

"I can."

"You're the one who can speak for them?"

"Yes."

(Šāhīn, meanwhile, was listening, and since he was already experienced, he mused to himself that his brother had been taken in already.)

"Agreed," said the eldest brother. "Come over here and let me pay you the bridewealth for the forty girls. Where are we to meet you?"

"First pay me the bridewealth,"[10] she answered, "and tomorrow, go and reserve a certain public bath for us at your expense. Stand guard at the gate, and as we go in you yourself can count us one by one—all forty of us. We'll go into the baths and bathe, and after we come out each of you will take his bride home by the hand."

10. According to Islamic law (*šarīᶜa*), the bridewealth (*fēd;* sometimes translated misleadingly as "bride-price"), although paid to the father, belongs to the bride; frequently, however, fathers do keep a portion of it. See Cohen, *Border Villages:* 87 n. 1; also Granqvist, *Marriage* I: 111 n. 1, 119–155; Jaussen, *Naplouse:* 57–62.

"Just like that?" he wondered.

"Of course," she assured him.

He brought out a blanket, she spread it, and—count, count, count—he counted one hundred Ottoman gold coins for each girl. When he had finished counting out the money, she took it and went straight out. Calling her friends over, she said, "Sit here! Sit under this tree! Each of you open your hand and receive your bridewealth."

"Eh!" they protested, "You so and so! Did you ruin your reputation?"

"No one's to say anything," she responded. "Each of you will take her bridewealth without making a sound." Giving each of them her money, she said, "Come. Let's go home."

After she had left their place, Šāhīn said to his brother, "Brother, she tricked me and took only the food. But she tricked you and got away with our money."

"Who, me?" the brother declared, "Trick me? Tomorrow you'll see."

The next day the brothers stayed at home. They went and reserved the baths at their own expense, and the eldest stood watch at the door, waiting for the girls to arrive. Meanwhile, the vizier's daughter had gotten up the next day, gathered all the girls, the king's daughter among them, and, leading them in front of her, headed for the bath with them. And behold! there was our effendi guarding the door.[11] As they were going in, he counted them one by one. Count, count, he counted them all—exactly forty.

Going into the baths, the girls bathed and enjoyed themselves. But after they had finished bathing and put on their clothes, she, the clever one,[12] gave them this advice: "Each of you is to shit in the tub she has bathed in, and let's line the tubs up all in a row." Each of them shat in her tub, and they arranged them neatly in a row, all forty of them. Now the baths had another door, away from the entrance. "Follow me this way," urged the vizier's daughter, and they all hurried out.

The eldest brother waited an hour, two, three, then four, but the girls did not emerge. "Eh!" he said, "They're taking a long time about it."

"Brother," said Šāhīn, "they're gone."

11. *Effendi,* a word of Turkish origin, now arabicized and anglicized, was originally an official title of respect equivalent to "Master" or "Sire"; it is now used in Arabic to mean only "gentleman."

12. The word *malᶜūne* (past participle of *laᶜana,* "to curse") is generally used to refer to someone who is clever and knows how to take care of herself (or himself, *malᶜūn*).

"But listen!" he replied, "Where could she have gone? They all went inside the bathhouse together."

"All right," said Šāhīn, "let's go in and see."

Going into the bathhouse, brother, they found the owner inside.

"Where did the girls who came into the bathhouse go?"

"O uncle!" replied the owner, "They've been gone a long time."

"And how could they have left?" asked the eldest brother.

"They left by that door," he replied.

Now, Šāhīn, who was experienced, looked in the bathing place and saw the tubs all lined up.

"Brother!" he called out.

"Yes. What is it?"

"Come here and take a look," he answered. "Here are the forty! Take a good look! See how she had them arranged so neatly?"

Finally the brothers went back home, wondering to themselves, "And now, what are we going to do?"

"Leave them to me!" volunteered Šāhīn. "I'll take care of them."

The next day Šāhīn disguised himself as an old lady. Wearing an old woman's dress, he put a beaded rosary around his neck and headed for the city. The daughter of the vizier, meanwhile, had gathered the girls, and she was sitting with them in a room above the street. As he was coming from afar, she saw and recognized him. She winked to her friends, saying, "I'll go call him, and you chime in with, 'Here's our aunt! Welcome to our aunt!'" As soon as she saw him draw near, she opened the door and came out running. "Welcome, welcome, welcome to our aunty! Welcome, aunty!" And, taking him by the hand, she pulled him inside to where they were. "Welcome to our aunty!" they clamored, locking the door. "Welcome to our aunty!"

"Now, girls, take off your clothes," urged the vizier's daughter. "Take off your clothes. It's been a long time since we've had our clothes washed by our aunty's own hands. Let her wash our clothes!"

"By Allah, I'm tired," protested Šāhīn. "By Allah, I can't do it."

"By Allah, you must do it, aunty," they insisted. "It's been such a long time since we've had our clothes washed by our aunty's hands."

She made all forty girls take off their clothes, each of them leaving on only enough to cover her modesty, and she handed the clothes to him. He washed clothes till noon.

"Come girls," said the vizier's daughter. "By Allah, it's been such a long time since our aunty has bathed us with her own hands. Let her bathe us!"

Each of them put on a wrap and sat down, and he went around bathing them in turn.[13] By the time he had finished bathing them all, what a condition he was in! He was exhausted.

When he had finished with one, she would get up and go put on her clothes. The vizier's daughter would then wink at her and whisper that she should take the wrap she was wearing, fold it over, twist it, and tie a knot at one end so that it was like a whip. When all forty girls had finished bathing, the leader spoke out, "Eh, aunty! Hey, girls, she has just bathed us, and we must bathe her in return."

"No, niece!" he protested. "I don't need a bath! For the sake of . . ."

"Impossible, aunty!" insisted the vizier's daughter. "By Allah, this can't be. Eh! You bathe and bathe all of us, and we don't even bathe you in return. Come, girls!"

At a wink from her, they set on him against his will. They were forty. What could he do? They took hold of him and removed his clothes, and lo and behold! he was a man. "Eh!" they exclaimed. "This isn't our aunty. It's a man! Have at him, girls!" And with their whips, each of them having braided her robe and tied knots in it, they put Šāhīn in the middle and descended on his naked body. Hit him from here, turn him around there, and beat him again on the other side! All the while he was jumping among them and shouting at the top of his voice. When she thought he had had enough, she winked at them to clear a path. As soon as he saw his way open, he opened the door and dashed out running, wearing only the skin the Lord had given him.

His brothers were at home, and before they were even aware of it, he showed up, naked. And what a condition he was in! Up they sprang, as if possessed. "Hey! What happened to you?" they asked. "Come! Come! What hit you?"

"Wait a minute," he answered. "Such and such happened to me."

"And now," they asked among themselves, "what can we do?"

"Now, by Allah," answered Šāhīn, "we have no recourse but for each of us to ask for the hand of his bride from her father.[14] As for me, I'm

13. The girls wear a small wrap (*mzāṭ*) for the sake of modesty.

14. The ceremony of asking for the bride's hand, or *ṭulbe*, is a formal part of the wedding process and cannot be dispensed with even when both sets of parents have agreed to the match privately. It would, however, be most unusual for the bridegroom himself to

going to ask for her hand. But as soon as she arrives here, I'm going to kill her. No other punishment will do. I'll show her!"

They all agreed, each going to ask for his bride's hand from her father, and the fathers gave their consent.

Now, the daughter of the minister was something of a devil.[15] She asked her father, if anyone should come asking for her hand, not to give his consent before letting her know. When Šāhīn came to propose, the father said, "Not until I consult with my daughter first." The father went to consult with his daughter, and she said, "All right, give your consent, but on condition that there be a waiting period of one month so that the bridegroom can have enough time to buy the wedding clothes and take care of all the other details."[16]

After the asking for her hand was completed, the minister's daughter waited until her father had left the house. She then went and put on one of his suits, wrapped a scarf around the lower part of her face, and, taking a whip with her, headed for the carpenter's workshop.

"Carpenter!"

"Yes, Your Excellency!"

"In a while I'll be sending you a concubine. You will observe her height and make a box to fit her. I want it ready by tomorrow. Otherwise, I'll have your head cut off. And don't hold her here for two hours!"

"No, sir. I won't."

She lashed him twice and left, going directly where? To the halvah maker's shop.

"Halvah maker!"

"Yes."

"I'm going to be sending you a concubine momentarily. You will observe her. See her shape and her height. You must make me a halvah doll that looks exactly like her. And don't you keep her here for a couple of hours or I'll shorten your life!"

"Your order, O minister," said the man, "will be obeyed."

---

make the formal request for his bride's hand, as in this tale; rather, this task is generally performed by the male elders of his extended family. Girls are given away in marriage by their fathers or grandfathers, in council with male elders of their families. Cf. Tale 20, n. 8; Tale 21, n. 13; and see Granqvist, *Marriage* II:9–11.

15. On the phrase "something of a devil" (*malʿūne*), see n. 12, above.

16. The buying of the wedding clothes (*kiswe*) for the bride (and frequently for some of her immediate relatives) is the responsibility of the bridegroom's family. See Granqvist, *Marriage* II:40–46; Grant, *People:* 55–56.

She lashed him twice with the whip and left. She went and changed, putting on her ordinary clothes, then went by the carpenter's shop and stayed awhile. After that she went and stood by the halvah maker's shop for a while. Then she went straight home. Changing back into her father's suit, she took the whip with her and went to the carpenter.

"Carpenter!"

"Yes, my lord minister!"

"An ostrich shorten your life!" responded the girl.[17] "I send you the concubine, and you hold her here for two hours!"

She descended on him with the whip, beating him all over.

"Please, sir!" he pleaded, "it was only because I wanted to make sure the box was an exact fit."

Leaving him alone, she headed for the halvah maker's. Him too, she whipped several times, and then she returned home.

The next day she sent for her slave and said to him, "Go bring the wooden box from the carpenter's shop to the halvah maker's. Put the halvah doll in it, lock it, and bring it to me here."

"Yes, I'll do it," he answered.

When the box was brought, she took it in and said to her mother, "Listen, mother! I'm going to leave this box with you in trust.[18] When the time comes to take me out of the house and to load up and bring along my trousseau, you must have this box brought with the trousseau and placed in the same room where I will be."

"But, dear daughter!" protested the mother, "What will people say? The minister's daughter is bringing a wooden box with her trousseau! You will become a laughingstock." I don't know what else she said [but it was no use].

"This is not your concern," insisted the daughter. "That's how I want it."

When the [bridegroom's family] came to take the bride [out of her father's house], she was made ready, and the wooden box was brought along with her trousseau.[19] They took the wooden box and, as she had

17. "An ostrich shorten your life!" This expression is particularly appropriate for the occasion because of the phonetic resemblance between the Arabic words for "ostrich" (*naʿʿ-āme*) and "yes" (*naʿam*).

18. In cultural practice, the trust (*ʾamāne*) is sacred. It is said, "He who has trusted you, don't betray him, even if you are a betrayer" (*mīn ʾammanak lā txūno, law kunt xāyin*).

19. The fetching of the bride (*ṭalʿit il-ʿarūs*) by the groom's family is a formal part of the Palestinian wedding. For details on how the bride is made ready, see Granqvist, *Marriage*

told them, placed it in the same room where she was to be. As soon as she came into the room and the box was brought in, she threw out all the women. "Go away!" she said.[20] "Each of you must go home now."

After she had made everyone leave, she locked the door. Then, dear ones, she took the doll out of the box. Taking off her clothes, she put them on the doll, and she placed her gold around its neck. She then set the doll in her own place on the bridal seat,[21] tied a string around its neck, and went and hid under the bed, having first unlocked the door.

Her husband, meanwhile, was taking his time. He stayed away an hour or two before he came in. What kind of mood do you think he was in when he arrived? He was in a foul humor, his sword in hand, ready to kill her, as if he did not want to marry her in the first place. As soon as he passed over the doorstep, he looked in and saw her on the bridal seat.

"Yes, yes!" he reproached her. "The first time you abandoned me on the shelf and took the food, I said to myself it was all right. The second time you threw me into the toilet and took the food, and I said all right. The third time you removed my body hair and made me look like a bride, taking the food with you, and even then I said to myself it was all right. After all that, you still weren't satisfied. You tricked us all and took the bridewealth for the forty girls, leaving each of us a turd in the washtub."

Meanwhile, as he finished each accusation, she would pull the string and nod the doll's head.

"As if all that weren't enough for you," he went on, "you had to top it all with your aunty act. 'Welcome, welcome, aunty! It's been a long time since we've seen our aunty. It's been such a long time since aunty has washed our clothes!' And you kept me washing clothes all day. And after all that, you insisted, 'We must bathe aunty.' By Allah, I'm going to burn the hearts of all your paternal and maternal aunties!"

Seeing her nod her head in agreement, he yelled, "You mean you're not afraid? And you're not going to apologize?" Taking hold of his sword,

---

II:51–55; cf. also Tale 11. For a discussion of the parting songs sung to the bride upon her leaving her father's house, see afterword to Group I, "Siblings"; and for examples, see Sirḥān, *Mawsūʿat* V:85.

20. For the bride to throw the women out of her bridal chamber would be considered immodest behavior and is therefore unacceptable. For the bridegroom to do so, however, would not be considered bad behavior, because people understand that he has a duty to fulfill.

21. For the bridal seat (*maṣmade*), see Tale 11, n. 4.

he struck her a blow that made her head roll.[22] A piece of halvah (If the teller is not lying!) flew into his mouth. Turning it around in his mouth, he found it sweet.

"Alas, cousin!" he cried out. "If in death you're so sweet, what would it have been like if you were still alive?"

As soon as she heard this, she jumped up from under the bed and rushed over to him, hugging him from behind.

"O cousin! Here I am!" she exclaimed. "I'm alive!"

They consummated their marriage, and lived together happily.

This is my tale, I've told it; and in your hands I leave it.

Afterword

In general, the five tales in this group portray the early stirrings of sexuality, when they are still subjective feelings and before formal arrangements for marriage have been made. Except for "Jbēne," the individuals in the tales, whether male or female, handle these feelings in a way that communicates them to those for whom they are intended. In "The Little Bird," the theme of sexual awakening is manifested in the bird's preparation for marriage. By collecting her trousseau, and by beautifying and putting herself on display, she arouses the interest of the sultan's son. In "Jummēz Bin Yāzūr, Chief of the Birds," the youngest daughter's request is ambiguous enough that the father can acquiesce without feelings

22. The bridegroom's anger here and his desire to strike his wife represent an exaggeration of a custom that prevailed in some parts of the country, particularly the north, where this tale was collected. Just before the consummation of the marriage (*daxle*—literally, "entry") the male relatives of the bridegroom slap him a few times. The purpose of this beating is to arouse his anger so that he can assert his manhood, in case he has been too preoccupied to be any good for the bride (*min xōf mā yinfaᶜš il-ᶜarūs*). His anger is further aroused by the women's singing and dancing around the bride at the *jalwe,* or "unveiling" (see Tale 35, n. 17). Before he arrives to unveil the bride, the women spread millet on the floor; he slips, and they have a good laugh at his expense. His anger thus thoroughly aroused, the groom gets up and beats his wife with a stick, after which she is expected to rise and kiss his hand. In other parts of the country (such as Arṭās in the south), however, the groom asserts his authority symbolically by touching the point of his sword to his bride's nose and forehead and then to each cheek; he then removes the veil with the tip of his sword. See Granqvist, *Marriage* II: 115; Sirḥān, *Mawsūᶜat* V: 87. As Granqvist notes (*Marriage* I: 10), however, customs vary from village to village, and it would be dangerous to generalize.

of shame. The girl is sending the message of her readiness, which Jummēz is able to decipher. In "Sackcloth," the sexual awareness begins even before the girl leaves home, producing feelings of confusion, shame, and guilt, especially since she seems to arouse a most unnatural passion in her father. Hence her desire to cover her body completely, so as to appear to be not only of the opposite sex but also a horrible freak whom no one would want to touch. Only later, when she has had more experience and feels secure at the palace of the king's son, is she able to accept her sexuality. Her dancing in public in the wedding dress her father had brought her is a declaration of her new awareness, her readiness to accept a mate. In "Šāhīn," the girl is the more mature of the two protagonists, and she awakens Šāhīn to his manhood. The emotional upheavals arising out of the first stirrings of sexuality are here shown not to be limited to young women: young men feel them also. Šāhīn must work through his frustrations and his confusion to assume the responsibility of his manhood.

In "Jbēne," in contrast, the girl attempts to hide or deny her sexuality. Her behavior differs from the straightforward courtship behavior shown in the other tales in this group. She is more concerned with the welfare of her family than with her own; thus, her feminine, "nurturing," character emerges in relation to them, not to the husband-to-be, even though they were not willing to accept the responsibility that might have prevented her abduction. The tale shows the poignancy of separation, the isolation of the new bride. Jbēne overcomes this isolation through acceptance of her mate, which in turn leads to reunion with her family. In "Jbēne," sexual identity must be drawn forth from a reluctant woman, and her sorrow over the loss of her home security overcome.

The narrative devices used in these tales reinforce the theme of sexual awakening and the attendant personality changes. While the use of disguise is common in folktales, it seems to be particularly appropriate here. In the last three tales in the group, the heroines or heroes put on some form of disguise in an effort to mask their confusion while in transition to the new identity. The first two tales share the metaphorical disguise of the bird symbol, thus conveying a culturally complex meaning that would be impossible to communicate directly. Jbēne's disguise of staining her body black literalizes the metaphor of ruining one's reputation; it serves as an appropriate symbol of her ambivalence and confusion, and of the shame or dishonor she might feel concerning her sexuality. She stains her body black not only to remain anonymous but also to protect her reputation and ward off possible advances from the son of the emir. Her longing for her parents is expressed in her ditty, which at the same time is instrumental in attracting the attention she is trying to avoid. Similarly with Sackcloth, if merely being a woman is sufficient to arouse unnatural passions, then her disguise transforms her into a monster of the opposite sex. The son of the king signals his readiness for marriage by his willingness to disguise himself as a woman, which, as can be seen from "Šāhīn," is a humiliating thing to do, especially if the disguise were to be discovered. Whereas in "Šāhīn" the feminine disguise is at first thrust on the hero against his will, he later assumes it voluntarily; here, then, the use of disguise helps to convey the role reversal on which the tale is based.

As a group, these tales also convey something of the power that women possess through their sexuality. The first half of "The Little Bird" presents us with the archetypal image of a girl ready for marriage who, having made all the preparations, sends out her signals to attract the male. She appears to be passive and receptive, prey to be hunted. On the other side we have the archetypal male, an authority figure with symbolic gun in hand, ready to assert his will. Yet he could not be more wrong than to assume that he can have the upper hand, either because he is a male or because of his social position, or both. In "Jummēz Bin Yāzūr," the lover risks his life by admitting his secret to his sweetheart. And in "Sackcloth," as we have noted, the king's son risks his masculinity by wearing women's clothes. Finally, in "Šāhīn," it seems that no matter what the vizier's daughter does to the hero, his attraction to her only increases. The images here are reversed: she is the hunter and he the hunted.

In the Introduction we discussed the potential for conflict between husband and wife, especially when they are not first cousins. In this group of tales we can glimpse the source of this conflict: the power residing in women's sexuality on the one hand and the superior social position accorded males on the other. In this respect the first and last tales in the group ("The Little Bird" and "Šāhīn") differ markedly from the others ("Jummēz Bin Yāzūr," "Jbēne," and "Sackcloth"), where the female is presented as having no concern but to be taken for a mate by the male. In "Šāhīn" and "The Little Bird," however, the roles themselves are put to the test. Whereas the male, as represented by the son of the sultan, with his hunting tools and pretensions, receives his power from the role endowed on him by society, the power of the female is from within, from her own being. It is the source not only of her procreative power, but also of her creativity, her playfulness. For only the female is presented as playful, her playfulness in the courtship ritual being an outward expression of the power of her sexuality.

Yet this playfulness has serious overtones, because in the end the private passion must be channeled into public behavior that is in harmony with the norms of society. As Šāhīn says, "We have no recourse but for each of us to ask for the hand of his bride from her father." In other words, legal and public sanction must be sought to validate private desire; otherwise, the whole process of courtship will remain at the level of a game. "The Little Bird" teaches us that underneath the charming acquiescence of Jbēne and Sackcloth lies a power that no man can master. And "Šāhīn" teaches us that behind the apparent role of male domination sanctioned by society there may lie another reality altogether.

The Quest for the Spouse

16. *The Brave Lad*

TELLER: Allah has spoken, and His word is a blessing!
AUDIENCE: Blessings abound, Allah willing![1]

There was once the king of a city who had a very beautiful daughter. He announced that he would give her hand to anyone who could kill the ghoul. He also let it be known that the ghoul would be easy to kill: all one had to do was remove three hairs from his head. If they were removed, the ghoul would die. The ghoul had been giving the people a hard time, eating them and their animals, and they wanted to be rid of him. He lived in a cave in the forest, not far from the city.

A lad in love with the girl but too poor to become the king's son-in-law[2] one day decided to try his fortune against the ghoul, even though he could not be sure if he would come back alive or not. No one except him dared agree to the king's condition.

The lad went to the ghoul's cave while it was still daylight, but did not find him at home. He was roaming about, looking for someone to eat. In the cave the youth found the ghoul's wife, who was a girl from their city. The ghoul had fallen in love with her and had abducted her. The moment she saw the young man, the girl gave him some advice. "You'd better go back where you came from," she said. "When the ghoul comes home in the evening, he'll make a feast of you."

1. The unusual opening formula, —*qāl alla w-qāl xēr* —*xēr inšālla* (literally, "Allah has spoken, and He spoke blessings"; "Blessings, God willing!"), carries profound significance: first, it glorifies the power of speech by attributing it to a divine source; second, it equates material blessings (*xēr*) with the Logos, the divine word; and third, it demonstrates the importance of folktales to the community, since the formula implies that telling them is a blessing. See also Tale 6, n. 1.

2. Perhaps he could not afford the girl's *fēd* (bridewealth, for which see Tale 15, n. 10). Furthermore, he could not possibly have been able to afford the costs of the wedding, which are borne entirely by the bridegroom's family, since for a king's daughter the festivities would have to be lavish. A Palestinian proverb says, "He who has money can have the king's daughter for his bride" (*illī ʿindo flūso, bint is-sulṭān ʿarūso*). See also Tale 15, n. 16.

But he refused to listen and stayed with her, telling her his story. The girl agreed to help him because she hated the ghoul, who had abducted her when she was engaged to her first cousin, whom she loved and who loved her. By helping the lad, perhaps she could get rid of the ghoul and go back to her cousin.

When the ghoul came home, he was growling from hunger. He had not been able to find anyone to eat. The girl hid the young man in the wardrobe.[3]

"I smell a human being," roared the ghoul as he came in.

"Nonsense!" replied the girl. "You brought that smell with you."[4]

The ghoul then ate whatever he could find and went to sleep. She lay down to sleep next to him. As soon as he was fast asleep, she plucked one of the hairs from his head.

"What's going on?" the ghoul grumbled, waking up.

"I dreamt you were drowning in the sea," she answered. "And by the time I got to you, your whole body was under water. Nothing was above except your head. So I pulled you by your hair to save you from drowning, but you woke up and woke me up, and it turns out I really was pulling your hair."

Believing her, the ghoul closed his eyes again, and no sooner was he fast asleep than she plucked another hair from his head. He woke, jumping up like a madman. "What's the matter with you?" he asked.

"I was dreaming," she lied, "that you and I were traveling together on a boat and I fell overboard. If I hadn't taken hold of your hair, I would certainly have drowned. And when you shouted at me, I woke up. It turns out I really was taking hold of your hair."

The ghoul, out of his stupidity, believed her again.[5] When he was

3. Older Palestinian houses, whose walls could be over one meter thick, had recesses in the walls for storing various things (see Tale 3, n. 6). With the introduction of cement, however, the walls were considerably reduced in thickness, and, because houses are constructed without closets, wooden wardrobes were introduced for storing clothing and household materials such as linens and towels.

4. *Il-ʾins fīk u-fī ḍyālak* is a formulaic expression meaning literally, "The human [smell] is in you and in your trail."

5. This is the only explicit reference to ghoulish stupidity in the tales. Ghouls can also be clever, as we shall see in Tales 19 (see n. 5), 29, and 33, though their proverbial cunning is not equal to that of women, as is evident here. A popular proverb says, "Women's tricks have defeated the tricks of the ghouls" (*ḥiyal in-niswān ġalabū ḥiyal il-ġīlān*).

Ghouls are said to be fond of eating human flesh, especially that of children (cf. Tale 6, again sound asleep, she plucked the third hair from his head, and he died, thus sparing her and the people of the city his evil.

In the morning the girl and the lad headed back to the city, taking with them whatever they could carry from the cave, and not forgetting the three hairs. The king, the princess, and the people of the city received them joyfully when they heard about what had happened. As for the girl, they celebrated her wedding to her cousin. And as for the princess, they celebrated her marriage to the lad, arranging festivities and beautiful nights.

We ate from their feast, left them, and came home.

17. *Gazelle*[1]

TELLER: [Not] until you testify that God is One!
AUDIENCE: There is no god but God.

Once upon a time there were three brothers.[2] Their father happened to be a king, and he said to them, "Listen! I'm about to die, and you have three sisters. He who comes to ask for the hand of any of them—don't even ask where he's from. Just give her to him in marriage."[3]

After the king died, the first suitor came to ask for the hand of one of the sisters, and he gave her to him.[4] The second also he married off, and

---

n. 12), and of having humans for mates. A proverb says, "The ghoul has devoured the whole world, except his wife" (*il-ġūl ʾakal kull id-dinyā ʾillā marato*). See afterword to Group I, "The Quest for the Spouse." For further reference to the ghoul figure, see Footnote Index, s.v. "Ghouls and Jinn."

For hair as a source of strength, cf. Tale 22. On the magical power of hair, see Leach, "Magical Hair"; on hair in relation to summoning the jinn, see Westermarck, *Ritual* I:353.

1. The gazelle (*ġazāle*) is frequently used as a metaphor for beauty in folk speech and popular culture, especially in songs. *Ġazāle* is not used as a girl's name. Cf. Tale 2, n. 1.

2. *Min hān la-hān illā ha-ṯ-ṯaliṯ ixwe*—literally, "From here to here, lo! these three brothers"; an unusual opening sentence that effectively makes the brothers appear suddenly out of nowhere.

3. The daughters' marriage here is especially urgent because the father is dying. If the brothers were to marry and become preoccupied with their own families, their sisters would be left in a vulnerable situation vis-à-vis the brothers' wives, who might not tolerate the sisters' presence. Under these circumstances, marriage to any husband is preferable to staying at home under the yoke of gratitude to the daughters of strangers (*tiḥt ijmīlit banāt in-nās*)—that is, their brothers' wives.

4. "He" here refers to the eldest brother, as the text makes clear two sentences on. See next note.

the third. Now the eldest brother, whose name was Ḥasan,[5] thought to himself, "Here I've married off the girls, and I have no idea where they ended up."

"Let's go," he said to his brothers. "We want to go hunting."

They went hunting, you might say, to the outskirts of our town here. And lo! a gazelle sprang among them. This one said, "She's my prey!" and that one said, "She's mine!" [Finally] they said, "Not for me, or for you. Let's make a ring around her, and he whose horse she passes near—she's his, and he becomes her hunter."

Now she was not really a gazelle. She was from the jinn (In the name of Allah, the Merciful, the Compassionate!).[6] She gazed at them, and, since a good person always stands out among his folk, she picked one of the brothers and passed right under his horse.

"All right, brothers," Ḥasan announced. "You must go back now. She's my quarry, and I'm going to chase her."

He gave chase, and as he approached her, the gazelle would run away from him. She kept this up [until they stood] below his oldest sister's town.[7] Once he arrived in the town, he had no idea which way the gazelle had turned. Where was he to go? After tying his horse, he looked around, and behold! there was the servantgirl of his oldest sister. "Mistress, mistress!" she called out to his sister. "That man tying his horse could almost be you. Perhaps you come from the same blood."

"Where is anybody going to come from to see me?" asked the mistress. "In any case, tell him to please come in!"[8]

When she asked him to come in, the brother could not believe his ears. He had not known where to find lodging. On entering, he discovered his

5. For "Ḥasan," see Tale 5, n. 4. The fact that Ḥasan is the eldest brother is unusual; see afterword to Group I, "Siblings."

6. This formula is pronounced to counteract the evil influence of the jinn, who are spirits and may be found anywhere. Because jinn are fond of possessing human beings, it is best to pronounce this formula frequently. See Tale 22, n. 8; cf. Tale 29, n. 6. On the use of distancing devices in the tales, see Introduction, "The Tales"; cf. Tale 5, n. 8.

7. In the hilly regions of Palestine, such as the area where this tale was collected (in Turmusᶜayya, district of Ramallah), villages are always built on hilltops, thereby commanding an unobstructed view in all directions. See Tale 5, n. 14.

8. *Qulīlo yitfaḍḍal*—literally, "Tell him to honor us with his presence." The verb *tfaḍḍal* is used throughout Palestine and other parts of the Arab world when inviting a guest into one's house. Its root, *faḍula,* carries a whole complex of meanings, including "to have the kindness to do something," "to deign," "to condescend," and "to be graciously disposed." Cf. Tale 42, n. 15; Tale 44, n. 12.

own sister. How happy they were! They celebrated with singing and dancing.[9]

"And what brought you this way, brother?" she asked.

"Gazelle brought me," he answered.

"Good," she said. "Now relax."

By Allah, in a little while her husband showed up.

"Welcome, welcome to our brother-in-law!"[10] he saluted him. "And what brings you to this part of the world?"

They held each other in friendly embrace, kissing each other on the cheeks. The host ordered dinner for his guest.

"By Allah," replied the brother. "Gazelle brought me."

"By Allah, I'm more than a match for a hundred hosts," returned the brother-in-law. "But I haven't been able to overcome Gazelle." (He meant hosts of jinn—In the name of Allah, the Merciful, the Compassionate!)

"By Allah, this is my lot," the brother replied.

In the morning he mounted his horse and moved on. Gazelle appeared and did as she had done before, slowing down, then running away as soon as he came near, until she came below the palace of the second sister. As the other sister had asked, so did this one: "Brother, what has brought you here?"

"Gazelle brought me, sister," he answered.

"Welcome, welcome!"

They had dinner and amused themselves, enjoying each other's company.

"I can overcome two hundred hosts," announced the brother-in-law, "but I'm no match for Gazelle."

The next day he again mounted his horse and moved on, with Gazelle jumping here and there, until she reached the town where his youngest sister lived and his third brother-in-law was. He said, "I have more power than three hundred hosts, but I can't overcome Gazelle."

That's right. Now, each of his brothers-in-law had given him a hair, saying, "If you're ever in a tight spot, just rub this hair, and before you know it we'll be there."

On the fourth day she again jumped here and there until she reached her own city. When they arrived there, he did not know which way she

9. *Qāmu ha-l-ifrāḥ*—literally, "They arranged festivities." See Tale 13, n. 10.

10. "Welcome, welcome!" (*ahlan wa-sahlan*) is an extremely common expression in the Arab world.

had turned. Stopping to visit an old woman in a hut, he said, "Here's the price of my dinner! Take it and go bring me dinner and some feed for my horse. And tonight, mother, I'd like to stay here with you."[11]

"One hundred welcomes!" replied the old woman.

They sat around chatting, and she asked him, "What brought you here, son?"

"Gazelle brought me," he answered.

"This Gazelle," she advised, "has suitors all over the world. See her castle? It's that one over there. And every time one of them comes asking for her hand, her father says, 'He who can move this mountain away from the front of my house can have her hand. And he who can't move it—I'll have his head.' And every morning you find him cutting off their heads."

"By Allah," he said, "it's all destiny and fate. I'm going to ask for her hand."

He came and asked this person and that, and they all said, "Don't go! You're a nice young man, and it would be such a loss if he were to cut off your head."

"It's no use," he replied.

Remembering the hairs his brothers-in-law had given him, he rubbed all three of them, and behold! six hundred hosts of jinn appeared. Gazelle, too, she loved him and came to his aid. He started on the mountain, and before day had risen, look! it was (In the name of Allah, the Merciful, the Compassionate!) as if there was no mountain there at all.

When the sun rose, it shone on her father's bed. "Alas!" he cried out. "He's going to take her, damn his parents!"

Now, there was one among the jinn who wanted Gazelle, but she did not want him because she preferred Clever Ḥasan. He and Gazelle always fought, but now that the mountain was gone, she overcame him. Taking hold of him, she hung him up by his hair.

She lived a month or two with Clever Ḥasan in the palace. And what a palace it was! Fit for a king! As she was used to roving, she said to him, "I'm going to roam for a while, and you look after yourself. This room you can open, and that room also. I'm going to take the air for a couple of weeks, and will be back."

11. The hero here assumes enough familiarity with the old woman to ask her to bring his dinner without a show of politeness, but when he suggests staying the night, he quickly interjects the word *mother,* thereby eliminating all untoward inferences. See Tale 8, n. 5.

Opening one room, he found treasure. And here were weapons. And here . . . [He opened them all] except a certain room. "This room," he thought to himself, "why did she give me its key and say, 'Don't open it!'? What's she hiding from me? By Allah, I've got to open it."

He opened it and found a young man hanging by his hair.

"Please!" he called out. "I beg you! Release me! I put myself at your mercy!"[12]

The young man begged so much that Ḥasan took pity on him and released him, and no sooner had he done so than the mountain returned as it had been. He looked around, and there was Gazelle! Realizing what had happened, she came running.

"Why do you give me so much trouble?" she scolded him. "May Allah give you as much trouble in return! Just like that, you released him! If I hadn't defeated him, do you think the mountain could've been moved, or anything else have happened for that matter?"[13]

Ashamed, he dragged himself below, while she went back up to deal with the man who had been bickering with her for so long.

"Who knows," he bragged, "but that this time I'll defeat you and take away your soul."

"And this time," she snapped back, "who knows but that I'll overpower you and finish you off. This time, I won't be satisfied just to let you dangle."

"What!" he mocked. "Go away! My soul is lodged in the kneebone of a certain tiger who lives in such and such a country. So, how are you to get hold of it?"

Now, her husband heard this, and he immediately set out for the country where that tiger was to be found. On his way he came upon three men arguing over their inheritance from their father. They were fighting over three things: a club giving anyone able to lift it power over

12. The expression *daxīlak* (I beg you) is generally heard in the cities and villages and is a less urgent request than *ṭanīb ʿalēk* (I put myself at your mercy), which is more common among the Bedouins. *Daxīlak,* from the root *daxala,* "to enter," means literally, "I have come unto you" or "I have entered your house [as a supplicant]." *Ṭanīb* comes from *ṭunub* (tent rope) and refers to the custom of touching the tent ropes, especially of a chieftain, when seeking another's help. The laws of hospitality and honor among the Arabs are such that the person whose help is being sought is duty bound to honor the request if it is within his power. See Granqvist, *Marriage* II:322n.1.

13. There is an unresolved contradiction in the narrative, because earlier the teller said Gazelle had defeated her enemy *after* the mountain was moved.

forty men, a magic carpet, and a cap of invisibility. Haggling over these things, one of them said, "No! I won't take this. It won't be fair." And another said, "No! I won't take that. I'll be the loser."

"What are you arguing about?" he asked.

"We're arguing about which of these three things was intended for whom. You judge for us."

"Gladly," he answered. "I'll help you decide."

Taking a stick, he stood at the top of a hill and said, "I'm going to throw this stick down into the wadi. He who can bring it back gets all three things."

"By Allah," they agreed, "this is fine."

Lifting up the stick, he hurled it away right to the bottom of the wadi. The three brothers went running after it. Putting on the cap of invisibility, he took hold of the club, mounted the magic carpet, and said, "Don't land except in the country where the tiger is to be found."

When he landed in that town, he came upon an old woman and her daughter. Introducing himself, he said, "Old lady, I'd like to stay with you."

"Welcome, welcome!" she responded.

She offered him some yogurt, and, to his surprise, it was reddish in color.

"Old lady," he asked, "why is this yogurt red like that?"

"Look here, son!" she answered. "Our town is surrounded. In this direction there's a giant scorpion, in that one a snake, in the other one a viper, and over there is a tiger. The sheep can't roam freely in any direction, and so they eat the dirt between the houses."[14]

"All right," he announced, "tomorrow morning I'm going to take your sheep grazing in the direction of the viper."

"But, dear son!" she protested. "The viper will bite you."

"No," he insisted. "I'm going to graze them."

Leading the sheep in the morning, he went roaming with them, and what did he find but that the grass was this high. The sheep fed on the tender tips of the grass. The viper came out, and lo! she had seven heads.

"Who's been grazing in my pasture?" she asked.

"A stranger who doesn't know any better," he answered.

14. In the region where the tale was collected (see n. 7, above), the soil is reddish in color.

"All right," she said. "You're a stranger who doesn't know better. Today, you came. Tomorrow, you'd better stay away."

He let the sheep graze till evening, then went home and stayed with the old woman. In the morning he went back.

"Who's been grazing in my pasture?"

"A stranger who doesn't know any better."

"All right. Today, you came; another day, stay away."

"Every day you claim you're a stranger who doesn't know better," she said to him on the third day. "I don't know [what you're up to]. Come down to the battlefield!"

He came down and cut off all her heads. People said, "The son of the old woman has killed the viper. He has opened such and such a direction!" In our town you might say he opened up Wadī l-ʿĒn. The whole town took their sheep grazing there.

The next day he said, "I want to go in the direction of the snake."

"You won't be able to kill this one, dear son," she protested.

"No," he answered, "I want to go."

As he had done to the viper, he did to the snake. The townspeople proclaimed, "The son of the old lady has opened up the second direction." [In our town] you might say it was the direction of Ez-Zāwye. The same thing he did with the scorpion and opened up that direction.

"I want to go in the direction of the tiger," announced Ḥasan the next day.

"No, son," said the old woman. "You opened up three directions, that's enough."

"No," he answered, "I want to go."

He pulled himself together and went. The tiger showed up and asked, "Who's grazing in my pasture?"

"A stranger who doesn't know any better."

"With me, there's no such thing as a stranger," responded the tiger. "Here, you must come down to the battlefield."

"You come down," Ḥasan challenged him.

A blow from this one and a blow from that one, and from here a blow and from there a blow. They kept it up till evening, and neither of them was able to win. The first day, the second, and the third, neither of them could win. The boy could not defeat the tiger, nor the tiger the boy.

On the fourth day, the tiger boasted, "Who knows but that I'll get the better of you and eat carrion over your belly."

"And who knows but that I will get the better of you," replied the other. "I'll eat a meal of flat bread rubbed with ghee and sugar,[15] drink a flask of wine, and kiss my delicate young lady—all on a mat spread on your belly."

Now, the old woman was eating her heart out over him. She said to her daughter, "Daughter, stick your head over the wall and see if your brother's getting the better of the tiger, or if the tiger's got your brother down."

Allah was on his side.[16] The girl peeked out, and listen! he was mouthing his boast. She rushed back in and said to her mother, "Yee! My brother is saying such and such and such."

"Yee, daughter!" said the mother. "Let's set to it."

So they quickly baked some flat bread and rubbed it with ghee and sugar, and the girl bundled it up and brought it to her brother, along with a flask of water and a straw mat. And by Allah, the moment the girl showed up, the lad (with Allah's help) threw the tiger to the ground. Taking the mat, he spread it on the tiger's belly, ate the sugared bread, drank the flask of water, and kissed the young lady. He cracked the tiger's knee open, and behold! there was the other man's soul in a snuff box this small. Reaching for it, he took and put it in his pocket and then came back—only to find the neighbors (Far be it from you!) wailing and lamenting.

"Well, mother," he asked, "I've opened four directions. So why are the neighbors wailing?"

"You should know, son," she answered. "There's a demon guarding the spring, and every year around this time he must have a bride. This year it's our neighbors' turn. They will dress her up and leave her in a room, and they don't know where the demon of the spring will take her."

"I was ready to leave for home," he said, "but now I've changed my mind."

In the morning they clothed the girl in a bridal dress and put her in the room so that the guardian of the spring could come take her and release the water for them and their animals to drink. By Allah, he did not take long to show up.

"Who's this sitting with my bride?" he roared.

15. "Flat bread rubbed with ghee and sugar"—*mafrūkiyye*.

16. *ʾAlla biddo y-jībhā*—literally, "Allah wanted to bring it [i.e., his luck]."

"By Allah, it's only me," answered the youth. "Stretch out your neck and take her!"

When the demon stretched out his neck, the lad cut off his head, and water gushed from the spring. And how pleased were the townspeople! They were overjoyed. Some of them said, "My sister's yours [for a bride]!" Others said, "My daughter's yours!"[17] While others were saying, "You have so much and so much money coming!"

"No! No!" he announced. "I'm not staying. Not for an inheritance, or for money!"

By Allah, he said, "Magic carpet, don't bring me down except [at the house] of such and such a family!" And when the carpet landed, he thought to himself, "By Allah, I'm going to see what's in this snuff box."[18] (You know that an unfortunate one remains so always.)[19] Taking hold of the snuff box, he struck it to open it, but it flew down into a well. "And what in the world's going to bring it back?" he thought. Then, remembering the hairs his brothers-in-law had given him, he rubbed them, and lo! some rams appeared. They threw themselves down into the water and kept stirring it until they recovered the box. After they recovered it, they fought [over it]. It came open, and lo! a bird flew up into the sky.

Again he rubbed his brother-in-laws' hairs, and a whole flock of birds, so thick they blocked the sun, appeared. They chased and chased the bird until they brought it to him. Holding on to it tightly, he said [to his carpet], "This time don't land except in Gazelle's town!"

He found Gazelle and her foe still sparring. "Who knows," he was saying, "but that I'll kill you and take away your soul?" And she was answering, "Not at all! Who knows but that I'll be getting the better of you and taking your soul away?"

"I told you where my soul was," mocked the other. "How are you going to get to it?"

17. In actual practice, a father or brother may sometimes offer his daughter or his sister for a wife under special circumstances, as for example when another man loses his wife or as a reward for great achievement.

18. "By Allah"—*wallah* or *wallāhi*—is not really an oath but is used more as an affirmative in discourse. Although many tellers use it to punctuate their narrative, the teller of this tale seems more fond of it than most.

19. This phrase is part of a proverb that is applied to someone who constantly gets into trouble: "A miserable [or unfortunate] one will remain miserable always, even if they hang twenty lanterns from his backside" (*il-matʿūs biẓal matʿūs, law ʿallaqū ʿa-ẓahro ʿišrīn fānūs*).

Ḥasan immediately squeezed the bird, showing no mercy.

"Ouch!" the jinni cried out. "By Allah, I'm in a tight spot."

"What!" she yelled back. "Are you mocking me?"

"No, by Allah," he confessed. "This time, I really am pressed."

Meanwhile, her husband kept tearing the bird's limbs. When he tore the bird's foot apart, the man's foot would fall, a wing from the bird, and a hand from the man—until there was nothing of him left at all.

The bird of this tale has flown, and now it's someone else's turn.

18. *Lōlabe*[1]

TELLER: Testify that God is One!
AUDIENCE: There is no god but God.

Once there was a king who had a son—an only son and no other. He made a vow.[2] If his son survived and grew up, he would run two channels

1. The name "Lōlabe" is not ordinarily used for girls; it means "spiral," and its applicability to the tale is obscure.

2. The making of a vow (*nid̲ir*), usually in connection with something or someone precious and in danger of being lost or harmed, such as a stray animal or a sick child, is a popular practice in the Arab world. The individual making the vow states it as a condition: if *A*, then *B*. *B* is supposed to be an act favored by the Deity and may include any of the following propitiatory acts: animal sacrifice for the sake of Allah or for the poor (*d̲bīḥa la-wajh il-lāh, la-l-fuqarā*); fasting (*ṣyām*) for a certain number of days; going on the hajj; performing a certain number of prostrations (*rakᶜāt*) in prayer; lighting candles in a saint's shrine (*maqām*) or a church (*knīse*), or buying articles that may be useful in these holy places; giving alms to the poor (*ṣadaqa*); and so forth. One or more of these acts are performed after the desired result has occurred, among which may be: the return of an absent one (*yrawwiḥ il-ġāyib*); the healing of a sick person (*yṭīb il-imrīẓ*); a woman's pregnancy (*tiḥbal il-mara*); the birth of a boy (*tjīb ṣabī*); or the release of someone from prison (*yiṭlaᶜ flān min is-sijin*).

The vow is believed to bring good results; the Deity seems to favor such "deals" and so fulfills His part of the agreement. Most Palestinian adults can recount tens, if not hundreds, of cases where the vow worked. Yet a vow is also a serious and dangerous affair, for it is always possible that the person making it may not be able to fulfill his side. Such nonfulfillment may anger the Deity, causing Him to inflict a revenge that may be worse than the original condition—in which case it would have been better not to have made the vow in the first place.

In the tale, the listener is made to appreciate the father's anxiety over the boy's life, and hence the need for the vow. We are told that the king "had a son—an only son and no other." The implication here is that other siblings had died young because the mother is unable to bear children who can survive (*biᶜišilhāš wlād*), and thus he is liable to die young too. A related concern of the father is not having an heir should his remaining child die.

into the city for the benefit of the poor and the destitute. One channel would be filled with honey, and the other with ghee.[3]

One day the boy grew up and started school, and an old crone began annoying him. Every day she would meet him and say, "Tell your mother to fulfill the vow, or I'll cut short your life!" But when he reached home, he forgot. The next day, she would wait for him on his way to school and say, "Tell your mother to fulfill the vow, or I'll cut short your life!" And he would answer, "But, grandmother, I keep forgetting."

"You forget," she said one day. Gathering some pebbles from the road, she put them in his pocket and said, "These stones are to remind you. The moment you put your hand in your pocket, you'll remember."[4]

"Very well," he said. But when he came home from school he changed clothes without putting his hand in his pocket. When they washed his clothes, his mother found the pebbles in his pocket. "Yee!" she thought to herself. "Allah forgive me! A king's son with a craving. O my little baby! It looks like he wanted to put candy in his pocket, but look, he put in pebbles." The moment he came home, she asked him, "Son, why did you put these pebbles in your pocket? My darling boy, if you've been craving something, tell me and I'll give you the money to buy it."[5]

"Ah yes, mother," he recalled. "No, I don't crave anything. Rather there's an old woman who meets me every day and says, 'Tell your mother to fulfill the vow, or I'll cut short your life.'"

"Yes, all right," she said.

The mother went up to see the king, and he gave orders, "Dig two channels, clean them well and paint them, and run honey in one and ghee in the other!" Now there was one who had news of the channels and who also knew the old woman. He was (Save your honors!) mean, a rascal.[6] He went to the old woman and called out, "Hey! Old lady! The sultan

3. Honey and ghee are worthy of a vow because both are highly desired and expensive. See Tale 1, n. 5.

4. The putting of stones or other heavy objects in one's pocket as a reminder of something is actually practiced.

5. The oversolicitous attitude of the mother, who invents a candy craving on the part of her son, is a realistic portrayal. The audience would appreciate this concern, however, because he is an only son.

6. The Arabic word for "rascal" here is *manjūs*, from the root *najusa*, "to be [ritually] impure or unclean." Hence, the narrator's interjection *ḥēša s-sāmᶜīn*, translated here as "Save your honors!"; but see Tale 15, n. 8.

has declared he will cut off the heads of all the old women." She locked herself in and hid.

Meanwhile, the king had the channels built, one for honey and the other for ghee. People scooped the honey and ghee up until there was no more. The old woman's neighbor came to her, saying, "Hey, neighbor! What's the matter? Why do you have yourself locked in?"

"O, dear neighbor," she answered, "so and so told me such and such."

"Yee! God help you!" exclaimed the other. "He's tricked you. Didn't you know the king was today fulfilling the vow he'd made for his son? He's had a channel dug for honey and another for ghee. You'd better hurry."

Taking with her a piece of cotton, two small pots, and a little glass, she set out. She sat under the king's palace by the channels and started soaking her piece of cotton and squeezing it into the glass. The few drops of honey she poured into one pot, and the few drops of ghee into the other. Now the son of the king looked over and found it was the old crone who used to pester him every day, and she was letting [whatever she could get] soak into the cotton. She was too late to get much. Waiting until she had filled her glass, he brought a pebble and threw it out the window right down at her glass, and lo! he spilled it. Looking up like so, she exclaimed, "Yee! So it's you, the son of the king! For over an hour I've been trying to fill this glass, and you've spilled it for me just like that! May Allah afflict you with Lōlabe, daughter of Lōlabe!"[7]

"Don't worry, old woman," said the boy. "Come around this way, and I'll replace it for you."

She brought the two pots with her, and he filled them up and said, "Go your way!"

Afterwards, he went to his mother and said, "Mother, prepare food and provisions for me. I want to go searching for Lōlabe."

"O my son, my darling! Son of worthy people! Where are you going to search?"

"No use," he insisted. "I'm going to search for her."

His horse having been prepared, he took the provisions and set out

7. *ʾAlla yiblīk ib-lōlabe.* Although falling in love is not considered to be bad or harmful for a boy, the old woman phrases her wish in the form of a curse (*daʿwe;* see Tale 24, n. 3), using the word *afflict*. We may thus conclude that the vow was not fulfilled properly or that it came too late, and that punishment for the boy had to follow.

with the crowing of the cock.[8] He traveled and traveled, moving from place to place, until he reached a castle on a hill in the wilderness. He must have been tired, for he lay down to rest by the wall of the castle. Looking out, Lōlabe saw him at the foot of the castle.

"Who are you?" she asked. "Are you Clever Ḥasan?" (I don't know his name.)[9]

"Yes," he answered.

"My mother's coming any moment, and she'll gobble you up. You'd better come up!"

And (if the story is to be trusted) she let down her hair, he hung on to it, and she pulled him up into the castle with her. Her mother arrived.

"Lōlabe! Lōlabe!" she called out. "Let your hair down for your mother! Your sad, miserable, and tired mother, who's eaten a hundred trees and a hundred cows and still hasn't had enough."

Lōlabe let down her hair and pulled her mother up. It is said, however, that as soon as she heard her mother's voice she blew on Ḥasan and changed him into a pin, which she stuck in her headband.

"You reek of human, human," said the mother when she came in. "Not for a little while, or since yesterday, but as of right now, even before sunrise!"[10]

"O mother!" replied Lōlabe. "It's you who goes running into all sorts of things! It's you who leaves early. As for me, I'm here in the castle. How could a human being possibly reach me?"

"I don't know," said the mother. "But you do smell of human."

"There is no human here," insisted Lōlabe.

Looking about, the mother noticed the pin in Lōlabe's headband.

"Lend me that pin so I can remove a thorn from my foot," she said.

"All day long you're wandering around running into things and knocking trees down under your feet," answered Lōlabe. "And if there were a thorn in your foot, it would've fallen out."

"No, daughter," groaned the mother. "This is a big thorn. Give me the pin so I can remove it."

8. Palestinian villagers used to—and some still do—depend on the cock's crow to signal morning and time to get up and go to work. Cocks are supposed to crow three times, punctuating the time from dawn to sunrise.

9. This curious interjection by the teller is as if to say that the hero should have his own name, not just the generic "Clever Ḥasan." See, however, n. 14, below; cf. Tale 5, n. 4.

10. *Rīḥtik ins, ins, lā min issa walā min ams; ʾillā ʾissa, qabl iṭlūʿ iš-šams* is an unusual varia-

Removing the pin, Lōlabe turned it into a watermelon, which she hid among their store of watermelons, and she gave her another pin to remove the thorn. Her mother passed it this way and that over her foot and gave it back. (Could it be true that a ghouleh would really want to remove a thorn?) She looked around again and said, "Give me that watermelon to eat."

"All day long you're running around in the wild to fill your belly," complained Lōlabe. "And now you've come to eat what I have in the house."

"By Allah," said the mother. "I'm really tired" (and I don't know what else), "go bring me a watermelon to eat."

Lōlabe went and rolled a watermelon over to her mother, who said, "Not this one! That one!" "Not this one! That one!" and so on, insisting so much that Lōlabe took hold of the watermelon and dashed it to the floor, spilling seeds all over. Now Lōlabe (if the teller is not lying) covered one of the seeds with her foot, while her mother set about licking up the watermelon—seeds, rind, and all—and started on her way out.

"Let me down," she said.

Lōlabe let her down, and the ghouleh went her way. She then took the watermelon seed and blew on it, bringing the boy back as he had been.

"Let's hurry out of here!" she urged. "If my mother came back now, she'd kill us both and devour you." She then brought henna and spread it over all the articles of everyday use in the house—the kneading bowl, the plate, the cooking pot. She did not forget anything, they say, except the mortar and pestle.

Taking the comb, the mirror, and the kohl jar with her, she came down with him. They gathered themselves together and traveled, traveled.

"O Lōlabe!" her mother called out when she came back. "Let your hair down for your sad and tired mother."

There was no answer. "She's kneading [the dough]," said the kneading bowl. "She's sifting [the flour]," said the sieve. "She's doing the laundry," said the washtub. The mortar and pestle was left, and it rang out, "Rinn! Rinn![11] The human took her and ran away!"

---

tion on the formula usually uttered by ghouls in this situation, which is simply "You smell of human" (*rīḥtik ins*). Note the three-part rhyming pattern: *ins, ams, šams*.

11. "Rinn! Rinn!" renders onomatopoeically the sound of a ringing bell. The behavior

She went running after them, following in their tracks. When Lōlabe looked back, she spied the ghouleh and her bitch behind them.

"My mother's following us," she said. "In a moment, she'll devour us."

Taking hold of her comb, she cast it behind her. It turned into a fence of thorns, and they moved on, running away from there.

"Chop, chop, my little bitch!" said the ghouleh, "and I'll chop with you till we open a path and follow him."

They chopped and chopped until they cleared a path and then followed in pursuit.

When she looked back, Lōlabe saw the ghouleh still behind them.

"She's catching up with us," said Lōlabe, and she threw the kohl jar behind her. It turned into a wall of fire.

"Pee, pee, my little bitch!" said the ghouleh, "and I'll pee too, till we clear a path and follow them."

They pissed and pissed till they made a path, then followed in pursuit.

When Lōlabe looked behind her, the ghouleh was still following.

"My mother's still on our heels," she said. "Now she'll devour us. We have only this mirror left."

Taking hold of the mirror, she tossed it behind her, and it turned into a pool that blocked the way for the ghouleh and her bitch.

"Lap it up, lap it up, my little bitch!" said the ghouleh to her helper, "and I'll lap it up too. If you burst, I'll sew you up; and if I burst, you'll sew me up again."

But how much water were they going to lap from this pool? They licked and licked until they both burst and died.

When Lōlabe looked back, she found them dead.

"It's all over," she said. "They're gone. Now we're free."

Pulling themselves together, they traveled and traveled. If their village was ʿArrābe, they came, you might say, to the famous oak tree by Maslaxīt.[12] Leaving her there (he didn't think it proper to bring her home like that), he said, "Wait for me here till I go tell my family and come back for you with a proper wedding procession and the sultan's royal band." After he had gone, Lōlabe climbed into the tree and sat down.

---

of the mortar and pestle is an apt metaphor for the spreading of rumor about a love relationship in a Palestinian village community.

12. This ancient tree in the plain of Battōv (upper Galilee) is used by the local people as a landmark. Cf. Tale 5, n. 5; Tale 30, n. 11.

Underneath the tree there was a well. The slavegirl of the king's household came to fill her jar from the well. Looking over into the water, she saw Lōlabe's reflection there.

"Alas!" she cried out. "Me with all this beauty in the well, and I'm a slave to a household of blacksmiths!"[13]

Smash! She hurled the water jug to the ground and went home, got another jar, and came back. Again looking into the water, she saw Lōlabe's reflection. She thought her reflection beautiful.

"What!" she exclaimed. "Me with all this beauty in the well, and I'm a slave to a household of blacksmiths!" Hurling her water jug to the ground, she was set to leave, when Lōlabe laughed from the tree. Looking up, the slavegirl saw her.

"So," she said. "It's you who's sitting up there, and I've been breaking my master's jars for nothing. Now they'll kill me. You'd better come down!"

Lōlabe climbed down.

The slavegirl, it turned out, was a witch. Holding the bride in front of her, she stuck her full of pins. When she stuck a pin in her head, it would turn into a dove's head, and her arms into dove's wings. She stuck and stuck her with pins until she had changed Lōlabe completely into a dove. She threw Lōlabe into the air, put on her clothes, and sat in the tree waiting for the son of the king. Arriving with the sultan's band, the son of the king passed under the tree and prepared to bring her down. And how did he find her, but sitting there [like a princess]? "Climb down!" he said, and he brought her down from the tree.

"Are you Lōlabe?" he asked when she came down.

"Yes."

"Why are your eyes like that?"

"Because I've been crying for you so much."

"Why are your nostrils like that?"

"Because I've been blowing my nose from crying so much."

"And why is your face like that?"

"Because I was slapping it so much, lamenting your absence."

13. This reference, *ʿabdit dār ḥaddādīn* (which could also mean, "a slave to a family named Ḥaddādīn"), is obscure, for we have just been told that she is a "slave of the king's household." Practitioners of all crafts, however, and blacksmiths in particular (perhaps because they were most often gypsies), were generally looked down upon, especially by the Bedouins.

"She is my portion and my fate," he said to himself, covering her face before anybody could see her. He sat her on a horse, and the procession started for home. As soon as they arrived at the palace, he took her inside and lived with her. "It's settled!" he convinced himself. "She must be Lōlabe." She herself kept insisting she was Lōlabe.

From that time the real Lōlabe started coming to their house, the palace of the king. She would fly to the kitchen and perch on the wall.

"Cook! O cook!" she would cry. "The son of the king, your master—is he happy or sad? Is he in the company of whites or blacks? Come, let us cry together tears of coral and pearl!" Perching on the wall, she would then weep, and pearls and coral would pour from her eyes. The cook would rush out to pick them up, and the food would burn. The first day, the food burned; the second day also. On the third day, the son of the sultan said [to his servants], "Tell the cook to come see me! I want to see what's the matter with him, why for the past two or three days the food's been burned so badly we haven't been able to eat it." They sent for him, and he came.

"Come here!" said the son of the sultan. "Why for the past two or three days have you been doing that to the food? Are you new at this trade?"

"Master, let me explain!" replied the cook. "Every day a dove comes, perches on the wall, and cries out, 'Cook, O cook! The son of the sultan, your master—is he happy or sad? Is he in the company of whites or blacks? Come, let us cry together tears of coral and pearl!' She stands on the edge of the wall and weeps and weeps, and coral and pearls pour down. Look how much I've already collected from what she's left behind!"

"When does she usually come?"

"She comes when I start to cook," he answered. "I go out to collect the coral and pearls. I get distracted, and the food burns."

"All right, this time you're forgiven. Tomorrow, take good care of the food!"

Going up to the roof, the son of the king lay in wait for her. When the dove came, she landed on the wall. "Cook, O cook!" she called out. "The son of the king, your master—is he happy or sad? Is he in the company of whites or blacks? Come, let us cry together tears of coral and pearl!" She was distracted, crying, when he crept up from behind, reached out his hand, and caught her. Taking her inside, he put her in his lap. As he stroked her, he found the pins planted in her body. Pull, pull! The first pin—her arm came back as it was. The second pin and the third—he kept feeling around, removing pins from her body, until Lōlabe appeared again.

"What's going on?" he asked. "Who did this to you?"

"A slavegirl came upon me," she answered. "Such and such happened to me, and she was the one who did this."

Now the other (she was a witch after all!) outwitted him. She caught him, changed him into a dove, and made him fly away. She then started to lord it over Lōlabe, making her sleep on a straw mat. He, too, would come flying around her window, land on the sill, and cry out, "O Lōlabe, Lōlabe! How are you faring in my father's house?"

"Mats under me and mats over me," she would answer. "It is the sleep of hardship, O my Yūsuf!"

Perched on her window, he would weep and weep till his eyes went blind, and then he would fly away. Coming back the next day, he cried out, "Lōlabe, O Lōlabe! How are you faring in my father's house?"

"Bedding under me and bedding over me," she answered. "It is the sleep of comfort, O my Yūsuf!"

Standing there, he cried, and she cried with him. When his eyes went nearly blind, he gathered himself and flew away. On the third day he came back, calling, "Lōlabe, O Lōlabe! How are you faring in my father's house?"

"Silk under me and silk over me," she answered. "It is the sleep of a vizier, O my Yūsuf!"[14]

Standing in the window, he cried and cried. Meanwhile, she had been waiting behind the window, and, reaching out her hand, she caught hold of him and removed the pins from his body.

They began their wedding celebrations all over again, holding a feast and making merry for many an evening. He married her. It was then announced in the city, "He who loves the sultan must bring a load of wood and some burning coals!" They burned the witch and scattered her ashes to the wind.

This is my tale, I've told it, and in your hands I leave it.

14. The first-person possessive of the name Yūsuf (Yūsufī) in Lōlabe's answer (*tiḥtī ḥarīr, fōqī ḥarīr; nōm il-wazīr, yā Yūsufī*) is used as a connecting rhyme, or near rhyme (*-bi* with *-fi*), with the question (*yā Lōlabi, wiš ḥālik fī dār abī?*). The question itself and all three answers form rhyming ditties that are apparently independent of the rest of the tale—which

Afterword

In contrast to the tales in the previous group, which explore subjective feelings associated with sexuality, the quest tales here concern the search for a bride as a public affair circumscribed by preexisting conditions. The interplay of social forces in the quest situation is similar in all three tales, receiving its clearest expression in "The Brave Lad." The very realistic narration in this tale, the absence of magic and the supernatural, itself gives a meaningful cultural context to the quest pattern. The teller relates this tale without distancing herself from the action, as if the events narrated came, or could come, from actual life. It seems perfectly natural for a lad to desire the king's daughter but be too poor to propose (see Tale 16, n. 2). His quest is realistically motivated, as is the girl's desire to help him. The tale's sense of realism is heightened for an Arab audience when the teller says the girl wanted to marry her cousin, whom she loved, and the ghoul had taken her against her will. From this tale we see the basic elements of the quest clearly: a male in search of a mate, a female receptive to his approach and willing to help him, and an authority figure who must be overcome before the maiden can be won.

In all three tales the initiation of the quest is constrained by the requirements of the social system. In "The Brave Lad" the fulfillment of the lad's private desire for the king's daughter is made contingent on the performance of a public duty—killing the ghoul. The same holds true for "Gazelle," where, in the process of obtaining the soul of the jinni from the tiger's kneebone, the hero rescues the town from the ravages of four other monsters. And in "Lōlabe" as well, the boy's quest is tied to a public function, namely, the fulfillment of a vow—an act that benefits everyone in the city, especially the poor and the destitute.

The purpose of the quest, it would appear, is to demonstrate the necessity of cooperation between the partners in order to ensure their success. Left to his or her own resources, neither partner would succeed. The girl in "The Brave Lad" did not know the secret of the three hairs before the young man came into the cave, and he in turn would not have been able to pluck them from the ghoul's head as she did. The boy in "Lōlabe" would not have been able to cast the magic spells on his own,

---

may explain why the teller was confused earlier (see n. 9, above) about the name of the hero.

and without him Lōlabe would not have risked the perilous journey out of the wilderness castle. And the young man in "Gazelle" would not have been able to move the mountain without Gazelle's help, nor would she have been finally able to kill her arch foe without his aid. Similarly, cooperation is necessary in the face of the hostility the young couple faces from their parents and from society. It affirms the breaking of the parental bond of authority and the creation of a new bond based on mutual love and partnership.

Yet within the framework of cooperation the roles are not equal. That of the female is more complex than that of the male, reflecting perhaps the complexity of her actual role in society, with marriage being for her a transition from one authority figure (the father) to another (the husband). The role of the male is to go looking for a mate, but beyond his needing the courage to start the quest, not much else is asked of him. In "Gazelle," even the quest itself is not initiated by the young man alone; Gazelle's role in it is substantial. She not only guides him to the right places where he can obtain help to move the mountain, but she also helps him in the task itself by overcoming the guardian jinni. Similarly in the other two tales: once the quest is initiated, the responsibility of seeing it through to completion falls to the women. The complexity of the female role is clear in "Lōlabe." After Lōlabe exerts her utmost to save the young man and herself from the clutches of her mother, he abandons her in the tree while he goes to obtain his parents' consent to bring home his bride—consent that apparently was not forthcoming, for the couple must suffer still further hardship before their marriage can be celebrated openly.

Seen in its cultural context, the quest itself appears as the price that young people who wish to select their own mates must pay for the freedom to make their own choice. The authority figure functions to preserve tradition by putting obstacles in the path of personal freedom for both sexes. In "Gazelle," the dying father instructs his sons to give their sisters to any suitors who come seeking marriage. Although exaggerated, this situation represents the practice even today. Because in traditional Palestinian and Arab culture the choice of a mate is of vital importance to the community, it cannot be left entirely up to the individual; the interests of the whole family must be taken into account as well. Those who insist on choosing for themselves, then, must be willing to make sacrifices to achieve their goals. In "The Brave Lad," the young hero must have enough courage to face the ghoul; and in "Gazelle," he must at least have the courage to face the tiger. In "Lōlabe," the successful union at the end must be earned by overcoming two sets of obstacles, one from the mother ghouleh, and the other (though not explicitly) from the boy's own parents.

Arrayed against the young couple in their struggle are the supernatural forces of the jinn, the subhuman forces of the ghouls, and the black forces of magic. What is the function of these forces, and why do they occur here? We notice, on closer examination, that only the authority figures are presented as ghouls or jinn. In "The Brave Lad" the ghoul is the husband, in "Lōlabe" the ghouleh is the mother, and in "Gazelle" the guardian of the mountain is a jinni—and, we presume, an agent of or surrogate for Gazelle's father as well. (The situation in this tale is complicated by the fact that Gazelle herself is said to be of the jinn.) Earlier (see Tale 6, n. 13; Tale 8, n. 8), we suggested that ghouls might represent exaggerated human appetites—hunger or sexuality—gone to excess. Here, the human appetite presented in ghoulish aspect is parental possessiveness, a force that aims to keep a son or a daughter in a state of perpetual childhood. Thus the parents at the beginning of "Lōlabe" forget about fulfilling their vow: they do not want to admit to themselves that their son has grown up. The love of a ghoul for his children is in fact proverbial in Palestinian folk speech. A person's excessive love for his or her children is said to be "like the love of a ghoul for his child" (*zayy imḥabt il-ğūl la-ʾibno*).

We therefore see that the behavior of the authority figure is part of a cultural pattern as well. Although in each tale the couple are ready for each other and for the match, the parents are reluctant to let go of their children. The image of Lōlabe, imprisoned by her mother in a wilderness castle, represents most poignantly the situation of marriageable girls. And the behavior of the fathers in "The Brave Lad" and "Gazelle" is not very different from that of Lōlabe's mother; they, too, keep their daughters beyond the reach of suitors, setting nearly impossible conditions for winning their hands. The situation in "The Brave Lad," moreover, underscores the point by presenting a second authority figure, a man who marries a girl against her will, as a ghoul. Thus the ghouls and jinn are imaginative representations of the obstructing forces as seen by the intending couple. In order for the couple to achieve their aim, these forces must be eliminated. Gazelle hangs her rival jinni by his hair, being unable to get his soul and kill him; as long as he remains alive, her relationship with her husband remains insecure. The necessity of overcoming the authority figures, then, is the very source of the narrative logic that turns them into monsters or ghouls, thereby justifying the couple's killing them with impunity.

Finally, the significant role that hair plays as a unifying image for the source of power in all three tales must be mentioned. In "The Brave Lad," the ghoul is killed by removing three hairs from his head. (Cf. the story of Samson, *Judges* 16.) By rubbing his magic hairs, the young man in "Gazelle" is able to summon the jinn; and Gazelle herself disables his rival when she hangs him up by his hair. Although these instances, which spring from ancient Semitic folklore, are, like Lōlabe's hair, removed from the domain of ordinary experience, the cultural context nevertheless helps to explain the significance of hair in the folk imagination. In Palestinian culture, hair is thought of almost as if it were a private part of the body, and both women and men, especially among the fellahin, cover their heads. Women with long hair, which is considered a mark of feminine beauty and a source of attraction to men, tie it in a bun and cover it. Indeed, a woman who lets her hair down in front of strangers is considered immodest, such behavior being interpreted as an act of allurement. In Tale 20, the king happens upon a girl combing her long hair and immediately falls in love with her; perhaps, then, Lōlabe's long hair, which has the power to attract a young man from a distant land, is the source of her magic power as well.

Group II

FAMILY

Brides and Bridegrooms

19. *The Old Woman Ghouleh*

TELLER: We are blessed with plenty!
AUDIENCE: Blessings abound, Allah willing!

The son of the king took the daughter of one of his father's viziers for his wife. As the girl was sitting in the bridal seat receiving congratulations, an old woman came in and said, "Niece, may your wedding be blessed!"

"And may Allah bless you too, aunty!" responded the bride.

"I'm sorry, my dear," the old woman said, "but I don't have any money to give you as a wedding present.[1] Would you accept these glass bracelets?"

The old woman then went home, waited until midnight, and returned. "Little bracelets, little bracelets!" she said, tapping on the door, "Open the door!"

The bracelets fell from the girl's wrists as she slept, and they opened the door. The old woman came into the house and woke up the bride. "Hush," she whispered, "don't let your husband know what's going on. Your father has just died." Immediately, the bride jumped out of bed and went with the old woman. If, you might say, their house was on the south side of town, the old woman took her in an easterly direction, until they arrived at a cave. When she came into the cave, the girl was met by a small ghouleh and a big ghoul, who took away her clothes and her jewelry and devoured her.

Now we return to the king's son. When he awoke in the morning, he found his bride missing. He told his father, and they started arguing with the vizier, accusing him of having taken his daughter back in secret. Another minister happened to be there, and he said, "I swear by Allah, O king! Your son can have my daughter.[2] Please don't get upset!" They sent for the cadi and drew up the marriage contract.

1. Traditionally, relatives and friends of the newlyweds offer money to the bride or groom as part of the wedding ritual known as *nqūṭ*. See Granqvist, *Marriage* I: 128–130.

2. On giving away a daughter, see Tale 17, n. 17.

Instead of wearing white like the last time, this time the old woman wore green.[3] Bringing a green bead with her, she said to the bride, "You must forgive me, niece, but I don't have any money as a wedding present. Please keep this bead to protect you from the evil eye."[4] Believing what the old woman said, the girl took the bead and hid it in her dress. When all the guests had left, she brought it out and put it on the table by her bed, along with her golden bracelets.

Just before dawn the old woman came back to the bride's house. "Open the door, beadling!" she said, "Beadling, open the door!" The bead came down and opened the door, and the woman came in and woke up the girl. "Don't let your husband know," she whispered, "but your mother is on her deathbed." The girl rose up to go with her. "Wear all your gold things," suggested the old woman. "The people expecting you know you're a bride."

In the morning the husband awoke to find that his wife had disappeared. He had a fight with her father, accusing him of having taken his daughter back. A third minister offered his daughter. This time, however, they decided to patrol all the roads leading out of town. They also stationed watchmen in all the streets. That evening the groom went in to his bride.

The old woman came wearing a blue dress and carrying a citron. "My dear," said she to the bride, "I don't have any money to give you as a present. Take this citron instead."

3. White is the color of purity; green the color of Islam. Both colors are worn by pious older women, especially after they have completed the religious duty of the hajj. See Kanaana et al., *Al-Malābis*: 44–45.

4. According to popular belief, all charms to ward off the evil eye, whether decorations on houses, beads worn by children, or beads hanging from cars' rearview mirrors or the necks of domestic animals, must be blue.

The belief that people can cause injury or damage to others or to objects they envy or desire simply by looking at them, although common worldwide, is particularly prominent in the Middle East. Protection from the evil eye is especially necessary on such a joyous occasion as a wedding, when the bride is exposed to the gaze (and therefore possibly the envy) of others. Songs against the evil eye are sung to the bride while she rides the camel, mule, or mare during the wedding procession (see Granqvist, *Marriage* II:62). In addition, the rice, salt, raisins or sweets, and other objects thrown at the bride or the newlyweds, aside from being emblematic of fertility, apparently serve to ward off the evil eye (see Granqvist, *Marriage* II:79n.2). For a discussion of Palestinian beliefs and practices concerning the evil eye, see Canaan, *Aberglaube*: 28–32; Einsler, "Das böse Auge"; see also the definitive article by Alan Dundes, "Wet and Dry, the Evil Eye," in *Interpreting*: 93–133 (with bibliography, pp. 265–276).

This girl was cleverer than the others, who did not say anything to their husbands.

"Keep this citron for me," she said to her husband.

"Who gave it to you?" he asked.

"It was the woman in the blue dress."

"Ah, yes!" he exclaimed. "This woman is a ghouleh."[5]

He stuck a knife in the citron, and they went to sleep. In the middle of the night the old woman returned and knocked on the door.

"Little citron! Little citron!" she called out, "Open the door for me!"

"And how can I open with a knife stuck in my heart?" answered the citron.

The newlyweds woke up. The bridegroom removed the knife from the citron, and it came down and opened the door. When the ghouleh came in, they pretended to be sleeping.

"My dear niece," said the old woman to the bride, "you'd better get up. Your only brother has just died."

Signaling her husband, the bride got up and went with the woman. A little later he, too, rose from bed and blew the whistle to alert the watchmen, who followed the old woman the moment they saw her. She started running, with the bride right behind her and the guards following, until they caught up with her just before she reached her cave. With a dagger they rent open her dress, and what did they find but that she had a goat's tail and donkey's hooves? From the tail down she had the shape of a donkey, with hair like a donkey's. And from the tail up she looked exactly like a human being. When she entered her cave, her eyes contracted and sparkled like flames.[6] The small ghouleh and the big ghoul started to bray. The guards entered the cave on the heels of the ghouleh, along with the bridegroom and the ministers who had lost their daughters. They killed all three ghouls and split their bellies open with their daggers.

Then, gathering up their daughters' clothes and the gold heaped in the cave, they went home.

And there we left them and came back.

5. The ghouleh in this tale is distinguished by her cleverness (cf. Tale 16, n. 5). Using tricks to gain her ends, she immediately secures the trust of the first two brides; indeed, they trust her to such an extent that they wear jewelry to their parents' deathbeds, something cultural norms do not allow.

6. On flames and ghouls, cf. Tale 33, n. 7. Although ghouls can take any shape, they

20. *Lady Tatar*[1]

There were three sisters, and each of them had a hen.[2] The eldest killed her hen and ate it. The second one did the same. After a while they started pestering the young one: "Why don't you kill your hen too? How long are you going to stay without meat?"[3]

"How am I going to slaughter it?" she responded. "And how much [meat] will there be to eat? This way, she'll lay an egg every day, and I'll eat the egg."

Becoming envious, the sisters took the hen and dropped it into the well of the ghoul while the young one was away.[4] When she came back and asked about her hen, she could not find it, and her sisters kept their secret. Searching for her hen, the young one discovered it in the well of the ghoul. When she went down into the well to bring back her hen, she found the ghoul's house inside the well dirty and his laundry piled up. She swept and mopped the floor, did the laundry and the dishes, and left the house sparkling clean.

As she was about to climb back out with her hen, the ghoul arrived. She hid under the stairs. Looking around, the ghoul found his house clean and everything in order.

"Who's been cleaning my house?" asked the ghoul. "I smell a human being!"

She was afraid to come out, so she stayed in her hiding place.

---

usually appear as in this tale—half human and half animal; see Footnote Index, s.v. "Ghouls and Jinn." For further references, see Granqvist, *Marriage* II: 169n. 1; for more on the physical features of ghouls, see Canaan, "Dämenonglaube": 17–19.

1. "Lady Tatar" is not a woman's name. The word *Tatar* means "Tartar" or "Turk" and is associated in people's minds with beggars and gypsies. *Yā tatarī, yā ġajarī* ("You Tartar! You gypsy!") is a form of name-calling.

2. In Palestinian villages families ordinarily raised animals in the yard. The mothers would designate a hen or two for each of her marriageable daughters so that they could sell their eggs to buy beads, thread, and other embroidery items in preparation for marriage. Because the hens were left to roam freely in the fields, when one was lost the girls would first search the abandoned wells for them. The villagers searched the wells for other lost animals and children too. See Tale 3, n. 4.

3. In another version of the tale collected from a different part of the country the opening sequence is more logical: upon slaughtering their chickens in turn, the first and second sisters offer their younger sister a thigh, then demand their share from the sister's hen. A similar sequence, involving babies, occurs in Tale 30.

4. On jealousy among sisters, see Tale 12, n. 6.

"Whoever cleaned my house like this," the ghoul said, "you may come out safely. Just come out!"

When the girl heard this, she emerged from her hiding place.

"You are my daughter," swore the ghoul. "I swear by Allah, and may He betray me if I betray this oath!"[5]

The maiden lived in his house, comfortable and happy. Every day she would sit in the sun by the mouth of the well and comb her hair. The king's geese would come to visit, and they taunted her: "Hey! Ghoul's daughter! Your father's fattening you up to make a feast of you!"

From that day on the girl grew thinner. Noticing her condition, the ghoul hid himself and found out what the story was.[6]

"The next time those geese come around," he said, "say to them, 'Tomorrow the sultan is going to slaughter you, pluck your feathers, have you cooked, and eat you.'"

When she said that to them, all their feathers dropped off. Having seen that, the sultan followed them the next day to find out what their story was, why their feathers had fallen out in a night and a day. Following them, he came upon the ghoul's daughter, and he found her appealing.[7] He asked her to marry him, but she said, "Ask for my hand from my father, the ghoul."[8]

The sultan came and asked for her hand from the ghoul, and he gave his consent. Before his daughter left his house for the sultan's palace, the ghoul said to her, "Don't speak to him, not even one word, until he says to you, 'O Lady Tatar, O Lady Tatar—her father the sun, and the moon her mother!'"

She went to live in her husband's palace. He would speak with her, but she did not answer because he did not know the words taught her by her father, the ghoul. When he saw that she was like that, the sultan married another woman, thinking his wife was mute.

5. *B-ʿahd alla, w-il-xāyin y-xūno alla*—literally, "I promise to Allah, and may Allah betray him who betrays this oath!" See Tale 13, n. 7; Tale 42, n. 7.

Ghouls are not always harmful creatures. In Tales 10 and 22, the ghouls are donor figures who, by giving the heroes advice, help them in attaining their goals. In Tale 28, as in this one, a ghoul acts as a father figure to a girl who has no one else.

6. In Palestinian culture weight loss indicates that something is seriously wrong with a person or an animal (as in Tale 13).

7. When the king sees the girl combing her hair, he is exposed to more of her charms and beauty than would ordinarily be permitted. See afterword to Group I, "The Quest for the Spouse."

8. The girl here is insisting on the proper form; see Tale 15, n. 14.

"By Allah," said the second wife one day, "I want to go visit my co-wife, the one who the sultan says is mute."

She went, and the ghoul's daughter received her and welcomed her. It turned out she could talk after all.

"What shall I make for you?" she asked. "I'd like to make you cheese pastry."[9]

She then commanded, "Get ready, oven!" and the oven set itself up. "Come here, flour, water!" and they came. Then she said, "Let the pastry become ready!" and it was done. Taking the tray full of pastry, she carried it into the oven. When she came back out again, the pastry in the tray was baked to a golden brown, and she and her co-wife ate of it.

Her co-wife became jealous, and when she went back home she said to her husband, "Your other wife's not mute at all. She can talk!" She related to him what had happened and said, "I'd like to make for you what she made for me."

"Come here, oven!" she commanded, but the oven did not obey. "Come here, flour!" but the flour did not come. She then went and set up the oven, brought the flour and the water herself. After she made the pastry, she took hold of the tray and went into the oven to do as her co-wife had done. She was burned in the oven, along with her pastry, and died.

Meanwhile, the king went back to the ghoul's daughter and talked with her, but she would not speak with him. He then decided to marry another woman, and this one too said, "I'd like to go visit my mute co-wife."

"What shall I make for you?" wondered the ghoul's daughter. "Let me prepare some fried fish." "Come here, kerosene stove!" she commanded, and it came. "Come here, frying pan!" and it came. Waiting until the oil in the pan was boiling hot, she put her hands in the oil, palm to palm, saying, "Palm over my palm, let the fried fish come!" The pan filled with frying fish, brown and crispy. She ate of it with her co-wife. But when her co-wife tried to imitate her, her hands were burned, the frying pan fell over on her, and she died.[10]

9. *Mṭabbaq* is a pastry made from flour, water, and cheese. The cheese is placed inside thin layers of dough, and after baking a sugar syrup is poured over the pastry.

10. The sequence of events in this tale, in which the second and third wives lose their lives through no fault of their own, reflects women's genuine concern about polygyny. Granqvist (*Marriage* II: 186–217) discusses the question of polygyny in Palestinian culture, offering many examples of proverbs, folk ditties, and songs, all centering on the bitterness of having a co-wife—for example, "A co-wife is bitter, even if she is honey in a jar" (*iẓ-ẓurra murra, lannhā ʿasal fī jarra;* p. 186). See Tale 30, n. 3.

Once more the sultan came back to the ghoul's daughter after having deserted her.[11] This time, however, he hid himself to learn if she was actually mute or if she could speak as his wives who had died had claimed. Hiding himself, he found her bored with her situation.

"I'm thirsty," she said. "Come give me some water!" The pitcher and the water jug started arguing over which of them was to bring the water for her. "If only," she sighed, "if only your master were to say to me, 'O Lady Tatar—her father the sun, and the moon her mother!' he would relieve us all."

As soon as he heard this, the sultan called out, "O Lady Tatar—her father the sun, and the moon her mother!"[12]

"Yes," she replied, "and two yesses."[13]

They lived happily, and there we leave them and come back here.

21. *Šōqak Bōqak!*

There was in the old days a king, Ṯāʾir by name, who had no children except an only son whose name was ʿAlāʾiddīn.[1] When he became of marriageable age, his parents urged him once, twice, and three times to let them find him a wife, but he always refused.[2] One snowy day he took his servant and went hunting. A doe sprang in front of them, and he aimed and shot her. The servant slaughtered her, and as her blood flowed to the ground, he said, "O master! May you find a bride who's like this blood on the snow."[3]

11. On husbands' desertion of their wives, see Tale 10, n. 8.

12. Ordinarily a couple do not call each other by their first names; a woman who does so in public, for example, would be considered overly familiar. See Tale 27, n. 1.

13. The girl's response here—"and two yesses" (*naʿamēn*)—indicates that she is pleased and willing to cooperate with her husband. The custom of using the dual form to indicate a friendly and receptive attitude applies to all greeting terms; thus the most popular response to "thank you" (*šukran*) is *ahlēn* ("two welcomes"), to "hello" (*marḥabā*), *marḥabtēn* ("two hellos").

1. The cultural emphasis on having many children shines through the telling syntax of the first sentence, which also sets the stage for the son being spoiled and his parents not being able to deny any of his demands (see n. 4, below). Cf. the opening sentences of Tales 14, 15, 18, 22, 27, 32.

2. Parents start putting pressure on a son—especially an only son—to get married quite early, soon after he reaches puberty, or from age fourteen or fifteen.

3. A striking image for the ideal standard of beauty in a woman: a fair complexion with rosy cheeks. Cf. Tale 2, n. 1.

Now, ʿAlāʾiddīn had seven cousins, and his parents had been wanting to marry him to one of them. But when he came home from the hunt, he said to his mother, "Mother, take away the bed of happiness and bring in the bed of sorrow.[4] Your son ʿAlāʾiddīn is sick, and there's no medicine or cure for him."

"O my son, my darling!" exclaimed the mother. "If your kingdom lacks something, we'll gladly provide it. And if your army's too small, we'll give you more soldiers."

"Impossible!" he replied. "If you fulfill my request, I'm well; and if not, I'm going to stay sick."

"All right, son. What is your request?"

"You must look for a bride for me whose face is like blood on the snow."

The city they lived in was the biggest in the whole kingdom. The mother went searching in the city, hoping to find a girl who fit the description, but she could find none. Finally she spied a hut on the side of Mount Mqallis, you might say.[5] "I still have to look in that hut over there," she thought to herself, "and, by Allah, I'm going to climb up to it." Mounted on a horse, she went up the mountain with her servants. When the owners of the hut saw them coming, they said, "This must be the king's wife. Let's go out and receive her."

"No one in the world will please my son like this one," thought the king's wife when she saw their daughter. Rushing home, she said to him, "Son, what a bride I've found for you! In all my life I've never seen anyone like her."

"Good!" he said.

So, they went asking for the girl's hand from her family.

"We are honored," they responded. "Is it possible we should find anyone better than you?" They accepted readily.

ʿAlāʾiddīn's family then went and made all the formal arrangements. They asked for the girl's hand, signed the marriage contract, and set out to bring the bride home, but her father put a condition on them. "My daughter," said he, "will not leave this house except riding on a dapple

4. The phrasing here—*qīmī frāš il-hanā, w-ḥuṭṭī frāš il-ḥuzun*—indicates that the son is spoiled. If the family had four or five children, the son's sickness would not have been put in terms of death and condolences, as here. See n. 1, above.

5. Mount Mqallis is the name of a mountain in the Galilee, south of the village of ʿArrābe, where the tale was collected.

gray mule and escorted by a regiment of Turkish soldiers marching to the sultan's royal band." His wish was granted, and the bride was brought to her new home.

Now the seven cousins stationed themselves by a doorway in the path of the wedding procession, where they knew the bridegroom would be passing.

"May Allah forgive our uncle's wife for having done such a thing to our cousin!" exclaimed the first one. "If only his wife weren't bald!" Another one jumped in with, "If only she weren't insane!" And another with, "If only she weren't blind in one eye!" "If only she weren't so rude!" said a fourth, and so on.

Hearing this, ʿAlāʾiddīn thought, "Alas! Because I've given her so much trouble, my mother has found me a girl with all these deformities."[6] Turning right around, he ran away. He did not go home.

In the same city the family had an orchard in which there was a palace, where he went and stayed by himself. They waited for him. Today he'll come. Tomorrow the bridegroom will arrive. A week went by, then a month, then forty days.[7] When forty days had gone by and the bride had still not seen her husband, she went to her mother-in-law.

"Do you really have a son, or don't you?" she asked.

"My dearest," answered the mother-in-law, "ʿAlāʾiddīn's my son. There's no one like my son. He's like this and like that."

"I believe you. Where is he?"

"Let me tell you, my daughter. Your husband has seven cousins. Such and such is their story, and we don't know how to bring him back, to convince him to come back home."

"In that case," said the bride, "ask my uncle[8] if he would fulfill my request, and I'll bring him back." The mother went and spoke with her husband, and he said, "Whatever she asks for, I'll have it made for her, so long as she brings him back."

"O uncle," said the bride, "I want you to have a tunnel dug for me, from my palace here to the one where he's keeping himself."

6. True to life, in the tale ʿAlāʾiddīn is kept from seeing his bride throughout the process leading up to his marriage; see Tale 35, n. 17.

7. In an article on the significance of the number forty (cf. Tale 10, n. 11), Stephan says, "Forty days after marriage the bride must visit her parents" ("The Number Forty": 217). It is also said that "he who has been with people forty days . . . knows their secrets and has become one of them" (Granqvist, *Birth:* 80).

8. "Uncle" (*ʿammī*) here means "father-in-law".

The king had a tunnel made right up to the steps of the palace where his son was. The bride then went into her husband's orchard, wandering around and laying waste to everything, ripping up plants here and breaking them there. She then came to a fountain. How beautiful was the scenery there! [Soon] the shrubbery around there was quite a sight. Turning her back, she went down into the tunnel and headed for home.

When the bridegroom came by later, what did he find but that the orchard, the fountain, and the beautiful scenery were all in ruin, broken and torn up?

Calling his gardener over, he said, "Come here and tell me who's been doing this to the orchard?"

"Please, master!" begged the gardener. "A houri came,[9] and I didn't know whether she was an earthling or a creature from the sky. In all my life I've never seen anyone like her. Her beauty could not be described by comparing her with anything—not the sun or the moon. She comes, my lord, and says to me, 'Gardener! Šōqak bōqak![10] Your head is down and your feet are up!' As soon as she says that, I lose all sense of myself, or even where I am, until she's ready to leave again, when she says, 'Gardener! Šōqak bōqak! Your feet are down and your head is up!' I have no way of knowing from where she comes or how she goes."

"About what time does she usually come?" asked the young man, and the gardener said she came at such and such time. "Fine!" said the king's son, deciding to keep a watch out for her. He waited and waited, until he caught her.

"Come here!" he said when he had caught her. "I'm tired. Let's go sit by the fountain and relax. Who are you?"

"I'm from the country of 'The Spoons and Ladles Are Where?'" she answered. "I'm the daughter of the king of that country."

"Very well, O king's daughter!" he said. "Let's sit and enjoy ourselves here by the fountain.

Now there was a beautiful gourd vine planted all around the fountain. "What's this?" she asked, and he replied it was a gourd planted for decoration. She recited:

9. A houri (*ḥūriyye*) is a beautiful nymph of the Islamic paradise; hence here, a woman of unearthly beauty.

10. The nonsense syllables "šōqak bōqak!" like "abracadabra," are meant to invoke a mood of unreality, which is reinforced later when the bride identifies herself as being from the country of "Spoons and Ladles." The translation of the magic phrase does not reflect the

"O Turkish gourd!
Around the fountain trailing
West of you,
I saw my darling
Sitting to take his ease
His hair he has given
As a net to catch the breeze

Let him moan and weep forever
Who took from my sight my lover!"[11]

But he did not understand her.

In a while he led her to a violet. "What's this, O son of the king?" she asked.

"It's a violet," he answered.

She recited:

"You can hear the violet sing:
'Of all flowers, I am king.
With my sword in hand,
I conquered the land.
Though for a month I'm here,
And away the rest of the year,
Yet my essence in a vial's
A cure for all life's trials.'"

But he did not understand her intention.

"Come," he said, "let's sit here and relax. Take this cigarette and smoke it." Lighting a cigarette, he offered it to her, and she said:

"What is the tobacco's fault
That in reeds you should roll it
And with fire burn it
To force out the smoke?

Let him be sad forever,
Who took from my sight my lover!"

---

power of the original (*šōqak bōqak! rāsak tiḥtak w-ijrēk fōqak!*), with its rhyme and repetitive staccato rhythm.

11. For the sake of preserving the rhyme some minor liberties were taken in the translation of this and some of the following poems.

Yet he did not understand her.

They walked a little further and came upon a mulberry tree. "What's this, O son of the king?" she asked, and he said it was a mulberry. She called out:

"O you mulberries!
O mulberries![12]
Dangling from the boughs,
Spreading by the leaves!

May his sin haunt him forever,
Who took from my sight my lover!"

And he still did not see her meaning.

"Let's go up to my palace," he suggested. "I want to show you my palace."

"I can't walk," she said. "My legs hurt."

"Impossible!" he said. "You'll not walk, you'll ride on my shoulders."

Carrying her on his shoulders, he was taking her up to his palace when she saw, O so many roses and flowers creeping along the walls of the palace. "What are these, O son of the king?" she asked, and he said they were roses and flowers. She then said to him:

"O flowers climbing up our walls!
If true what I fear,
That you who are here
To your seven cousins
Have given ear,
How helpless you are,
And to me, how far!"

But he did not understand.

As he was taking her up, she rubbed her foot against a thorn on a rose bush. Blood flowed from the scratch, and she cried out, "Ouch! You wounded my foot!"

"Would that my hand and foot were both broken," he answered, "rather than your foot scratched!" Pulling out the royal handkerchief, he bandaged her foot with it.

12. On the use of fruit to symbolize sexuality, see Tale 12, n. 1.

"If my father were to go asking for your hand from your father," he said, "would he give you to me?"[13]

"Yes," she answered.

When he had brought her up to the palace, he said, "For the sake of Allah, let me sleep a while on your knee."

She let him put his head in her lap, and he fell asleep. Stealing away by the bottom of the stairs, she went straight home.

"Uncle's wife!" she said, "Tomorrow, he'll be back."

"O, my daughter!" said the other, "May Allah hear you and let my son come back!"

Now, the household of the king had been wearing black in mourning. "Take off these black things," said the bride to her mother-in-law, "and put on beautiful clothes! Decorate the house! It's certain. He's coming home tomorrow." She then went up to the king.

"Uncle," she said, "send out a party to receive ʿAlāʾiddīn. He's coming back home."

"How can I send anybody out?" asked the king. "What if he should refuse?"

"He won't refuse," she answered. "He's going to come."

The king sent members of his court, and they went to bring ʿAlāʾiddīn back. As for him, he came straight with them. On their way up the stairs, the king's son of course went ahead of the others. Meanwhile, his bride had called a servant over, given her a plate, and said, "As soon as the king's son comes up, throw this plate in front of him." The servant stood behind the door and threw down the plate as soon as he came up. He cried out:

"Pox upon her
Who hurled to the floor
The plate that came crashing!"

His bride answered him:

"And pox upon him
Who pulled out the scarf—

13. Customarily it is the mother who finds the bride and makes the preliminary arrangements (as in the tale), and the father who makes the official request. See Tale 15, n. 14; cf. Tale 42, n. 11.

The scarf of the kingdom put,
As bandage to my foot!"

"Were you the one then whose foot I bandaged?" he cried out, and came running over to her.

They lived happily ever after, and may Allah make life sweet for all my listeners!

22. *Clever Ḥasan*[1]

TELLER: Once upon a time—but first a prayer of peace for the Virgin!
AUDIENCE: Peace be to her!

Once upon a time there was a king who had an only son and no other. One day the father died. Taking his mother with him, the son said, "Mother, let's go traveling around these lands. We ought to have some fun."

With her on one mare and him on another, they went out and traveled, traveled, traveled. They came upon a man sitting at the crossing of three roads.

"Hey, uncle!" called out the boy.

"What do you want?" the man answered.

"What road is this?" asked the boy.

"This one's the Road of Safety," the man replied. "That one's the Road of Regret, and the other's a road that sends but does not bring back."

"I'm taking the Road of No Return," announced Clever Ḥasan.

"O Clever Ḥasan! For the sake of Allah! For the sake of the Prophet! For the sake of Jesus and Moses!"[2]

"Never!" said the youth. "I must take this road."

"But you will surely die!"

"Let that be as it may!" declared the boy. "When my life span has run out, let me die."[3]

1. On the name "Clever Ḥasan," see Tale 5, n. 4.

2. This is probably the order of holiness as perceived by the Muslim folk in Palestine. It is interesting to note, however, that the teller is a Christian woman, as the opening invocation indicates.

3. *ʾAnā w-ʿumrī*—literally, "I and my life span [are in the hands of Allah]!"

Setting out on that road, he came upon a giant with his head in the sky and his feet on the ground.

"Peace to you!"

"Welcome!" said the giant. "But, Clever Ḥasan, who's given you permission to pass this way?"

"I want to pass!" insisted the lad.

"This means war!"

"So be it!"

Drawing his sword, Clever Ḥasan struck him a blow which cut off his legs and threw him to the ground.

"Ouch!" roared the giant. "No one has ever been able to defeat me before. Here, take the keys to my palace! You and your mother can stay in it."

They stayed in the palace. Of course, what does a king have to do but go out hunting and shooting? One day, he went out to take the air, and his mother took pity on the black giant. Every day she would bring some cotton and wash his legs, dressing them with iodine until they healed. They fell in love and married,[4] without Clever Ḥasan knowing what was going on behind his back. She became pregnant and gave birth, to a boy the first time. Becoming pregnant again, she gave birth to a boy the second time.

"What am I going to do?" she asked. "If Clever Ḥasan finds out, he's going to cut off my head."

"Come," said the giant, "Do you see that orchard full of pomegranate trees? No one has ever gone into that orchard without being torn to pieces."

"It's a simple matter then," said the mother. Taking some turmeric, she dyed her face yellow.[5]

"May you be well again, mother!" said Clever Ḥasan when he came home. "What's the matter, mother? What happened to you?"

"Nothing's really the matter, son," she answered. "I just want to taste the pomegranates from that orchard over there before I die."[6]

4. The reference to marriage here is a euphemism for an illicit sexual relationship. Legal marriage, as we have seen, follows a form prescribed by social and religious traditions. See afterword to Group I, "Sexual Awakening and Courtship."

5. The mother colors her face yellow to look sick. Compare the behavior of the woman in Tale 7 (see n. 2) and the fourth wife in Tale 30.

6. For pomegranates, see Tale 35, n. 1.; for craving, see Footnote Index, s.v. "Pregnancy and Childbirth."

"That's easy, mother," he said. "Supply me with enough provisions to take care of my needs there and back."

Mounting his horse, he traveled. Arriving, he came upon a sheikh sitting there.

"Peace to you!" the lad hailed him.

"Welcome!" replied the sheikh.[7] "Had your salaam not come first, I would have gobbled you up and licked the flesh off your bones! Where are you going, Clever Ḥasan?"

"By Allah, most venerable sheikh, I'm on my way to get some pomegranates for my mother."

"Ho! Ho!" laughed the sheikh. "I've been sitting here for the last twenty years, and I'm still waiting to taste those pomegranates. But until now, no one has ever gone into that orchard and come out alive."

"Allah will deliver me," replied Ḥasan.

"Now, O Clever Ḥasan," said the sheikh, "what you must do is go straight in, without looking left or right. If you turn this way or that, you're dead! Pick the pomegranates, put them in the saddlebags, and come right out!"

"Yes, sir!" said Clever Ḥasan, and he went straight in. He filled the saddlebags, adding three extra pomegranates for the sheikh, and came out. He gave the pomegranates to his mother, and she said to the giant, "You said he would die, but here he is back, just like a monkey!"

"I don't know how he could have done it," he replied. "No one has ever gone in there and come out alive."

"You've done well, son," she said to the lad. "You can go now. Allah bless you!"

The following day, the giant said, "Look here! There's a melon patch, and no one who goes into it ever comes out alive."

She did the same thing, dyeing her face with turmeric and lying in bed. "O my head!" she moaned.

"What's the matter, mother?"

7. "Sheikh" has several meanings in Arabic, not all of which have carried over into English. In the Palestinian dialect the word refers most frequently to the religious teacher or leader (*xaṭīb*) who calls the faithful to prayer (*'āḏān*) and leads them in performing it (cf. Tale 6, n. 3). Yet the word is also commonly used as a respectful form of address for or reference to an older man, the implication being that age confers knowledge and wisdom.

The use of this word in the present context is at once ambiguous and revealing, since the sheikh's response to Ḥasan's salaam is the formula uttered by ghouls after the initial greeting by the young hero. It will be noted that the ghoul in Tale 35 (see n. 3) is also introduced as a sheikh; the ghouls here, however, are helpful figures, whereas the one in Tale 35 is not.

"By Allah, son, I have a yearning for watermelons."

"That's easy, mother," he said. "Give me enough provisions to get there and back."

She gave him the provisions, and he ran, ran, until he arrived. Again he came upon a sheikh at the gate. "Peace to you, O uncle sheikh!"

"Had your salaam not come first," responded the sheikh, "I would have gobbled you up and licked the flesh off your bones! What do you want?"

"I want a watermelon from this patch," the lad announced.

"I've been sitting here for the last ten years, and I've never seen anyone who was able to bring out even one melon. Those who go in never come out."

"Allah's the final judge, for me as well as for them," said Ḥasan.

The sheikh said to him the same as the other had, "Go straight in. If you turn this way or that, you're dead!"

Going right in, the youth filled a sack with watermelons, taking three extra melons for the aged sheikh. Pulling himself together, he came out of there fast. A thousand followed him (In the name of Allah!) but they were not able to catch him.[8] Carrying the melons with him, he brought them to his mother, thinking she would be happy.

"Yee!" complained the mother to the giant, "You said he would die, but here he is, back with melons just like a monkey!"

"What can I do?" asked the giant. "I don't know how he does it."

Taking the melons, the mother ate some and said to Ḥasan, "Thank you, son! May Allah reward you with plenty!"

"Your last resort is to ask for the water of life," the giant said. "He'll never be able to bring the water of life! It'll take him at least seven days and seven nights just to get there."

"O my son, my darling! My finger is burned and it needs the water of life to make it well."

"Mother," he said, "prepare enough provisions to get me there and back."

Taking his provisions with him, Clever Ḥasan started on his way. He carried with him a razor, a pair of scissors, some cologne, scented soap, and clean clothes. When he reached the land of the ghoul, he greeted him, "Peace to you, uncle ghoul!"

8. A thousand devils is meant, but the teller avoids mentioning them explicitly because that is supposed to gather them, whereas mention of the name of Allah drives them away (see Tale 29, n. 6; cf. Tale 17, n. 6).

"Welcome, Clever Ḥasan!" replied the ghoul. "Had your salaam not come first, I would have gobbled you up and licked the flesh off your bones!"

Coming down from his horse, the lad trimmed the ghoul's eyebrows, his beard, mustache, and hair; washed him with the scented soap; splashed him with cologne; and gave him fresh clothes to wear.[9]

"May Allah give you pleasure, as you gave me," exclaimed the ghoul. "What can I do for you, Clever Ḥasan?"

"I want to fetch the water of life for my mother."

"Listen," said the ghoul, "I'm going to send you to my sister. She's a month older than me, but a whole age wiser. If you find her grinding sugar, with her breasts thrown back, approach her and suck at her right breast and then at her left. But if you find her grinding salt, with her eyes sparkling red, take care not to go near her!"

"Yes, sir!" said Clever Ḥasan, and he went straight ahead. He found the ghouleh grinding sugar, with her breasts thrown back over her shoulders. When he had sucked at her right breast, she called out, "Who was it that sucked at my right breast? He's now dearer than my son ʿAbd ir-Raḥīm." When he had sucked at her left breast, she asked, "Who was it that sucked at my left breast? He's become dearer than my son ʿAbd ir-Raḥmān." She then said to him, "You've sucked at my breasts, so I can't possibly harm you. But my children are eleven ghouls, and if they see you, what're they going to do to you? What am I to do with you?"

Soon her children came home, and when she heard their voices she blew on him, turning him into a needle which she stuck into her dress. Her sons arrived.

"We smell a human being!" they announced.

"The human smell's in you and your trails," she answered.

"Impossible!" they insisted. "There's a human smell here!"

"Guarantee his safety!" she said.

"He's our brother in God's promise, and may Allah betray him who betrays this oath!"

She brought Ḥasan back as he was. "Welcome!" they said, hugging and kissing him. (Of course, he had now become their brother.)

"Who among you will take Clever Ḥasan to bring the water of life?"

9. The ghoul's wild appearance is evident here from the context. Ghoulishness is equated with wildness and the absence of the marks of civilization; hence, by calling the ghoul "uncle," by trimming his mustache and beard, and by giving him fresh clothes to wear, the boy civilizes him. See Tale 6, n. 4.

One of them said he needed ten days for the journey, and another said nine days, but the youngest said he could take him there and bring him back in seven minutes. Carrying Clever Ḥasan on his back, the ghoul flew with him.

"How big does the world look to you?" he asked.

"As big as a wheat sieve," replied Ḥasan.

"How big does the world look to you now?"

"As big as a flour sieve."

"And now?"

"As big as a piaster."[10]

"That's it!" announced the ghoul," "We're there. Come down now. See that gate over there? You'll find the door leaning to the side. Set it back in place. Then you'll see dogs and horses. Take the meat away from the horses and put it in front of the dogs, and take the barley away from the dogs and give it to the horses. Take this empty pitcher with you and put it at the edge of the fountain. Bring back a full pitcher, and don't turn left or right. Come straight out and slam the door quickly when you leave!"

Clever Ḥasan went right in, and did as the ghoul had told him. He fixed the door, switched the meat and the barley, put the empty pitcher down, picked up the full one, turned his back, and came straight out.

"Trap him, O gate!" shouted the devils.

"It's been forty years since I've been opened!" came the answer.

"Catch him, O hounds!"

"It's been forty years since we've tasted meat!"

"Hold him, O horses!"

"It's been forty years since we've tasted barley!"

Meanwhile, Ḥasan ran until he reached the ghoul, who put him on his shoulders and flew off.

"Welcome!" said the ghouleh when they arrived. "Allah be praised for your safety!"[11]

"Who's going to take him back to his uncle?"[12] they asked among themselves.

10. The progression here from the large wheat sieve (*ġurbāl*) to the flour sieve (*munxul*) to the small piaster (*qirš;* see Tale 5, n. 16) indicates that the ghoul is flying higher and higher with Ḥasan.

11. The common expression (*l-ḥamdilla ʿa-salāmtak*) is a form of congratulations for a safe return from a journey or recovery from an illness.

12. "Uncle" (here, *xāl*—literally, "maternal uncle") refers to the ghoul who sent Ḥasan on to his sister, the ghouleh who adopted him.

"I'll complete the favor I did him," volunteered the youngest, "by taking him back to his uncle."

Taking him on his shoulders, the ghoul flew back with him to his uncle.

"Here's your horse back!" said the big ghoul.

"Yes," said Ḥasan, bidding him good-bye. He then mounted his horse and moved on.

On his way back to his mother, the king's daughter saw him from her balcony.

"Clever Ḥasan!" she called out. "Stop here awhile!"

"No," he said, "I don't want to stop."

"By my father's head," she swore, "and by Allah, who gives him power over other people's heads, if you don't stop by I'll have yours cut off!"

Ḥasan came over to see her. Now, she was clever and took away the pitcher with the water of life, giving him one full of ordinary water in its place. She then fed him lunch and sent him on his way. He went straight to his mother and knocked on the door.

"O despair!"[13] the mother cried out when he knocked. "Here he is, still alive, O Slave of Blessing!"

"By Allah," the giant exclaimed, "I have no idea how he could have come back."

"Welcome back, son!" she said. "Allah be praised for your safety!"

She kissed him, taking away the pitcher. "And now," they said to each other, "What are we going to do?"

"Ask him where his strength lies," suggested the giant.

"O Clever Ḥasan, my son," she asked him one day, "where does your strength lie?"

"On my head are seven hairs," he answered. "If you cut them, all my power will be gone."[14]

"Come here," she said, "and let me remove the lice from your hair."

She sat down to delouse him and pulled the seven hairs from his head. When she gave him a bit of thread, he did not have the strength to break it.

"O Slave of Blessing!" she called out. "Come over and cut off his head!"

13. *Yī, ya xaytī*—literally, "Alas! O my sister!"

14. On hair, see Tale 16, n. 5.

"No, mother!" begged Ḥasan. "I'm your son!"

"Never!" said the mother. "Cut off his head!"

They chopped off his head, gouged out his eyes, and cut his body into four pieces, which they put in a box that they threw into the sea. The following day some fishermen found a box that had been washed ashore by the waves. "By Allah," they said, "this will make a good present for the king's daughter. We're going to present it to her."

Taking the box with them, they came to the daughter of the king, and the moment she saw them, she knew. "Alas!" cried she, "Oh! What a loss, Clever Ḥasan!" She took him from the fishermen, giving them ten dinars and sending them on their way. "So! Your mother did you in!" she said to him, opening the box. "How much did I advise you, but you didn't listen!"

With the water of life at hand, she connected the foot to the leg and rubbed them with the water, and (Allah granting the power) it healed. She then connected the arms, the back, and the shoulders. Lastly, she placed the head in place and rubbed it with the water, and behold! he sneezed.[15]

"Where am I?" he asked.

"You're with me, O Clever Ḥasan," she answered. "Where are your eyes?"

"They gouged them out before they slaughtered me. My little brother has them."

"Don't worry!" she said, and set about feeding him broth of squab and chicken every day.[16] She fed him these nutritious broths daily until he grew as strong as a camel.

"I'm going back to kill the giant," he announced.

"And how are you going to kill him?" she asked. "First you must get your eyes back. Take some trinkets with you and call out, 'Bracelets, O girls! Rings, O girls!'[17] Your brothers will come out and ask how

15. His sneezing shows that the operation has been successful, for immediately afterward he asks, "Where am I?" According to folk belief, if a sick person sneezes, he or she will get well. One can also call down a curse upon somebody, "May you not sneeze!" (*rētak ma b-tiʿṭas*)—meaning, "May you die!" Folk expressions also use sneezing to convey the same meaning, for example, "Someone hit him over the head, and behold! he never sneezed afterward" (*ḍarabo ʿa-rāso, yam mā ʿiṭsiš*).

16. These broths are believed to be very nutritious and also easy to digest (*xafīf ʿa-l-miʿde*—literally, "light on the stomach").

17. *ʾAsāwir yā banāt, xawātim yā banāt* is a common traveling salesman's cry.

much you want for them. Say you don't want money, you want eyes. What's in your left hand for the left eye."

Ḥasan did as she advised him. "Ah! Yes!" his little brother piped up. "By Allah, my brother's eyes are on the window sill. Wait till I get them for you." Taking the eyes with him, Ḥasan threw down all his trinkets, saying, "On your way now!"

When he had come back, the king's daughter put his eyes back in place and he became better than before, even more youthful than he had been. Having got his eyesight and his strength back, he said to the king's daughter, "I'm going over to kill them one by one."

"O my sweetheart, my soul!" she pleaded with him. She nearly died begging him to stay. "Never!" he said, mounting his horse. Taking his sword with him, he headed straight for the door and knocked.

"Who is it?"

"I'm Clever Ḥasan!" he announced.

"Yee!" she screamed, "It's the death of me!"[18]

"You didn't say that when you had me slaughtered," said her son. "You had me quartered. But by Allah, I'm going to tear you to pieces—you and your Slave of Blessing!" First he cut the giant's throat over her knee, then he slaughtered the two boys and the girl[19] and tore them to pieces in front of her. "As for you," he said, "I'm not only going to kill you, I'm going to tear you to shreds. I bring you here whole and hearty, and you betray me by marrying the slave whose legs I cut off!"

He tore her apart and threw the pieces away. Then he demolished the palace and took all the giant's treasure, sending it to the king's daughter.

One day the king asked his daughter, "Don't you want to get married?"

"Yes, father, I do," she answered. "Let it be known in town that I want to get married."

It was made public that the king's daughter was ready to marry, and the notables—the viziers, the pashas, and the beys—came passing under her window, expecting her to choose one of them by tossing an apple over his head, but it was no use.[20]

Meanwhile, Clever Ḥasan put on a tattered sackcloth. He had also got

18. Same as in n. 13, above.

19. The girl was not previously mentioned. On the ratio of two males to one female, see Tale 42, n. 12.

20. Pashas and beys were high civil or military officials in the Ottoman Empire; they also represent honorary titles conferred by the Ottoman rulers on selected notables from leading Palestinian families.

The practice portrayed here, wherein the girl chooses her mate by throwing an apple hold of a sheep's stomach, which he had ripped open and put on his head. He then came and walked under the window of the king's daughter's palace. Recognizing him, she threw the apple down over his head.

"Yee! What shame!" some exclaimed. "What a disaster!" said others. Each had her own words, and the father refused. He did not want to give her to him.

"Never!" she insisted. "I won't take another!"

"If you must marry him," he said, "you'll marry him in the house of desertion."[21]

"Fine," she said. "I accept."

They were married and lived together in isolation. Time passed, and her father was at war. Clever Ḥasan had an old, worn-out mule, and when the war started he rode it into battle. "Ḥā! Ḥā!" he egged his mule on, and people abused him, spitting on him and cursing: "Damn your father and his father who took you for a son-in-law by giving you his daughter!"

When he had left these people behind and there was no one around to see him, he brought out his magic ring.

"Magic ring!" he called out.

"Your servant at your command!" came the answer.

"I want a green mare the like of which has never been seen, and I want a gold-plated sword."

Immediately, a green mare appeared, a green suit of armor, and a golden sword. He went down to battle, and—slit! slit!—he slit throats till sunset. A third of the enemy was destroyed. On his way back to town, riding his mule and wearing his tattered clothes, whoever saw him spat on him.

The next day he went to battle, and again people were cursing him and spitting on him as he passed through. When he had gone some distance and there was no one around to say "There is no god but God!"[22] he dismounted from his mule.

(or, in some versions, a handkerchief) over his head, derives from the Indian tradition (in Sanskrit, *swayaṁvara*—literally, "self-choice"), the most prominent example being the Nala and Damayantī episode in the *Mahābhārata*. For an extensive discussion of this institution in the "occidental" folktale, see Cosquin, *Les contes indiens:* 317–346.

21. The reference here to the "house of desertion" (*bēt il-hijrān*) is mistaken, since "desertion" is an institutionalized status applicable to wives rather than daughters. See Tale 10, n. 8; cf. Tale 35, n. 12.

22. This is an interesting way of saying that there were no other people around, the assumption being that if anyone were around, that person would be a Muslim.

"Magic ring!" he called out.

"Your fortune's at your fingertips!" came the answer.

"I want a red mare, a red suit, and a gold-plated sword."

Down to battle he went, and—slit! slit!—he cut throats until another third of the enemy was gone. Pulling himself together, he went home as people spat on him.

On the third day he mounted his mule and came down, and when he reached a deserted spot, out came the ring.

"Magic ring!"

"Your fortune's at your fingertips!"

"I want a white suit, a white mare, and a sword that will give me the upper hand in battle."

"Fine. Right away!"

Clever Ḥasan came down to the field of battle. Meanwhile, the king, hearing about the knight who came and killed a third of the enemy every day, said, "By Allah, I want to go and see the knight about whom the people have been talking."

Clever Ḥasan came down to the battleground, killed the remaining third, and went back home riding the white mare. When people saw him and realized who it was they had been spitting on, they thought something strange was going on and went to speak to the king about it. When the king saw Ḥasan, he was overwhelmed.

"Your husband," he asked his daughter," what's his name?"

"His name," she answered, "is Clever Ḥasan, the son of King So-and-So."

"You married the son of King So-and-So!"

"Yes."

The king came forward and embraced Ḥasan, saying, "I'm really sorry, dear son-in-law!"

He had it announced in town that there was to be a feast of seven days and seven nights to celebrate the marriage of Clever Ḥasan to his daughter. The townspeople were invited to feast for the whole week at the king's expense, in celebration of Clever Ḥasan's wedding.

And may every year find you in good health!

23. *The Cricket*[1]

TELLER: Testify that God is One!
AUDIENCE: There is no god but God.

Once there was a woman who could not get pregnant and have children. One day she cried out, "O Lord, would you grant me a little girl, even if she's nothing more than a cricket!" It so happened that Allah heard her plea, and she became pregnant and gave birth to a cricket. A day went and a day came, and the cricket grew up. Once upon a day she wanted to get married.

"Mama," she said, going to her mother, "I want to get married."

"What can I do for you?" asked the mother. "You must look for a bridegroom as small as you are."

The cricket went away, and came upon a camel.

"Baʿ! Baʿ!" said he. "Will you marry me?"

She answered:

> "Cricket, cricket, your mother!
> And you are cousin to the whore.
> I'll put the gold in my sleeve,
> And talk to my mother some more."[2]

"O mama!" she said to her mother. "His eyes are very big, his head is very big, and his ears are very big. All of him is very big."

"No!" said the mother. "This one's not your size. Don't marry him."

Back to the camel the cricket went, and said, "I don't want to marry you."

1. The chirp of the cricket (*xunufse*) is the most pervasive summer sound in the country. Stephan says that *xunufse* (which he translates as "scarabee") is a "term given to unimportant, ugly people who, notwithstanding their inferiority in beauty, have a high opinion of themselves" ("Palestinian Animal Stories": 181). Although *xunufse* may also mean "scarab" or "beetle," the imitative sound ("tzee, tzee, tzee") used later in the tale makes it clear that the teller intended it to refer to the cricket.

2. "Gold" in this ditty refers to bridewealth (see Tale 16, n. 2); "cousin" most likely signifies "husband" (Tale 27, n. 1).

Traditional Palestinian women's dress has long, flowing sleeves in which small objects can be placed.

Although the meaning of the cricket's ditty is obscure in the present version of the tale, other versions shed some light. In a Palestinian version recorded by Stephan (see n. 8, below), the cricket's suitors at first insult her by calling her a *xunufse* (see n. 1, above) and telling her to get out of the way. When she responds with the first half of the ditty recorded here, they propose marriage, whereupon she asks them to place the gold in her sleeve.

She wandered around some more, and met a bull.

"Ba'! Ba'!" said he. "Will you marry me?"

She answered:

"Cricket, cricket, your mother!
And you are cousin to the whore.
I'll put the gold in my sleeve,
And talk to my mother some more."

She went to her mother and said, "O mama! His eyes are large, his head is large, and his ears are large. All of him is large."

"Better not marry him," said the mother.

Back to the bull went the cricket. "I don't want to marry you," she said.

She went away, and walked and walked until a little mouse found her wandering about and chirping, "Tzee, tzee, tzee."

"What're you looking for?" he asked.

"I'm wandering around looking for a bridegroom."

"Will you marry me?" he proposed.

She answered:

"Cricket, cricket, your mother!
And you are cousin to the whore.
I'll put the gold in my sleeve,
And talk to my mother some more."

"O mama!" she said to her mother. "His eyes are wee, his head is wee, and his ears are wee. All of him is very small."

"Yes," said the mother, "this one's your size. Marry him."

So back to the mouse the cricket went. "Yes," she said, "I'll marry you." And she went to live with him in his house.[3]

One day (it is said) their clothes became dirty, and they wanted to go somewhere to wash them. "Well," they said, "let's go look for water. Where shall we go?" They wandered about, with her walking behind him, and both of them going "Tzee, tzee, tzee," until you might say they reached the Sea of Acre.[4] Looking over this sea, they said, "Well, how

3. The behavior of the cricket up to this point and her mother's approval of it are not conventional. The girl's bold request for a husband, the mother's telling her to go out and find one on her own, and her direct confrontation of suitors would all be unacceptable forms of behavior in the society.

4. The "Sea of Acre" refers to the shores of the Mediterranean around the city of Acre (see Tale 24, n. 2). Commonly, when a married couple goes somewhere, especially in the villages, the wife walks behind her husband.

is this going to be enough? There's barely enough water here to get our clothes wet." They turned around and went down to the Sea of Tiberias.[5] They searched everywhere, up and down, but found no water. "There isn't enough water for us anywhere!" they exclaimed.

As they wandered, they saw a donkey's hoofprint with a little water in it. Calling her husband over, she said, "These waters will be enough for us to wash ourselves and our clothes, with some left over."

"Fine," he answered. "Let me go and get some soap."

He went over to Acre to bring the soap, and she sat at the edge of the hole.

"By Allah," she said to herself as she sat waiting, "I might as well wash myself until he gets back." Down into the water she went, and washed herself, but she could not climb back out. She tried and tried, but she failed.

As it happened, a man on a horse passed by. Hearing the pounding of his horse's hooves, she called out to him:

> "O uncle, riding your horse
> And jingling your bell!
> Say to the mouse,
> 'The Flower of the House
> In the treacherous water fell.'"

The horseman cocked his ear to listen. "Eh!" he thought, "Who is this talking?" Meanwhile, she was saying:

> "O uncle, riding your horse
> And jingling your bell!
> Say to the mouse,
> 'The Flower of the House
> In the treacherous water fell.'"

"And if you don't tell him," she added, "may your bottom get stuck to your horse!"

The rider went his way, and by the time he reached Acre he had forgotten what the cricket had said to him. When he had finished his business in the city, he went home and tried to get down from his horse, but he could not. Again and again he tried, without success. He called his wife and children to help him, and they pushed and pulled, but they failed. Then he remembered what the cricket had bid him do. "Eh!" he

5. Palestinians use the name "Sea of Tiberias" for the Sea of Galilee.

exclaimed, "It seems as if Allah has heard the call of the one who put this spell on me. I might as well go look for the mouse. But how am I ever going to find him?"

He went back to Acre and searched around the shops, asking their owners, "O uncle, did the mouse come in here? O uncle, did the mouse come in here?" The people in the marketplace looked at him in wonder. "What's this?" they asked among themselves, laughing. "Who is this man, riding around looking for a mouse? What's the matter with him? Is he crazy?"

As he was asking about, however, the mouse heard him. The rider, having searched and searched without success, went back home and dismounted easily. He was no longer stuck to his horse.

Now the mouse ran about his business. He stole a piece of meat from the butcher and a bar of soap from the grocer, and he ran back—"tzee, tzee, tzee"—until he arrived. When he discovered his wife had fallen in the water, he went crazy with fear for her. Putting the things he was carrying down on the edge of the hole, he lowered his head into the hole, but he could not reach her. He put his ear in the hole, his paw, then all parts of his body, and still he could not reach her. What was he going to do? He turned his back and dangled his tail in the water.[6] Taking hold of it, she was able to climb out.

"See what you've done!" she started blaming him. "You went away and left me, and I fell into the sea."

"How could I have helped it?" he answered. "Come, make us some *kubbe*[7] and let's have lunch."

She set to it, my little darlings, and prepared the food. They ate lunch, washed themselves and their clothes, and hung them out on the bushes till they were dry. Then they folded their clothes, and—"tzee, tzee, tzee—went home to the mouse's hole.[8]

This is my tale, I've told it, and in your hands I leave it.

6. Because it is impolite to turn one's back on other people, the teller apologizes for the mouse ahead of time ("What was he going to do?"). In other versions of this tale, the mouse dangles his penis in the water. In either case the apology is appropriate.

7. *Kubbe* is a meal consisting of bulgur (*burġul*) that has been soaked in water and mixed with lean ground lamb and diced onions. It may be eaten raw, although more usually it is baked.

8. "The Cricket" is one of the most popular children's tales in Palestine and occurs very frequently in collections of Palestinian folktales. Two versions recorded by Stephan H.

Afterword

This group of tales deals with the marriage relationship, focusing on the newlyweds themselves and the pressures they experience regarding their choice of mate and their sexuality. Because (despite the emphasis on endogamy) none of the couples are cousins but rather are strangers to each other, they must learn to establish patterns of communication and to adapt to each other's needs and observe each other's limits. The tales explore ways in which success may be achieved in marriage, especially in the initial phases of the relationship, immediately following the wedding.

"The Old Woman Ghouleh" shows us some of the confusion a young bride must feel in her new environment. She has had little choice in the matter of her marriage, her role having been passive throughout the whole process, and everyone, including her husband, is a stranger to her. She does not know who is a friend and who is an enemy. In this situation the bride is quite vulnerable, and the tale shows that a marriage can get off to a bad start when she does not immediately place her trust in her husband to protect her from the potential evil around her. When, however, as in the case of the third bride, this trust and the communication that automatically goes with it are present from the beginning of the relationship, the couple can cooperate to overcome obstacles.

In "Lady Tatar," in contrast, the burden of communication is thrown on the husband rather than the wife. Here the husband learns that if he communicates with his wife by treating her as she desires, she is more than willing to cooperate with him and share his life. At the beginning of the tale the lack of communication leads to frustration and multiple marriages; at the end, however, mutual understanding and harmony prevail. This tale also focuses on the bride, who, having been mistreated at home and then adopted by a stranger, is shown to need a good marriage relationship.

Whereas the first two tales in the group focus on the problems facing the women in a marriage relationship, the second two, "Clever Ḥasan" and "Šōqak Bōqak!" shed light on the pressures faced by the men. "Clever Ḥasan" is a composite of two tales that are rarely brought together as here. The first half, the story of Ḥasan and his mother, could have been

---

Stephan are included among the nineteen tales set down in his "Palestinian Animal Stories and Fables"; another version ("Little Beetle") appears in Crowfoot, "Folktales": 165–167.

classified under Group I, "Children and Parents," for, like Šwēš, Šwēš!" it depicts a conflict between mother and son that centers on the mother's sexuality. The second half is usually narrated separately as the adventure story of a young hero who defeats the enemies of his potential father-in-law. By juxtaposing these two disparate tales, using the figure of Clever Ḥasan as a unifying device, the teller spotlights one of the major conflicts a young man faces upon marriage: being caught between his mother and his wife. No less important, the tale also shows a corresponding conflict for the bride: being caught between husband and father. The juxtaposition of the two tales, then, demonstrates that husband and wife can achieve a harmonious relationship only when, through cooperation and by having sufficient strength of character to be independent, they have been able to overcome the negative influence of their parents. In "Šōqak Bōqak!" parental pressure is felt in yet another way. Anxious for their only son to have offspring, the parents urge him to marry before he is ready. His fears about his manhood and what his bride might look like drive him from home, and it then becomes the task of his sexually more mature wife to bring him back.

Of course, the mutual suitability of the partners is essential for a harmonious marriage relationship, and, given the dynamics of the Palestinian social system, the question of mate choice is of utmost importance in the lives of the newlyweds (see also afterword to Group I, "The Quest for the Spouse"). Naturally, both bride and groom have much to worry about when their families choose their mates. Conversely, the family becomes anxious when the children make their own choices. The ideal balance is achieved when the mate selected is suitable to both parties. In this light, the last three tales in the group reveal an interesting pattern. In "Šōqak Bōqak!" the son discovers that the mate chosen by his family is the one he would have chosen for himself, and in "Clever Ḥasan" the father realizes that his daughter's choice of husband is the one he would have made for her. A perfect compromise between individual desire and family requirements is struck in "Cricket," which explores the very dynamics of mate choice. Although the tale does not outwardly conform to the norms of the culture (young maidens simply do not go out looking for husbands, nor would their mothers allow them to), it nevertheless does present the criteria essential for the ideal mate. The daughter's anxiety about finding a husband is moderated by her mother's concern that he be a proper match for her physically, economically, and socially. Thus the daughter chooses the ideal mate, but only on the advice and approval of the mother. Under these conditions, husband and wife solve the problems they encounter in daily life through a combination of mutual affection, cooperation, and proper behavior based on each mate fulfilling her or his culturally prescribed role.

Husbands and Wives

24. *The Seven Leavenings*[1]

TELLER: Testify that God is One!
AUDIENCE: There is no god but God.

There was once in times past an old woman who lived in a hut all by herself. She had no one at all. One day when the weather was beautiful she said, "Ah, yes! By Allah, today it's sunny and beautiful, and I'm going to take the air by the seashore.[2] But let me first knead this dough."

When she had finished kneading the dough, having added the yeast, she put on her best clothes, saying, "By Allah, I just have to go take the air by the seashore." Arriving at the seashore, she sat down to rest, and lo! there was a boat, and it was already filling with people.

"Hey, uncle!" she said to the man, the owner of the boat. "Where in Allah's safekeeping might you be going?"

"By Allah, we're heading for Beirut."

"All right, brother. Take me with you."

"Leave me alone, old woman," he said. "The boat's already full, and there's no place for you."

"Fine," she said. "Go. But if you don't take me with you, may your boat get stuck and sink!"[3]

No one paid her any attention, and they set off. But their boat had not gone twenty meters when it started to sink. "Eh!" they exclaimed, "It looks as if that old woman's curse has been heard." Turning back, they called the old woman over and took her with them.

1. The tale's title probably derives from a cycle of tales revolving around a single theme. Here only two episodes were narrated.

2. The storyteller had the seashore by the city of Acre in mind. For a discussion of the significance of the city of Acre (ʿAkkā) in the history of Palestine, see "Topographical Researches in the Galilee" by Aapeli Saarisalo, which opens thus: "There is hardly any city in Palestine or in the whole world which has seen more history than Acre, Jerusalem perhaps excepted." Cf. Tale 43, n. 8.

3. For a discussion of the curse, see T. Canaan, "The Curse in Palestinian Folklore."

In Beirut, she did not know anybody or anything. It was just before sunset. The passengers went ashore, and she too came down and sat awhile, leaning against a wall. What else could she have done? People were passing by, coming and going, and it was getting very late. In a while a man passed by. Everyone was already at home, and here was this woman sitting against the wall.

"What are you doing here, sister?" he asked.

"By Allah, brother," she answered, "I'm not doing anything. I'm a stranger in town, with no one to turn to. I kneaded my dough and leavened it, and came out for pleasure until it rises, when I'll have to go back."

"Fine," he said. "Come home with me then."

He took her home with him. There was no one there except him and his wife. They brought food, laughed, and played—you should have seen them enjoying themselves. After they had finished, lo! the man brought a bundle of sticks this big and set to it—Where's the side that hurts most?—until he had broken them on his wife's sides.

"Why are you doing this, grandson?"[4] the old woman asked, approaching in order to block his way.

"Get back!" he said. "You don't know what her sin is. Better stay out of the way!" He kept beating his wife until he had broken the whole bundle.[5]

"You poor woman!"[6] exclaimed the old lady when the man had stopped. "What's your sin, you sad one?"

"By Allah," replied the wife, "I've done nothing, and it hadn't even occurred to me. He says it's because I can't get pregnant and have children."[7]

"Is that all?" asked the old woman. "This one's easy. Listen, and let me tell you. Tomorrow, when he comes to beat you, tell him you're pregnant."

4. "Grandson" here (*sittī*) is literally "O Grandmother!"; see Tale 7, n. 3.

5. Although hitting a wife is frowned upon, it is nevertheless accepted and entails no guilt or secretiveness. The behavior described here, however, is highly improbable.

When wife beating does occur, the society usually assumes that the woman is at fault; and in cases of sterility or lack of offspring, it is the woman who seeks treatment. Indeed, if there are no children a man is generally expected to turn against his wife and to seek another. His relatives might encourage him to divorce the first wife, inciting him against her and finding faults with her. A man is more easily forgiven if he hits a wife who does not have children.

6. *Yā xāybe*—literally, "O you who have failed!"

7. Inability to get pregnant and have children is the most common theme in all the folktales in this collection. See Tale 1, n. 3.

The next day, as usual, the husband came home, bringing with him the needed household goods and a bundle of sticks. After dinner, he came to beat his wife, but he had not hit her with the first stick when she cried out, "Hold your hand! I'm pregnant!"

"Is it true?"

"Yes, by Allah!"

From that day on, he stopped beating her. She was pampered, her husband not letting her get up to do any of the housework. Whatever she desired was brought to her side.

Every day after that the wife came to the old woman and said, "What am I going to do, grandmother? What if he should find out?"

"No matter," the old woman would answer. "Sleep easy. The burning coals of evening turn to ashes in the morning." Daily the old woman stuffed the wife's belly with rags to make it look bigger and said, "Just keep on telling him you're pregnant, and leave it to me. The evening's embers are the morning's ashes."[8]

Now, this man happened to be the sultan, and people heard what was said: "The sultan's wife is pregnant! The sultan's wife is pregnant!" When her time to deliver had come, the wife went to the baker and said, "I want you to bake me a doll in the shape of a baby boy."

"All right," he agreed, and baked her a doll which she wrapped and brought home without her husband seeing her. Then people said, "The sultan's wife is in labor, she's ready to deliver." The old woman came forth. "Back in my country, I'm a midwife," she said. "She got pregnant as a result of my efforts, and I should be the one to deliver her. I don't want anyone but me to be around."[9]

"Fine," people agreed. In a while, word went out: "She gave birth! She gave birth!"

"And what did she give birth to?"

"She gave birth to a boy."

Wrapping the doll up, the wife placed it in the crib. People were saying, "She gave birth to a boy!" They went up to the sultan and said she

8. This popular proverb—*jamrit il-lēl bit-ṣabbiḥ ramād*—signifies that passions will cool with the passage of time.

9. The old woman's desire to have no one else at the birth is contrary to the practice in the culture. Granqvist (*Birth:* 58) says, "As many [women] as possible like to come. When . . . related that when she gave birth to her son she had ten women round her all the time, it may have been no exaggeration. If only they have time all the woman neighbors come."

had given birth to a boy.[10] The crier made his rounds, announcing to the townspeople that it was forbidden to eat or drink except at the sultan's house for the next week.[11]

Now, the old woman made it known that no one was permitted to see the baby until seven days had passed. On the seventh day it was announced that the sultan's wife and the baby were going to the public baths.[12] Meanwhile, every day the wife asked the old woman, "What am I going to do, grandmother? What if my husband should find out?" And the old woman would reply, "Rest easy, my dear! The evening's coals are the morning's ashes."

On the seventh day the baths were reserved for the sultan's wife. Taking fresh clothes with them, the women went, accompanied by a servant. The sultan's wife went into the bath, and the women set the servant in front of the doll, saying to her, "Take care of the boy! Watch out that some dog doesn't stray in and snatch him away!"

In a while the servant's attention wandered, and a dog came, grabbed the doll, and ran away with it. After him ran the servant, shouting, "Shame on you! Leave the son of my master alone!" But the dog just kept running, munching on the doll.

It is said that there was a man in that city who was suffering from extreme depression. He had been that way for seven years, and no one could cure him. Now, the moment he saw a dog running with a servant fast behind him shouting, "Leave the son of my master alone!" he started to laugh. And he laughed and laughed till his heartsickness melted away and he was well again. Rushing out, he asked her, "What's your story? I see you running behind a dog who has snatched away a doll, and you're shouting at him to leave the son of your master alone. What's going on?"

"Such and such is the story," she answered.

This man had a sister who had just given birth to twin boys seven days

10. "In Palestine of today, it is the women who announce the birth of a child" (ibid.: 80). See Tale 32, n. 5.

11. See the section entitled "Feast for Boy" in ibid.: 78–80.

12. Granqvist notes that "after the birth the midwife comes every day, morning and evening. For seven days the child is rubbed with oil; salt and oil mixed together" (ibid.: 98) In the section entitled "Child's First Dress and Bath" she notes further that when "he is seven days old they wash him. After seven days and after fifteen days. Then after forty days. [One of her informants] says in the same connection that the seventh day is called 'the day of the bathing,' and adds, 'at his bathing the neighbors are given something to eat'" (p. 101). On the custom of going to the baths, see Tale 25, n. 1.

before. Sending for her, he said, "Sister, won't you put one of your boys at my disposal?"

"Yes," she said, giving him one of her babies.

The sultan's wife took him and went home. People came to congratulate her. How happy she was!

After some time the old woman said, "You know, grandchildren, I think my dough must have risen, and I want to go home and bake the bread."

"Why don't you stay?" they begged her. "You brought blessings with you." I don't know what else they said, but she answered, "No. The land is longing for its people. I want to go home."

They put her on a boat, filling it with gifts, and said, "Go in Allah's safekeeping!"

When she came home, she put her gifts away and rested for a day or two. Then she checked her dough. "Yee, by Allah!" she exclaimed. "My dough hasn't risen yet. I'm going to the seashore for a good time." At the shore she sat for a while, and lo! there was a boat.

"Where are you going, uncle?"

"By Allah, we're going to Aleppo," they answered.[13]

"Take me with you."

"Leave me alone, old woman. The boat's full and there's no room."

"If you don't take me with you, may your boat get stuck and sink in the sea!"

They set out, but in a while the boat was about to sink. They returned and called the old lady over, taking her with them. Being a stranger, where was she to go? She sat down by a wall, with people coming and going until late in the evening. After everybody had gone home for the night, a man passed by.

"What are you doing here?"

"By Allah, I'm a stranger in town. I don't know anyone, and here I am, sitting by this wall."

"Is it right you should be sitting here in the street? Come, get up and go home with me."

Getting up, she went with him. Again, there was only he and his wife. They had no children or anybody else. They ate and enjoyed themselves, and everything was fine, but when time came for sleep he fetched a

13. Aleppo (Ḥalab) is a major city in Northern Syria. It is inland, with no direct access by sea from Acre.

bundle of sticks and beat his wife until he had broken the sticks on her sides. The second day the same thing happened. On the third day the old woman said, "By Allah, I want to find out why this man beats his wife like this." She asked her, and the wife replied, "By Allah, there's nothing the matter with me, except that once my husband brought home a bunch of black grapes. I put them on a bone-white platter and brought them in. 'Yee!' I said, 'How beautiful is the black on the white!' Then he sprang up and said, 'So! May so-and-so of yours be damned! You've been keeping a black slave for a lover behind my back!' I protested that I had only meant the grapes, but he wouldn't believe me. Every day he brings a bundle of sticks and beats me."

"I'll save you," said the old woman. "Go buy some black grapes and put them on a bone-white platter."

In the evening, after he had had his dinner, the wife brought the grapes and served them. The old woman then jumped in and said, "Yee! You see, son. By Allah, there's nothing more beautiful than the black on the white!"

"So!" he exclaimed, shaking his head. "It's not only my wife who says this! You're an old lady and say the same thing.[14] It turns out my wife hasn't done anything, and I've been treating her like this!"

"Don't tell me you've been beating her just for that!" exclaimed the old woman. "What! Have you lost your mind? Look here! Don't you see how beautiful are these black grapes on this white plate?"

It is said they became good friends, and the husband stopped beating his wife. Having stayed with them a few more months, the old woman said, "The land has been longing for its people. Maybe my dough has risen by now. I want to go home."

"Stay, old lady!" they said. "You brought us blessings."

"No," she answered. "I want to go home."

They prepared a boat for her and filled it with food and other provisions. She gathered herself together and went home. There, in her own house, after she had sat down, rested, and put her things away, she checked the dough. "By Allah," she said, "it has just begun to rise, and I might as well take it to the baker." She took it to the baker, who baked her bread.

This is my tale, I've told it, and in your hands I leave it.

14. As noted in the Introduction ("The Tales and Authority in Society"), older women are thought to be asexual; the husband is therefore more ready to believe in his wife's innocence after the old woman confirms her interpretation of "black on white." Cf. Tale 8, n. 5.

25. *The Golden Rod in the Valley of Vermilion*

Once, long ago, there was a merchant. An important merchant. Every Friday the wives of the other merchants came to visit his wife, and they would go out to take the air, enjoying themselves at the public baths and then returning home.[1] Days went and nights came. One day the wives of the merchants came calling on her, and she went out with them. One of them happened to be wearing a beautiful black velvet dress, and the wife of the big merchant liked it very much. Home she went, and how angry she was! Who was that wearing such a dress but the wife of a merchant lesser than her husband, while she herself didn't have one? When her husband came home, he found her scowling.

"What's the matter, dear wife?"

"How could it be that the wife of Merchant So-and-So should wear a dress like that while I go without?"

"Well," he answered, "is it such a big matter?"

He went and cut for her a piece of cloth from the same material, and she had it made into a dress and wore it. She stood in front of the mirror. Now, she was a good-looking woman with fair skin, and the dress was black. She thought she was very beautiful. What did she say?

"Oh! How beautiful is the black on the white!" she exclaimed.[2]

"What!" said her husband. "You so and so! You've taken the black slave for a lover behind my back!"

"No, husband, no!" she answered. "I only meant my black dress."

"I don't believe you. You're in love with the black man."

O black, O white! she tried to reason with him, but it was no use. Taking hold of her, he started beating her. Then he tied her up by her hair to a hook hanging from the ceiling, and every day after that he would bring a bundle of sticks, beat her until he had broken them all on her sides, and then hang her back up.

1. Public baths do not exist in the villages. In the old days well-to-do city folk did not bathe at home but rather went to the public baths. The women would make a picnic out of the trip; they took food and musical instruments with them and would dance and sing and generally enjoy themselves. Cf. the trip to the public bath in Tale 24; see also Jaussen, *Naplouse:* 67–69.

2. In many regions of Palestine women's dress, before embroidery has been added, is black. Because velvet is considered one of the most luxurious of cloths and whiteness of skin a mark of beauty (cf. Tale 13, n. 2), it is understandable why the merchant's wife would find herself attractive. The sequence of events here is similar to that in the second episode of Tale 24.

On Friday, at the appointed hour, the wives of the merchants came to visit her. Entering, they called to her, and her servant came out to receive them. "She's bathing," said the servant. "Wait awhile." Later she said, "She's getting dressed, she's putting on makeup, she's decorating her eyelids with kohl"—and so on.

"But the day's nearly gone!" they murmured. "Let's go in and see what's going on." Her servant started to cry, but she let them in, and behold! their friend was hanging from the ceiling. Untying her, they sat her down. "What happened?" they asked. "What's the story?"

"Such and such is what happened," she said, relating her story.

Now, every day, while her husband was beating her, he would ask, "Is there anyone richer than me?"

"No."

"Is there anyone handsomer than me?"

"No."

"Is there anyone more manly than me?"

"No."

Whatever he asked, she always answered, "No." When she told her friends that her husband asked her these questions every day, one of them—a sly one—said, "Why don't you say to him, 'Yes, there is,' and if he asks who, tell him, 'The Golden Rod in the Valley of Vermilion.' He'll go looking and will be away a month or two. Meanwhile, you'll take a rest from all this beating until he comes back. And when he does come back, Allah will take care of it." Tying her up again, they left.

When he came home in the evening, he set about beating her.

"Is there anyone richer than me? More handsome than me?"

"Yes, there is."

"Who?"

"The Golden Rod in the Valley of Vermilion."

"By Allah," he swore, leaving her untied, "I'm going to have to go look for him. If I really do find him, then Allah will have forgiven you; but if I don't find him richer, handsomer, and more manly than me, may the Lord help you!"

Leaving her, he turned around and headed straight out. He traveled the first day, the second, and the third. Then on his way he was surprised to see a creature on the road. She was half bitch and half human. He asked her about the Golden Rod and she said, "Straight ahead!" Moving on, he met another creature, half fish and half human. He asked her, and she too said, "Straight ahead!" He went on until he reached a city, where he asked and people gave him directions. When he had got the directions, he went to the Golden Rod's house.

"Welcome! Welcome!" the Golden Rod received the merchant. "So, you've finally come!"

"Yes, I've come."

"You've accused your wife falsely," he said. "Your wife didn't do anything wrong. She did in fact have her dress in mind, but you accused her of [loving] the black slave and have come here to see if there's anyone richer, handsomer, or more manly than you. Isn't it so? Well, listen and let me tell you my story."

"Tell it to me," said the merchant.

"Allah knows," began the Golden Rod, "I too was once a married man. The first wife I had was my cousin. She used to bring me a cup every evening, and after I drank it I would roll over, not feeling a thing. 'By Allah,' I said to myself one day, 'this cup she gives me—I'm going to dump it down my collar and turn over as if drunk, then I'll see what she's up to.'

"She brought me the cup, and I did like this, spilling it down my neck, then I rolled over. No sooner did she see me in that condition than she went straight to the kitchen, ladled food onto a platter, and carried it, along with a pitcher full of water and a lantern, out of the house.

"I followed her, keeping well behind. By Allah, I followed her, and she kept moving till she reached a cave. She went into the cave, and lo! there was a black slave. No sooner did she go in than he set to abusing her. 'Damn your father and your mother!' he cursed. 'You've taken so long, I'm nearly dying from hunger.'

"'Well, I had to wait until I'd put him to sleep, until I'd finished my house work . . .'

"So, she served him the food and he ate.[3] When he had finished eating and drinking, she asked, 'What do you have for me to eat and drink?' He said there was a scrap of moldy bread and a bit of wormy smoked fish. She took them and ate, and then she embraced him and slept by his side. I stayed outside till they had gone to sleep. When they were fast asleep, I came in to them, cut off his nose, wrapped it in a handkerchief, and left. Waking up, she nudged him like this and found him dead. She rent her dress, beat her breast, and then headed home.[4] Waiting until she had gone

3. On the association of food with love and courtship, cf. Tale 15, n. 3.

4. For a discussion of dress, see Tale 12, n. 3. Granqvist gives the following description of the "demonstration of grief": "As soon as the last breath is drawn, the women present

ahead, I followed her, keeping well behind, but when we were close to home I struck out on a different path and got here ahead of her. I went back to bed and pretended to be fast asleep, just as I was before she went out. She came in, made her bed, wrapped a bandage around her head and fell asleep.[5] When I woke up in the morning, I saw that she had bandaged her head.

"'What's the matter, dear wife?' I asked.

"'I just got news my cousin's dead,' she answered.

"'And how long are you going to mourn for him?'[6]

"'A whole year,' she said.

"'No!' I objected. 'Four months will be enough.'

"She mourned four months," continued the Golden Rod, "and when she came out of mourning she said she wanted to go to the baths. I brought her a bouquet of flowers, perfumes, and toilet articles.[7] You should have seen the basket! It was full to the brim, except that I had put her cousin's nose among the articles. Taking the basket with her, she went to the baths, bathed, and came back home. She stood in front of the mirror to put on makeup and adorn herself, and, as she was searching among the things in the basket, her lover's nose came into her hand. She sprang up in anger, wanting to tear me to pieces.

"'Stop where you are!' I commanded. 'Let half of you stay human, and the other half turn bitch!'

"Tell me, merchant, did she or didn't she meet you on the way? And your poor wife who had meant only her new dress—what wrong did she do?

"Now," continued the Golden Rod, "having put a spell on her, I left her to guard such and such a place. Then I asked for the hand of my other

---

give vent to unrestrained sorrow. Each time a new woman enters, she beats her breast. . . . The women loosen their hair and tear at it. . . . Women tear their dresses. They blacken their faces and their hands with soot, and sometimes they even put dust and ashes on their heads" (*Muslim Death:* 53). Cf. Tale 12, n. 9.

5. Women, but not men, wrap a bandage around their heads when ill.

6. "The wife of a man who has died mourns for a year. The mourning consists in the following: not to wash her head kerchief, not to bathe, not to make herself beautiful, not to wear her best clothes, colored clothes, and not to blacken her eyes. . . . Ḥamdiye: 'According to [religious] law, the period of mourning is forty days, but the dead man's wife may mourn for a year, his sister for a year, and his mother all her life, if she wishes to do so" (Granqvist, *Muslim Death:* 107).

7. This is an accurate description of the preparations for going to the baths. Toiletries, towels, and a change of clothes were put in baskets, which were carried by the servants. Cf. Tale 24.

cousin and married her. Before long she, too, started to do the same thing as the other one. One day I spilled the cup and pretended to be drunk, while she went straight to the kitchen, ladled the food, and headed out. I followed her from a distance, and she too came to a cave, where a black slave shouted at her the same things. Then they ate, embraced, and slept. Waiting until they were fast asleep, I went in to them and cut out his tongue. He died. When she came to bid him good-bye, she found him dead. She beat her breast until she had had enough; then, pulling herself together, she left. No sooner did she leave than I followed, taking a different path when we were close to home. Having gotten there before her, I went to sleep. In the morning she had a bandage around her head.

"'What's the matter, dear wife?'

"'By Allah, I just got news my cousin's dead.'

"'How long are you going to mourn for him?'

"'I want to mourn six months,' she said.

"'No,' I said. 'Four's enough.'

"Four months she mourned, and when her mourning was over I brought her a bouquet like the other one and all the other things, putting them in a basket, her cousin's tongue among them. She went to the baths, and when she came home she stood in front of the mirror to beautify herself, and her cousin's tongue came into her hand. She rushed at me, screaming and wanting to tear me up.

"'Stop where you are!' I commanded. 'Half of you is human, let the other half turn fish!'

"I left her under a spell in such and such a place. Tell me, did she or didn't she meet you on the way?"

"Yes," the merchant answered. "She did."

"And your wife," asked the Golden Rod, "whose mind was only on her dress, what did she do?

"Anyway," he continued, "I asked for the hand of my third cousin and married her. Before long she, too, started to behave like the others. I did the same thing, spilling the cup down my collar and rolling over. When she saw me in that condition, she opened the wardrobe and took out a copy of the Qurʾān. Putting it under her arm, she took a candle with her and set out. I followed, walking behind her. She walked till she was out of the city and had come to the seashore.

"'Open up, O sea!' she called out. 'Let the lover see his beloved!'

"With the power of the Almighty," he said, "the sea parted and she walked in.

"'For you and for the one with you,' said the sea in parting. Not realizing she was being followed, she thought the Qurʾān was intended. I went in right behind her. When she came to an arched doorway, she said, 'Open, arched door! Let the lover see his beloved!'

"'For you and for the one with you?' he asked.

"'For me and the one with me,' she answered.

"Coming into a room she knocked on a door. He opened, and behold! he was a youth—handsome like a sweet basil plant.

"'Welcome, welcome!' he said. 'Did you finally get here, sister?'

"'By Allah,' she answered. 'Yes, I did.'

"'And what kept you so long?'

"'You know,' she answered, 'a woman's destiny's not in her own hands.'

"By Allah, she went inside with him. Setting the Qurʾān down, they read until they had their fill. Then they talked, and he put the sword between him and her. They lay down and went to sleep.

"'By Allah,' I said to myself, 'he didn't do anything, and she didn't do anything. So, I'm going to bring back for her a small token that would cause him no harm.'

"Waiting until they were asleep, I went inside. Since he had long hair, I approached and cut a small lock from the top of his head and tied it up in a handkerchief. As fate would have it, his soul was in that lock of hair, and he died.[8] When she woke up, she wanted to bid farewell to her brother. 'Brother, brother!' she called out, but she found him dead. She beat her breast, tore her clothes, and left, taking the candle and the Qurʾān with her.

"I stood aside until she had passed, then followed her.

"'Open, arched door!' she said, when she reached it. 'The lover will see his beloved no more!'

"When she reached the sea, the same thing took place. Once we were past the sea and had arrived in the city, I struck out on a different path and got home before her. I went to sleep just as she had left me. Meanwhile, she came in, wrapped a bandage around her head, lay down, and went to

8. For hair as a source of strength, see afterword to Group I, "The Quest for the Spouse"; for other references, see Footnote Index, s.v. "Hair."

We cannot help observing the sexually oriented symbolic reference not only in the name of the tale and its hero, but also in the three items he removes from his wives' lovers (nose, tongue, and lock of hair)—all lend themselves comfortably to psychoanalytic interpretation.

sleep. When I woke up in the morning, I found she'd put a bandage around her head.

"'What's the matter, dear wife?' I asked.

"'By Allah, I just got news my brother's dead.'

"'And how long are you going to mourn for him?'

"'I want to mourn six months,' she answered.

"'No,' I said. 'A year.'

"She mourned a year, and when she was out of mourning she did the same as the others had done, going to the baths and coming back to put on her best and make herself up. When she found the lock of hair among the toilet articles, she sprang up. She wanted to tear me into pieces. 'Stop where you are,' I commanded, 'and turn into a cat!' And here she is! You see her always sitting in my lap. And your poor wife—what wrong did she do? Her mind was only on the dress. As for me, I'm not going to marry another one. It's all over."

When the Golden Rod had finished his story, the merchant regretted how he had treated his wife. He was now anxious to go home and was about to excuse himself and leave, when his host said, "Wait a moment. I'm going to give you a present for your wife. She's a good woman and worthy of respect, and her mind was only on her dress."

The merchant went home very happy. He was now eager to please his wife. As soon as he reached his town, he went to his house. "Dear wife," he said, "I did you wrong. By Allah, he's richer and better than me in all respects. And here, he's sent you a present with me." Pulling out the present, he gave it to her, then went and sat down some distance away from her. She opened the package to see what kind of present it was and found a mirror in it. No sooner did she look in the mirror than she disappeared. The Golden Rod had snatched her away and married her.

This is my tale, I've told it, and in your hands I leave it.

26. *Minjal*

Once upon a time there was a woman. She had for a neighbor a charming rogue who knew how to enjoy life. "By Allah," said he one day, "I'm going to play a trick on her and take away one of the family's yoke of oxen." Waiting until the husband had gone to the fields to plow (they had another team of oxen which he did not take with him) the neighbor disguised himself and called out, "Ho! I have names for sale! Who wants a beautiful name? I sell names!" The woman was baking bread outdoors in her clay oven.[1] "Hey, uncle!" she cried out, "Come, come! Let me see! What are you selling?"

"I sell names," he answered. "What's your name, uncle?[2] Let me see if it's beautiful or not."

"By Allah," she replied, "my name's Minjal."[3]

"What!" exclaimed the salesman. "What's this Minjal? Is that a name fit for a woman? Why, that's nothing more than a piece of iron. Are you crazy enough to accept a name like that?"

"Very well, uncle," declared the woman. "Come, sell me a name. How much does one cost?"

"By Allah, cousin," he replied, "a beautiful name—I'll sell it to you for a yoke of oxen."

"Fine," she agreed. "Come, let me see what kind of a name you're going to sell me."

"By Allah," he said. "I'm going to call you, 'Mistress of All and Flower of the House.' Go in and take a bath. Then wear some nice clothes, pile up whatever mattresses you have, and make a bridal seat for yourself. Lock the door and sit on the mattresses. If your husband should come to the door, calling, 'Hey, Minjal! Hey, Minjal!' don't pay him any attention, even if he stands out there all day. Not until he calls you, 'Mistress of All and Flower of the House.'"[4]

"Fine, uncle," she said. "May Allah reward you! What do you want for payment?"

"I want that team of oxen."

1. The "clay oven" (*ṭābūn*) is a small structure housing an earthen oven used for baking bread and for some cooking. Villagers usually build the oven at some distance from their living quarters in order to avoid its smoke, most commonly at the edge of the road closest to the house. The *ṭābūn* is a circular structure a yard high and with a diameter of about a yard; its smooth clay walls house two compartments, the lower for the fire and the upper (usually lined with pebbles over a metal sheet) for baking the bread. See Tale 6, n. 8; Tale 39, nn. 3, 4.

2. She addresses him as "uncle" (see Tale 14, n. 7), and he returns the same form of address. Had he initiated the dialogue, he would have addressed her as "sister" (*yaxtī*) if they were of the same age or as "maternal aunt" (*xāltī*) if she were older.

3. *Minjal* means "scythe" or "sickle" in Arabic. It is not used as a girl's name in Palestine.

4. *Sitt il-kul u-zēnt id-dār*—literally, "Mistress of All and the Beautiful One of the House." Like "Minjal," this name is not ordinarily used. Here, combined with changing clothes, bathing, and acting like a bride, the new name is a harbinger of the new relationship to be established between the wife and her husband.

"Go ahead and untie it," she agreed.

The salesman went ahead, untied the oxen, and took them. The woman then went in, combed her hair, put on her best clothes, and if they had a couple of old mattresses she piled them up and sat on them like a bride. Locking the door from the inside with the key, she sat waiting on the bridal seat.[5]

It was raining, and her husband was plowing.[6] It had rained on him and on the team. Poor man! He came home from the field dripping with water. Knocking on the door, he called out, "Minjal! Minjal!" No answer. He pounded on the door and banged against it shouting, "O Minjal! O Minjal!" until he was exhausted. Meanwhile, his wife was sitting inside, feeling frustrated.

"You can say 'Minjal' till you rot!"[7] she finally said. "I've bought a new name."

"Who did you buy it from?"

"From a traveling salesman."

"And how much did he sell it to you for?"

"I paid with the team of oxen."

"What is this name that you've bought?" he asked.

"My name is now Mistress of All and Flower of the House," she answered.

"By Allah, O Mistress of All and Flower of the House," he swore, "I don't even want to go into the house you're in. If I find others as crazy as you, I'll be back. But if I can't find anyone so crazy, I'm not coming back. You can keep your name, and you can keep the house." Leaving the team in the lower part of the house,[8] the man then turned and left.

5. For the bridal seat, or *maṣmade,* see Tale 11, n. 4.

6. "The plough," says Frances Newton, "is a very simple wooden affair with one handle. The ploughing season begins with the 'early rains,' due about the middle of October. The peasant takes his plough down . . . [and] sharpens the triangular iron share in the blacksmith's forge. He makes any repairs to the wooden part, and the yoke, that may be necessary. Then, driving the pair of oxen before him, and riding on a donkey with the plough, he sets off for the 'field' or portion of the village lands allotted to him. These communal lands are apportioned by the drawing of lots each year at the beginning of the ploughing season" (*Fifty Years:* 39).

7. *Y-manjil ḥālak u-yijdib bālak*—literally, "May you be scythed and your attention scattered!"

8. The "lower part of the house" is *qāᶜ il-bēt.* Traditional Palestinian village homes usually consisted of one large room with a two-level floor, two-thirds of it being higher than the other third. "This larger portion is called the 'Mastaba,' and is occupied by the human

It was pouring rain. He went, you might say, to the cemetery of the Christians[9] and took shelter by the side of a big rock. Taking off his clothes, he sat under this rock by the cemetery of the Christians. In the morning some Christian women came to visit. One like Ḥanne—her children died in their youth; another, like Badīʿa—her brother died a young man.[10] This one had lost a son, that one a daughter, and another a father or a mother. Anyway, they came to visit the graves and found this naked man.

"Brrr!" he shivered. "Allah protect you, sisters! Please give me something to cover my nakedness."

"What sort of creature are you, uncle?" they asked.

"I came back from the grave," he answered, "and I'm bringing good news. The dwellers of these graves are all going to be coming back home, and they're all naked. Go bring some clothes, and tomorrow you'll find your loved ones here. They're all going to be coming back."

"By Allah, is it true what you're saying, uncle?"

"Yes, it's true."

The women went running back to their houses. She who had lost a daughter brought her her jewelry, and she who had lost a young son brought him his suits. Oh! What clothes they were! Each one had prepared a bundle. You should have seen what these Christian women brought together—the bundles and the jewelry! They went and gave it all to the man in the cemetery.

"When will the dead be coming back, uncle?" they asked.

---

element of the family. The lower half is used for the non-human element. Cows and camels, horses, donkeys, cocks and hens, even pigeons, are all part of the family, and are housed under the one roof. . . . Along the edge of the raised part of the floor a line of shallow depressions, or mud troughs, form the mangers for the cattle standing on the lower level. This does not result in any unpleasant conditions for the household, as the lower part is swept daily, and in most cases is kept spotlessly clean. The animals are all turned out to pasture or to work, during the day" (Newton, *Fifty Years:* 33). See Tale 3, n. 6; Tale 15, n. 5; and Canaan, "Palestinian Arab House," esp. XIII: 33–39 ("House of the Peasant"). See also Jäger, *Das Bauernhaus in Palästina*.

9. There actually is a small Christian community in the village of ʿArrābe, in the Galilee, where this tale was collected. Perhaps the storyteller is hinting that the character in the tale might have gotten away with tricking just the small Christian group but not the whole village community.

10. Ḥanne and Badīʿa are women in the village's Christian community; the men mentioned below (Šiblī, Xalīl, and Ṣāliḥ) are related to these women, as husbands, sons, or brothers.

"Come back tomorrow at this time," he answered, "and you'll find them dressed and waiting for you. But take care not to talk in front of anyone about this! Come by yourselves, because only the Christians will be coming back."

After the women had gone home, he took the bundles, tied them together, and ran away. The next morning the Christian women came back to the graveyard—nothing had changed. "Yee!" they cried out, "By Allah, that man must have tricked us." Back home they rushed and told their men what had happened. He who had a donkey or a nag mounted it and set out. Šiblī, Xalīl, Ṣāliḥ—whoever had lost a bundle of clothes mounted his animal and set out to search for the man. Meanwhile, he had found a place, a cave, where he deposited the big bundle and left. As they were searching, they came by him.

"O uncle," they asked, "didn't you happen to see a man with such and such a description carrying some bundles?"

"Yes, uncles," he answered, "he just passed this way. But on your animals, you can't follow him since it's so muddy. Better take off your shoes and leave your animals here. You'll catch up with him in a moment."

"Is that true, uncle?" they asked.

"Yes, it's true."

Dropping their shoes from their feet, they left the animals behind. "Leave them with me," he reassured them. "I'll take care of them." But no sooner did they turn their backs than he gathered the shoes and sandals, tied the animals together, and, dragging them behind him, set off. The men ran and ran till they were tired. They could barely breathe, but, not finding anyone, they came back. And see! Where was he? He was already far away. Pulling themselves together, they went home.

The man, you might say, left his town behind and traveled until he came to a village like Il-Iᶜzēr, Rummāne, and Id-Dēr, where the farmland is below the village.[11] As he approached he saw a farmer plowing. Waiting until he was even with him, he said out loud, talking to the nag he was riding, "Easy! Easy! May Allah damn your owner's father! If someone were to offer me a meal, even if it's nothing more than lentil soup, I'd give you to him in exchange."[12]

11. Il-Iᶜzēr, Rummāne, and Id-Dēr (Dēr Ḥannā) are all villages in the upper Galilee, north of Nazareth, close to ᶜArrābe, and fit the description of the setting in the story—that is, a hillside village with agricultural lands in a valley at the foot of the hill. Cf. Tale 17, n. 7; Tale 44, n. 11.

12. By asking for lentil soup, the man makes the deal more appealing to the farmer.

When the farmer heard this, he cried, "O uncle, what did I just hear you say?"

"By Allah," answered the other, "I was just saying that if anyone were to offer me a meal of lentil soup I'd give him this horse in exchange."

"Wait, wait, uncle!" shouted the farmer, "I'll bring you something in a moment."

Off he went, running to his wife. "Come, come!" he said, "Right away, boil some water and make a little lentil soup."

"What's the story, my man?" she asked.

"You won't believe this," he replied, "but we're getting a draft horse for a dish of lentil soup."

She went ahead, ground some lentils, and placed the water over the fire.

"Prepare a feeding trough, woman," he said.[13] "Plant a stake here, and tie one end of a rope to it and the other end to my foot, and let me check if there's enough room for people to pass behind the horse without getting kicked."

When she had prepared the trough, driven in the stake, and tied the rope to his foot, he said, "Pass behind me, wife, and let me see if the nag could reach you if you passed behind her and she kicked." Turning around, she walked behind him. He kicked, throwing her down. And lo! blood all over and she had miscarried. "Die and to hell with you! Right now I want to go after the blue nag, which is more valuable to me than anything. And when I come back, I'll deal with the situation here."

Meanwhile, by the time they had prepared the feeding trough and the soup and had tested how she would pass behind the horse—by that time the other man had untied the farmer's yoked team and (begging the listeners' pardon!), having crapped on the tip of the ox goad, stuck it in the ground and made off with the animals. Coming back down, our brother in Allah did not find the horse, his own team, or anything else. And when he saw the goad, he said, "By Allah, this man has tricked me. And even if my wife has miscarried, what bothers me most, by Allah, is how he could have managed to climb up the goad and shit. How could he have

Because Palestinian fellahin usually produce and store a year's supply of lentils, they are always available and soup can be easily and quickly prepared. Cf. Tale 36, n. 8; Tale 44, n. 14.

13. The feeding troughs are located on the raised part of the floor of the house. Some homes were designed such that people coming into the house had to walk between the animals to get to the *masṭaba*. See n. 8, above, where reference is made to "mud troughs."

done it? How could he possibly have sat on the tip of the goad and shat?"[14]

Having collected the Christian women's clothes, the horses, and the draft animals, the man came back home, only to find his wife still sitting like a new bride on the piled-up mattresses. "O Mistress of All and Flower of the House!" he cried out. "By Allah, many other crazy people like you have I found." And he lived with her, accepting her with her faults.

This is my tale, I've told it, and in your hands I leave it.

27. *Im ʿĒše*

TELLER: Testify that God is One!
AUDIENCE: There is no god but God.

Once there was a man, and he had a daughter. He and his wife had no other children except this daughter, and her name was ʿĒše. One day people from another town came to ask for ʿĒše's hand. They asked for her hand, took her for a bride, and departed.

The days passed. ʿĒše became pregnant and gave birth; she had a boy.

"Abū ʿĒše!"[1] said the mother.

"Yes. What do you want?" he replied.

"Our daughter has given birth to a boy," she answered, "and we ought to go visit her. What are we going to take her?"[2]

They took her a bolt of cloth, they took her a pitcher of oil.

Later the mother said, "O Abū ʿĒše! We want to take ʿĒše a sheep, maybe a ewe."

They traveled and came upon a shepherd with some ewes.

"O uncle!" Abū ʿĒše said to him, "We ask in Allah's name that you sell

14. It should be noted that the ox goad has a nail sticking out of its tip.

1. Customarily, husbands and wives do not call each other by their first names (cf. Tale 20, n. 12). Until the birth of their first child, the newly married couple call each other "cousin"; thereafter they address each other, and are addressed by others, as "Abū . . ." ("Father of . . .") and "Im . . ." ("Mother of . . ."). A man is generally named after a son, even if he has many daughters and no sons. Thus Abū ʿĒše's name prefigures his emasculation later in the tale (see n. 6, below). ʿĒše is a common girl's name in Palestinian and Arab society.

2. It is a social imperative to visit a daughter who has given birth, especially if she is married outside the village and it is her first child, and particularly if it is a son. The parents bring presents, usually consisting of clothes for the baby and nourishing food for the mother.

us a ewe good for slaughter. But it has to be a good one; fat must be dripping from its nose."[3]

The shepherd brought out the first ewe, but Im ʿĒše said to him, "No! We want the fat to be dripping from its nose!" He went and brought back a ewe with snot dripping from its nose—and what a state she was in! She was tottering. And there was Im ʿĒše saying, "Yes. This is the one we want."

"That's fine," said the shepherd.

They took their ewe and walked on. As they approached ʿĒše's town, they looked and, behold! the surface of the earth was cracked. The ground had cracks in it.

"Abū ʿĒše!" the mother called out.

"Yes."

"By Allah, this land of ʿĒše's is thirsty. Let's pour out the pitcher of oil and water it." They poured it out.

Before they arrived, look! there was a tree shaking like this in the wind.

"Abū ʿĒše!"

"Yes."

"By Allah, this olive tree of ʿĒše's is shivering from the cold. Let's wrap this cloth around it." They wrapped it around.

When they came close to town, they found a watchdog whining.

"Abū ʿĒše!"

"Yes."

"By Allah, this dog of ʿĒše's is hungry. Let's feed him these provisions." They fed him what they had brought.

They arrived, came in, and she said to her daughter, "By Allah, daughter,[4] we brought you oil, cloth, and meat. But we found your land thirsty and watered it with the oil; we found your olive tree cold and wrapped it with the cloth; and we found your bitch hungry and fed her the meat."

"Never mind, mother!" ʿĒše said. "But take care not to tell anyone! Those who ask you, tell them 'we brought what we brought,' and don't let anyone know what you did!"

In two or three days Im ʿĒše said to her husband, "You go home, Abū ʿĒše, look after the chickens and the house, and I'll stay a few more days to help ʿĒše, since she's an only child and now has a baby."

After the father had left for home, ʿĒše said to her mother, "Mother,

3. Generally, the fatter the meat, the more nourishing and the tastier it is thought to be.

4. "Daughter" here (*yammā*) is literally "O mother!"; see Tale 7, n. 3.

you stay with the baby and look after him, and let me go out and gather a few pieces of wood." She left the baby with her mother and went to the countryside in search of wood.

The baby started crying. "Poor boy!" thought Im ʿĒše. "By Allah, maybe his head's itching from lice." She went and heated water in a cauldron until it boiled. She then dropped the baby in it, lifted him out, and put him back to bed.

When ʿĒše came home, her mother said, "You see, your son was crying from the lice and the dirt. Here I've washed him and put him to sleep, and from the time I put him in bed he's had his head down and he's been sleeping."

ʿĒše waited. Now the baby will wake up. In a little while he'll wake up. She went to check on the boy and found him dead.

"O you daughter of a cursed father!" she said. "This baby's dead! Soon my husband will be coming home from Hebron, and he'll kill you. You had better go home!"

Im ʿĒše went home, and found that her husband had locked himself in.

"O Abū ʿĒše! Open!"

"No. You'll kill me!"

"Open!"

"No. You'll kill me!"

"What did you do?"

"I slaughtered the chickens."

"That's all right! Open up!"

"I spilled the jar of oil."

"To hell with it! Just open!"

"No. You'll kill me!"

"What did you do?"

"I said to the cow, 'Give me some food!' but she wouldn't. So I slaughtered her."

"Let it be a sacrifice! You're worth everything. Just open!"

"You'll slaughter me!"

"Why? What did you do?"

"The camel was chewing his cud. I said to him, 'Give me some food!' but he wouldn't. He came at me, and I covered my pecker with a cauliflower leaf. He goes and bites me, eats the leaf, and eats my pecker too!"[5]

5. "Pecker" here is *zuburtī*, the feminine form of the more common *zubrī*. The use of the feminine form—or, in effect, the diminutive, as if to say "my little pecker"—is actually part of the overall gender pattern of the tale: we note, for example, that the tale is named

"Alas! Alas!" cried Im ʿĒše. "Nothing in the world mattered like your balls, and now you're a gelding!"[6]

The bird of this tale has flown—and a good evening to all!

Afterword

The issues addressed in these tales can touch on any established marriage relationship. We find sexuality, which was a central theme in the "Brides and Bridegrooms" group, a vital issue here as well. It is clearly articulated in the last tale, "Im ʿĒše," in which the couple are willing to tolerate each other's mutual follies and even the loss of their material possessions. The one loss the marriage cannot sustain, that of the husband's virility, poses a problem for both husband and wife. For the husband it represents a source of anxiety and fear about himself. We have already come across this anxiety in "Šōqak Bōqak!" (Tale 21), where the young man, married before he is ready, runs away in fear and must be seduced back by his more mature wife. Here we see it again in the second half of "The Seven Leavenings" and in "The Golden Rod in the Valley of Vermilion," where the husband asks, "Is there anyone handsomer than me? . . . more manly than me?"

With regard to what these tales reveal about sexuality, we find that the attitudes applicable to women are different from those applicable to men. Cultural practice dictates that women should be modest and not express their sexuality openly, yet women are not presented as being anxious about their sexuality. On the contrary, as we saw from earlier tales (e.g., "Šahīn" and "Šōqak Bōqak!") and from "Im ʿĒše" here, they are open in their approach to this question and honest in their feelings. The dark side of sexuality emerges from "The Seven Leavenings" and "The Golden Rod," where the men's fear or anxiety about their virility is projected as the women's sexual voraciousness, as we see from the behavior of the Golden Rod's three wives. This projection is condoned by the society. If the husband is sexually unsure of himself, the wife is assumed to be at

after ʿĒše's mother and not her father; that the parents take their daughter a ewe (for which two separate words of feminine gender—*šā* and *naʿje*—are used); that the dog they encounter is a bitch (*kalbe*); and that ʿĒše loses her son and Abū ʿĒše his masculinity.

6. *Kul šī fdāk, fdāk, ġēr bezātak w-ixṣāk*—literally, "Let everything be a sacrifice, a sacrifice, except your testicles and your emasculation!"

fault; she must, as in "The Seven Leavenings" and "The Golden Rod," be having an affair with the black servant. (It is interesting that the literalized metaphor of "black on white" is used as a central image in both tales.)

Equally as important as sexuality in a marriage relationship, and integral to it, is the question of offspring. A complex of problems for men and women alike arises out of the association of sexuality with virility and fertility. A man feels more manly and powerful when he has fathered many children, particularly sons, and society confirms this feeling by offering repeated congratulations and favorable comments on his manliness. The absence of male offspring makes a man vulnerable to social criticism, and he would be urged to marry another woman. Feeling inadequate when the marriage is infertile, he starts to question his manliness and vents his frustration by beating his wife ("The Seven Leavenings"). Lack of offspring is even more problematic for the woman. If for the husband male children represent manliness and virility, for the wife they are an essential part of her identity; indeed, a woman without a son has practically no identity, and no security in life. "The Seven Leavenings" is a case in point: before pregnancy the wife is guilty of a great sin, but once she claims to have conceived, her husband dotes on her and treats her with utmost respect.

Although it is mentioned explicitly only in "The Seven Leavenings," absence of offspring (of sons in "Im ʿĒše") is at the core of the couple's problem in each of these tales. This point is made clearly in the case of Minjal, who, alone among all the married women in the tales, is called by her first name—a name that denotes an ordinary tool—rather than "Im So-and-So." As her clever neighbor says of her name, "What! That's nothing more than a piece of iron!" In the other tales as well, there is a certain degree of tension between husband and wife. With time on their hands and no children, the males become dissatisfied with their wives and start finding fault with them.

The tales in this group focus on the relationship between husband and wife at a certain stage in the marriage. Several open with a stagnating relationship, often caused by the absence of children, and end with a transformation. Fulfillment may be brought about through children ("The Seven Leavenings"), by finding the right partner ("The Golden Rod"), or by a change in character. "Minjal" is a pivotal tale, in this respect, for it shows the possibility of renewal. In "Minjal"—as in "Lady Tatar" (Tale 20), but at a later date in the marriage relationship—the woman insists on being addressed in a certain way, thereby guaranteeing respect for herself. But now two marriage relationships are portrayed: the one between Minjal and her husband, the second between the gulled farmer and his wife. The contrast between the two women could not be any clearer. In the second relationship the teller emphasizes the greed and cruelty of the husband, whose wife, though pregnant, is less important to him than a workhorse—merely another useful tool, though admittedly more precious than a scythe.

Family Life

28. *Chick Eggs*

TELLER: Once upon a time, O my listeners . . . but not until you bear witness that God is One.
AUDIENCE: There is no god but God!

Once there was a girl, the daughter of a co-wife.[1] And, as everybody knows, a co-wife's daughter usually turns out meaner than her own mother. Her stepmother hated her, always saying to her "Come here" and "Go there" and giving her endless work to do.

The stepmother had a daughter of her own about the same age. One day she said to her mother, "Mother, I want to go to the countryside with my sister to gather wood." "Go ahead," said the mother.

After the girls had left, lo! a salesman was crying his wares:

"Chick eggs, chick eggs for sale!
Will get a girl pregnant without a male!"

Now, the woman had been wanting to do away with her co-wife's daughter. She called the salesman over, bought two eggs from him, and cracked them in a pan. For her own daughter she fried two ordinary eggs in a separate pan. When the girl came from gathering wood, her stepmother fed her the chick eggs.

A day came and a day went, and the girl was sitting in the sun. The woman said to her, "O girl, come remove lice from my hair." The girl kept shifting her position and wriggling like this from the heat.[2] One moment she'd say, "O my father's wife, I want to move into the shade," and the next moment she'd say, "O my father's wife, I want to move back into the sun."

1. The entire tale is told from the point of view of the stepmother; hence the "good" girl in the tale is initially seen as "mean"—meaner than her own mother. Even though the first wife is presumably dead, from the perspective of the second wife her undesirable influence in the house is still felt through her daughter.

2. Sensitivity to heat is a sign that a woman is pregnant.

The woman went to her husband. "Look here, my man!" she said. "Your daughter's pregnant."

"Speak again," he exclaimed, "and say it's not so!"

"No, by Allah," replied the wife, "she's pregnant. And if she isn't, you can have whatever you want."

A day went and a day came, and the girl's pregnancy began to show. The woman said to her husband, "O man, get rid of her!"[3]

"I will," he answered. "Prepare some provisions, and I'll take her and do away with her."

The wife brought together a cow pie (she said it was bread), a donkey turd (she said it was stuffed cabbage), and ass's urine (she said it was ghee). She put these things for her in a basket and waited.

The man took his daughter to a place where there was no one coming or going, then said, "Daughter, wait for me here! I'm going for a walk and I'll be right back."

The sun set and it was getting dark. The place was rough, rocks everywhere! with no one coming or going. What was she to do? She said:

"Father, you're taking so long to crap
The thyme has started to sprout!"[4]

In a while, look! an old man on a white mare was approaching.

"O girl," he said, "what are you doing here?"

"It's my fate," she answered. "I came here."

"And what are these things you're carrying?"

She answered, "This is bread," and he said, "May it be so, God willing!"[5]

"This is stuffed cabbage."

3. The society generally accepts that illicit pregnancy is a crime punishable by death, although all such sins are not automatically so punished. See afterword to Group I, "Siblings," and the section on sexuality in the Introduction ("The Tales and Authority in the Society").

4. Thyme is a component of *zaʿtar,* which may be considered the Palestinian national dish. The herb, together with other herbs as well as solid ingredients such as roasted wheat and garbanzo beans, is ground into a fine powder. Bread is dipped in olive oil and then into the *zaʿtar,* all being accompanied by fresh green vegetables. Although this meal is usually eaten for breakfast, it forms part of the staple diet in the Palestinian household. See Granqvist, *Marriage* II: 176; Crowfoot and Baldensperger, *Cedar:* 71ff.; Dalman, *Arbeit* I: 342, 454, 543.

5. In the original the stranger's response consists of only one word, *inšālla* ("Allah willing!"), for which see Tale 6, n. 1.

"May it be so, God willing!"

"This is ghee."

"May it be so, God willing!"

Then he said, "Look here, do you see that cave?"

"Yes," she answered.

"You must go sleep in it," he continued. "Three or four ghouls will arrive. One of them will come limping, and right away you must remove the thorn and bandage his foot."

She gathered herself and went up to the cave, and before long the ghoul with the limp arrived, just as the man had said. She went over to him and removed the thorn from his foot and bandaged it. "No one is to devour her!" he announced. After that they would bring some of what they had caught for her to eat. By Allah, a day went and a day came, and she gave birth.

She was absent ten, maybe twelve months or more. Her father said to his wife, "By Allah, I want to go back to the place I left my daughter. I want to find out what became of her." He went back to the place he had left her. Looking in the distance, he spied a cave with smoke rising from it.

"If you're my mother," said the girl, "come in. If you're my uncle's daughter, come in; if you're my sister, come in; and if you're one of my relatives, come in. But if you're my father, keep out!"

He begged so much to be forgiven that she opened for him. When he entered, she felt shy in front of him and went to hide her child.[6]

"Daughter, it's enough!" he said. "You must come home now."

"No, father," she answered. "Not only do I not want to go back, it didn't even cross my mind. I'm alive and comfortable. Allah's looking after me."

"You can't stay by yourself in this rocky wilderness," he insisted. "You must come home with me!" He swore divorce and forced her.[7] She prepared herself, and they set out.

As she was leaving, she said by the door of the cave, "Father, I forgot my kohl pencil." She went back for it. Then again she would get as far as

6. Such is the father's authority that the girl still feels shame in front of him even though he has abandoned her.

7. Swearing divorce is a serious oath, made to exert moral pressure on someone to do something. If the condition of the oath is not fulfilled, the swearer is legally bound to divorce his wife, although a *fatwā* (legal way out) is usually found for him. See n. 9, below.

from here to there and she'd say, "I forgot my little bottle of kohl." She could not find it in her heart to go back home and leave her baby behind.

They had not been on their way for long when again she said, "Father, I've forgotten such and such a thing."

"Why are you taking the long way around this, daughter?" the father finally asked. "If you have a son, bring him along!"[8] Lifting the baby, she wrapped him and brought him with her.

Now, the ghouls used to bring her everything—money, gold, jewelry, and clothes. They would carry it with them and bring it to her. She took a little of everything, wrapping it in a bundle and loading it on the donkey. They set out on their journey, the grandfather placing the child in front of him.

When his wife saw them, she said, "You didn't leave your daughter in the wilderness. You put her in the lap of luxury! Exactly where you took your daughter, you must take mine!" "Fine," he said. "Let's go."

She went and prepared real bread and stuffed grape leaves for her daughter. Her father took her and left her in the same place he had left his first daughter.

"Daughter," he said, "I want to go take a crap." In a while the same old man appeared. "What's this?" he asked. Red with anger because her father had abandoned her, she answered (Far be it from my listeners!), "Shit!"

"And this?"

"Shit!"

"And that?"

"Shit also!"

He would say "God willing" every time, and all her food turned into that which she had named.

"Do you see that cave?" he asked. "Go up to it. Three or four ghouls will arrive. One of them is huge and will be limping from a thorn in his foot. Take hold of his foot and twist it like this to increase his pain."

The girl made her way up to the cave. The ghouls came, and she did as the man had told her. "Cut her up and devour her!" said the big ghoul. They ate her all up, leaving only the liver and lungs, which they hung by the entrance to the cave.

8. The father's gesture here indicates acceptance of his daughter's trespass and his forgiveness of her, in spite of the social pressure he will face. In fact, a little later on, when the man places the child in front of him on the donkey, he shows a hint of pride in his grandson.

Now, by Allah, the mother did not wait long for her daughter. "Go bring her!" she said to her husband. "It's been long enough. Just right." He went. In the meantime she gathered the daughters of their relatives and neighbors, and she said to them, "Sing! When my husband returns in a while, he'll give you all gold and necklaces. Sing!"

Reaching the cave, the father found nothing of his daughter, only the liver and lungs hanging by the door.

Meanwhile the girls were singing, and the mother was dancing in their midst.

The father, however, was cursing her, "O you daughter of damned parents! Nothing did I find but this liver and lungs hanging by the door of the cave. Hey, you! Your parents be damned! I found nothing but this liver and lungs hanging by the door of the cave."

She, on the other hand, was saying to the girls, "Sing! Sing! Do you hear my husband calling? He's saying, 'Sing! Sing!'"

When he arrived, the husband said to her, "Get out of here! You are divorced! If people usually swear divorce three times,[9] I hereby swear a hundred times." He divorced her, and his daughter stayed with him.[10]

The bird of this tale has flown; one of you owes another one.

29. *The Ghouleh of Trans-Jordan*

Once there was a poor man. One day he said to his family, "Let's cross over to Trans-Jordan. Maybe we can find a better life there than we have here."[1] They had (May Allah preserve your worth!)[2] a beast of burden.

Crossing eastward, they came upon some deserted ruins.[3] When they found an empty house in the ruins, they wanted to move into it. A

9. According to Islamic law, the divorce becomes legally binding after the third time a man says "I divorce you," since he is not permitted to remarry the same woman more than three times.

10. Cf. the ending of Tale 9. The behavior of the co-wives in both these tales confirms the observation of Joseph Jacobs that "the envious step-mother of folktales was originally an envious co-wife" (*Indian Fairy Tales:* 248).

1. Traditionally, nomadic and seminomadic tribes crossed the River Jordan back and forth to graze their herds, often making use of ruins and caves for their camps.

2. *ʾAjallak allāh*—literally, "May Allah exalt you!" See Tale 15, n. 8.

3. From the description in the tale, the "deserted ruins" (*xirbe*) apparently occupy an area the size of a whole village.

woman came upon them. "Welcome!" she said to the man. "Welcome to my nephew![4] Since my brother died, you haven't dropped in on me, nor have you visited me."

"By Allah," he answered, "my father never mentioned you to me. And in any case, we came here only by chance."

"Welcome!" she replied. "Welcome! Go ahead and stay in this house."

Now, the house was well stocked with food, and they settled in. The man had only his wife and a daughter. They would cook meals, and in the evening the daughter took the woman her dinner. She lived in the southern part of the ruined town, and they lived in the north, with some distance between them.

One evening the girl went to bring the woman her dinner. She came up to the door, and lo! the woman had thrown to the ground a young man with braids like those of a girl gone astray, and she was devouring him.[5] Stepping back, the girl moved some distance away and called out, "Hey, Aunty! Aunty!" The ghouleh shook herself, taking the shape of a woman again, and came to the terrified girl.

"The name of Allah protect you, niece!" exclaimed the ghouleh.[6]

"A black shape crossed my path," the girl explained, "and I became frightened."

Taking the dinner from the girl, the ghouleh said, "Don't worry! I'll wait here until you get inside the house." But she followed her to the door of the house to find out what the girl was going to say to her mother.

"How's your aunt?" asked the mother.

Now the girl was a clever one, and she answered, "When I got there, I found her sitting quietly with her head in her lap, like this."

After the ghouleh had gone back to her house to finish what she was eating, the girl said to her mother, "Mother, it turns out our aunt is a ghouleh."

"How do you know she's a ghouleh?" asked the mother.

4. On the ghouleh's calling the man "nephew," see Tale 6, n. 11.

5. The description here derives from earlier standards of male beauty. Men used to grow and braid their hair, with long braids considered a standard of handsomeness and not (as it would be today) a sign of effeminacy.

6. *Ismalla ʿalēki*—literally, "May the name of Allah be upon you!" The name of Allah protects from all evil, which is thought to be lurking everywhere. In situations where there may be danger, when a child falls or cries out in fear, or when a baby wakes up from sleep, the name of Allah is invoked. Cf. Tale 17, n. 6; Tale 22, n. 8; see Hanauer, *Folklore:* 141–157.

"I saw her eating a lad with locks like those of a seductive girl," said the girl.

Her husband was sleeping. "Get up, get up!" she said. "It turns out your aunt is a ghouleh."

"What! My aunt a ghouleh! You're a ghouleh!"

"All right," the wife replied. "Sleep, sleep! We were only joking with you."

When he had gone back to sleep, they went and filled a sack with flour. They brought a tin can full of olive oil and (May it be far from the listeners!) the beast of burden. Loading the provisions on it, they called upon the Everlasting to watch over their journey.[7]

Meanwhile, the man slept till morning, and when he woke he found neither wife nor daughter. "So," he thought, "it seems what they said is true." He mounted to the top of the flour bin and lowered himself in.[8]

After sunrise the ghouleh showed up, but when she went into the house, there was no one there. Turning herself back into a ghouleh, she started dancing and singing:

"My oil and my flour, O what a loss!
Gone are the masters of the house!"

When he heard her singing and prancing about, the man was so scared he farted, scattering flour dust into the air. She saw him.

"Ah!" she cried out. "You're still here!"

"Yes, Aunty!" he answered.

"Well, come down here," she said. "Where shall I start eating you?"

"Eat my little hand," he answered, "that did not listen to my little daughter."

After eating his hand, she asked again, "Where shall I eat you now?"

"Eat my beard," he answered, "that did not listen to my wife."[9]

And so on, until she had devoured him all.

7. *Qālin yā dāyim*—literally, "They said, 'O Everlasting One!'" Note that the teller does not actually say the women started out on their journey. The custom of calling upon Allah at the start of any journey is so deeply ingrained in the Palestinian people that merely saying "Yā alla" (O Allah!) is equivalent to saying "Let's go!"

8. Large bins (*xawābī;* sing., *xābye*) in which provisions such as lentils, wheat, and dried figs were stored from one year to the next were part of the structure of older Palestinian houses.

9. *Kulīnī min ilḥaytī, illī ma smiᶜt min imraytī*—literally, "Eat me from my little beard, because I did not listen to my wife."

Now we go back to the girl and her mother. When they had reached home, the mother said to her daughter, "She's bound to follow us and turn herself (God save your honors!)[10] into a bitch. She'll scratch against the door. I'll boil a pot full of olive oil, and you open for her. When she comes in, I'll pour the oil over her head."

In a while the ghouleh came and scratched at the door, and the girl opened for her. No sooner had she gone in the door than the woman poured the oil onto her head. She exploded, and behold! she was dead. There was no moisture in her eye.[11]

In the morning the woman filled the town with her shouts, and people rushed to her rescue.

"What's the matter?" they asked.

"Listen," she said. "There's a ruin, and it's full of provisions. It was protected by a ghouleh, and here! I've killed the ghouleh. Any one who has strength can go load up on wheat, flour, and oil. As for me, I'll be satisfied with the food in the house where we stayed."

30. *Bear-Cub of the Kitchen*

Once there was a king who had three wives.[1] One day a mosquito crept into his nose.[2] Try as he would, he could find no doctor or medicine, east or west, that could cure him. It did not come out, and soon his nose had swollen up, like this. "It's all over," they said. "The king is going to die."[3] One day, as he sat contemplating his condition, the mosquito said

10. *Bᶜīd min is-sāmᶜīn*—literally, "May it be far from the listeners!" Cf. n. 2, above.

11. The emphatic proverbial expression *mā fī bᶜēnhā l-balle* is used, as here, to confirm that someone is really dead. See Dundes, "Wet and Dry, the Evil Eye," in *Interpreting:* 108–110 and passim.

1. As there is no mention of offspring in the first sentence, the audience would assume that the king married more than once to beget children.

2. The mosquito is the symbolic equivalent of possession by an idea the man is unable to get rid of. Coupled with the striking symbol of the swollen nose, the entire image may be profitably interpreted in sexual terms.

3. A man who is about to die without offspring has sufficient justification to marry again. As we have seen (Tale 20, n. 10), public pressure against polygyny is strong. A man with a wife and male children has no justification for taking another woman; indeed, his action might be interpreted as a desire for sex, a shameful motive. Considering the absolute importance accorded to male children, however, social pressure itself might in fact cause a man without offspring to become sick unto death—for in a way, such a man is already dead

to him, "Look here, I'll come out of your nose, and you will get well. But will you take me for your wife? I'm from the jinn (In the name of Allah, the Compassionate, the Merciful!), and I must be free to do with your wives as I see fit."[4] He wanted to be cured, and thinking he could manage just as well without his other wives, he said, "All right, just come out!"

Out the mosquito jumped, and behold! it was a girl (Praise be to her Creator!) so beautiful she took one's mind away. "These wives of yours," she said, "where am I going to send them?"

"You're free," he answered.

"I want to pluck their eyes out, and you will put them in a well and send them only a pitcher of water and a loaf of bread every day."

"So be it!" he said.

She gouged out their eyes and put them in a bottle which she sent to her jinn family for safekeeping, then she had the women thrown into a well. The king married her.

By Allah, it turned out (so our tale comes out right)[5] that his three wives were all pregnant.[6] The first gave birth, and by Allah, she delivered a boy. "Are we going to let him live like this?" asked the others. "Let's eat him." His mother divided him, giving a piece to each of them and eating two-thirds of him herself. One of the women found she did not have the heart to eat her piece, and since it would not have filled her anyway, she saved it. When the second gave birth, they did the same thing. When the third gave birth, she said, "Why for Allah's sake don't we save this boy? He might be helpful to us."

"Impossible!" objected the others. "We divided up our children, and yours is to remain alive?"

"Give me back the leg I gave you!" demanded one.

---

before his physical demise. People say, "What a shame! He's going to die without having left children behind" (*yā ḥarām, biddo y-mūt balā ma y-xallif*).

4. In giving the new wife a jinn origin, the tale further excuses the man by transferring the guilt he would feel at marrying again from himself to her. When a man takes a new wife, people frequently talk about how unfair (*ẓulum*) it is to the old wife, who had served and taken care of him. Anticipating the inevitable conflict with her co-wives, then, the wife here protects herself ahead of time.

5. On the storyteller's interjections, Tale 5, n. 8.

6. Palestinian folk strongly believe that if a woman cannot bear children and the husband takes a new wife, they will get pregnant at the same time. A popular proverb says, "If not for jealousy, the princess wouldn't have gotten pregnant" (*lōlā l-ġīre mā ḥiblit il-ʾamīre*).

"Give me back the shoulder!" said the other.

"Here!" she said to them. "You take back the leg, and you the shoulder. As for me, I want to keep my son. Who knows but Allah? He might be useful to us."[7]

A day went and a day came, and the boy grew up, his three mothers nursing him. What else would you expect from the child of a tale? He grew up in no time at all. And no sooner did he start crawling than he began to dig a hole at the bottom of the well. As he grew bigger, the hole became larger. One day he looked, and lo! the hole he had made led to his father's kitchen. He would then go into the kitchen and take meat, rice, and whatever else he could find, tying it all in a bundle and stealing away to feed his mothers. After that, he would take a handful or two of salt, dump it into the pot, and turn his back.[8]

Now, the king would fire one cook and hire another, but it was no use. Then they said, "Let's keep watch. Maybe somebody sneaks into the kitchen and puts salt in the food." One day the cook caught him red-handed. "All right," he said. "You're taking the food. But what makes you do this?" Word was sent to the king, and he said, "Bring him to me!"

"Why did you do that?" the king asked when the boy was brought in.

"Why not?" answered the boy. "Why did you have their eyes plucked out and then have them dropped into the well? I'm their son."

"So!" they all exclaimed. "The king has a son!" They called him Bear-Cub of the Kitchen, and from then on it was, "Here comes Bear-Cub of the Kitchen!" and "There goes Bear-Cub of the Kitchen!" After that he took food and water to his mothers, and looked after all their needs.

His father's wife became jealous of him.

"O my head!" she complained. "O my arms! O my legs!"

"What do you need?" asked the king, and she answered, "I want pomegranates from Wādī is-Sīb." (Whoever goes to this wadi never comes back alive.)[9]

"And who would dare go to Wādī is-Sīb?" asked the king.

"Send Bear-Cub of the Kitchen," she answered.

7. Although the teller does not specify which wife says this, the social context would indicate it was the eldest. By saving her son to serve them, she gains an advantage over them. On the utilitarian view of children, cf. Tale 10, n. 7; see Tale 40, n. 5.

8. Putting salt in the food creates conflict between a husband and his new wife, for it gives the man the impression that his wife cannot cook.

9. Wādī is-Sīb, the name of an imaginary location, may be translated as the "Valley of Oblivion." Cf. Tale 36, n. 2.

Bear-Cub of the Kitchen went, and somehow came back and brought pomegranates. And what! All hell broke loose. "Bear-Cub of the Kitchen has gone to Wādī is-Sīb and come back safely!" they all shouted.

Now, his father's wife—how frustrated she felt! She was ready to crack. "What am I going to do?" she asked herself. "This time I want to send him to the region where my people live. They'll kill him for sure, and he won't come back."

"O my heart!" she moaned. "O my this, O my that!" and I don't know what else.

"What's the matter?" asked her husband.

"I want Bear-Cub of the Kitchen to bring me medicine from such and such a place."

"Go, son," said the father.

Bear-Cub of the Kitchen gathered himself together and went. Allah helping him from above, he found her entire family—her mother, father, and brothers—gone. There was no one left in the palace except a little girl with a mass of disheveled hair as big as this.

"Where's your family?" he asked.

"They've gone out," she answered.

Looking this way and that, he spied some bottles on the shelf.

"Well," he said, "what's in these bottles?"

"In this one," she answered, "is my mother's soul, and in that one is my father's. This one here contains the soul of my brother So-and-So, and that one there has the soul of my sister who lives in such and such a place."

"And these that sparkle," he asked, "what are they?"

"These," she answered, "are the eyes of my sister's co-wives, who live in such and such a place."[10]

"And what will cure these eyes?"

"The medicine in this bottle," she replied. "If the eyes are rubbed with some of this medicine, they'll stay in place and will be cured."

"Fine," he said. "And what are these ropes here for?"

"Whoever takes hold of these ropes can take the palace and the orchard with him wherever he wants."

"And this small bottle over here," he continued, "what's in it?"

"This is my soul," she answered.

10. Although the English word *co-wife* is connotationally neutral, the Arabic *ẓurra* (pl. *ẓarāyir*) is derived from the root *ḍarra*, meaning, "to harm." See Tale 20, n. 10.

"Good," he said. "Wait a moment and let me show you."

First he cracked her soul, then the souls of her brother, mother, and father. Then, taking hold of the ropes, he headed home from the direction of Bāb il-Hawā.[11] What clouds of dust he raised! You might have thought two or three hundred horsemen were on their way. The whole town rushed out, and what a commotion there was! When he came closer, they exclaimed, "But this is Bear-Cub of the Kitchen, and he's brought the palace, the orchard, and everything else with him!"

His father's wife looked out her window, and behold! there was her family's palace. You couldn't mistake it. And how her eyes sparkled! Her soul was in his hand.

"Come here!" he said. "Just like you plucked out my mothers' eyes and then left them in the well, right now I'm going to crack your neck."

He cracked her neck. Then, bringing his mothers out of the well, he took them down to the bath and put their eyes back in place. They were cured. He took his place by his father's side, and the wives came back just as they had been before.

Its bird has flown, and now for another one!

31. *The Woman Whose Hands Were Cut Off*

TELLER: May Allah bless the Prophet!
AUDIENCE: Allah bless him!

There was a man whose wife had given birth to a daughter and a son and then died. One day the man himself died, and the children remained alone.

They had a hen that laid an egg every day. They would eat the egg for breakfast and wait till the following day. It so happened one day that the hen stopped laying. "I must go check inside the coop," said the girl to herself. She went down into the coop to search the straw, and behold! she found a pile of eggs, and under it was all her father's money. Her father, it turned out, had been saving his money under the straw in the chicken coop. "Here, brother," she said when he came home, "I've found the

11. Bāb il-Hawā is literally "Gate of the Wind." In the hilly regions of Palestine, where most villages and towns are located on hilltops (as is the village of Turmusᶜayya, district of Ramallah, where this tale was collected), the approach to the town is always through the valley. The western breeze blows up these valleys from the Mediterranean. Cf. the first poem in Tale 21; see Tale 5, n. 5; Footnote Index, s.v. "Geography."

new place where the hen's been laying eggs." She did not tell him about the money. They brought the eggs out and ate one every day.

One day, when the boy had grown up a little, she asked him, "If someone were to show you the money saved by your mother and father, what would you do with it?"

"I'd buy sheep and cattle," he answered.

"Brother," she said to herself, "you're still too young."

Time passed, and she asked again, "If someone were to show you the money saved by your mother and father, what would you do with it?"

"I'd get married," he answered.

"Now you're older and wiser," she said, "and I want to get you married.[1] Such and such is the story."

She took her brother with her, and they went searching in this world to find a bride. Before long they came upon a girl living in a house all by herself.[2] The lad married her, and she became pregnant and gave birth first to a girl. In the middle of the night, the woman got up, devoured her daughter, and smeared the lips of her sleeping sister-in-law with blood. When they woke up in the morning, she said to her husband, "Your sister's a ghouleh, and she has eaten our daughter. Come take a look at her lips."

"Why did you eat the girl?" he went and asked his sister.

"By Allah, brother," she answered, "I didn't eat her."

The young man did not say anything. He just waited.

The following year, his wife gave birth to a boy, and she got up in the middle of the night and ate him, again smearing her sister-in-law's lips with blood. Becoming suspicious of his sister, the brother did not say anything to her. "I must kill her," he said in his mind.

In a few days he said to her, "Come, let's you and I go into the countryside." When they had gone some distance, he sat her down under a tree by a well and said, "So, this is how you treat me, eating my children!"

"By Allah, brother," she answered, "I didn't eat them."

Drawing his sword, he cut off her hands and her feet, and she called down a curse upon him: "Brother, may a thorn get stuck in your foot that no one can pull out." Allah heard her prayer, and a thorn got stuck in his foot on his way home. As he approached the house, he found his wife

1. For a discussion of the motherly role of the sister, see Tale 7, n. 4.

2. We have here an indication that something very unusual is going on, for, although old women may live by themselves, girls in village society are simply not permitted to do so. Cf. Tale 42, n. 3.

chasing after a rooster and realized she was a ghouleh.[3] Not daring to go in, he ran back the way he had come.

Now we go back to his sister. As she was sitting by the mouth of the well, lo! a female snake came up to her panting and puffing with fear. "Hide me," she begged, and the girl hid her under her dress. In a while a he-snake showed up puffing and asked her, "Have you seen a she-snake?"

"Yes," she answered. "There, she's fallen into the well."

The male dropped himself into the well, and the female, coming out from under the girl, called after him, "Explode! Here I am!" The male burst and died. The female, meanwhile, rubbed like this on the girl's stumps, and her hands came back as before. She then rubbed the girl's legs, and her feet came back as they had been. Then the girl went her way. She found a husband, got married, and had children.

One day her brother, who had been wandering around looking for someone to pull the thorn from his foot, but without success, came to his sister's doorstep. He did not realize it was his sister's house, but the moment she saw him she recognized him, while he had not recognized her. She had in the meantime said to her children, "When a man who limps comes by here, keep asking me, 'Mother, tell us the story of the man who cut off his sister's hands and feet.'"

"What's your problem, uncle?" she asked, calling him over.

"There's a thorn in my foot," he answered, "and nobody's been able to pull it out."

"Come here and let me see," she said, and doing with the pin like this, behold! the thorn jumped over there. Rising to his feet, he kissed her hands.

"Stay and have dinner with us," she said.[4]

He sat down to eat, and the children said again and again, "Mother, tell us the story of the man who cut off the hands and feet of his sister." The mother began to tell the tale, and at the end she said to them, "I'm the one whose hands and feet were cut off, and this man here's your uncle."

The moment he heard this, they all got up and hugged each other.[5]

The bird has flown, and a good night to all!

3. For a similar situation involving a ghouleh chasing a rooster, see Tale 6, nn. 7, 8.

4. For "dinner" (*ġadā*), see Tale 14, n. 10.

5. The sister forgives her brother, even though he does her harm. Cf. afterword to Group I, "Siblings"; see the section on brother/sister relationships in the Introduction, "The Tales and the Culture."

32. *Nᶜayyis (Little Sleepy One)*[1]

TELLER: Once there was a king—and Allah's the only true King. Let him who has sinned say, "I beg Allah for forgiveness!"

AUDIENCE: May God grant us remission from our sins!

Once there was a king who had an only son and no other. His name was Nᶜayyis, Little Sleepy One, and his father loved him very much and indulged him. One day the daughter of the king of the jinn fell in love with him and stole him away from his father.[2] There was no place left in the world where the king did not ask about his son, but he could not find him.

In that country there were three girls who were spinners. They used to spin their wool, sell it, and eat from what they earned. When they grew sleepy while spinning at night, they would sing:

"O Nᶜayyis[3]
Go away from here!
To us you're no cousin
Or a brother dear.
Go to the princess instead
She will clothe and indulge you
And keep you well fed."

Now, there were scouts in the town searching for the son of the king, and they heard the song of the spinners. To the king they rushed and said, "O Ruler of the Age, we've found your son!"

"Are you sure?"

"Yes, we've found him!" they answered. "We heard a girl sing:

'O Nᶜayyis
Go away from here!

1. The name Nᶜayyis, the diminutive form of *naᶜs* ("sleepiness"), is not used for children. Here the use of the word is deliberately ambiguous (see n. 3, below).

2. In the Palestinian patrilineal family system, the children belong to the father. This tale was used as an example in the Introduction to elucidate the relationship between father-in-law and son's wife. For lore concerning the jinn, see Hanauer, *Folklore:* 140–157, esp. 140–143, where a story of a similar disappearance is offered. For other references, see Tale 36, n. 3.

3. Here "Nᶜayyis" means "Little Sandman." The double meaning of this word (as a child's name, "Little Sleepy One," and as "Little Sandman") creates the basic semantic confusion on which the tale is based.

To us you're no cousin
Or a brother dear.
Go to the princess instead
She will clothe and indulge you
And keep you well fed.'"

"Ah, yes!" exclaimed the king. "This must be my son."

"Go, bring the girls!" The order was given, and the guards went and brought the first one.

"Young woman," said the king, "do you know Nʿayyis?"

"Yes, my lord," she answered. "He comes to me every night."

"Good," they said to her and brought her to live in the palace, where servants and attendants waited on her. She ate and drank her fill, doing no work and feeling no fatigue, and stopped feeling sleepy. When two or three nights had gone by, they asked her, "Young woman, have you seen Nʿayyis?"

"No, by Allah," she answered, "I haven't seen him in a couple of nights."

The king married her to his cook and sent after the second one.

"Young woman," he asked, "do you know Nʿayyis?"

"Yes, my lord. Day and night he's with us."

They bathed and clothed her and put her in the palace where she lived in bliss and comfort. When she had rested and slept enough, she stopped feeling sleepy.

"Have you seen Nʿayyis, young lady?" the king asked.

"No, by Allah, my Lord," she answered, "I haven't seen him in two or three days."

The king married her to the baker.

"Have you been seeing Nʿayyis, young woman?" the king asked the third girl when they had brought her.

"Yes, my lord. Every night I see him."

They did with her as they had done with her sisters, settling her in the palace. She turned out to be more clever than her sisters. Every time they asked her, "Did you see Nʿayyis, young woman?" she would answer, "Yes, my lord. Every night I see him."

For a month, two, three, four, she said she had seen him every night. Finally the king said to his wife, "Take this pair of bracelets. Give them to her, and ask her to pay for them. If she can come up with the money, then she really has been seeing Nʿayyis. If not, then she's a liar."

"Here, young woman," the wife said, "take this pair of bracelets and bring me their price from Nʿayyis."

"Yes, my lady," replied the girl.

That night, she sat up in bed, crying and calling out:

"O Nʿayyis
Go away from here!
To us you're no cousin
Or a brother dear.
Your father has given me
This pair of bracelets
How am I to pay the treasury
The price of this jewelry?"[4]

And how she cried! When she had called out three times, lo! a voice said, "The key's in the wardrobe, and the wardrobe's full of treasure. Reach in and take what you want." Opening the wardrobe, she took out the price of the bracelets, laughing happily.

"Here, uncle," she said, "take the price of the bracelets."

"So," thought the king, "it's true, my son's still alive."

She had stayed another three, four months (Allah knows how long!) when the king brought her a ring.

"Bring me the price of this ring from Nʿayyis," he said.

"Right away, my lord," she answered and went back to her bed, crying and calling out:

"O Nʿayyis
Go away from here!
To us you're no cousin
Or a brother dear.
Your father has given me
This ring
And how am I to pay the king
The price of this precious thing?"

Again the voice said, "The key's in the wardrobe, and the wardrobe's full of treasure. Reach in and take what you want!" Taking out the price of the ring, she gave it to her uncle.

4. Some liberty was taken with the song's last line in order to preserve the rhyme. Rendered literally, it would read: "And where am I going to reach for its price?" (*u-ḥaqqo mnēn aṭūl*).

One day Nʿayyis himself came up to see her and said, "Young woman, my wife's pregnant, and you must stuff your dress with rags and pretend you're pregnant until nine months are up."

Wrapping a bandage around her head, she made a point of going to see her uncle every once in a while.

"Uncle, I'm pregnant."[5]

"Yes, daughter. What do you want?"

She said she wanted a piece of liver, and he brought her three.[6]

"O uncle, I want squabs. O uncle, I want this, and I want that," she kept asking. Whatever Nʿayyis's wife down below craved, the girl would ask the king for. Then Nʿayyis would come and take it to his wife below.

Her pregnancy over, the jinn wife gave birth first to a boy.

"Here, young lady," said Nʿayyis. "Take this baby and hide it inside your underwear. Then cry out, 'Mother, I've given birth!'"

Putting the baby in her undergarments, the girl came to the top of the stairs.

"Master!" she cried out. "I've had the baby."

"In the name of Allah, the Compassionate, the Merciful!" exclaimed the king.

Bringing the baby out, they washed and dressed him. Then they looked after her, wrapping a bandage around her head and putting her to bed.

She brought the boy up, and how handsome he was—the son of royalty! The king was crazy about him.

The jinn wife became pregnant again, and the girl did as before. The wife gave birth to a boy, and the girl took him and hid him in her underwear.

"Uncle, I've given birth!" she cried out. "Mistress, I've given birth!"

They spoiled her more and more, giving her four wet nurses to help her. What can you say? She was now a queen!

The wife became pregnant and delivered a third time, giving birth to a

5. A wife normally addresses her father-in-law as "uncle" (*ʿammī*). Here, however, the woman's situation in the king's household is ambiguous. She calls the king "uncle" when announcing her pregnancy, but at other times she addresses him as *sīdī* ("sir" or "master").

The tale here abridges the process of announcing the pregnancy to the king. Normally, a pregnant woman would first tell her mother-in-law or sister-in-law, and they in turn would make sure the news reached the father or father-in-law. Cf. Tale 24, n. 10.

6. Pregnant women are accorded special treatment. They are offered what is considered to be heavy and nourishing food, mostly meat, especially the internal organs of lamb (cf. Tale 2, n. 2). See Footnote Index, s.v. "Pregnancy And Childbirth."

girl. And the same thing that had happened with the two boys also happened with the girl.

One day Nᶜayyis came up, bringing her three candles, and said, "During the call to prayer on Thursday evening, light these candles." On Thursday evening, she did just as he had said, putting one boy on this side of her, the other on the other side, with the girl in the middle, and lit the three candles.[7] When the jinn wife saw her, she cried out, "Alas! Alas! The human woman has done me in!" And she exploded and died.

"May you never rise again!" Nᶜayyis cursed her, tearing down the palace over her and coming back up again.

"Master, come see Nᶜayyis!" shouted the spinner girl. "Mistress, come see Nᶜayyis! Hurry! Hurry!"

When they rushed down to see their son, he said, "I was married to a jinn woman, and these children of mine are from her. But if it weren't for this girl here, by Allah, I would never have come back. I want to marry her."

They had a wedding celebration that lasted seven days and seven nights. Music was playing and people were dancing. Our master married our mistress—and may every year find you in good health!

AUDIENCE: And may Allah save your tongue!

Afterword

The general theme that unites the tales in this group is that of conflicting loyalties. The conflict usually centers on the male and arises out of his responsibilities as the head of his own household or as a member of an

7. Thursday evening (*lēlt il-jimᶜa*)—literally, "The night of Friday"—extends from sunset Thursday to sunrise Friday. Because Friday is the Muslim holy day, its onset the night before is considered a propitious time for the performance of religious duties and the granting of wishes and prayers. Actually, candles are not lit in any Islamic rites; it is therefore interesting to note that the narrator of this tale is a Christian woman from Gaza.

Exorcism is frequently practiced among Palestinian folk for the cure of minor illnesses, especially those affecting children that are thought to have been caused by the evil eye. One common method of driving out the evil spirit causing the illness would be for the child's mother or grandmother to put a piece of alum on the fire and, as it bubbles and smokes, to pass her hand over it and then over the affected part of the body while reciting a precise formula. Cf. Tale 35, nn. 18, 19.

extended family. In the last tale in the group, "Nʿayyis," the source of the conflict is not so much the responsibility a mature man must shoulder but rather the duty a young son owes his parents by remaining within the fold of the extended family.

"Chick Eggs" and "Bear-Cub of the Kitchen" demonstrate the potential for divided loyalties in a polygynous situation. In the first the man must attend both to his present wife and to his daughter, who represents her own mother in the household. In the second the aging king's loyalty is divided between his older wives, who unite to fight the beautiful new wife; she in turn protects herself by taking revenge ahead of time. In both tales the husband is emotionally manipulated by the wife, either through the children ("Chick Eggs") or by pretended sickness ("Bear-Cub"). And here again, as in all the other tales embodying a polygynous situation (Tales 3, 5, 6, 7, 9, 20, and 35), the first wife, either directly or through her children, is vindicated against those who follow her.

In "The Ghouleh of Trans-Jordan" and "The Woman Whose Hands Were Cut Off" the source of the conflict is the extended family. The man in the first tale is caught between his conjugal family (his wife) and his natal family (his supposed aunt), and he chooses at his peril to align himself with the latter against the former. In "The Woman Whose Hands Were Cut Off," somewhat the reverse situation obtains, with the man choosing to believe his wife over his sister. In either case the male is in a difficult situation vis-à-vis the females for whom he is responsible. Predictably, however (cf. Tales 7, 8, 9), the sister in the latter tale is honest and kind to her brother, forgiving him even before he asks for forgiveness and welcoming him into her own family.

Despite the supernatural machinery, the conflict in "Nʿayyis" is also between natal and conjugal families. In this tale, as in "Lōlabe" (Tale 18), the parents have an only son who is torn from them by supernatural forces, and in both cases these forces are overcome so that the son may return to his family. In "Bear-Cub," the teller presents the beautiful woman who wrests the king from his wives and his three sons in the metaphorical guise of the jinn. In "Nʿayyis," however, no transitional devices are provided to help mediate the connection between jinn and human in the mind of the listener; the teller endows the jinn wife with an absolute existence, separate from that of the human domain, and the listener must make the imaginative leap between the two domains unaided.

We may therefore conclude that the jinn wife in "Nᶜayyis" is a very beautiful woman who captivated the son to such an extent that she made him renounce his parents. The implicit moral to be drawn from all three tales is that the bond between the son and his parents (particularly when he is an only child) is, or should be, so strong that it would take a supernatural power to break it.

Group III

SOCIETY

33. *Im ʿAwwād and the Ghouleh*[1]

Once upon a time there were some women who agreed to meet on a certain day to go wash their clothes at the spring on the edge of town.[2] As they were discussing the matter, a ghouleh who had hidden herself behind a retaining wall nearby heard what they agreed to do that day.[3] On the appointed night, toward dawn, she came to the one among them whose house was on the outskirts of town and made as if she were one of the women who had promised to go to the spring. The woman to whose house she had come was called Im ʿAwwād. Calling out from the outside door of the house, the ghouleh said, "Hey! Im ʿAwwād! Let's go! Tie your dirty clothes in a bundle, and let's go do the laundry!"

"Who is it?" asked Im ʿAwwād.

"I'm Im So-and-So," answered the ghouleh.[4]

"All right," said Im ʿAwwād.

It was the middle of the month, and the moon was bright.[5] Thinking it was daylight already, she put her laundry in a tub and lifted it.

"Bring your son with you," suggested the ghouleh. "We might be a while."[6]

She brought her son with her, and the two women walked, with the ghouleh in front. When they had gone just beyond the last houses in town, Im ʿAwwād looked and saw that the feet of the woman walking in front of her were making sparks.[7] Realizing the woman was a ghouleh, Im ʿAwwād was afraid.

"I want to go back," she said.

"Why?"

1. On the name Im ʿAwwād," see Tale 27, n. 1. ʿAwwād is a common boy's name.

2. In the old days the women got up and, in groups, went early (at the time of the dawn call to prayer) to wash their clothes at the spring. They then dried the laundry on trees and bushes. Cf. the ending of Tale 23.

3. For a description of these retaining walls, see Tale 12, n. 11.

4. Presumably, the ghouleh can take any shape she wants. Cf. Tale 6, n. 10; Tale 19, n. 5; and the situation in Tale 29.

5. The reference here is to the lunar calendar by which the moon is full at mid month.

6. The assumption here is that the boy is still nursing.

7. It is characteristic of ghouls that their feet make sparks as they walk. Ghouls are generally associated with flames, sparks, and redness. Cf. n. 10, below; Tale 19, n. 6.

"I forgot my husband's tunic,"[8] she replied, "and he'll kill me if I don't wash it. Here! Take this boy and go ahead, and I'll catch up with you."

Putting down the washtub, and the boy by its side, she went running back to her husband.

"Heat up the oil, you whose house is in ruins!"[9] she cried out, knocking on the door. "Now she'll come and eat us before anyone can come to our help."

By the time the ghouleh had finished eating the boy, she came back to eat Im ʿAwwād and her husband.

"O Im ʿAwwād!" she cried out from behind the outside door. "Here's ʿAwwād's little prick! Make it into a little wick!"[10]

When the man heard this, he said to his wife, "What you've been saying is true, damn your parents! This is a ghouleh!"

The ghouleh dug under the door until she could stick her head and neck inside, and Abu ʿAwwād poured the boiling oil over her head.[11]

"Do it again!" she cried out, and he answered, "My mother didn't teach me how."[12]

The ghouleh's head exploded, and she died.

Its dust has scattered, and now for another one![13]

8. The *dimāye* resembles a tunic to some extent: a full-length, long-sleeved shirt, it covers a man's body from neck to feet, with a frontal opening extending the whole length of the garment. Today some men wear a Western suit jacket over the *dimāye*, but many still wear the aba over it. For a description, see Kanaana et al., *Al-Malābis:* 203–205.

9. The strong curse *yā xarīb il-bēt* anticipates the destruction of the family at the hands of the ghouleh.

10. This striking image (*xuḏī zbērit ʿawwād sawwīhā fitīle*) bears out earlier remarks connecting the ghouleh with sexuality (see afterword to Group I, "Siblings"). Furthermore, by coupling the image of the wick with that of the male member, it links sexuality and fire-related imagery as well (see n. 7, above).

11. Cf. the ending of Tale 29.

12. A ghoul must be killed with one blow; see Tale 3, n. 8.

13. *Ṭār iʿjājhā uʿalēku badālhā*—literally, "Its [swirling] dust has flown, and upon you—another in its place." A bird image is implied in this unusual formula; see Tale 13, n. 11.

34. *The Merchant's Daughter*

TELLER: Once upon a time . . . O my listeners, let him who loves the Virgin hail her with blessings of peace!

AUDIENCE: Peace be with her!

Once there was a merchant, a big merchant, the biggest of all the merchants, and he had an only daughter. He did not have a wife; she had died. He used to pamper his daughter very much, and she spent her days at home with no one to keep her company.[1] When the time came for pilgrimage, he thought, "I'd like to go on the hajj." He made preparations, but his daughter asked, "And how can you leave me all by myself?"

"Don't worry," he answered. "I'll have all the daughters of my fellow merchants come visit you, and they'll stay with you every night. You have nothing to worry about during the day."

"Fine," she agreed, and he went to ask the other merchants to send their daughters over.

"Of course," they said.

Every day after that the girls came in the evening, one after the other, until they had all arrived. One night, as they were sitting around chatting, they craved something.

"Yee! By Allah," they said, "we'd like to have some dried figs, some raisins, and some dates from the cellar below. Who'll go get them?"

This one said, "I'm afraid," and another said she too was afraid. Finally one of them said, "I'll go down." So down she went, and she was reaching for things when lo! she came upon a ghoul in the cellar.

"Hmmm!" he hummed. "You keep quiet, or I'll eat you!"

"Yes," she said. "I'll keep quiet."

Pulling herself away, she went home to her family.

"What's become of her?" asked the other girls. "She's been gone a long time. Why don't you, So-and-So, go see what happened to her."

So, down to the cellar she went, and lo! there was the ghoul.

"You keep quiet, or I'll eat you!"

"Yes, I'll keep quiet."

She too went home. So did the third and the fourth one, until the merchant's daughter was all by herself. What was she to do, poor girl? Where

1. On the pampering of girls, see Tale 8, n. 3; Tale 12, n. 2.

was she to turn? "Why don't I go down," she told herself, "and see what the matter is. Why those girls went and didn't come back."

So down she went to see, and she came upon the ghoul.

"Listen here," he said. "You keep quiet, or I'll eat you!"

"Yes," she answered, "I'll keep quiet."

What am I going to do, Lord, and where will I turn?[2] She found, you might say, a bit of wheat in the cellar—and in the old days they used to grind the wheat by hand.[3]

"Why don't I take some of this wheat," she thought, "and sit down to grind it?" Bringing the wheat, she prepared the grinder and sat down to grind. The ghoul sat opposite, grinding with her.

Now, they had a neighbor whose name was Abū Xalīl. "Why don't I tell our neighbor," she thought. "Why don't I call him over without the ghoul knowing I'm calling?" Now, in the old days they used to sit and grind, singing and chatting. She then sang:

"Sharpen your long sword, sharpen!
O neighbor, Abū Xalīl,
Black he is, with a crest.[4]
Together we're grinding meal."

And the ghoul sang back:

"Grind, my father's daughter, grind!
The night ahead is long,
The amount of grain is small.
When the wheat's ground up
I'll suck the meat off your bones."

Im Xalīl and Abū Xalīl were still up, sitting around talking, when all of a sudden he said, "Listen! Listen, Im Xalīl!"

2. The narrator of this tale frequently assumes the characters' identities by articulating their thoughts directly, as here, without bothering to add the necessary transition, "she said."

3. An ethnographic comment from the teller. The grinder referred to here, used for grinding grain, consists of two circular slabs of volcanic rock each about two inches thick and two feet in diameter. The stones are placed on top of each other with the fulcrum in the middle. The woman sits on the floor with legs outstretched, the grinder between her knees, and she turns the wooden handle, which is inserted near the top stone's rim. The grain is fed by hand through the fulcrum opening and emerges from the circumference coarsely ground. Women frequently sat facing each other in pairs, taking turns at the handle and singing songs (as in the tale) to relieve the tedium.

4. The crest and the black color convey the impression of a strange and reptilian creature, ghoulish but different in appearance from the ghouls we have encountered so far.

"What?" she asked.

"Our neighbor's daughter," he whispered. "I wonder what's happening with her." They listened a while, and lo! she was singing again:

"Sharpen your long sword, sharpen!
O neighbor, Abū Xalīl,
Black he is, with a crest.
Together we're grinding meal."

Whereupon came the response:

"Grind, my father's daughter, grind!
The night ahead is long,
The amount of grain is small.
When the wheat's ground up
I'll suck the meat off your bones."

"By Allah," said Abū Xalīl. "I'm going over to see what the story is." Having sharpened his sword, he jumped over the wall between the houses and went to his neighbor's. Looking in, he found her at the grinding stone with the ghoul facing her. He rushed upon him with the sword and killed him. He died, poor fellow!

The girl then told him her story. "It was like this," she said. "The girls went down to the cellar, and each of them in turn went home, leaving me all by myself." She told him the whole story. "It's all right now," said Abū Xalīl, going to look out the door. He saw (May it be far from you!) a donkey with its saddlebags still on it. Bringing them over, he stuffed the ghoul's head in one bag and the body in the other and loaded them back on the donkey.

The donkey already knew the way home, and when he got there the ghoul's mother said, "Yee! How good my son is! Allah bless him! Here, he's sent us a feast, but who knows what else he went to do?" Taking the feast he had sent out of the panniers, she removed its clothes, dipped it in hot water and skinned it, and put it in a caldron on the fire. Then she went and invited her paternal and maternal aunts and her other relatives, and they sat down to the feast. As they were eating, behold! his ring came into her hand. "Yee!" she screamed (the distant one!). It's her son![5]

5. In n. 2, above, we saw how the narrator interchanges the first- and third-person pronouns to achieve a sense of immediacy in the narration. Here, to mitigate the effect of the catastrophe, the narrator switches from the first person to the third in the middle of what would otherwise be a direct quotation. Cf. Tale 5, n. 13.

She got up from the table. What was she to do? How was she to find out who had done that to her? She bought rings, bracelets, and earrings and went around calling out, "Girls! I have rings! I have bracelets and earrings!" As she passed in front of the merchant's house, the girl saw her.

"Come over!" she called out.

"What do you want?"

"I want to buy something from you," said the girl.

Coming over, the woman said, "Listen, I don't sell things for money, but only for a new story."

"Well," said the girl, "sit down while I tell you a story."

Then she told her the story of the ghoul, what she had done with him, how the girls had all gone home, and how they had loaded him on the donkey. Now (the distant one!), the mother's heart was boiling over.

"Yee!" quavered the girl. "You're scaring me."

"Don't worry!" said the woman. "It's only because I've eaten *mluxxiyye* and fava beans, and my stomach's upset."[6]

Anyway, she gave her earrings, bracelets, rings, and whatever else she wanted for nothing, and went on her way. What was she to do? She then went home and talked it over with her relatives. "What are we to do?" they asked, "now that we know who his murderers are?"

"Well," she said, "we're going to ask for her hand. We'll say I have a son, and we want her as a bride for him."

"Fine," they agreed. "Let's do it."

Taking two or three men with her, they set out. Who is her guardian, now that her father is in the hajj? Told that it was Abū Xalīl, they went to see him.

"O Abū Xalīl," they said. "We want this girl. We want, we'd like to be, in-laws to you." What else they said, I don't know.

"Uncles," he responded, "I'm not related to her. I'm not her paternal or maternal uncle. I'm only her neighbor, and her father has entrusted her to my care. And the Prophet himself bade us take care of our neighbor, and our neighbor's neighbor, down to the seventh neighbor."[7]

6. *Mluxxiyye* (*Corchorus olitorious,* or Jew's mallow) and fava beans are rarely eaten together. *Mluxxiyye,* a leafy green vegetable used in a lamb stew that is served over rice, is supposed to be difficult to digest, as are fava beans (for which, see Tale 8, n. 4; Tale 36, n. 1).

"My stomach's upset" (*qalbī biġlī*)—literally, "My heart is boiling."

7. This is a very well known and often-quoted *ḥadīṯ* (saying, or tradition) of the Prophet. A popular proverb also confirms this concern: "Ask about the neighbor before

"We'll take care of her," they said. "We'll provide for her, we'll buy her things." They dazzled him.

"That's fine," he said. "But what am I to say to her father when he returns?"

"Don't worry," they answered. "He won't say anything when he sees all that we've brought for her. He won't say anything."

"All right," he agreed. "It's nothing unusual. Everyone gets married."

After buying the trousseau, they came and prepared the bride. The ghouleh then came with a few people, claimed the bride, and left.

When the bride arrived at her new home, the ghouleh's house, she found it poverty stricken. It was the house of poor peasants. The ghouleh also had a daughter (May it be distant from you!) who was ugly and lame, her body twisted and deformed all over.

Now, the ghoul's mother lit the fire and put a huge caldron on it, filling it with water. "In a moment," she thought, "I'm going to slaughter her and cook her on the fire. But first, until the water boils, I might as well go invite my relatives." Then, forcing the bride into a burlap sack, she sewed it shut over her.

The poor girl sat in the sack. She happened to have some gum, so she started chewing: "Chew, chew, white gum! Chew, chew, red gum! Chew, chew, blue gum! Chew, chew, yellow gum!" Her sister-in-law, the pitiful one, called out to her, "Hey, sisten-in-law!" (She couldn't talk properly.)

"What do you want?" asked the other.

"Give me some gum!"

"And how can I give you anything? I can't stretch out my hand. Make an opening in the mouth of the sack so I can give you some."

"I'm afraid you might nun away" (that is, "run away").

"Don't worry," the girl reassured her. "I won't run away."

The ghouleh's daughter fetched a knife and cut away a stitch, while the girl inside loosened a few more stitches, then reached out her hand and gave her a bit of gum. The ghouleh's daughter chewed and chewed, while the other was making a wider opening in the mouth of the sack until she was able to pull herself out of it. Now that she was out, what was she to

---

you ask about the house" (*ʾisʾal ʿan il-jār qabl id-dār*). The cultural importance of neighbors is accurately reflected in the tale. Because people tended to live in the same house for generations, they had the same neighbors for many, many years. Hence, neighbors were sometimes closer to a family than their own relatives, sharing sorrowful and joyous occasions.

do? How was she to act? Dragging the dim-witted girl over, she slaughtered her, put her in the caldron, and fled. And what did she do then? She went up to the roof and waited.

Meanwhile, the ghouleh arrived with her guests. "Yee!" she exclaimed. "It looks like my daughter (Allah bless her!) has already slaughtered her and put her on the fire. And here, she's almost done. Allah bless my daughter!"

The food served, they sat down to eat, but the daughter's scalp came into the mother's hand and she recognized it. "Yee!" she screamed. This is her daughter (the distant one!).

Now, the bride, while they were eating, sneaked into a room and found it full of money and treasure.[8] Filling her pockets, the front and other parts of her dress, she pulled herself together and got out of there. She walked and walked, until she came to a carpenter's shop.

"Listen, uncle!" she said.

"Yes."

"Won't you make me a dress of wood?[9] I'll pay you as much as you want."

"Yes," he answered, "I'll make you one."

"In that case," she suggested, "hide me here in your shop until you finish it. And if someone should come by, beware of telling them you've seen me!"

He hid her behind the planks of wood and set to making her dress. Now (the distant one!), the ghouleh, her insides burning (her daughter and son were gone!) came chasing the girl. She ran here and there, and whomever she saw she asked, "O uncle, haven't you seen a bride all decked out and perfumed?"

"No."

"O uncle, haven't you seen a bride all decked out and perfumed?"

"Not at all. We haven't seen anyone like that."

She kept running from one direction to another, always returning to the carpenter and asking him, and he always answered her, "Not at all," until he had finished the dress. The dress finished, the girl put it on and walked away.

8. Hoarding treasure is a consistent feature of ghoulish behavior throughout the tradition. Cf. Tales 19 and 29.

9. This dress, meant to protect the merchant's daughter from the depredations of the ghouleh, is unique to this tale, and the connection between wood and evil influence is obscure. Cf., however, Tale 8, n. 6; Tale 35, n. 9.

"What's your name, niece?" those who saw her on the road asked, and she answered, "My name is Little Woodling." The ghouleh too, running back and forth, asked her, "Little Woodling, have you seen a bride all decked out and bustling?"

"Not at all," she answered. "I can't see, and I don't know. I haven't seen anybody."

Now (the distant one!), the ghouleh kept running and searching until she burst and died. And the girl took off her wooden dress and went home. When her father came back from the hajj and heard the story, he blamed his neighbor for what he had done, marrying the girl off without his permission. After that they lived in bliss and happiness, and may Allah save the mouths of my listeners!

35. *Pomegranate Seeds*[1]

There was once a woman who had no children except an only daughter whom she indulged.[2] She had a pair of golden slippers made for her. The mother loved her daughter very much and would send her to the sheikh for lessons. (In the old days there were no schools; the sheikhs were the teachers.)[3] Early one morning the girl went to the house of the sheikh and found him skinning a little boy and devouring him.[4]

She gathered herself and ran away, not returning to her mother. "If I return to my mother," she thought, "she'll want to take me back to him,

1. "Pomegranate Seeds" is not actually used as a girl's name. Because pomegranates are deep red when ripe, the name is meant to convey health and beauty (cf. Tale 21, n. 3). "The bride is often compared to a pomegranate for beauty," say Crowfoot and Baldensperger (*Cedar:* 111) in an account of Palestinian lore about the pomegranate (pp. 111–112). Canaan says it is generally believed that "every pomegranate has one seed which has come from heaven" ("The Child": 166). Elsewhere ("Plant-lore": 160) he adds that city Muslims "take great care not to drop or lose any of the seeds, since that might be just the one which came from paradise," citing the following proverb: *Ir-rummān bi-mallī l-qalb ʾīmān*" ("Pomegranates fill the heart with faith"). See n. 19, below.

2. Through this detail the teller intimates that the girl will inevitably get into some kind of trouble. See Tale 8, n. 3; Tale 12, n. 2.

3. For a definition of *sheikh,* see Tale 22, n. 7. In the old days sheikhs were responsible for the education of children whose parents could afford to send them to school (see Granqvist, *Birth:* 140–155; Grant, *People:* 171; Sirḥān, *Mawsūʿat* V: 12–14). It was not, however, a common practice to send girls to school (see Granqvist, *Birth:* 276).

4. The sheikh is never explicitly stated to be a ghoul, although his ghoulishness is implied throughout.

and he'll devour me. I'd rather not stay in this place at all." She ran away in fear, leaving one of her golden slippers by the doorstep. One slipper fell off, while the other remained on her foot as she ran. She came to a shopkeeper.

"O uncle!" she pleaded, "It's now evening, and I'm a stranger in town. Won't you let me sleep here tonight, in your shop?"

"Yes, my daughter,"[5] he replied, "why not?"

He left her in his shop and went home. Who came to her? The sheikh. He said to her:

"Tell me, Pomegranate Seeds!
What strange sights did you see,
When by the doorstep of the master
You forgot your golden slipper?"

She answered:

"I saw him praying and fasting,
The eternal Lord worshipping."

The sheikh tore up all the cloth, turning the big shop upside down, and left. When the owner came to open his shop and check on the girl, he found it all torn up. "Oh! My son!"[6] he cried out. "Help, people, help!" The townspeople felt sorry for him. They brought a tray and collected money for the goods he had lost.[7] He beat the girl until he nearly killed her. "Have pity!" they reproached him. "Why are you beating her?[8] Could she have torn up your shop?"

Eventually the girl made her escape to another town. She came to a grocer who sold ghee, sesame oil, sugar, and olive oil.

"O uncle!" she begged him, "Won't you let me sleep here tonight?"

"Yes, my daughter," he replied, "why not?"

The sheikh came to her at night, and he said:

5. The shopkeeper, we note, calls the girl "my daughter" (*yā bintī*); if he were actually her uncle, he would address her with the same form she uses for him—*yā ʿammī* ("O my paternal uncle!"). See n. 11, below.

6. "Oh! My son!"—a literal translation of *yā waladī* (meaning, "Oh! My [poor] son!"), which is a common exclamation expressing a sense of loss and not a call for the son to help.

7. The custom of relatives and neighbors collecting money for a family in distress is still practiced. Cf. Tale 43, n. 6.

8. The translation here attempts to convey the emotional complexity of the common expression *Ḥarām!* (literally, "It is forbidden!"), which, aside from its literal meaning, also

"Tell me, Pomegranate Seeds!
What strange sights did you see,
When by the doorstep of the master
You forgot your golden slipper?"

She answered:

"I saw him praying and fasting,
The eternal Lord worshipping."

The sheikh poured the olive oil into the sesame oil, mixing them together with the ghee, the rice, and the sugar. Then, turning his back, he left.

In the morning the owner opened his shop. "Oh! My son!" he lamented, beating his breast. As they had done for the other one, the people collected money for this one.

The girl meanwhile pulled herself together and left. "Where am I to go?" she wondered. "I've nowhere left except this tall tree here. Live or die, I'm going to climb it. He won't see me up there."[9] She climbed and sat up in the tree, looking like the full moon, like a doll.[10]

In a while the king came to water his horse by the pool under the tree, but the animal shied. The king looked up and saw a maiden like the full moon sitting in the tree.

"Young woman!"[11] he called out, "Are you human or jinn?"

"By Allah, I'm human," she answered. "From the choicest of the race."

"Come down and ride behind me!"

She was hungry. She had not eaten in two days (and of course the Son

---

combines the idea of having mercy with the notion of guilt for wrongdoing ("Why are you beating her?").

9. In the folk imagination, wood appears to offer protection against the forces of evil. Cf. the English folk expression "Knock on wood," and Tale 34, where the merchant's daughter escapes the clutches of the ghouleh by hiding in a wooden dress; see also Tale 8, n. 6; Tale 34, n. 9.

10. On the moon and feminine beauty, see Tale 2, n. 1.

11. *Bint,* in the expression *yā bint,* "Young woman!" means either "girl" or "daughter." We thus note an important but subtle difference in the forms of address used by the shopkeeper and by the king. The possessive pronoun in the shopkeeper's address, *ya bintī* ("my daughter"), eliminates in the minds of the listeners any possibility of sexual reference, whereas the king's address leaves that possibility distinctly open. The storyteller's apology—"She was hungry . . . (and of course the Son of Adam cannot live if he does not eat)"—immediately before the girl's agreeing to ride behind the king on the horse confirms this observation.

of Adam cannot live if he does not eat). She collected herself, came down, and rode behind him. He took her to his mother and said, "Mother!"

"Yes, son."

"I've captured a treasure. If you like me, you must like her. And if you love me, you must love her."

"Of course, son," she said. "Like my own eyes." The mother brought the girl up until she became a young woman, lovely like the moon.

"Mother!" said the king when the maiden came of age, "I want to marry her."

"Marry her," said the mother.

The king married her, and she became pregnant and gave birth to a boy. When she had given birth to her first son, the sheikh came to her in the night. He said:

"Tell me, Pomegranate Seeds!
What strange sights did you see,
When by the doorstep of the master
You forgot your golden slipper?"

And she answered:

"I saw him praying and fasting,
The eternal Lord worshipping."

Snatching her son away from her, he smeared her hands and mouth with blood and disappeared.

In the morning the servant went up to the master's quarters: "O Master, she's all bloody!"

"Don't worry about it," the king said.

The next time, the sheikh did with the second son as he had done with the first and disappeared. The king questioned his wife, but she would not say a word, neither yes nor no. She was afraid to speak.

The third time, she gave birth to a girl. The sheikh came, seized the baby, and disappeared.

"That's it!" announced the king. "She's hereby deserted! Put her in a separate house!" [12]

"But," protested the servants and his mother, "tomorrow she'll devour us and our children!"

12. *Ḥuṭṭūhā b-bēt il-hijrān*—literally, "Put her in the house of desertion." See Tale 10, n. 8, on desertion as an institutionalized status for women.

"No!" insisted the king, "I won't get rid of her. I'll leave her in separate quarters." And every day after that he himself came to give her food through the window.[13]

One day the king decided to go on the hajj.[14] He said to himself, "I might as well go see what Pomegranate Seeds wants."

"Pomegranate Seeds!" he said, "What do you want from the Ḥijāz?"

"I only want the box of myrrh[15] and seven switches of pomegranate wood," she answered. "And if you don't bring them, may your camels start dropping blood and pus, and stop you from coming back!"

He traveled and traveled. He bought the whole world but forgot the box of myrrh. Halfway home, the men were going to leave the camels behind. They had collapsed, and not one of them was able to move.

"Boys!" said the king, "I've forgotten something." He went back and started asking around, "O Uncle, do you happen to have the box of myrrh and seven whips of pomegranate wood?" People laughed at him, snickering, "What's with you, uncle? Are you crazy? Are you in your right mind? By Allah, this thing you mention, we've never heard of it before."

He asked a second person, and a third. Finally, he came upon a clever one, who said, "What are you looking for, O hajj?"[16]

"I want the seven whips of pomegranate wood and the box of myrrh," replied the king. "How much do they cost?"

"Fifty dinars."

"Here! Take a hundred, and let's finish with this business!"

Taking the money, the other went to an orchard and cut seven switches of pomegranate wood. He then went back to the market and bought a

13. In all the tales in this collection in which the husband becomes estranged from his wife (cf. Tales 10, 20), he still loves her regardless of her supposed fault.

14. As we have already seen (cf. Tales 7, 12, 34), going on the hajj is the standard method in the tales for sending a man on a journey; cf. Tale 7, n. 7.

15. The Arabic word *ṣabr* carries several meanings, among which are "patience," "prickly pear," "aloe," and "myrrh." It is unclear which of the last two meanings is appropriate here, as both of the substances referred to are quite bitter. We opted for "myrrh," first because the word itself is derived from the Arabic *murr* ("bitter") and second because the aloe plant is not native to Arabia, whereas myrrh is. Cf. Tale 45, n. 8.

16. The word *hajj* refers both to the act of pilgrimage (its usual meaning in English) and to the pilgrim himself (sometimes rendered in English as "hajji"). As a form of address (*yā ḥajj!*; fem., *ḥajje*) it indicates respect for the person thus addressed, whether he or she has been on the hajj or not. It is, however, the preferred form of address for those who have in fact performed the religious duty of pilgrimage, taking precedence even over Abū Flān (Father of So-and-So) and Imm Iflān (Mother of So-and-So).

small amount of bitter myrrh, put it in a box, and brought it, along with the whips of pomegranate wood, saying, "Please accept these!"

Before the king had even reached them, the camels were running.

"Here you are!" he said to his wife.

A short time after the hajj, the king wanted to marry again. It was the unveiling of the bride[17] (people everywhere!), and the king was about to remarry. Pomegranate Seeds started whipping the box of myrrh with the pomegranate switches, crying out:

"O box of myrrh, give me patience![18]
To his school I went and found him
Devouring a boy. I ran away,
Dropped my slipper there—
O box of myrrh, give me patience!
Then I climbed the tree,
And the king married me.
I gave birth to the first ones—
O box of myrrh, give me patience!
Then I gave birth to the girl,
And they told him I was a ghouleh—
O box of myrrh, give me patience!"

She had not finished, when lo! the wall split open[19] and she saw her children walking out of it. Children of kings, like full moons they were! And what were they like? Well behaved and very, very handsome.

17. The unveiling (*jalwe*) refers to the part of the wedding ceremony at which the bridegroom unveils the bride, a custom that is practiced differently in different parts of the country (cf. Tale 15, n. 22). It is a particularly important part of the ceremony, because it may be the first time a bridegroom sees his bride, as is presumed to be the case in our tale. Granqvist (*Marriage* II: 115–119) gives a complete and vivid description of this ritual; see also ʿArnīṭah, *Al-Funūn:* 138. For a sample of a *jalwe* song, see Dalman, *Diwan:* 254–261.

18. Because *ṣabr* means both "myrrh" and "patience," it is obvious that the tale, through a form of sympathetic magic, relies on the power residing in words—specifically, their ability to carry more than one meaning—to effect the exorcism. See n. 15, above.

19. On exorcism, see Tale 32, n. 7.

Concerning the efficacy of pomegranate switches, Crowfoot and Baldensperger (*Cedar:* 112) offer the following account: "Now because the pomegranate tree had power over evil spirits, in the days when madness was believed to be caused by possession and beating in vogue as a cure, a beating with pomegranate branches was considered peculiarly efficacious. This appears in the oft told tale of the lunatics who lost their feet. The poor madmen, let out for the day, went to bathe their feet in a pool and got them so mixed that they could not sort them out. . . . At last a wise sheikh came by, to whom they told their trouble. He, bringing a pomegranate rod, then gave each of them a good beating on his feet. Each madman as he felt the pain knew his feet for his own and took them out of the water."

"Children!" she said to them. "Your father's getting married, and tonight's the night of the unveiling. Go there, and walk right in! When people stop you to ask who you are, say to them, 'This is our father's house, and you, the strangers, are going to kick us out?'[20] Don't listen to anyone! The girl will sit in her father's lap, and you boys one on each side of him."

They went and entered the bridal room. When the king beheld them, what a sight they were! He stopped looking at his bride, to see what she was like.

"Get out of here!" the people around shouted at them. "What a disaster you are! Damn your father and the fathers of those who gave birth to you!"

"This is our father's house," they answered, "and you, the strangers, are going to kick us out?"

"Where's your father from?" the king asked them, taken by surprise. "Who are you? Who's your mother?"[21]

"We're the children of the one who lives in the house of desertion," they answered.

"Speak again," he said, "and tell me the truth!"

"That's the way it is," they answered.

"What's the bride's name?" asked the king, and they told him it was Ṣālḥa.

"Ṣālḥa's hereby divorced as of last night!" announced the king. "Seven servants are to go escort the queen here!"

They went and accompanied the queen, and the celebration turned out to be for him and his children.

Hail! Hail! Finished is our tale!

36. *The Woodcutter*

Once upon a time there was a poor man, a woodcutter. Every day he would bring a bundle of wood, sell it, and eat from his earnings. One day, before setting out to the woods in the morning, he roasted a handful

20. This expression is a reformulation of a popular folk expression, *ʾId-dār dār abūnā, w-iju l-ġurub yitḥūnā* ("The house is our father's house, and the strangers have come to kick us out").

21. The order of the questions here is significant in terms of the Palestinian definition of

of fava beans to entertain himself along the way.[1] He walked along munching on them, taking the road to Bāb il-Wādī. As he approached the well belonging to the house of Yūsif is-Slīman,[2] the one in the middle of the road, he tossed a bean up in the air—but it did not land in his mouth, it fell right into the well. Driven by his poverty and his sadness over its loss, he squatted by the mouth of the well and cried out:

> "Oh! My fava bean,
> My protection against hunger!
> Oh! My fava bean,
> My protection against hunger!"

And how he cried over the loss of that bean!

Now, the well, in it they say there were (in the name of Allah, the Compassionate, the Merciful!) dwellers.[3]

"Hey uncle, leave us alone!" they answered him.[4] "What's the matter with you? You hurt our ears with all this din!"

"I want my fava bean back," he answered, crying again:

> "Oh! My fava bean,
> My protection against hunger!"

---

self, with the king's first concern in establishing the identity of his children being not in terms of kinship or lineage but in the father's place of origin.

1. Like the lentil (see Tale 26, n. 12), the fava bean is an important source of food for the Palestinian fellah, especially for breakfast. As the tale demonstrates, it is highly valued, and many proverbs and folk sayings attest to its importance, such as: *mā tqūl fūl, ġēr ta-yṣīr fī l-iʿdūl* ("Don't call them fava beans until they're in the basket"—in other words, "Don't count on something until you have it") and *b-tinballiš fī ṯimmo fūle* ("A fava bean doesn't [have time to] get wet in his mouth"—said of someone who cannot keep a secret). See Tale 8, n. 4.

2. Bāb il-Wādī is the way leading out of the village of ʿArrābe, upper Galilee, where the tale was collected. Yūsif is-Slīmān and others mentioned later on are members of the community and neighbors of the teller. Thus the narrator of this tale places the action concretely in her village (cf. Tale 30, nn. 9, 11). For other references to ʿArrābe in these tales, see Tale 5, n. 14.

3. The dwellers in the well are jinn; for more on wells, see Tale 3, n. 4. In "Haunted Springs" (p. 153), Canaan states, "It is an old and wide-spread belief in all Semitic countries, that springs, cisterns and all running waters are inhabited"—and at the end of the article he lists 120 such "inhabited" springs throughout Palestine. Jaussen ("Le cheikh Saʿad ad-din": 150) says, "Ils [les djinn] sont très nombreux et habitent en tous lieux; mais ils fréquentent particulièrement les régions désertes, les puits, les sources." For Palestinian jinn tales, see al-Barghūthī, *Ḥikāyāt jān;* for a comprehensive discussion of the jinn in the Arabic tradition, see al-Jawharī, *ʿIlm al-fūlklūr* II: 359–467; for Palestine in particular, see Canaan, "Dämonenglaube": 2–28. For other references, see Tale 32, n. 2.

4. Polite forms of address are so deeply ingrained in Palestinian (and Arab) social behavior that even the jinn are presumed to observe them correctly.

"Uncle!" they said, "Is it worth all this din? Here! Take this wooden bowl—whatever you tell it to fill with, it will fill, and you can eat something other than these fava beans."[5]

Taking the bowl with him, he went back home. He brought it into the hut with him, locked the door, and said, "Wooden bowl, fill up with rice and meat, topped with yogurt sauce!"[6] And what do you think happened? Before he even had time to look, the bowl had filled with rice and meat, and with sauce covering them. And what now, you might ask? He ate until he could barely move, and every day after that—evening, morning, and noon—he would tell the bowl to fill with whatever food he wanted to eat. He then ate and threw away the rest.

One day he felt bored. "Am I just going to sit around in this shack?" he asked himself. "By Allah, I want to go out and have a good time. But what am I going to do with this bowl?" Then he said, "By Allah, I'm going to leave it with our neighbor"—you might say at the house of Im Falāḥ. Going over to her house, he knocked and said, "Hey, Im Falāḥ, Allah save you! Would you mind keeping this wooden bowl in your house and taking care of it? And mind, don't wreck it while I'm gone by saying to it, 'Wooden bowl, fill with rice and meat; or with cracked wheat, noodles and tomato sauce!' and then eating from it! I'll be gone for a couple of days to have a good time, then I'll be back."

No sooner had he turned his back than Im Falāḥ said, "Wooden bowl, fill with rice and meat, topped with yogurt sauce!" And what! They had barely time to look, when it became full to the brim. The whole family ate till they were stuffed.

"Yee! By Allah, he'll never see it again. We have an old bowl just like this one, and when he comes back we'll give it to him instead. May he never eat! He's all by himself, and we're a whole family. What does he need it for?"

Coming back, the woodcutter knocked on their door, "Im Falāḥ!"

5. The *bāṭye* is a large wooden bowl used by women to knead the dough for the family's bread. After rising, the dough was taken to the bakery in the same bowl, which the women carried on their heads. Peasant families traditionally used the *bāṭye* to serve meals for the entire household. See n. 6, below.

6. The traditional style of Palestinian cooking facilitates the use of the *bāṭye* for serving food. Meat (usually lamb), when available, is stewed with a vegetable (*yaxnī*) and served over rice. Meat stewed in yogurt sauce (see Tale 40, n. 6) and served over rice (*mansaf*) is considered a special dish, and is served to guests on formal occasions, such as wedding celebrations (*jīze*), baptisms (*ʿimmād*), circumcisions (*thūr*), and completing the roof on a house (*ʿaqde*).

"Yes, brother. What do you want? Do come in, please!"

"For the sake of Allah," he answered, "give me back the wooden bowl. I'm dying of hunger, and I want to go home and eat."

She gave it back to him, or so he thought, and he took it home.[7] Right away he said, "Wooden bowl, fill with rice and meat, topped with yogurt sauce!" He waited and waited, but it did not fill. "Fill up with cracked wheat and noodles! Fill up with rice and lentils![8] Fill up with this or that!" But it did not fill. Nothing at all happened.

When he went to see Im Falāḥ about it, she said, "I don't know what you're talking about, brother. That's the one you brought here and I gave it back to you. What can I do?"

So back to the well he went, and—splash!—dropped it in and started moaning:

"Oh! My fava bean,
My protection against hunger!"

"What's the matter with you?" asked the dwellers in the well. "Didn't we give you the wooden bowl?"

"It's ruined," he answered. "It's no good any more."

"Well, then," they said, "take this mill! If you turn the handle to the right, it'll grind gold; and to the left, silver."

Well, he took it with him and went home. Locking the door of his hut, he sat down to grind. Every day he would grind a bit and put it in his pocket, then he would go enjoy himself in Acre, Haifa, or Nazareth. When he had done this for nearly a month, he started to worry. "What if someone should come," he thought, "tear down the door of this shack, and steal the mill?" Taking it to another neighbor, you might say to Nōxa's house, he said, "O Im Yāsīn![9] For the sake of Allah, won't you keep this little mill in your house for me while I'm gone?"

"Yes, brother, you can leave it here. What's going to happen to it?"

7. "Or so he thought" (*qāl*)—literally, "he said," but frequently used as a transitional device (like the English "say" or "well") in a variety of contexts.

8. The simple and inexpensive peasant meal of *mjaddara* consists of rice and lentils, cooked together in water with some olive oil and served with fried onions or a tomato salad, or both. We note the downward progress of the woodcutter's requests: he asks first for rice and meat, then for progressively less fancy and more easily available foods. Cf. Tale 26, n. 12.

9. Nōxa is a neighbor of the narrator; we note that she is called by her first name when referred to indirectly, but in direct address she is "Im Yāsīn" (cf. Tale 27, n. 1).

"Meanwhile," he said, "Allah save you! don't use it for grinding gold and silver by turning the handle to the right or to the left!"

No sooner had he turned his back than she set it down and said, "Come, let's try this mill!" And behold! what was the result? The woman went crazy with happiness.

In a day or two, he came back.

"O Im Yāsīn, for Allah's sake, give me back the mill!"

Taking what she gave him home, he turned the handle this way and that, but it did not grind anything. He spread his legs and sat down. Turn the handle this way, turn the handle that way, till he was exhausted, and still no result.

"Damn your owner's father!" he cursed it.[10]

Back to the well he went, and—splash!—he dropped it down to the bottom and repeated his lament:

"Oh! My fava bean,
My protection against hunger!"

"Hey, uncle!" they said. "You've destroyed our peace! Didn't we give you the wooden bowl and the little mill? What more do you want?"

"People have robbed them from me," he complained.

"Well," they responded, "in that case take this stick back to the people you left them with and say to it, 'O my stick, keep flitting, on the side of this neighbor hitting!' and it'll keep on bashing them until they return your things."

Back home he went, straight to Im Falāḥ. "Give me back my wooden bowl!" he said.

"But we already gave it back to you," she insisted.

"All right, then," he said:

"O my stick, keep flitting,
On the sides of Im Falāḥ hitting!"

And the stick went ahead and beat her and her family until it had softened them up.

"Please, brother," they begged. "For the sake of Allah, may He damn your father and your wooden bowl! Go, take it! It's the one over there on the shelf."[11]

10. On this curse, see Tale 1, n. 6.
11. For "shelf" (*sidde*), see Tale 15, n. 5.

He took it and went home. After he had tried it out and made sure that it worked, he left it there and went to Im Yāsīn's house, where he said:

"O my stick, keep flitting,
On the sides of Nōxa hitting!"

The stick hit her over and over, until she said, "There's your mill over there! Go take it, and may Allah damn your father and your mill!"

He took it home, tried it out and found it worked, and lived in comfort from then on.

This is my tale, I've told it, and in your hands I leave it.

37. *The Fisherman*

Once there was a fisherman who lived all by himself in a shack. Every day he caught some fish and sold them, saving a few for his neighbor to cook for him. Because he was by himself and had nobody, she took pity on him. One day he thought, "Am I to keep imposing on my neighbor like this? By Allah, I'm going out to the coffeehouse for a cup of coffee, and when I come back I'll prepare the fish myself." He put the fish down, covering them with a platter, and went to the coffeehouse, where he sat down to sip a cup of coffee. When he came home, he discovered his house had been visited. While he was gone, a board had dropped from the ceiling, and three daughters of the king of the jinn had come out. One of them had cleaned the fish, another had fried them; then they had left, having first done his dishes and put his house in order.

When he came back, he uncovered the fish and found them all cleaned, scraped, and cooked exactly the way he liked them. "By Allah," he thought, "my neighbor must have taken pity on me and come in to prepare the fish for me." The next day, he went to her house. "Here!" he said. "Take these fish, neighbor, and may Allah reward you! Yesterday you came in and prepared the fish for me at home."

"No, brother," she answered, "I did no such thing. I wouldn't dream of going into your place while you're out."

Going to an elderly barber,[1] he said, "Sir, I want to tell you a story. Yesterday, such and such happened to me."

1. The assumption is that the barber is reputed for his knowledge and wisdom. In the village economy of old the barbers performed several functions, including primitive surgery. They would know what was going on in the village better than anyone else.

"Sir," answered the barber, "tomorrow, put the fish down and hide behind the window. Then you'll see who comes into your place and does them for you."

Well, he went and caught a few fish and sold what he wanted to sell, leaving only as many as he could eat. Bringing them home, he covered them with the platter and said, "By Allah, I'm going out to the coffeehouse for a cup of coffee, and when I come back I'll prepare them myself." Going out, he turned and stood guard behind the window. The board dropped, and three girls came down. And what girls they were! You might say they were nothing less than daughters of kings. One of them swept the house, the other scraped the fish, and the third put things in order. Quick as a wink, he did not wait for them to finish but opened the door. Two of them disappeared, and the youngest one remained.

"It's settled," she said. "Fate has decreed I'm yours.[2] Besides, I don't dare go back home now. My parents will kill me."

Taking her in, he lived with her. He sent for the cadi, who drew up a marriage contract, and he married her and lived together with her. In two or three days he said, "Are we going to stay in this shack? You already know what I do for a living."

"Don't worry," she answered. "Leave it to me!"

She sent for people, put out a bid on a house, and had one built opposite the king's palace. When she took possession of the house, she furnished and arranged it, and then lived together with her husband.

One day she got up early in the morning and went to the roof to hang out her laundry, when the king saw her.

"To whom does this woman belong, people?"

"This is So-and-So's wife."

Sending for the fisherman, he said, "I want your wife."

"O Ruler of the Age," begged the fisherman, "how can I give you my wife?"

"I don't know how you're going to manage it," responded the king, "but I want her. I'll set an impossible task for you, and if you fail to do it, I'll cut off your head and take your wife."

"What is it?"

2. The word *xalaṣ*—"It's settled"; literally, "It is finished"—is frequently heard in (Eastern) Arabic conversation, particularly when agreement on an issue has been reached. It may also be used to preempt discussion or argument, as in the present context.

The expression *anā qisimtak*—"Fate has decreed I'm yours"; literally, "I'm your portion"—is based on the word *qisme,* sometimes rendered in English as "kismet."

"I want you to bring me a grapevine, to be planted in the evening. And in the morning I want to get up and find one bunch of grapes on it. I want to eat from it with my whole army, and it should stay exactly as it is."

The fisherman went crying to his wife.

"It's finished," he lamented. "I'm going to die."

"Don't be afraid," she said. "Go back to the shack we were in and call out, 'You whose height is two hand-spans and whose hat is two finger-lengths, come out!' and a creature will appear. Say to him, 'My mistress Xaddūj bids you tell my mistress ʿAyyūš to give me a branch of the grapevine growing in front of her house.'"[3]

"All right," he said, and went to call out as she had taught him, bringing back with him a branch of the vine. He went and dug by the door of the palace, planted it, and then headed home.

In the morning, it is said (and if the teller is to be trusted), the king came and found a full-grown grapevine with one cluster of grapes on it. He cut it down and ate from it with all his army, and it stayed exactly as it was. The king then excused the fisherman. But what was he to do? He wanted the fisherman's wife. Waiting a week or two, he sent for him again.

"What do you want, my lord?"

"I want your wife."

"O Ruler of the Age! O son of worthy people! My wife?"

"This time," said the king, "you must bring me a loaf of bread. I will eat from it with my army, and it should stay exactly as it is. Otherwise, I'll cut off your head and take your wife."

Again he went crying to his wife, saying, "Such and such is the story."

"Don't worry," she answered. "Go and call on the same one you called on last time, and say, 'Give me the loaf of bread sitting on the shelf in my family's house.'"

The fisherman went, called out, and the creature came. "My mistress Xaddūj," said he, "bids you tell my mistress ʿAyyūš to give me the loaf of bread sitting on the shelf in her family's house." The creature disappeared and then came back with a loaf of bread and said, "Here, master!"

Bringing the bread with him, the fisherman put it in front of the king, who ate from it with all his army, and it stayed exactly as it was. The fisherman then took the bread home with him.

3. Xaddūj and ʿAyyūš are diminutive forms of two popular women's names, Xadīje and ʿĒše. Cf. the title of Tale 27.

"It's no use," declared the king finally. "Whether it cracks, or whether it rings,[4] I want the fisherman's wife."

And again he sent for him, and said, "I want you to bring me an infant the moment he's born, naked and with his umbilical cord still attached. I want this infant to tell me a tale that's all lies, from beginning to end."

"My lord," said the fisherman, "by the honor of your womenfolk, I beg you!"

"No use," answered the king.

Back to his wife went the fisherman, weeping.

"What's the matter?" she asked.

"Such and such is the story," he answered.

"Fine," she said. "My sister's just now giving birth. Go stand by the door of the shack and call out again. Tell the creature to wait until she's given birth, then have him wrap the baby in a piece of cloth and bring it to you."

The fisherman went and called the creature out, saying to him, "My mistress tells you to give me the baby her sister's giving birth to right now."

"Wait until he's born," replied the creature.

The fisherman waited by the door of the shack, and when she had given birth, the other wrapped the baby in a piece of cloth and brought him.

"Hurry!" urged the fisherman's wife, "Take and put him in front of the king, and don't worry about anything!"

The fisherman carried the baby in his arms to the king's palace.

"Peace to you!" declared the infant the moment they came in.

When they had brought him a chair and the baby sat down in it in front of the king, he said, "O Ruler of the Age, I want to tell you a tale."

"Please go ahead," responded the king, and the infant began his tale:

"By Allah, O king, in the old days I used to go around selling olive oil loaded on a rooster. One day the rooster's back broke. I was going around wondering what to do for him, what to use on him, when someone much like yourself showed up.

"'Young man,' said he, 'you've got no recourse but walnuts. Crush a walnut and rub it on the rooster's back, and it will heal.'

"So I went, got hold of a walnut, and crushed and spread it on the rooster's back. In the morning I woke up and found a tree on his back,

4. *Ṭaqqat rannat*—a folk expression meaning "Come what may."

and it was loaded with walnuts. Even with forty pickers up in it, not one could see the other; and with forty gatherers under it, not one could reach out and touch another.

"Well, I brought pickers and gatherers and had the tree picked and the nuts gathered. Then I looked up and saw one nut still hanging from the tip of the topmost branch. I reached for a handful of dirt and threw it to knock the walnut down, and that handful spread into a plain the size of Marj Ibn ʿĀmir on top of the tree.[5] I hired a team of yoked oxen, and set to plowing the plain and planting it with sesame. A caravan passed by and said, 'Young man, what're you planting?'

"'By Allah,' I answered, 'I'm planting sesame.'

"'No,' they said. 'By Allah, it's a waste of this soil to plant sesame in it. It's better to plant watermelons.'[6]

"So I hired laborers and had the sesame seeds picked up, one by one. When they were finished, I counted the seeds and found one missing. As I was going around looking for it, I found it in an ant's mouth. With me pulling in one direction and the ant in the other, the seed split and the ant got away with one half and I with the other. I pressed it out, and it yielded a ton of sesame oil.

"After that I started planting watermelons in the plain. I would no sooner plant the seed than the watermelon would grow behind me as large as a big jar.[7] I wanted to cut open a watermelon, so I took hold of one and did like this with the knife, and what should happen but that it slipped from my hand into the watermelon. Taking off my clothes, I jumped inside the watermelon and found I was in a market of butcher shops.[8] As I was wandering around looking for the knife, I found it with one of the butchers. With me pulling in one direction and he in the other, we ended up fighting over the knife. Eventually, I snatched it away from him and struck him a blow that killed him. Then I pulled myself together and came out. And here I am, O Ruler of the Age! I came directly to see you. Whatever you want, I'm ready to do it."

5. "Marj Ibn ʿĀmir," otherwise known as the Plain of Esdraelon, is the fertile plain (*marj*) stretching from Jinīn to Nazareth in the northern part of the country.

6. In fact, soil that is good for watermelons is also good for sesame.

7. The jar (derived from *jarra*), made of red clay, is round or oblong in shape and holds about twenty gallons. These jars were used for storing an annual supply of olive oil or for holding water hauled in from the spring. See Newton, *Fifty Years:* 36.

8. The markets in old Arab cities with a casbah (e.g., Jerusalem, Damascus, Tunis, and Fez) tend to be divided along professional lines, and thus include such markets as this *sūq il-laḥḥāmīn,* consisting of butcher shops.

"Uncle," said the king to the fisherman, "take this boy away, and may Allah bless you and your wife! And never again will I claim her."[9]

The fisherman took the boy back to his family, and he lived with his wife in peace and comfort.

This is my tale, I've told it, and in your hands I leave it.

Afterword

These tales take for their theme the relationship between the individual and society, where family bonds and obligations do not necessarily dictate the standard of conduct. In this group the fabric of society in operation is shown, with the values of helping those in distress and of neighborliness present or assumed in all of them. The women in "Im ʿAwwād" go to the spring to wash their clothes in groups, both for protection and because people like to be together. In "The Merchant's Daughter," the neighbor not only comes to the girl's rescue, but he also assumes the father's role in marrying her off. Pomegranate Seeds is helped by the shopkeepers, who, out of a sense of social (and moral) obligation to help the helpless, take her in for the night; and when their shops are turned upside down, the shopkeepers' neighbors in turn assist them by collecting money. In "The Woodcutter," the standards of honesty and fair dealing are broken only at the risk of severe and justified punishment. And in the last tale of this group, the fisherman's in-laws help him in a difficult situation, and his neighbor at the beginning of the tale cooks for him, taking pity on him because he is alone and has nobody.

Yet in spite of the social harmony that is presumed to reign, the collectivity does break down. These tales show how disorder can arise when individuals attract negative forces simply by virtue of possessing things or qualities that the rest of society covets. Indeed, envy is considered an active force, its instrument the evil eye; and although the eye is not explicitly mentioned in any of the tales, its power is nevertheless present, symbolized in the first three tales by the actions of the destructive ghouls. As demonstrated in "Im ʿAwwād," it is not easy to protect oneself from these forces, which are "supernatural" not in the sense of being beyond

9. *Bēnī w-bēnhā ʾalla*—literally, "Between me and her, there's Allah," i.e., she is forbidden to him.

nature but rather in being beyond human control. Although presented in terms of ghoul and jinn imagery, the behavior of these forces resembles that of human beings—as seen in the modesty of the fisherman's jinn wife, which prevents her from returning home after having visited a man's house for fear of parental retribution; or in the greed of the ghouleh in "The Merchant's Daughter," who has amassed a large hoard of treasure but does not use it to benefit her family.

Three broad categories of possessions—which accurately reflect the concerns of the society—attract these negative forces: children, wealth, and sexuality. In "Im ʿAwwād," the simple fact of having a male child is the source of envy, for aside from their economic value to the family, sons are also its source of power in the society. Boy children are envied for their own sake, and parents frequently take precautions to protect them from the evil eye. The woodcutter's sudden acquisition of wealth is envied by his neighbors, whose greed resembles that of the ghouleh in "The Merchant's Daughter." And in "The Fisherman," the extreme beauty of the wife sets her apart from other women, thus drawing the power of envy to her, and her sexuality turns her into an object that the king wishes to possess. In "The Merchant's Daughter," the forces of evil converge upon a single girl living by herself without a male protector. Men would assume that someone in her position is easily available, and they would be eager to take advantage of her if they could. Pomegranate Seeds is made to suffer because she is a special creature. She is so special that her mother had a pair of golden slippers made for her, and she is envied for her beauty and her faithfulness. Her encounter with the schoolmaster/sheikh at the beginning of the tale carries clear sexual overtones, and her flight from one place to another may be seen as an attempt to escape the bad reputation that keeps following her. She must struggle for many years to regain her reputation and her honor in the face of strong public pressure, represented by the people who curse her children and urge the king to marry another woman at any cost.

Group IV

ENVIRONMENT

38. *The Little She-Goat*

TELLER: Testify that Allah is One!
AUDIENCE: There is no god but God.

Once there was a she-goat who had three kids. She used to say to them, "You stay here. I'm going to bring you some grass." Every day she went grazing until she was full, then she came home with grass for them and said:

"O my kids! O my kids!
Open the door for me!
The grass is on my horns
And the milk is in my teats."

They would then open the door for her.

One day the hyena saw her as she was leaving and discovered where her kids were.[1] "By Allah," he said to himself, "I'm going to eat them." Now, the she-goat, before going out, would caution her kids, "If anyone should come and say, 'Let me in,' be careful not to open the door." Because the mother's tail had been chopped off, she said to the kids, "If someone should come and say to you, 'Open for me, I'm your mother,' check first if the tail is chopped off or not. If not, then it can't be me. Don't open the door!"

The hyena went to the cave where the kids were and called out:

"O my kids! O my kids!
Open the door for me!
The grass is on my horns
And the milk is in my teats."

"Turn around," they bleated, "and let us see your tail."

Turning around, he displayed his tail, and lo! it was not chopped off.

"Go away!" they said. "You're not our mother."

What was he to do? He wanted to trick them so he could eat them. To the ant he then went and said, "Chop off my tail so I can eat the kids of the little she-goat."

1. For the hyena, see Tale 4, n. 7.

"No," answered the ant, "I won't chop off your tail unless you go to the threshing floor and bring me a measure of wheat."[2]

So to the threshing floor he went and said, "O threshing floor, give me a measure of wheat so I can give it to the ant, and the ant will then chop off my tail so I can eat the kids of the little she-goat."

"I won't give it to you," replied the threshing floor, "unless you bring a team of oxen to tread the wheat on me."[3]

The hyena then went to the oxen and said, "Yoked team, come tread the wheat on the threshing floor, and the threshing floor will give me a measure of wheat, and the measure of wheat I'll give to the ant, and the ant will then chop off my tail so I can eat the kids of the little she-goat."

"We won't go treading," replied the oxen, "unless you tell the spring to give us water to drink."

Going to the pool by the spring, the hyena said, "O pool, let the team of oxen come and drink so that they will tread the wheat on the threshing floor, and the threshing floor will give me a measure of wheat, and the measure of wheat I'll give to the ant, and the ant will then chop off my tail so I can eat the kids of the little she-goat."

"Let the team come and drink," said the pool.

So the team of oxen went and drank at the spring, then they trod the wheat on the threshing floor, and the threshing floor gave a measure of wheat to the ant, and the ant chopped off the hyena's tail.

Back he went to the kids of the little she-goat and called out:

2. Like the *sanāsil* (see Tale 12, n. 11), the threshing floors (*bayādir;* sing., *bēdar*) are a characteristic feature of the Palestinian countryside. The threshing floor, says Conder in his accurate description, is "a broad flat space, an open ground, generally high; sometimes the floor is on a flat rocky hill-top, and occasionally it is an open valley, down which there is a current of air; but it is always situated where most wind can be found. . . . The size of the floor varies, from a few yards to an area of perhaps fifty yards square, and rich villages have sometimes two such floors" (*Tent Work* II:259). See also Grant, *People:* 136. There is a rich folklore associated with the harvest season in Palestine, some of which is recorded in Crowfoot and Baldensperger, *Cedar:* 15–23.

3. Oxen, yoked in teams of two or four, are the animals most commonly used for threshing grain, although other animals, such as horses, donkeys, mules, and occasionally camels, may be hitched together for this purpose as well. The grain is trampled, sometimes under the animals' feet, but more frequently by a heavy wooden sledge (*mōrij*) hitched to one of the beasts, on which a boy sits and drives the animals. "A number of recesses," says Conder (*Tent Work* II:259), "are sunk in under the side of the sledge, and in these small rough pieces of hard basalt . . . are let, which, acting like teeth, tear the corn." See also Grant, *People:* 137; Newton, *Fifty Years:* 42.

"O my kids! O my kids!
Open the door for me!
The grass is on my horns
And the milk is in my teats."

"Show us your tail," they bleated again.

He showed it to them, and, seeing that it was chopped off, they opened the door for him. In he came and gobbled them all up.

When the little she-goat came home, she discovered the hyena had eaten all her kids. To the blacksmith she then went and said, "Make me iron horns, and make them so sharp I can stab the hyena and get my kids back from his stomach."

The blacksmith made her a pair of iron horns as sharp as knives. The little she-goat put them on, rushed to the house of the hyena, and stomped on the roof.

"Who's pounding on my roof?" roared the hyena. "You've shattered my jars of oil."[4]

"I'm the little she-goat of the twisted horns," announced the goat. "Come on out and let's fight!"

The hyena came out. Piercing him this way and that with her horns, the little she-goat ripped open his stomach and pulled her kids free.

This is my tale, I've told it, and in your hands I leave it.

39. *The Old Woman and Her Cat*[1]

Once there was an old woman who had a cat. One day she brought some milk home, and the cat came and lapped it up. Feeling angry, she cut off his tail.

4. For these jars, see Tale 37, n. 7.

1. For folklore about cats in the Holy Land, see Hanauer, *Folklore:* 265–270. "The cat," he notes (p. 265), "is liked by the Moslems, it is said, for the following reason. When the Prophet was a camel-driver, he was asleep one day in the shade of some bushes in the desert. A serpent came out of a hole and would have killed him had not a cat that happened to be prowling about pounced upon and destroyed it. When the Prophet awoke he saw what happened, and, calling the cat to him, fondled and blessed it. From thenceforth he was very fond of cats."

"Meow! Meow!" he cried. "Give me back my tail."

"Give me back my milk," demanded the old woman.

"And how am I going to bring back the milk for you?" he asked.

"Go bring it from that ewe over there," she answered.

Going to the ewe, the cat said, "Ewe, give me some milk, and the milk is for the old woman, and the old woman will then sew my tail back on."

"Bring me a branch from that tree over there," said the ewe, "and I'll give you the milk."

So to the tree he went and said, "O tree, give me a branch, and the branch is for the ewe, and the ewe will give me some milk, and the milk is for the old woman, and the old woman will then sew my tail back on."

"Go tell that plowman over there to come plow under me," replied the tree.

To the plowman then he went and said, "O plowman, come plow under the tree, and the tree will give me a branch, and the branch is for the ewe, and the ewe will give me some milk, and the milk is for the old woman, and the old woman will then sew my tail back on."

"Bring me a pair of shoes from the cobbler," said the plowman.[2]

He went to the cobbler and said, "O cobbler, give me some shoes, and the shoes are for the plowman, and the plowman will plow under the tree, and the tree will give me a branch, and the branch is for the ewe, and the ewe will give me some milk, and the milk is for the old woman, and the old woman will then sew my tail back on."

"Bring me two loaves of bread from that bakerwoman over there," answered the cobbler.[3]

The cat then went to the bakerwoman.

"Bakerwoman," he said, "give me two loaves of bread for the cobbler, and the cobbler will give me some shoes, and the shoes are for the plowman, and the plowman will plow under the tree, and the tree will give me a branch, and the branch is for the ewe, and the ewe will give me some milk, and the milk is for the old woman, and the old woman will then sew my tail back on."

2. The type of shoe referred to here (*madās*) is no longer common among Palestinian landholders. In the old days these simple shoes were made entirely from the type of rubber used for tires. For a photograph, see Schmidt and Kahle, *Volkserzählungen* II: pl. 36.

3. The business of constructing the clay outdoor oven known as the *ṭābūn* (see Tale 26, n. 1), of keeping it hot with the proper fuels (see n. 4, below), and of baking the bread falls to the woman.

"Bring me a bucketful of manure from that pile over there," said the bakerwoman.[4]

So, bringing a bucket full of manure, the cat gave it to the bakerwoman, and she gave him two loaves of bread. Taking the bread, he gave it to the cobbler, and the cobbler gave him the shoes, which he gave to the plowman, who plowed under the tree. The tree then gave him a branch, which he gave to the ewe, who gave him the milk. Taking the milk with him, he went running back to the old woman.

"Meow! Meow!" he cried. "Why don't you sew my tail back on?"

The old woman took the milk and sewed the cat's tail back on, and they became friends again.

The bird of this tale has flown; are you ready for the next one?

40. *Dunglet*

Once there was a woman who had no children. Her husband was a plowman, and every day they had a hard time finding someone to take food out to him.[1] They had a few sheep, and one day, as the wife was sweeping out their pen, she cried out, "O seeker, your wish be granted! May I become pregnant and have a boy, even if it is a piece of dung!"[2]

It was as if Allah Himself had spoken with her tongue.[3] When she gave birth, she delivered a pile of dung. All those present at the birth gathered

4. The dry manure of nearly all the domestic animals in Palestine, particularly that of goats, sheep, cattle, and camels, makes an excellent fuel for the *ṭābūn* when mixed with pressed olive pulp (*jifit*) and the husks of grains. Hence the "pile" the bakerwoman refers to may contain other types of fuel in addition to manure. Perhaps because manure is superior (and relatively scarce) as a fuel, both the word for this pile of fuels (*mizbale*)and that for the act of fueling the *ṭābūn* (*tizbīl*) are derived from the word for manure, *zibil*. For more details on *ṭābūn* fueling, see Kanaana, "Al-Ṭābūn" (15:80–84).

1. Plowmen occur frequently in the tales, reflecting the peasant milieu that characterized Palestinian society. See Tale 26, n. 6.

2. Because the woman cannot have children, she asks for strange offspring. This wish, which occurs elsewhere in the collection (see Tale 1, n. 3; Tale 8, n. 1), seems to represent a type of bargain with Allah, since He has not seen fit to "feed" her with children. For the first part of the invocation, yā ṭālbe yā ġālbe, see Tale 13, n. 1.

3. See Tale 8, n. 2, on this metaphor.

up the dung and threw it outside, but lo! a piece of it rolled under the wardrobe.[4] The woman became very, very sad.

One day, while kneading the dough, the wife called out, "O Lord, if only you had given me a son, he would have taken the food out to his father!"[5] And behold! the piece of dung jumped out from under the wardrobe and said, "Mother, I'll take the food to my father."

The woman set to preparing the food, bringing together some yogurt and seven loaves of bread, and she gave it to Dunglet, who carried it to his father.[6]

"Welcome!" said the father when he saw him in the distance. "Welcome, Dunglet, and the path that led Dunglet, who's bringing his father the yogurt and the seven loaves!" And behold! Dunglet answered, "Death to Dunglet and the path that brought Dunglet, who ate the yogurt and the seven loaves and has come to follow them up with his father and the yoked oxen!"[7] He then devoured his father and the oxen.

Going back home, he found his mother kneading dough.

"Welcome!" she said. "Welcome, Dunglet, and the path that led Dunglet, who's coming to help his mother with the kneading!"

"Death to Dunglet," he answered, "and the path that brought Dunglet, who ate the yogurt and the seven loaves, finished off his father and the oxen, and has now come to follow them up with his mother and her dough!" He then devoured his mother.

The next day he went to visit his father's sister, and found her patching her roof.[8]

"Welcome!" she said. "Welcome, Dunglet, and the path that led Dunglet, who's coming to help his aunt with the patching."

"Death to Dunglet," he answered, "and the path that brought Dunglet, who ate the yogurt and the seven loaves, finished off his father and

4. See Tale 24, n. 9, on having many women present at a birth.

5. Children are an economic asset; they start helping with the domestic and agricultural work from an early age. See Tale 30, n. 7; cf. Tale 10, n. 7.

6. Yogurt is a major item in the peasant diet. With bread it makes a whole meal, and village families rely on this combination, together with olive oil and fresh vegetables, for sustenance, especially during the summer months. Cf. Tale 36, n. 6.

7. Geography dictates the type of draft animal used for plowing. Although a team of oxen is the most common, in the terraced hill country (see Tale 12, n. 11) a donkey (or a pair), a mule, or a horse may be used, and in the desert camels are sometimes used (singly).

8. The roofs of village houses were usually made of a mixture of mud and straw, laid over a wooden platform. Just before the rains (in October), the women patch their roofs with a fresh layer of this clay.

the oxen, his mother and her dough, and has now come to follow them up with his aunt and her clay!" He then devoured his aunt.

The following day he went to visit his mother's sister, and found her doing the laundry.

"Welcome!" she said. "Welcome, Dunglet, and the path that led Dunglet, who's coming to help his aunt with the washing."

"Death to Dunglet," he answered, "and the path that brought Dunglet, who ate the yogurt and the seven loaves, finished off his father and the oxen, his mother and her dough, his aunt and her clay, and has now come to follow them up with his second aunt and her laundry!" He then devoured his second aunt.

The next day he went to visit his grandmother, and found her spinning.

"Welcome!" she said. "Welcome, Dunglet, and the path that led Dunglet, who's coming to help his grandmother with the spinning!"

"Death to Dunglet," he answered, "and the path that brought Dunglet, who ate the yogurt and the seven loaves, finished off his father and the oxen, his mother and her dough, his aunt and her clay, his second aunt and her laundry, and has now come to follow them up with his grandmother and her spinning!" He then devoured his grandmother.

On his way home he ran into a wedding procession.

"Welcome!" people said. "Welcome, Dunglet, and the path that led Dunglet, who's coming to help us celebrate the wedding!"

"Death to Dunglet," he answered, "and the path that brought Dunglet, who ate the yogurt and the seven loaves, finished off his father and the oxen, his mother and her dough, his aunt and her clay, his second aunt and her laundry, his grandmother and her spinning, and has now come to follow them up with the bride and groom!" He then devoured the bride and groom.

As he was walking down the street, he met two blind men who were trying to cross it.

"Welcome!" they said. "Welcome, Dunglet, and the path that led Dunglet, who's coming to help us with the crossing!"

"Death to Dunglet," he answered, "and the path that brought Dunglet, who ate the yogurt and the seven loaves, finished off his father and the oxen, his mother and her dough, his aunt and her clay, his second aunt and her laundry, his grandmother and her spinning, the bride and the groom, and has now come to follow them up with the blind men!"

One of them pulled a little knife out of his pocket and gashed Dunglet's belly. All the people he had devoured came tumbling out, and everything went back as it had been.

41. *The Louse*

Once a louse married a flea.[1] One day guests came to visit them.

"O wife," said the flea. "Won't you get up and make us some dinner?"[2]

Getting up, the louse kneaded unleavened loaves and went outside to bake them in the oven.[3] But when she reached in, she could not bring them out. She ran to her husband the flea and said, "I wasn't able to reach them." So out he went and came toward the oven to reach for the loaves, and behold! he landed in the heart of the oven.

The louse waited for him, but he did not come back. Back to the oven she went, and lo and behold! he was burned to a crisp—*qaḥmašāne*.[4] He was as charred as charcoal.

Going then to the dump, she smeared herself with soot.[5]

"What's the matter, O louse?" asked the dump. "Why are you smeared with soot?"

"I'm smeared with soot—*saxmāne*," answered the louse, "for my husband the lost one—*ṭaršāne*—who fell into the oven and burned to a crisp—*qaḥmašāne*."[6]

1. In the popular imagination the louse and the flea are thought to belong to the same species, the louse being the female and the flea the male. This belief probably received linguistic confirmation from the gender of each word in Arabic; *qamle* ("louse") is feminine in form, and *barġūṯ* masculine.

2. For "dinner" (*ġadā*), see Tale 14, n. 10.

3. The reference here is to the *ṭābūn*, for which see Tale 6, n. 8; Tale 26, n. 1; Tale 39, nn. 3, 4.

4. Although our policy in translating these tales has been to produce a readable English text without intrusions from the original language, an exception had to be made in this case. Because the tale builds up to a crescendo, not only of action but also of sound, leaving out the rhyming motif would have been equivalent to taking away part of the action.

5. For "dump" or fuel heap (*mizbale*), see Tale 39, n. 4. Soot would be available at or near the dump because that is where the remains from the *ṭābūn*—ashes as well as charred pieces of wood—are thrown. Women smear their hands and faces with soot in mourning, at the death of male relatives in particular. Granqvist (*Muslim Death:* 53) says, "A woman takes pride in expressing her violent sorrow. And she knows it will be spoken of in the village." For more on "demonstration of grief," see Tale 25, n. 4; cf. Tale 1, n. 11. See also Jaussen, *Naplouse:* 338.

6. The Arabic text throughout has "cousin" (rather than "husband"), for which cf. Tale 6, n. 2.

"As for me," said the dump, "I'm collapsing."

Toward evening a flock of sheep came that way.

"What's the matter, O dump?" they asked. "Why have you collapsed?"

"I've collapsed—*hailāne,*" answered the dump. "The louse is smeared with soot—*saxmāne*—and the flea has fallen into the oven and burned to a crisp—*qaḥmašāne.*"

"As for us," said the sheep, "we're going lame."

In the morning they passed by an olive tree.

"Why, O sheep," asked the tree, "are you lame like this?"

"We're lame—*ʿarjāne,*" they answered. "The dump has collapsed—*hailāne*—and the louse is smeared with soot—*saxmāne*—for her husband the lost one—*ṭaršāne*—who fell into the oven and burned to a crisp—*qaḥmašāne.*"

"As for me," said the tree, "I'm withering."

A bird came to perch on the tree.

"What's the matter, O olive tree?" asked the bird. "Why are you withered?"

"I'm withered—*šalallāne,*" answered the tree. "The sheep are lame—*ʿarjāne*—the dump has collapsed—*hailāne*—and the louse is smeared with soot—*saxmāne*—for her husband the lost one—*ṭaršāne*—who fell into the oven and burned to a crisp—*qaḥmašāne.*"

"As for me," said the bird, "I'm plucking my feathers."

The bird then went to drink at the spring.

"What's the matter, O bird?" asked the spring. "Why are you plucked?"

"My feathers are plucked—*maʿṭāne,*" answered the bird. "The olive tree is withered—*šalallāne*—the sheep are lame—*ʿarjāne*—the dump has collapsed—*hailāne*—and the louse is smeared with soot—*saxmāne*—for her husband the lost one—*ṭaršāne*—who fell into the oven and burned to a crisp—*qaḥmašāne.*"

"As for me," said the spring, "I'm drying up."

Bedouin Arabs[7] came to get water at the spring and found it dry.

"What's the matter, O spring?" they asked. "Why are you dry?"

"I'm dry—*našfāne,*" answered the spring. "The bird's feathers are plucked—*maʿṭāne*—the olive tree is withered—*šalallāne*—the sheep are

7. The original expression has only the second term, *ʿarab*—the most common form of reference to the Bedouins among the Arabs themselves.

lame—*ʿarjāne*—the dump has collapsed—*hailāne*—and the louse is smeared with soot—*saxmāne*—for her husband the lost one—*ṭaršāne*—who fell into the oven and burned to a crisp—*qaḥmašāne*."

"As for us," declared the Bedouins, "we're breaking our jars."

They broke their jars and headed back to their camp. Some other Bedouins ran into them.

"Why, O Arabs," they asked, "are your jars broken?"

"Our jars are broken—*kasrāne*," they answered. "The spring is dry—*našfāne*—the olive tree is withered—*šalallāne*—the sheep are lame—*ʿarjāne*—the dump has collapsed—*hailāne*—and the louse is smeared with soot—*saxmāne*—for her husband the lost one—*ṭaršāne*—who fell into the oven and burned to a crisp—*qaḥmašāne*."

"And as for us," these nomads exclaimed, "we're getting out of here—*raḥlāne!*"

Afterword

This group differs fundamentally from all the other tales in the collection. Because they are "formula" tales, requiring a verbal precision that becomes part of the content, there is little room in them for tellers to show individuality in weaving the narrative. Also, being formulaic, they are circular in structure, with the end contained in the beginning. They therefore do not reflect social reality in the same way the other tales do; rather, they serve an analogical function, as models of that reality. The regularity and security of the social world is reflected in the predictable organization of each tale—the prescribed order that must be followed for the next step to be achieved. Thus, as a group, the tales show individuals as existing in harmonious interdependence with the environment, both animate and inanimate. In the first three tales disharmony is produced by upsetting one of the links in the chain of relationships, thereby triggering a process of readjustment in all the other links until equilibrium is restored. In "The Louse," in contrast, one of the links in the chain has been destroyed, and the damage reverberates throughout the system, causing harm to all its components and preventing the restoration of equilibrium. Thus an action that appears inconsequential at the microscopic level, when multiplied throughout the chain, can damage the entire community.

Despite the similarity in form, the tales are nevertheless marked by differences in detail that set each apart from the others. "The Little She-Goat," one of the most popular children's tales in the country, lends itself to allegorical interpretation, with the she-goat standing for the underdog and the hyena (which in some versions is represented as a ghoul) representing oppressive authority. With courage and community cooperation, the she-goat is able to liberate her children from the belly of the monster. It is instructive to observe how the alliances in the tale are worked out. Even though the hyena can get help from the other animals as long as he gives something in return, the domestic goat is the only animal that receives help, from the blacksmith, with no conditions attached; thus human beings and domestic animals are in alliance against the forces of the wild. Like "Dunglet," the tale teaches us that, despite his awe-inspiring appearance, the monster is not so fearful after all.

The dialectic of domestic versus wild on which the tale of the she-goat turns helps us understand the next tale, "The Old Woman and Her Cat." Although the cat is a domestic animal, it has not totally lost its wild impulses and so does not hesitate to lap up the old woman's milk as soon as an opportunity presents itself. This observation is confirmed by the fact that few households keep cats as pets. In the villages, where food has traditionally been scarce, little is left over for pets; cats therefore lead a semiwild existence, living on the scraps tossed to them and on what they can hunt in the fields or steal from people's homes. Thus the cat's theft of the old woman's milk would not be an unusual occurrence; it would, however, be unusual for the old woman to keep a cat when she could not feed it. The taming of the cat, then, seems to be the point of the tale. By acting selfishly in lapping up the milk, the cat, although acting according to its nature, is behaving in a manner contrary to the norms of the society. And the routine of sending him out to regain his tail is a way of teaching him the meaning of cooperation and interdependence. The theme of nature versus culture, in fact, is prominent in Palestinian folklore, and the cat is often used emblematically to typify the sort of creature that, no matter how refined it appears to be, still preserves its wild nature underneath.

In many respects, "Dunglet" is similar to "The Little She-Goat." In both tales the ghoulish figure is overcome by being slashed in the belly so that those he had devoured may return to their previous condition. The belly thus serves as a central image to convey concretely the idea of greed, which the ghoul usually personifies in the tales. Both tales, like all folktales, champion the weak underdog against the strong and powerful.

In "The Little She-Goat," the hyena was seen to represent oppressive authority. The tale of "Dunglet," too, deals with a social evil, namely, the oppression of children by adult members of the extended family. We note that the initial wish to have a child is utilitarian: the family needs someone to take the food out to the father. Further, wherever the child turns, all his relatives perceive him only in terms of his usefulness to them. He seems to exist only insofar as he can be of use. Certainly, in such an environment the child would harbor an intense resentment toward his family, and the figure of Dunglet may therefore be seen, from the child's point of view, as a justified magnification of that resentment.

Yet "Dunglet" is a more complex tale than would appear at first sight. It demonstrates clearly the organic relationship (discussed in the afterword to Group V) between the human world and the supernatural, which, taken together, form a unitary reality. In "Dunglet," as in "Sumac!" (Tale 8), the wish for strange offspring originates in the mind of the mother; the ghoulish figure, in other words, is a symbolic externalization of conditions already existing within the social system. The harmonious functioning of the individual within this system is presumed to be the normal state of affairs. The individual's thought process, although invisible, is nevertheless understood to be as "real" as are material manifestations of reality. Hence, Dunglet's mother can act upon the world merely by wishing. Socially isolated because she has no children, in her despair she challenges her destiny by asking for something absurd (cf. Tale 1, n. 3). Indirectly, the tale admonishes its listeners against having evil thoughts, for the possibility exists that this evil will materialize and harm others. It is this sort of "materialization" of thought that lies behind the belief in the evil eye (alluded to in the preceding afterword to Group III and discussed in Tale 19, n. 4).

The tale of "Dunglet" also demonstrates clearly the relationship between ghoulishness and appetite, and teaches an important lesson about the metaphorical significance of "devouring." Palestinian mothers threaten their children with the devouring ghoul from an early age, and even though no one knows what a ghoul looks like, each has his or her own image of it. That is why it is said that ghouls can take any shape. Now, Dunglet is the shape that his mother's hunger takes: he is an eternal belly, always devouring but never satisfied; he has the power to destroy anyone who can see him, especially members of his family. The only way to destroy him is to pierce his belly, the locus of his appetite, yet the only ones who have the power to do so are the blind men, who cannot even see him. In short, those who are themselves hungry cannot liberate themselves from the illusion of his power; they have been "devoured," overcome by the power of appearance.

As for "The Louse," this tale provides a kind of model for the sympathy that people feel for each other in case of disaster. Here we find the reverse of the process of identity discussed in the afterword to Group III: although the individual derives his identity from the collectivity, that collectivity in turn shares the fate of the individual. Thus the collectivity is understood in its native context to be not necessarily an oppressive force, but a community of feeling wherein an individual's fate can act upon the society at large and hence affect its destiny.

Group V

UNIVERSE

42. *The Woman Who Fell into the Well*

Once there were some men who had been out selling, you might say, charcoal and were on their way home.[1] As they were traveling, one of them said, "God forsake you![2] By Allah, we're hungry!"

"O So-and-So!" they said. "Stop by and ask for something for us."

Stopping by a house to ask for something, he found a woman at home.[3]

"I entreat you in Allah's name, sister," he said, "if you have a couple of loaves of bread, let me have them for these cameleers. We're on the road from faraway places, and we're hungry."

"Of course," she said, and reached for the bread, giving him what Allah put within her means to give—a loaf, maybe two.

And, by Allah, on his way out of the house, he stumbled over a dog tied to a tree. Startled,[4] the man fell backwards, and behold! he ended up in a well that happened to be there. It was a dry well and held no water at all.[5]

"There is no power and no strength except in Allah!" exclaimed the woman.[6]

"O sister," the man cried out, "lower the rope and pull me out!"

Throwing him the rope, the woman started to pull him out but when he almost reached the mouth of the well her strength failed her. His weight grew too heavy for her, and she fell into the well with him.

"There is no power and no strength except in Allah!" exclaimed the man. "But don't worry, sister. By Allah's book, you're my sister!"[7] And they sat together for a while.

1. For traveling salesmen, see Tale 4, n. 3.

2. *ʾAlla yiqṭaʿkum*—literally, "May Allah cut you off, or abandon you [on the road]!" This is more an expletive than a curse.

3. It is an accepted practice for merchant-salesmen traveling in remote villages to ask for food at private homes; people would distinguish between them and beggars.

The woman here is by herself, without male "protectors." As we have seen from Tales 10 and 35, this situation has considerable potential for complication. Cf. Tale 31, n. 2.

4. As we find out later on in the tale, the man is startled by the dog charging him.

5. On wells, see Tale 3, n. 4.

6. This exclamation, *lā ḥawla wa-lā quwwata illā b-illāh,* is used frequently, especially in situations that are beyond individual control. It is usually abbreviated, as here, to *lā ḥawla wa-lā* ("There is no strength and no . . .").

7. *ʾInti uxtī fī ktāb alla* is a binding declaration of honorable intention, carrying the moral weight of an oath (for which, see Tale 13, n. 7; and cf. Tale 20, n. 5).

Now, her brothers were seven, and with their plowman they were eight, and they were all out plowing the fields.[8] In a while the plowman showed up.

"Hey, So-and-So!" he called out. "Hey, So-and-So!" But she did not answer.

After a while, she called out from the well, "Pull me out!"

When he had pulled her and the man out, she said, "Such and such is the story, and please protect my reputation. By Allah, this man is like my brother. Protect me, and don't tell my brothers. They'll kill me. And come harvest time, when my brothers pay your wages, I'll add two measures to your share. Just don't tell on me!"

"Fine," said the plowman.

A day went and a day came, and they harvested the grain and threshed it. He took his wages, and the sister gave him extra.

"What did you do this year," asked his wife, "that So-and-So's household gave you extra?"

"By Allah," replied the man, "he who protects another's reputation, Allah will protect his reputation in turn."

"Impossible!" she insisted. "You must tell me what happened, or else you'll worship one God and I another!"

"By Allah," he said, "there was a girl who had fallen into a well with a man, and I pulled her out."

Now the wife, when she sat together with the other women, used to say, "Did you know? So-and-So—my husband pulled her out of the well, and she had a man with her!"

This woman told that one, and so on, until her brothers got hold of the news.

"We must kill her," they said.[9]

The girl, catching on to their intentions, ran away at night. Eventually she came to a tent, and lo! there was a young man in this tent, living together with his mother. They let her stay with them, and the mother would bring food in to her.[10]

Now, the man was a bachelor, and his mother said, "Son, by Allah,

8. On plowing, see Tale 26, n. 6.

9. See Tale 28, n. 3.

10. A Bedouin tent (*šaq*) is usually divided by a curtain separating the women's quarters from the men's. The curtain can be lifted when there are no strangers around. See Jaussen, *Moab:* 75.

this girl has filled my eye. She's very nice, and I'd like to approach her for you."[11]

"Yes, mother," he said. "If you want me to marry her, speak with her."

"O So-and-So!" said the mother. "What do you think? My son—I have no one but him. What do you say to my marrying you to him?"

"I'll marry him," the girl replied.

She married him. After that, she became pregnant and gave birth to a boy whom she called Maktūb. Then she became pregnant again and delivered, giving birth to a girl whom she called Kutbe. Again she became pregnant and delivered, giving birth to a boy whom she called Mqaddar.[12]

Meanwhile, her brothers were roaming the countryside looking for her. One day, coming by where she was, they said, "By Allah, it's getting late, and we'd like to take shelter with you for the night." (See how destiny works!) After they came in and sat down, their host prepared them the dinner which Allah placed within his means, and they ate. The father kept saying, "Come here, Maktūb! Go over there, Kutbe!" The whole time it was like that, "Kutbe this, Maktūb that, and Mqaddar this!"[13]

As they were sitting after dinner, they said, "Let us tell of our adventures."[14] Then they said, "The first tale's on the host."

"All right," he said. "I'd like to tell you about what happened to me in my time. Where are you folks from?"

"By Allah," they answered, "you might say we're from the hills around Hebron."

"By Allah," he said, "I had an adventure when I was a young man of twenty."

"Please proceed!" they said.[15]

"By Allah," he began his tale, "we were salesmen, traveling in your

11. This detail clearly illustrates the mother's role in the marriage of her son. See Tale 21, n. 13.

12. We note (as in Tales 10, 22, 32, and 35) the ratio of two males to one female. The children's names, Maktūb, Kutbe, and Mqaddar, are all variations on the theme of fate, and are not used in actuality. The first means "that which is written"; the second refers to the writing itself (fate); and the third means "that which is decreed." See Tale 7, n. 9.

13. The father here is obviously proud of his children and intent on showing them off to his guests.

14. The word translated here as "adventure," *xurrafiyye,* could also mean "folktale," but the setting and the host's tale make it obvious that the narration of stories of personal adventure, or memorates (*nahfāt, nawādir, sawālif, xarārīf*), is intended.

15. For "Please proceed!" (*tfaḍḍal*), see Tale 17, n. 8.

part of the country. One day we were hungry. 'So-and-So!' said my companions, 'Stop off and beg a few loaves for us.' By Allah, I stopped by this girl—May Allah protect her reputation! 'For the sake of Allah, sister,' I begged, 'if you can spare us a couple of loaves of bread! We're camel drivers, and we're traveling.' By Allah, reaching for some loaves of bread, that noble woman[16] handed them to me and said, 'Brother, make sure to sidestep the trunk of that tree. There's a dog tied to it, and it might charge you. Take care not to fall into the well.' And by Allah, folks, she hadn't even finished her words of warning, when the dog rushed at me. And he no sooner attacked than I was startled and fell into the well."

Now the plowman, who was traveling with them, said, "I must go out. I have to pee!"

"No!" her brothers responded. "Don't go out until the host finishes his tale."

"By Allah," continued their host, "when I fell into the well, a girl looked in and said, 'There is no power and no strength except in Allah. There's no one here who can pull you out.' Her brothers were seven and with the plowman they were eight, and they were all out in the fields. 'For the sake of Allah, sister,' I begged her, 'lower the rope and pull me up!' And, by Allah, that decent woman—May Allah protect her honor!—dangled a rope down and started to pull me up, but when I was almost to the mouth of the well my weight was too much for her and she fell into the well with me."

The plowman again said, "I want to go pee," but her brothers answered, "Sit!"

"By Allah," the host went on, "who should show up but the plowman? 'Here I am!' she said, after he had called to her. Lowering a rope, he pulled her out. 'Brother,' she pleaded with him, 'such and such is the story.'"

Now she herself was listening. Where? In the tent she sat, listening to her husband's tale.

"I have to go take a shit!" said the plowman.

"Sit!" the brothers said. "Wait till the host tells his tale!"

"By Allah, friends," continued the host, "the man pulled us out, and I came this way."

16. *Bint il-ḥalāl,* for which see Tale 14, n. 2.

No sooner had he said that than she burst out with a ululation[17] from behind the divider in the tent, and then came in to where they were sitting and said, "You're my brother, and you're my brother."

"You," exclaimed the brothers, "are here!"

"Here I am," she answered, "and I've called my children Maktūb, Kutbe, and Mqaddar."

The bird has flown, and a good night to all!

43. *The Rich Man and the Poor Man*

Once upon a time there were two sisters, married to two brothers, one very, very rich, and the other very, very poor.[1] One day the sister married to the poor one went to visit the wife of the rich one and found her preparing stuffed cabbage leaves for dinner. She sat on the doorstep, but her rich sister did not say to her, "Come in, sister, and sit down inside."[2] When she brought the cabbage out of the boiling water, the rich sister gave the ribs of the leaves to her children but did not say, "Here, sister,

17. Ululation (*zaġrūte;* pl., *zaġārīt*) is a high-pitched, euphonious trilling sound made by Arab women on joyous occasions.

1. This combination of sisters married to brothers is fairly common and highly desired, especially among first cousins, the assumption being that two first cousins are better than one. Frequently, in-laws decide they like the first sister and decide to bring a younger sister into the family as well by marrying her to another son. Sometimes a woman marries the eldest son and, if her mother-in-law is dead, may take charge of the family and bring in her sister; or, if the father-in-law is dead, she may prevail on her husband to wed his younger brother to her sister in order to avoid having a stranger for a sister-in-law (*silfe;* pl., *salafāt*). For a discussion of the relationship among the wives of brothers, and for comments relevant to this tale, see the section on *salafāt* in the Introduction ("The Tales and the Culture").

Concerning the hostility that is presumed to exist among *salafāt*, Granqvist quotes the following ditty, which lumps sisters-in-law together with co-wives: *lēlt is-silfe, aṣbaḥit mixtilfe / lēlt iẓ-ẓurra, aṣbaḥit minẓarra* ("The morning after the sister-in-law [came into the house], I woke up feeling out of sorts / The morning after the co-wife [came into the house], I woke up feeling harmed"); see *Marriage* II: 186–187.

On rivalry and jealousy between sisters, see afterword to Group I, "Siblings"; and Tale 12, n. 6. The situation here is exacerbated by the wealth of the one sister and the poverty of the other.

2. The teller is concerned to show the cruelty of the rich sister, who does not invite her own sister in, even though Palestinian custom requires that food be shared with a pregnant woman in a state of craving. See nn. 4, 5, below.

take some and eat them." Putting her head in her hands, the poor one sank deep into thought.

"What are you doing, sister?" she asked.

"My husband has brought me cabbage and meat," replied the sister, "and I'm going to stuff the cabbage leaves for the children to eat."[3]

Now the wife of the poor brother had recently become pregnant, and she craved the food. When she smelled the cabbage, she sighed.[4] "Alas!" she thought in her heart. "Would that I had even one of those cabbage ribs to eat!"[5] But she was ashamed to say anything to her sister. She sat and sat, and then prepared to leave, but the other did not say, for example, "Stay, sister, until the cabbage leaves are done so you can have some"; or, "Stay and have lunch with us." She did not say anything.

The wife of the poor man went straight home to her husband. "My man," she said, "we must buy some cabbage and make stuffed cabbage leaves for the children. And, by Allah, I too have a craving for it. I was visiting my sister, and she didn't say to me, 'Take this and eat it, even if it is only a rib of cabbage.'"

Her husband was employed by the vizier. "Very well," he said. "I'll save my wages for the whole week, and we'll buy cabbage and meat. You prepare the meal, and we'll invite the vizier to have dinner with us."

He saved his money for a week and bought a kilogram and a half of

3. Stuffed cabbage (*malfūf*) is one of the most popular of Palestinian dishes. The description of its preparation is abbreviated in the tale. The cabbages are first boiled and then separated into leaves from which the ribs are removed. The boiled ribs are popular as snacks for the children while the meal is being cooked, or they may be inserted under or among the rolled leaves in the saucepan. The stuffing consists of minced lamb, rice, ghee, and condiments (salt, black pepper, and turmeric and/or cumin), and whole cloves of peeled garlic are added among the stuffed leaves. Stuffed cabbage, when cooking, has a characteristic aroma.

4. Granqvist discusses cravings in *Birth:* 38–43. Regarding smell, she says, "The same woman had once cooked something which gave a very strong smell and then a woman relative said to her, 'Do not forget! In the next house dwells such and such a woman and she is in a certain condition thou must give her some of the food!' She at once took some down to her" (p. 42). See Tale 2, n. 2; and Footnote Index, s.v. "Craving."

5. "In general," says Granqvist, "if a person cannot satisfy his desire for a special food this harms him. If he can see the food, it is also harmed and in that way they who eat of it. People are afraid to eat food which another has longed for. They say that his soul is in it" (*Birth:* 43). So also, Canaan: "Bis zum heutigen Tage zeigt der weitverbreitete Sprachgebrauch die selbständige Wirkung der bösen Seele; *manfūs* = er ist beseelt; *nafsuh fīhā* = seine Seele ist darin (= er wünscht es)" ("Dämonenglaube": 43). Cf. our note on the evil eye, Tale 19, n. 4.

meat, a kilogram and a half of rice, and some cabbages. She stuffed the cabbage leaves and cooked them, and dinner was ready. Because they were inviting the vizier, they borrowed a mattress from one neighbor, a cushion from another, and plates and cutlery from others.[6]

When the vizier arrived in their hut, they seated him on the mattress, while the husband sat next to him on a straw mat and she sat in front of them, serving the stuffed cabbage leaves. Before she was aware of what she had done, and in spite of herself, she farted.[7] "Yee!" she cried out, "may my reputation be ruined! And I had to do this in front of the vizier. Earth, open up and swallow me!" The earth, so the story goes, opened up and swallowed her.

Down under the surface of the earth she went, and where did she find herself but in a souk bustling with shops and people. It was a whole world, just like the souk in Acre or even a little bigger.[8] Now, her husband and the vizier did not know where she had gone. They waited and waited, but when she did not come back, they served the stuffed cabbages and ate them. Then the vizier went home.

Meanwhile, the wife went around the marketplace. "Has anyone seen my fart?" she asked. "Tell me the truth, brother! Haven't you seen my fart?"

"What fart, sister?" people answered. "Folks must be crazy where you come from." A group gathered around her, and she told them what had happened, from the beginning to the end. "By Allah, dear aunt," they said, "you are right to be looking for it," and they all, the police and the townspeople, went searching around with her. "Who has seen the fart?" they cried out. "Who has seen the fart?"

"Here I am!" he answered, surprising them. And how did they find

6. The reciprocity described here is typical of life in Palestinian villages. People often borrow mattresses and bedding, particularly when they have an important guest; frequently the donors come and offer their help without being asked, as in Tale 35 (see n. 7).

7. Breaking wind in public is extremely embarrassing, for both men and women. If a man were to do it in a public gathering, he would subsequently avoid the place where it happened and the people who were then present. This subject seems to be popular for gossip and humorous entertainment. A popular tale has it that a king once broke wind in assembly. Mortified, he left the country—but on returning forty years later, he discovered that people still remembered the incident.

8. Acre, formerly the administrative and commercial center of the northern district, is, like Jerusalem, a walled town, with meandering souks inside it. For more detail, see Tale 23, n. 4; Tale 24, n. 2.

him but sitting in a cafe with his legs crossed like an effendi, all bathed and wearing a cashmere suit with a fez on his head.[9] Gathering around him, they started to blame him for what he had done. "How could you have done what you did to this poor woman?" they said. "You escaped against her will, and embarrassed her in front of the vizier."

"I was pressed tight inside her, utterly uncomfortable," he defended himself. "Now that I've escaped, I've bathed and dressed up, and I'm having a great time. Why not?"

"All right," they said, "now that you've done what you did and blackened this woman's name, how will you compensate her?"

"Her reward," he answered, "will be that every time she opens her mouth to say something, a piece of gold will fall from it. And you, sister," he added, "just say, 'Let the earth open and bring me up!' and it will happen."

"Let the earth open and bring me up!" she said, and behold! gold fell from her mouth, and the earth opened and brought her back up. It was early evening, and her husband was sitting at home. "What happened to you, dear wife? Where did you go? What did you do?" As she was telling her story, pieces of gold were falling from her lips.

She went and bought a rosary and recited prayers of praise to Allah. Gold was falling from her mouth the whole time. They became very, very rich.

"Right now," she said to her husband, "this very moment, you must buy us a house like a king's, complete with servants, slaves, and furniture!"

Before twenty-four hours had passed, her husband had already bought her a mansion to vie with the king's palace, all furnished and with servants. It is said she put on clothes just like those of the king's wife, living in her mansion with servants all around her.

9. Fezzes were a common headdress for men during the time of the Ottoman empire, especially in cities among the upper and professional classes. The more familiar Palestinian headdress, the *ḥaṭṭa* (*kuffiyya*) and the *iʿgāl,* came into prominence during the revolution of 1936, with the rise of Palestinian nationalism.

Cashmere (*ġabānī*) is a cloth woven with "silk and woolen thread. It has a white background, with gold, black, red, and yellow threads running through it. It was popular at the beginning of this century for the manufacture of abas and headdresses (*ʿimam*)." See Kanaana et al., *Al-Malābis:* 330.

The "suit" referred to here is not a Western-style suit, with trousers and a jacket, but rather formal village dress, which consisted of the flowing robe (*qumbāz*), worn over long cotton pantaloons (*sirwāl*), gathered in at the middle with a leather belt, and covered with the (cashmere) aba.

When a few days had passed, the rich brother's wife remembered her sister. "Yee!" she said, "my poor sister was craving food and came to visit, and I didn't offer her even one bite of the stuffed cabbage. There are still some scrapings left at the bottom of the pot, and, by Allah, I'm going to take them to her myself." Scraping the bottom of the pot, she put what she found on a plate. When she arrived at her sister's old shack, she found someone else living there. She asked about her sister, and they said to her, "Where have you been? You sister has bought a house fit for a king, and now she's living in it."

Taking the plate of scraps over to the new house, she knocked on the door. A servant and some slaves appeared. "What do you want?" they asked.

"I want to see my sister," she answered.

"Wait till we ask our mistress," they said.

"By Allah, dear sister," she said when she came in, "I forgot to invite you to eat when you were visiting us, and now I've brought you a plateful of stuffed cabbage."

"No! No!" replied the other sister, "take the food home with you. Thank you very much, and may Allah increase your blessings!" She called her servants and said, "Fill silver plates full of every kind of food in the kitchen, put them on a large silver platter, and send it home with her. Take it over yourselves!"

"For the sake of Allah," the visitor asked, "what did you do to get all this?"

"Such and such happened to me," replied her sister.

As soon as she arrived home, the wife of the rich man told her husband the story she had just heard. "Right now," she said, "immediately, you will invite the vizier and bring the ingredients for stuffed cabbage, and I'll do as my sister did."

"Listen, wife!" said the husband, "Allah has blessed us with more than we need. We are content in our life, and we don't need anything more. Your sister was a poor woman, may God help her! Why don't you just forget about all this?"

"No!" insisted the wife. "You must invite the vizier."

So he went and bought the makings for stuffed cabbage leaves and invited the vizier. The vizier came to dinner, and she sat in front of them to serve the food. She pressed and squeezed in order to fart, putting so much pressure on herself that she forced out a little fart. "Let the earth open up and swallow me!" she exclaimed, and the earth opened and swallowed her.

She went down below, only to find it nighttime, with rain falling and the streetlamps all out. How miserable it was all around!

"Yee!" she thought, "may my reputation be ruined! What have I done?" She walked around the streets, reeling in the darkness and the rain. People meeting her would ask, "What's the matter with you, aunty? Where are you going, aunty?"

"I'm looking for the fart," she would answer.

"What fart, aunty?" they asked, and she said, "Such and such happened to me." She told them her story.

As before, they all went asking about, until they heard him. "Here I am!" he squeaked. They found him, you might say, taking shelter from the rain in a dank animal pen, all wrapped up in a piece of coarse cloth and shivering from the cold. "Who wants me?" he asked. "What do you want from me?"

"Such and such you did to this poor woman!" they blamed him. "Why did you embarrass her in front of the vizier?"

"I was sitting inside her, warm and happy," he answered, "and she kept pressing and squeezing till she forced me out against my will, to fend for myself in this cold darkness."

"Very well. How then are you going to compensate her?"

"Her reward," he replied, "will be that every time she opens her mouth to say something, snakes and scorpions will spring from it and bite her."

No sooner had she said, "Let the earth open and take me back up!" than snakes and scorpions sprang from her mouth and bit her. When she was by her husband's side, he asked, "Well, what did you do?"

"I neither did nor found anything," she answered. She was telling her take while snakes and scorpions fell from her mouth and bit her until she died.

"You got what you deserved," said her husband then. "May you never rise again!"

He went and married another woman, happy to be rid of his first wife.

44. Maᶜrūf the Shoemaker

Once there was a shoemaker—a poor man with his wife and children, just like the son of Yūsif il-Xaṭīb, who is new to the craft.[1] All day he mended shoes—save the listeners!—so he could make two or three piasters and buy bread for his children.[2] I mean, he was making ends meet. One day his wife said to him, "You know, husband, I have a strong craving for *knāfe*.[3] It's a long time since we've had it, and we want you to bring us a platter full of *knāfe* with honey."[4]

"Wife," he asked, "how are we going to do that?"

"I don't know how," she answered, "but get it you must!"

Every day the poor man saved a piaster or two until in a week or two he had saved thirty, forty piasters and gone to the market, where he bought her a platter of *knāfe*. Carrying it along, he brought it home and gave it to her. But when she tasted it and found it was made with sugar rather than honey, she took hold of the platter and tossed the *knāfe* out.

"I told you I wanted a platter of *knāfe* with honey, not with sugar syrup!" she complained.

Now, Maᶜrūf, he was short-tempered, and he became furious. Reaching for the stick, he set to beating her, turning her this way and that until the stick was broken. Out she came running, and she went straight to the cadi to bring her case against her husband. The cadi sent after Maᶜrūf, and he came and found her there.[5]

"Why, my son," asked the judge, "do you beat your wife and insult her? And why don't you satisfy her needs?"

"Your excellency," answered Maᶜrūf, "may Allah give you long life! I'm a poor man. My condition's such and such, and my occupation's such

1. Yūsif il-Xaṭīb is a shoemaker in the village. When addressed directly, a young person with no children is usually referred to by his or her first name. In third person reference, however, it is common to use the *kunya* form, "son of . . ." (*ibin*) or "daughter of . . ." (*bint*). In either case, circumstances determine whether the name of the father or that of the mother is used, but use of the former is more frequent for both genders.

2. ". . . shoes—save the listeners!" (*ḥēšā s-sāmᶜīn*)—for which, see Tale 15, n. 8.

3. *Knāfe* is a famous Palestinian dessert made from sheep's milk cheese (see Tale 13, n. 2), over which finely shredded dough is placed. After baking, sugar syrup (or honey) is poured over the still-hot dough, and the dessert is served warm.

4. For honey, see Tale 1, n. 5.

5. The judge here (*qāḍī*, anglicized as "cadi") is a magistrate who interprets Islamic law (*šarī ᶜa*) and renders judgment according to it. Cf. Tale 14, n. 3. The term *qāḍī* also refers to civil court judges.

and such. She asked for a platter of *knāfe,* and for two weeks I scrimped until I was able to save its price. I went to the market, bought it for her, and brought it home, but when she tasted it and found it was made with sugar she said she didn't want it. So she took it and threw it out."

"It's all right, son," said the cadi. "Here's half a pound! Go buy her a platter of *knāfe,* and make peace between you!"

The judge made peace between them, giving them the half-pound, and they went to the market and Maᶜrūf bought his wife the platter of *knāfe.* Giving it to her to carry, he said, "Go!" She went home, and he stayed behind.

"By Allah!" he swore, "no longer am I even going to stay in the same country where this woman is to be found!"

He stayed away till sunset, then found a ruined house where he leaned against a wall and waited for daylight so he could run away. And, by Allah, while he was inside the house, toward morning he felt a giant come upon him before he even knew what it was.

"What are you doing here?" asked the giant.

"By Allah," answered Maᶜrūf, "I'm running away from my wife, and I want to get as far away as possible."

"Where do you want to go?"

"I want to go to Egypt."

Reaching for him, the giant, who was from the jinn, picked him up and set him down in Egypt. Earlier he was in Damascus, but before day broke he was in Egypt. Now, he used to have a neighbor in Damascus called ᶜAlī who had since moved to Egypt, where Allah had blessed him and he was now a big merchant. As Maᶜrūf was wandering about early in the morning, people saw him. He was a stranger, they could tell.

"Where are you from, uncle?"

"From Damascus."

"When did you leave Damascus?"

"I left this morning," he answered, "and I arrived this morning."

"Crazy man, crazy man, crazy man!" they shouted, gathering behind him and clapping. "Crazy man, crazy man!" they taunted him, following him around, until they passed in front of the merchant ᶜAlī's. Looking carefully at Maᶜrūf, ᶜAlī recognized him. He chased away the boys following him and called him over.

"Come here!" he said, although Maᶜrūf had not yet recognized his old neighbor. "Where are you from?"

"I'm from Damascus."

"When did you come from Damascus?"

"I left this morning."

"What!" exclaimed ʿAlī, "You left Damascus this morning, and you're now here in Egypt! Are you crazy? By Allah, those boys were right to follow you around. Don't you recognize me?"

"No."

"Do you remember you used to have a neighbor in Damascus called ʿAlī?"

"Yes."

"I'm your neighbor ʿAlī."

"You're ʿAlī!"

"Yes, I'm ʿAlī. Come with me."

He went and bought Maʿrūf a suit of clothes, a fez, and (saving your honors!) a pair of shoes. He also bought him socks and fitted him out properly. It was as if Maʿrūf had taken a different shape. He was quite a sight now! And on top of all that, ʿAlī gave him a hundred pounds.[6]

"Take this hundred pounds," he said, "and spend from it until you're able to find some kind of work. And if anyone should ask you, don't say, 'I left Damascus this morning and arrived here this morning.' Say you're a merchant, and you came ahead of your merchandise, which is following you by sea." He wanted to make Maʿrūf look important. Giving him the hundred pounds, he said, "Take this, and go in Allah's safe keeping!"

Maʿrūf went on his way. Upon meeting Šāfiʿ, he would give him some money.[7] When he met another person, he would give him some money.

"Where are you from, uncle?" people would ask.

"I'm from Damascus."

"What are you doing here in Egypt?"

"By Allah," he would answer, "I'm a merchant, and I arrived ahead of my merchandise, which is following me by sea."

"What's this?" people wondered, seeing him squander his money. "We've never seen anything on this scale before. What a generous man! If he weren't really an important merchant, he wouldn't be throwing money around like this!"

His reputation spread, and when he had used up the hundred pounds

6. For "pound" (*lēra*), see Tale 5, n. 16. On neighbors, see Tale 34, n. 7; and on mutual cooperation, see Tale 35, n. 7; Tale 43, n. 6.

7. For Šāfiʿ, the raconteur, see Introduction ("The Tellers").

he came to another merchant and borrowed two thousand, saying, "I'll pay you back when my merchandise arrives."

Again he went around, casting his money like seeds, distributing it among the poor. Whomever he met, he would just reach in and give him a handful, until the money was gone. He then went to another merchant and borrowed four thousand, distributing it the same way. What a reputation he achieved! Whichever way he turned, people said, "The merchant Maᶜrūf! The merchant Maᶜrūf! What a merchant this is, who just appeared in our country! We've never seen, we've never heard of anyone so great."

Who heard about him? The king. And the king had a daughter—you should see that daughter!

"Councillor!" he called.

"What do you want, O Ruler of the Age?" asked the vizier.

"A merchant has arrived in our country, the like of whom we've never heard of or seen. He's made the city rich with the money he's distributed, and his merchandise has yet to arrive. He's come here ahead of his goods. I want to send after him and invite him to dinner, and I want to marry my daughter to him. This way we'll gain him and his merchandise. What do you think?"

"Yes, O Ruler of the Age!" answered the vizier. "This is your business. Who am I to raise objections?"

"Go see him," said the king, "and say to him, 'You're invited, and you must have dinner with the king.'"

The vizier went, searched for him, and found him.

"Mr. Merchant Maᶜrūf!" he said.

"Yes!"

"The king sends you his greetings, and says your dinner tonight will be with him."

"Of course," answered Maᶜrūf. "Why not? Am I too good for the king?"

Pulling himself together, he went to the king, who had prepared him a table—brother, what a spread! They turned their attention to it and ate dinner. Everything was just fine.[8] They brought desserts. Anyway, they ate till they had had enough. After they had finished, washed, and sat down, the king said, "You know, Merchant Maᶜrūf."

8. *W-ib-amān illāh*—literally, "They were in the peace of mind (or contentment) provided by Allah."

"Yes?" answered Maʿrūf.

"I want you to be my son-in-law," said the king. "I want to give you my daughter in marriage. What do you say?"

Maʿrūf mused over this, then he said, "O Ruler of the Age, would anyone hate to be the king's son-in-law?"

"Councillor," said the king. "Call the official here!"[9]

The vizier called the cadi. A marriage contract for the king's daughter was drawn up, and the king prepared a feast for them.[10] He bought her a handsome trousseau, vacated one of his palaces, and brought Maʿrūf in to her. After they had been together as man and wife, the king said to his son-in-law, "This is the treasure chest of the kingdom, you can take what you want. And this money lying outside the chest is for you to spend as you like. You can replace it when your merchandise arrives." And so saying, he handed him the key to the treasury.

Now, brothers, every morning Maʿrūf would visit with the king, stay awhile, then go up and fill his pockets with money, which he distributed in the city before coming back home. This went on for ten, fifteen, twenty days, till the money outside the chest was gone. Reaching for the treasury then, Maʿrūf opened it and gave away from that money too.

By the time the king had realized his mistake the treasury was nearly empty, and the money outside it had already vanished.

"My vizier," said the king, "save me!"

"The owner saves his own property, O Ruler of the Age!" replied the vizier. "What happened?"

"This man has squandered all the spare money outside the treasury, and now even it is nearly empty. It's already been two months, and we haven't seen his merchandise or anything else. We're afraid he's a liar. What have we gotten ourselves into?"

"By Allah, it's not my fault," said the vizier.

"And now, what are we to do?" insisted the king.

"By Allah, O Ruler of the Age," answered the vizier, "no one can expose a man better than his wife. To your daughter, then!"

Sending for her, the king said, "Daughter, the situation is such and

9. The official referred to here is the *maʾzūn,* whom the *qāḍī* (see n. 5, above) authorizes to oversee the legal aspect of the marriage ceremony, such as the signing of the contract. See n. 10, below.

10. For a discussion of the marriage contract, see Granqvist, *Marriage* II: 23–29; and for the wedding feast, ibid. 14–23. Jaussen gives a brief description of the complete wedding ceremony in *Naplouse:* 67–84.

such, and we're afraid your husband may be a liar. Why don't you sound him out and see if he really does have goods coming or not, then send me word?"

"Fine," she said, and went home.

That evening, after visiting with the king, Maᶜrūf went home. His wife became coy with him, teasing him with questions: "By Allah, cousin, when's your merchandise arriving?" and "What's become of it?" and "How . . ." She kept up this coyness until he fell for her trick and chuckled.

"What's the matter?" she asked.

"By Allah," he answered, "I don't have any merchandise or anything else. I'm a poor man whose life story is such and such," and he told her his story.

"What!" she exclaimed.

"By Allah," he replied, "I've told it to you as it is."

"What can I say to you?" she answered. "We've been together as man and wife, and it would be a shame for me to betray you. But if my father were to find out, what might he not do to you? You tricked him, took his daughter, and spent his money. And even if my father doesn't kill you, those merchants whose money you took will do so. So, better get up! Let's go!"

Going down to the stable, she made a horse ready for him, putting provisions in the saddlebags. "Take care," she added, "not to stay in this country, where someone may bring up your name. Wherever they hear of you, they'll want to kill you. If my father asks me in the morning, I'll say, 'He got news of his merchandise and had to go see about it.' As for you, run as fast as you can! Beware of staying in this country!"

What was Maᶜrūf to do? Mounting the horse, he sped out of there. Brother, he stayed here one day and there another until he had been going for Allah knows how long. One day his provisions ran out, and hunger pricked him. Traveling on a road by a village, he saw a farmer planting the fields below the village and parallel to the road.[11] As he passed by him, he greeted him, "Hello!"

"Welcome!" answered the farmer.

"O uncle," he asked, "would you happen to have a loaf of bread for

11. The setting described here fits the villages discussed in Tale 5, n. 14; Tale 17, n. 7; Tale 26, n. 11. On plows and plowmen, see Tale 26, n. 6; Tale 40, n. 1.

me to eat?" Maʿrūf was something to look at! Seeing a man with royal robes, a horse, and a saddle—it was like another world to the farmer, and he said, "Yes, brother. Stop by and honor me with your presence."[12]

When Maʿrūf joined him, the plowman halted his team, took his rough cloak,[13] spread it on a rock, and said, "Sit down here until I go bring you some food. My house is right over there." Going up to his house, he said to his wife, "Woman, such and such is the story. Make us a bit of lentil soup and crumble some bread into it!" Ah! What was he to do? That was all he had.[14] His wife was lively, and she made the food quickly.

Meanwhile, Maʿrūf said to himself, "This poor man—I've held up his work. I might as well get up and help him out with the team until he comes back with the food." Taking hold of the plow, he shouted at the animals. He plowed a furrow, and in the course of the second the plow hit against something. He prodded the animals with the goad, and they pulled against the root that snagged the plow. And behold! it gave way to a door leading to a tunnel. Stopping the team, Maʿrūf went down into the tunnel. And what, my dears, did he find but sealed pots full of money! Seeing a ring by the mouth of one of the jars, he took it up. Now, the ring was dirty and covered with dust, and he wanted to wipe it off, but no sooner had he done like this with it than a being shook himself up.

"Your servant, master!" he said. "Order and wish, and it will be done!"

This being was the jinni residing in the ring.

"I want all this treasure outside," said Maʿrūf, "loaded on mules and camels."

No sooner had he said this than it was all outside, loaded on camels and mules.

"I want a hundred camels loaded with cloth," continued Maʿrūf. "I want a hundred mules loaded with sugar. I want this, I want that. I want gold, I want precious stones. I want soldiers. I want, and I want . . ."

Now, that poor plowman—he had barely come down with the food

12. On the verb *tfaḍḍal* ("stop by and honor me with your presence"), see Tale 17, n. 8.

13. The *bišt* resembles an aba in shape and general structure, except that it is made of hand-spun wool thread. Formerly worn by poor people, by fellahin at work, and by shepherds during the winter season, it is no longer in use. See Kanaana et al., *Al-Malābis:* 214, 303.

14. The raconteur, Šāfiʿ, who is himself a farmer like the one described here, apologizes for the man because lentil soup is humble fare and would not be offered to guests if other food were available; cf. Tale 26, n. 12.

when he looked, and behold! he saw a king with his army. It was as if all hell had broken loose. Eh! Eh! He took one step back and one forward, but Maᶜrūf, seeing him, called him over. "Come, come!" he said, "Bring me that tray!" Putting the tray in front of him, he ate the food, then he scooped handfuls of gold into the tray until he had filled it. After that he turned around and marched in front of his merchandise, dear brothers, till he reached his father-in-law's territory.

In the morning, the king sent for his daughter.

"So, daughter?" he asked.

"By Allah, father," she answered, "the other night while we were sleeping word came that the merchandise was on its way, and he went to pick it up."

Eh! How pleased was the king! The poor daughter, on the other hand, was only trying to let her husband escape so no one could catch and kill him.

Meanwhile, Maᶜrūf, as he approached his father-in-law's domain, sent a messenger out to let the king know his son-in-law was on his way with the goods.

Gathering the army and his cabinet, the king came out to receive his son-in-law. And behold! What a shipment it was, my dears! Look, it was like asking for what you want with your own tongue. Whatever you could possibly want was to be found there.

Coming into the city, Maᶜrūf paid back four thousand pounds to those from whom he had taken two, and eight thousand to those who had given him four. The rest he sent away for keeping in his father-in-law's storehouses—the gold in one room, the jewelry in another, the rice here, the sugar there, the goods, the cloth . . . It was like the end of the world! He filled the whole place with goods.

"See, my vizier!" said the king. "Didn't I tell you!"

The vizier was a shrewd man; nothing was lost on him.[15] "This couldn't be mere merchandise," he thought. "So many diamonds, and so much gold! Something isn't right here!" Now, in the course of his evening visits with the king and his son-in-law, the vizier spied the ring and recognized what it was.

"O Ruler of the Age!" he said, "By Allah, we're bored, and we'd like to have a party in the orchard, just for me and you and the merchant

15. "Shrewd man," *ibin ḥarām,* is literally "illegitimate son" (hence, "bastard"), the opposite of *ibin ḥalāl* (cf. Tale 14, n. 2). For the vizier, see Tale 5, n. 9.

Maʿrūf, your son-in-law. Let's take food and drink with us, and have a good time entertaining ourselves together."

"Yes, my vizier," responded the king, "why not?"

The next day the king spoke with his son-in-law. What was he to say? He accepted. But his wife, the king's daughter, saw the ring and recognized it. "Why don't you give me this ring?" she asked. "Leave it here with me."

"No," said Maʿrūf.

"Listen to me," she repeated, "and leave the ring with me. Here, give it to me right now, and let me keep it."

"No," he said again, refusing to give it to her.

By Allah, brothers, the following day they prepared themselves, taking servants with them who carried the things down to the orchard and left. Only the king, his son-in-law, and the vizier remained. The vizier acted as their servant. After they had eaten and were content, he served the king and his friend with wine, "Your cup! Your cup!" My dears, he kept pouring wine and giving to them to drink until they fell over. They were both finished—the king and his son-in-law. And no sooner had they fallen over—no sluggard he!—than the vizier snatched the ring from the man's finger and rubbed it.

"Your servant, master! Order and wish, and it will be done!"

"I want you to dump these two behind the mountain called Qāf," ordered the vizier.[16]

Taking them up, the jinni hauled them away. Meanwhile, as soon as he had gotten rid of them, the vizier went home. When did he go? In the evening. And where did he straightaway go? To the palace of the king's daughter. He wanted her. Of course, he wanted to have control of the kingdom and everything else there. But the moment she saw him coming back by himself the girl knew what had happened. She was a clever one.[17] And when he called on her, she opened for him.

"Where are my father and my husband?" she asked.

"What do you need your father and your husband for?" he replied. "Don't even bring them up! I'm now king, and I'm also your husband."

"Did you really get rid of them?"

"They're indeed gone!"

16. In Islamic cosmology this mountain, the *jabal qāf,* surrounds the terrestrial universe.

17. For "clever one" (*malʿūne*), see Tale 15, n. 12. Interestingly, much harsher terminology is used for the vizier (see n. 15, above).

"I was only looking for the truth," she said. "I want the truth. Will I find anyone better than you? I wanted to be rid of them anyway. Welcome, welcome!"

Brother, she became all-welcoming for him. "One hundred welcomes!" she said again.

"By Allah," he said, "this is the most blessed hour."

Receiving him with more welcomes, she brought out whatever food she had prepared for her husband and her father and served him with her own hands. And brother, how important she made him feel! After they had finished dinner and eaten fruits and desserts, they spent some time chatting with each other and feeling contented. Then it was time for sleep, and the vizier took off his clothes and lay in bed, saying, "Take off your clothes."[18] Removing some of her clothes, but leaving on a nightgown, she lay down next to him, but when he reached out his hand to touch her she jumped up.

"What's the matter?" he asked.

"What's the matter with you?" she replied. "You want to sleep here, but don't you know that a spirit resides in your ring. Take it off right now and leave it on that table over there! Tomorrow morning you can put it back on, but now it would be a shame. It's forbidden."

All that and I don't know what else, until he said, "By Allah, you're right." And going over to the table, he left the ring there and came back to bed, again lying down next to her. But no sooner did he reach for her than up she jumped again.

"What's the matter now?" he asked.

"We forgot to lock the door," she replied. "I want to get up and lock it. Someone might walk in on us."

Then she went straight to the table on her way to the door, took hold of the ring, and rubbed it.

"Your servant, master! Order and wish, and it will be done!"

"Take this dog," she commanded, "tie him up, and throw him over there by the pillar." When that was done, she said, "Bring my husband and my father back from wherever you left them!"

The jinni went and brought them back, and they found the vizier tied up by the pillar. Now, the king—he wasn't asleep, brother!—drew his sword and struck the vizier a blow, and lo! his head was rolling.

18. The teller here is going beyond what is normally permissible in social discourse. He would certainly not have ventured that far if children were present during the telling.

"Drag this dog away!" he commanded, and it was done. The vizier was thrown over the palace walls, and the king put his son-in-law as vizier in his place. Thereafter he and his son-in-law lived in comfort and bliss, and may Allah make life sweet for all my listeners!

45. *Im ʿAlī and Abū ʿAlī*

Once, long ago, there was a poor outcast of a man, and no one was willing to give him work. His name was Sparrow,and his wife's name was Locust. One day she started to grumble.

"Don't you fear Allah?"[1] she said. "Your children are dying of hunger. Don't we need to eat? Don't we need to drink? Why don't you find some work?"

"There is no work I can do," he answered.

"In that case," she continued, "come let me sew straps on this pouch, which has a copy of the Qurʾān in it (he couldn't read or write), so you can hang it over your shoulder. Every Thursday go to the cemetery,[2] and you're bound to bring home some bread for your children."

"By Allah that's a good suggestion," he said, "except that I don't know how to read."

"And do you think anyone's going to be listening to what you're reading?" she asked. "Just take hold of the Qurʾān, open it, and mumble something."[3]

Strapping the Qurʾān across his shoulder, he went to the cemetery, opened the book, and stood there, you might say reading from it. Wherever he saw people gathering around a fresh grave, he stood by them and mumbled as if reading.

"Make way for the sheikh!" people shouted. "Let the sheikh have a

1. *Yā wēlak min alla*—literally, "Woe to you from Allah!"

2. Muslims commemorate the dead on Thursdays, usually observing three Thursdays following the day of death. On the first, the immediate family brings food to the cemetery, and on the second and third Thursdays relatives and friends from other villages may bring food. Cakes, dates, boiled eggs, fresh fruits, bread, meat pies, and other easily portable food items are left at the cemetery as alms for the poor on behalf of the soul of the deceased. See Granqvist, *Muslim Death:* 155–158.

3. If someone among those receiving alms is able to read, he may recite something from the Qurʾān on behalf of the soul of the deceased, and the relatives will thereupon shower him with gifts of food.

place to sit! Bring fruits over here for the sheikh! Gather the cakes for the sheikh!"

His bag full, he went home and emptied it out for his children. They ate from it from one Thursday to the next.

The following Thursday, as chance would have it, the mother of the king's wife died.

"Go call the sheikh!"

They went and said to him, "Come to the king's wife. Her mother has died, and she wants to give you alms."

Taking the Qurʾān with him, he went and mumbled something, swaying from side to side. The king's wife gathered a little from everything she had brought and gave it to the sheikh, saying, "Venerable sheikh, will you come back next Thursday?"

"I'm at your service," he answered.[4]

On the third Thursday he went to see her. Now, the king's wife was in her ninth month and was expecting at any moment.

"Honorable sheikh," she said, "you must divine for me.[5] What am I going to have? A boy? Or a girl?"

"What am I going to do?" he thought. "If I say 'a girl' and she has a boy, the king will cut off my head. And if I say 'a boy' and she has a girl, he'll cut off my head. What a trap this is! What am I going to do? What a mess you've gotten yourself into, Sparrow! May fate let you down, Locust! How did you manage to get Sparrow into this fix?"

"There!" he said to his wife when he went home. "You weren't satisfied until you made me work. What's this mess I've gotten myself into?"

"Is that all?" she answered. "Divine for her, and whatever you feel like saying, say it. And on the day of reckoning, Allah will help."

When he came to see the king's wife the following day, she asked, "Did you, Allah willing, do the divination?"

"Yes, by Allah," he answered. "I read your fortune in the sand. You're going to have a boy and a girl."

"Will I give birth in the palace upstairs, or downstairs?" she asked.

4. *ʿAlā rāsī*—literally, "On my head."

5. Various kinds of divination were practiced in the old days. The type referred to here is divination by means of sand (*fatiḥ b-ir-ramil*): random lines were drawn with the fingers in a pile of sand, and then the future was predicted from the direction and shape of the lines (see Amīn, *Qāmūs:* 268; Donaldson, *Wild Rue:* 194). Women still practice divination at social gatherings in Palestinian homes by reading coffee grounds. In this ceremony, an emptied Turkish coffee cup is turned upside down on its saucer and the semiliquid remains are

"You'll give birth upstairs and downstairs," he said.

And so, the following day, behold! a messenger came from the king's wife.

"What news of the king's wife?"

"When she was in the palace downstairs," he reported, "she went into labor. 'Go bring the midwife!' they said, but while waiting for her she gave birth to her first baby. Thinking she had finished, they took her to her room upstairs in the palace, and when the midwife arrived she said there was still another baby inside her, and she gave birth to it upstairs."

Now, she had told the king that the sheikh had divined for her and had said she would give birth to a boy and a girl upstairs and downstairs. When the news reached the king, the good news that his wife had given birth to a boy and a girl, he said to Sparrow, "It's settled! From now on I'm going to let you divine everything that may happen around here." The king then showed him his favor, giving him what fate decreed should be his share.

"Woe to you, Locust!" said Sparrow when he went home. "The king says such and such, and I can't read or write. How can I divine for the king?"

"When the day of reckoning comes," she answered, "Allah will come to the rescue."

One day the king went down to the orchard to take the air and lost track of time. When he came to do his ablutions so he could pray, he took off the royal ring and put it aside. Now, there was a boy roaming the fields and tending a flock of ducks and geese. A one-eyed goose, while pecking around, happened to swallow the ring, and the boy was afraid to tell the king. When he had finished his ablutions and prayed, the king looked around for the ring; not finding it, he sent for the sheikh.

Now we go back to the boy, who went to sit by the gate. "The sheikh will find me out and tell the king," he thought, "and he'll cut off my head." Sitting by the gate, he waited, and when the sheikh came by he said, "I throw myself on Allah's mercy and yours. Such and such is the story, and I was too scared to tell the king for fear he'd cut off my head. I want you not to say anything. I'm afraid if the king knew he'd cut off my head."

---

allowed to trickle down the sides; the reader then divines the future from the shapes she sees inside.

"Don't worry," said the sheikh.

Going in to see the king, the sheikh said, "Yes, Your Majesty!"

"Such and such is the story of the ring," the king said.

"Your Majesty," said the sheikh, "do you keep geese and turkeys?"

"Yes."

"Your Majesty," continued the sheikh, "there's among them a one-eyed goose. Send someone to bring that one-eyed goose over here."

They went and searched and found it was true. There was a one-eyed goose. Taking hold of it, the sheikh slaughtered it, slit its gullet, and pulled the ring out before the king and the vizier, who were looking at each other [wondering], "What kind of creature is this, who has this knowledge?" The king accepted the ring and rewarded the sheikh, who gathered himself and went home.

Not many days had gone by when the sultan's treasure chest was stolen.

"Send for Abū ʿAlī!" he said. "Send for Abū ʿAlī!"

When the sheikh came in, the king said, "You have forty days to divine who stole the treasury."

Again he went to his wife, crying out, "What a misfortune, Locust! You really got me into a mess! Where did the treasure chest disappear to, and how should I know who took it when I don't even know how to count? How am I to know when the forty days are up?"

"Don't worry, my good man," she said. "I'll count out forty pebbles and put them in your pockets. Every day, after you finish evening prayers, throw one of them away until they're all gone. Then you'll know the time's up."

Counting out forty pebbles and stuffing them in his pockets, she said, "After prayer in the evening, just before you eat dinner, throw one of them away."

That evening, after he had finished praying, he threw one of the pebbles away and said "Heh! This if the first of the forty."

Now, the treasury had been robbed by forty thieves.

"If tomorrow the sheikh were to divine in the sand," they whispered among each other, "he'd expose every single one of us. Let's go check up on him."

They sent one of them to check, but no sooner had he reached the door of the sheikh's house than the thief heard him say, "Heh! This is the first of the forty." Back to his mates he ran.

"Listen!" he said, "By Allah, before he even saw or became aware of me he knew who I was, because no sooner did I come near the house than he said, 'Heh! This is the first of the forty.'"

But they did not believe him, and one of them who thought himself clever said, "Tomorrow, I'll go myself."

The following day, just as it was turning dark, the thief headed for the house of the sheikh, who had barely finished evening prayer when, taking a pebble from his pocket, he tossed it out and said, "Heh! This is the second of the forty."

Back the thief went running, as fast as he could, and said to his mates, "Listen! By Allah, he's found us out one by one. It's best for us to knock on his door, go in to see him, and try to negotiate." So four or five, you might say, of the sensible ones among them went to Abū ᶜAlī's shack in the evening. One of them came forward to knock on the door, and lo! the sheikh was saying, "Heh! This is the third of the forty."

"You see, by Allah," they whispered among themselves, "he knows each and every one of us." Then, going in to see him, they said, "We've come to you, O sheikh, so that you can save our souls."

"Allah is the only savior, my children," he said.

"We know," they continued, "that you've been divining to locate the sultan's treasury. We're the ones who stole it."

"Yes," he answered, "I knew all along it was you."

"All right," they said, "we'll bring it back, but we beg you not to tell on us."[6]

"You see that I know all," he said. "If even one para is missing, I will tell.[7] Make absolutely sure not to spend any of it."

"Absolutely not!" they assured him.

"In that case," he replied, "bring it here to me and, for the sake of Allah, I'll let you go free. I won't say anything to the king."

Away they went, took up the chest, and brought it in to the sheikh. No sooner had they left than he went to see the king and said, "Your Majesty, the treasury has turned up."

"In only three days it turned up!" exclaimed the king.

"Yes."

"Where is it?"

6. For *daxīlak* ("We beg you"), see Tale 17, n. 12.

7. The para was a very small unit of Ottoman currency; see Tale 5, n. 16.

"At my house. Send someone to fetch it."

When they had gone, gotten the treasure chest, and come back, the king declared, "From now on, I won't even move anything from one place to another without consulting Abū ʿAlī. And I won't walk from here to there except with Abū ʿAlī at my side."

"O Ruler of the Age," the vizier broke in, "this man's condition is disgusting. Does someone like him walk with kings?"

"What does it have to do with you?" answered the king.

Now, in a distant country there was a prince whose palace was on an island in the sea, and he wanted to hold a party in it for the other kings, including our king.

"My vizier," said the king, "I want to send for Abū ʿAlī. Let us take him with us."

"Why Abū ʿAlī?" complained the vizier. "He doesn't know how to talk, how to sit in company, or even how to eat."

"Impossible," said the king. "I want to take him with me."

"The orders are yours to give," replied the vizier, "and the advice is yours to follow."

Sending for Abū ʿAlī, they gave him a new suit of clothes with an aba and made him look good, and the king took him along to the palace. But no sooner had they arrived than they saw him leave the assembled kings, go running down the stairs, and sit outside on the sand. "Now my wife will be baking bread," he said to himself, moving his hands as if baking bread. "Now my wife will be cooking," he thought and made cooking motions in the sand with his hands. Meanwhile, the king's eye was on him.

"God knows what's going on," said the king to the vizier. "Abū ʿAlī's divining something in the sand."

Abū ʿAlī was now saying to himself, "Heh! Now she's finished cooking. Heh! Now she's serving the food. Come eat, children! Come, come, come!"

"Let's go! Let's go!" said this king to the other kings. "Let's go! Abū ʿAlī's calling us. God knows what's going on!"

And down came all the guests, running after the king. (See how the Lord can show his mercy!) No sooner had the guests rushed out of the palace than it came tumbling down. It turned out the ground on which it had been built was loose. Everyone stood, looking at it in amazement.

"See, my vizier," he said, "what would have happened if we hadn't brought Abū ʿAlī with us?"

But as they were standing around looking at the remains of the palace, lo! a bird with a locust in its beak flew into the king's sleeve. The king held it in his sleeve without knowing what it was.

"Abū ʿAlī," he said, "tell me what's in my sleeve?"

"By Allah, O Ruler of the Age," answered Abū ʿAlī, "tales and complaints are neverending. If not for Locust, Sparrow wouldn't have been caught!"

The king shook his sleeve open, and behold! a sparrow with a locust in its beak flew out.

"See, my vizier," he said. "Even I didn't know what was in my sleeve."

"Abū ʿAlī! Abū ʿAlī!" everyone exclaimed as they went home.

"What next, O Ruler of the Age!" said the vizier. "A natural imbecile who speaks whatever comes into his head trusting to Allah's mercy, and what he says just happens to come out right! Just let me give him this one test, and if he passes, I'm convinced. But what if he doesn't pass?"

"You can do with him whatever you like," said the king.

"Good," said the vizier, and he brought together a plate of prickly pear, one of honey, another of yogurt, and a fourth of tar. Covering them all with a platter, he said, "Send for the sheikh."

"Abū ʿAlī," he said when the sheikh arrived, "you must tell me what's under this platter."

This poor man—how could he know?

"By Allah, Your Excellency," he said, "we've seen days blacker than tar and more bitter than myrrh.[8] But Allah has also blessed us with days whiter than yogurt and sweeter than honey."

"How about it now!" exclaimed the king. "What do you say, my vizier?"

"Nothing," answered the vizier. "I'm convinced."

This is my tale, I've told it, and in your hands I leave it.

Afterword

Relations in these tales not only go beyond the familial and societal but transcend the physical environment as well. Here the relationship is between the human and the divine, as based on a human being's acceptance

8. For "more bitter than myrrh" (*ʾamarr min iṣ-ṣabir*), see Tale 35, n. 15.

of God's will as it is manifested on a day-to-day basis. Wisdom consists precisely in this continual trust in God's ultimate design for the universe.

The major characters in this group exhibit simplicity of heart and lack of guile, qualities that enable them to stay in touch with the workings of destiny. The woman who fell into the well does not hold a grudge against her brothers; she understands the social constraints that force them to behave as they do, yet she does not foolishly expose herself to their harm by remaining passive. Her actions demonstrate a dynamic acceptance of the workings of fate. In "The Rich Man and the Poor Man," this acceptance takes the form of contentment with one's lot in this life. The poor man's wife has a good relationship with her husband and does not aspire to become rich but is rewarded nevertheless, whereas the rich man's wife has a bad relationship with her husband, is not contented with her wealth, and becomes possessed with an all-consuming envy that in the end destroys her. Despite her poverty, the wife of the poor man does not envy her sister. Her craving for food stems from a biological need, and she tries to satisfy it within the limitations of her means. Her behavior exhibits qualities of generosity and innocence totally lacking in her sister.

In "Maᶜrūf the Shoemaker," the title character's innocence is projected as boundless and unselfconscious generosity, which evokes an even more generous response on the part of the unseen powers that reward him. Because this innocence is powerless against evil, as represented by the vizier, it needs outside support to survive—which Maᶜrūf's second wife unfailingly provides. And in "Im ᶜAlī and Abū ᶜAlī," the main character is a sort of divine fool who is also a husband and a father. His major worry concerns providing his family with enough food, yet his simple actions in earning his living echo with deep meaning for the perceptive listener. No doubt all four of these tales are moral, or philosophical, tales, but fortunately they are not moralistic. They provoke thought based on simple acceptance of fate at the level of everyday experience.

A word of explanation is necessary at this point. One frequently finds pejorative references to the people of the Middle East as "fatalists," even by prominent scholars. Yet fate has a different meaning in the Islamic and Arab worlds than in the Christian and Western worlds. To the Westerner, the notion of fate implies a blind force that controls everything. Belief in this force would negate the belief in freedom of will that forms the ethical basis for the culture of individualism prevalent in Europe and North America. To Christians in the West, this belief would also negate one's conviction that God was so graciously disposed toward this world that He was incarnated to "save" it. To a Muslim, in contrast (and to Christian Arabs), fate is not a blind force but simply the will of God, who is the essence of mercy and compassion. Certainly the characters in our tales are not fatalistic. They act, and they reap rich rewards. Action is rewarded, not fatalistic acceptance.

Fate has a different meaning, and it functions differently, in each tale. It is not only a system of belief about the world but also an attitude of acceptance of that which is—even when it appears to be incredible, as in the last tale. There are no random events or coincidences; everything that happens is God's will. The man and the woman in "The Woman Who Fell into the Well" both readily accept what befalls them, exclaiming, "There is no power or strength save in Allah!" upon falling into the well. Whether as a humble shoemaker or the king's son-in-law, Maᶜrūf accepts his destiny with equanimity. Like Abū ᶜAlī, he exhibits a quality of trust in Allah that shields him from all harm. His generosity is literally selfless: he has no self to protect. The same holds true for the poor man's wife, whose generosity of spirit does not diminish even after she acquires immense wealth.

In "The Rich Man and the Poor Man" and "Im ᶜAlī and Abū ᶜAlī," fate works like a supernatural force that brings magic into the world; it is the creative power that shapes events, combining the usual with the unusual—or, as in these two tales, transforming the usual into the extraordinary. It is aided in this process by the creative power of language, which is the silent partner in all literature. The creative role of language in the folktale is made explicit in the last tale, where the pun on the name of the character and his use of imagery at the end serve to bridge the gap between the imaginative and the real.

By shaping events in time, fate also shapes the plots of the tales. Only when the events in time are understood to unfold according to a meaningful sequence does the notion of plot make sense. This process works most clearly in "The Woman Who Fell into the Well," where one action inevitably leads to another and another, until finally the woman is reunited with her brothers. Here again, language helps us to understand how fate works, the names of the children in the tale (Maktūb, "that which is written," and Kutbe, "the writing") providing the necessary clues. Although these names would be perfectly acceptable for a boy and a girl, they do not occur in actuality. Their use here exemplifies the metaphorical significance of writing to indicate the fixity of fate. It is said that one's fate is "written on one's forehead," or of an event, that it was "written," that is, it was bound to happen. Yet even though the order of events is preordained, new combinations—new plots—are continuously brought into being, such as the marriage of the traveling salesman to the woman and the birth of their children. Thus fate works both as a creative and a determinative principle.

Acceptance of fate is wisdom, and wisdom in these tales is ascribed to women as well as to men. The wisdom of men tends to innocence and passivity, whereas that of women tends to thinking and action. The king's daughter is far more skilled in the ways of the world than is Maᶜrūf, and it is Im ᶜAlī's drive and her practical advice that help her husband prosper. In "The Rich Man and the Poor Man," the women are the dominant figures, while the husbands are merely passive spectators in their wives' evolving drama. This group of tales, then—which were narrated by both men and women—makes an important statement about the position of women in the society. Indeed, it is clear upon reflection that the tales all along have acknowledged women's centrality in the social structure and their equality (if not superiority) to men in those fields of action in which men are supposed to excel. The tale of the woman who fell into the well exemplifies the whole collection in this regard. The woman in this tale is not passive; her generosity, first in giving the man the bread and then in attempting to pull him out of the well, commits her to a course of action that will change her life. Rather than sitting around, passively waiting for her brothers' vengeance, she runs away at night. She gives the children their names and is—as the teller makes clear from her narrative style—the very center of the family.

Folkloristic Analysis

Each tale is introduced here by both its English and its Arabic name, and by the name and age of the teller (when available) and her or his place of residence.

Tales are identified as to Type following Aarne and Thompson's *Types of the Folktale* (abbreviated as "AT"); citations for international parallels to the tales included here may be found in that volume as well. Motif numbers are drawn from Thompson's *Motif-Index of Folk-Literature.*

In the "Parallels" section, we have listed Arabic parallels according to their geographic proximity to Palestine, beginning with the Mashreq and moving westward to Egypt and North Africa. For multiple entries within a geographic location, authors are listed in alphabetical order and entries are separated by semicolons (although multiple entries for a single author are separated by commas). A book or article title may be found by reference to the Bibliography; in cases where an author has multiple publications, the specific date of publication is given in parentheses. Roman numerals always indicate volume number, whether for book or for journal (for journal abbreviations, see Key to References, p. xix); arabic numerals indicate either page number (when directly preceded by a colon) or tale number (when no punctuation comes before), or, very occasionally, the number of a journal issue (following a roman numeral and preceding a colon). In addition, tales are cited by title.

Only tales drawn from the Arabic tradition are cited as parallels as such, or as variants. We do draw attention, however, to parallels deriving from other countries in the Middle East (notably Israel, Iran, and Turkey) and from areas on its periphery (Greece, Italy, Central Asia, India). References from culturally more remote areas are occasionally cited when particularly appropriate. Except for the Palestinian references, we cannot claim that our survey of Arabic parallels is exhaustive, although we did search the accessible major resources thoroughly (including Nowak's comprehensive—though with regard to AT typology occasionally spotty—*Beiträge*) and feel confident that it is fairly broad.

We have tried, in our survey of motifs, to be as thorough as possible. One difficulty we did encounter, however, was the absence of motif numbers for many narrative details encountered in the Palestinian and Arabic traditions. Motifs are arranged alphabetically.

Although this book, we believe, fills a gap in the scientific study of the Palestinian folktale, we must acknowledge other significant contributions to the field. The most important (and the most frequently cited) is the excellent collection by Schmidt and Kahle, *Volkserzählungen aus Palästina,* set down in the village of Birzeit in the early part of this century. Considering that their work was done before the availability of portable recording equipment, we can only marvel at the size of their collection—132 items, all transliterated—and the degree of accuracy in the transcription of the village dialect in which the tales were narrated. The primary interest of the authors, however, was linguistic and religious, and so these areas receive the greatest emphasis in their scholarly paraphernalia. Thus the authors provide in their introduction a fairly complete grammar of the Palestinian dialect, as well as a sizable glossary at the end; and the footnotes tend to emphasize biblical parallels. The importance of this work cannot be overestimated, particularly because it makes the Arabic tales accessible to Western readers through facing-page translations into German.

Another valuable work is Hanauer's 1935 *Folklore of the Holy Land* (which is still in print), a charming collection of folk narrative material dealing with beliefs about cosmology, the jinn, plants, and animals. It also contains folktales, saints' legends, Juha tales, and tales illustrating proverbs. Although this work describes the wealth of the Palestinian tradition well, including the Palestinian Jewish tradition, we suspect that the author tampered with the material somewhat by embellishing it for effect.

More recently, particularly since the founding of *TM* and *TŠ,* the Palestinian folktale has received much serious attention from Palestinian and other Arab scholars and writers, most notably al-Sārīsī, Sirḥān, and al-Khalīlī. These writers do show an awareness of the importance of dialect in setting down the tale, but only Sirḥān does so consistently. Al-Sārīsī's first book (1980), which contains only a sampling of folktales, is adapted from his master's thesis in the Department of Arabic at the University of Cairo, and with his training in folkloristics, his approach is the most scholarly of the three. Although some of his material on methodology, which was appropriate to his thesis, is extraneous in the book, the author does devote much attention to the study of the social context. In 1985 he published the complete texts of the tales he collected for his graduate research in the refugee camps in Jordan, but the awareness of both author and tellers was obviously focused on village life in Palestine—that is, predating refugee-camp days. Sirḥān's study, which focuses on the Palestinian customs and beliefs that underlie the tales, is also valuable, particularly his analysis of the role of the hero, the role of women, and the importance of social relations in understanding the tales. Finally, we have al-Khalīlī's work, which is certainly the most doctrinaire of the three, because his approach invariably concerns class struggle. If used cautiously, such an approach can yield useful insights, for undoubtedly the conflict between haves and have-nots does exist in folktales. Yet an overweighted emphasis on class is bound to distort the nature of the material. Indeed, all three authors suffer from too much analysis, with the tales receiving relatively little space in the books.

This note would not be complete without mention of Hilma Granqvist, even though her work is not primarily in the folktale. Having devoted her entire career to the study of Palestinian ethnography, she is the giant to whom subsequent researchers must look to achieve familiarity with the anthropological context that animates the folktales. Her work is thorough and forms a necessary adjunct to the study of this material—as readers will by now have seen from our frequent references to her work in the footnotes, to corroborate our own insights and to provide further evidence of their validity.

1. ṬUNJUR, ṬUNJUR. Narrated by Fāṭme, fifty-five, from the village of ʿArrābe, Galilee (also Tales 9, 11, 23, 24, 26, 36, 38, 43; see Introduction, "The Tellers").

   Type 591—The Thieving Pot.

   Parallels: None.

   Salient Motifs: D1605.1 Magic thieving pot; T548.1 Child born in answer to prayer.

   Thompson's comment (*Folktale:* 78) that this type is restricted to a relatively small area in Europe (basically, Scandinavia) seems to hold true for the Arab cultural area as well. We have not been able to locate any parallels, nor does Nowak list any in her index. The motif of wishing for a child (T548.1) is used as an introduction to bring the magic pot into being, thereby integrating the themes of poverty and lack of offspring.

2. THE WOMAN WHO MARRIED HER SON (ʾIllī tjawwazat ibinhā). Narrated by an eighty-two-year-old woman from the village of Rafīdya, district of Nablus.

   Type 705—Born from a Fish.

Parallels: Palestine—al-Khalīlī (1979) 10 "The Woman with Cut-Off Hands"; al-Sārīsī (1985): 137–140 "Gazelle," 228–230 "End of an Unfaithful Woman." Syria—Ramaḍān: 109–111 "The Apple of Pregnancy." Egypt—Dorson (1975): 159–163 "Falconer's Daughter." Sudan—al-Shahi and Moore 9 "The Wife and the Prince's Son," 10 "The Heron and the Crescent Bird." Tunisia—*Contes de Tunisie:* 29–32 "La jeune fille qui naquit d'un pomme."

Salient Motifs: B535.0.7 Bird as nurse for child; D1601.12 Self-cutting shears; H151.5 Attention attracted by hints dropped by heroine as menial: recognition follows; K1816 Disguise as menial; K1911.3.2 True bride takes house near husband. This eventually secures his attention; N365.1 Boy unwittingly commits incest with his mother; Q414 Punishment: burning alive; S22 Parricide; S51 Cruel mother-in-law; T579.8 Signs of pregnancy; W181 Jealousy.

Although the tale related here lacks the usual opening for this type (i.e., Motifs T511.1 Conception from eating fruit, and T578 Pregnant man), the complete type is actually more common in the Palestinian tradition. One version we collected contains this opening, as do the versions cited above (al-Khalīlī [1979]; al-Sārīsī [1985]: 228–230). The parallelism in detail among all versions cited is quite close, with the Egyptian version coming the closest, including almost identical phrasing for the servants' questions and the mistress's answer (*Q:* Lady, O lady, whose house is next to ours, / Haven't you got some grapes for the craving that is ours? *A:* Shame, shame . . . / The falcon and the peacock nursed me, / Now the Sultan's son has impregnated his mother, / And her craving hits nobody but me! / Scissors, cut off a piece of his tongue / So that he will not tell on me).

In his discussion of this type, Thompson (*Folktale:* 123) notes that it shares narrative elements with other tales of slandered wives. It is important to note, however, that the mother/son incest that forms part of the narrative structure of all the Arabic parallels cited is not part of Type 705 as analyzed by Thompson. In fact, *The Types* does not include any tales in which incest is committed; rather, all those listed (*Types:* 566) are instances in which it is averted.

3. PRECIOUS ONE AND WORN-OUT ONE (Il-ġālye w-il-bālye). Narrated by a man in his seventies from the village of Rammūn, district of Ramallah (also Tale 20).

Type 301—The Three Stolen Princesses.

Parallels: Palestine—ʿAbd al-Hādī 26 "Clever Ḥasan"; Bauer: 182–186 "The Two Brothers"; Littmann (1905) 8 "The Feather-Bird" (opens with Type 550); al-Khalīlī (1979) 9 "The Three Apples." Syria—Oestrup 6 "Les trois princes et l'oiseau d'or." Iraq—Qaṣīr

(1970) 2 "The King and His Three Sons." Egypt—Artin Pacha 6 "Les trois fils du sultan." Algeria—Galley: 116–145 "Mohamed ben es-sulṭān." General Arabic—Chauvin IV 181 "Les trois frères"; Nowak, Types 155, 177, 195 (but not 300, as listed on p. 408). Other parallels in Galley: 150–151, and in Nowak under each type. Cf. Boratav 22 "L'aigle du monde souterrain"; Walker and Uysal 1 "Blind Padishah and His Three Sons"; Surmelian 1 "Apples," and 15 "Alo-Dino."

Salient Motifs: C742 Tabu: striking monster twice; G84 Fee-fi-fo-fum; G530.1 Help from ogre's wife; G532 Hero hidden and ogre deceived by his wife when he says he smells human blood; G634 Genie sleeps with eyes open; H95 Recognition by bracelet; H1471 Watch for devastating monster. Youngest brother alone successful; K2211.0.1 Treacherous elder brother(s); N681 Husband (lover) arrives just as wife (mistress) is to marry; R111.2.1 Princess(es) rescued from lower world; T92.9 Father and son rivals in love.

The bulk of Thompson's discussion (*Folktale:* 53) centers on the "Bear's Son" theme (Part I of the six-part analysis of this type), which is missing from all the Arabic examples. Furthermore, Part VI of the analysis restricts the conflict to one between the hero and "impostors." Significantly, in all the versions cited here the "impostors" are members of the hero's immediate family—his brothers (Algeria, Egypt, Iraq, and Syria) or his brothers and father (Palestine). The Arabic tale therefore uses the type to focus on a very important issue in the culture: the relationship among brothers. Sibling rivalry motivates the tale from the start, taking the place of the Bear's Son motif in the narrative structure. This rivalry is translated in the course of the tale into sexual jealousy, which leads the brothers to betray the hero so that one of them can wed the beautiful maiden he rescues. The version offered here brings out the Oedipal implications of this rivalry clearly. In view of the thematic importance of polygyny in this corpus, we note that our tale further adapts the type to focus the conflict on the struggle between the son of one wife (Worn-out One) and the children of the other (Precious One), who are aligned with their father. The fact that, in contrast to all the other Arabic examples, the tale is named after the wives leads us to conclude that Palestinian tellers consider the conflict to be between the co-wives rather than among their children.

4. ŠWĒŠ, ŠWĒŠ. Narrated by a woman in her seventies from the village of Jabʿa, district of Hebron (also Tales 7, 27, 41, 42).
   *Type 1477**—Old Maid Tells Wolf to Come to Bed.
   Parallels: None.

Salient Motifs: B600 Marriage of person to animal; K1984.5 Blind fiancée betrays self. Mistakes one object for another; K2214 Treacherous children [son]; S21 Cruel son; X120 Humor of bad eyesight.

Although we have not been able to locate an exact parallel, a similar incident is presented humorously in "The Wishing Tree," recorded by al-Juhaymān (II 19). In this tale, the head of a household, wanting to find out the most secret desires of his wife, mother, and sister, informs them about a tree that fulfills wishes. He hides inside the trunk of the tree, and each betrays her secrets to him. The mother declares her wish to marry their shepherd. After telling his mother to prepare herself to receive the shepherd that night, he disguises himself as the shepherd and goes into her tent, having first eaten plenty of garlic, onions, and other gas-producing substances. Sitting in a corner of the tent, away from his mother, who had in the meantime beautified herself to receive her husband, the man pollutes the air with flatulence. Driven to despair, the mother cannot wait for daylight, at which time she insists on being divorced from the shepherd. Her son, pretending it had been difficult to arrange the marriage in the first place, reluctantly agrees.

5. THE GOLDEN PAIL (Minšal iḏ-ḏahab). Šāfiᶜ, sixty-five, from the village of ᶜArrābe, Galilee (also Tales 8, 10, 15, 25, 44; see Introduction, "The Tellers").

Type 531—The Clever Horse.

Parallels: Palestine—ᶜAbd al-Hādī 61 "Who Is Worthy of the Kingdom?" (exact parallel), 29 "The King of China's Daughter"; Campbell (1954): 48–57 "The Story of the Bashak"; al-Sārīsī (1985): 178–180 "The Magic Horse." Syria—Oestrup 5 "Le fils cadet du marchand." Lebanon—al-Bustānī: 185–197 "Clever Ḥasan." Iraq—Stevens 39 "Melek Muhammad and the Ogre." General Arabic—Nowak, Types 171, 176, 197 (parallels following each). Cf. Kunos: 134–142 "Cow-Peri"; Surmelian 6 "Bird-Peri," 13 "Hunter's Son."

Salient Motifs: B211.1.3 Speaking horse; B401 Helpful horse; B470 Helpful fish; B548.2.1 Fish recovers ring from the sea; B571 Animals perform tasks for man; D840 Magic object found; E80 Water of life. Resuscitation by water; H911 Tasks assigned at suggestion of jealous rivals; H931 Tasks assigned in order to get rid of hero; H1213 Quest for remarkable bird caused by the sight of one of its feathers; H1321.1 Quest for water of life; K775.1 Capture by taking aboard ship to inspect wares; L111.8 Heroes sons of wife not favorite of king; Q112.0.1 Kingdom as reward; W195 Envy.

In his comment on this tale Thompson observes that the tradition is "not always coherent," using the example of the pen in the story ("for it is not always clear why the hero should have a pen and what good it is to serve in the tale") to corroborate his observation (*Folktale:* 62–63). The Arabic versions cited do not seem to suffer from lack of coherence. On the contrary, the version included here, like the others, is woven together well, with the action progressing from the feather (the pen in the type) to the bird, and so on. It forms part of a cycle of adventure tales (centering on the exploits of a hero with the generic name—"Clever Ḥasan" or "Clever Mḥammad") popular with Arab raconteurs. Collectors also seem fond of these tales, for they predominate in the available literature over the sort of household tale that constitutes the bulk of this collection. Although belonging primarily to Type 531, this version also takes the sibling rivalry that underlies the narrative in Type 550 (as in the example from Oestrup) and makes it the motivating force for beginning the action. And, not surprisingly, the rivalry here is between brothers who are sons of co-wives, the son of the less desired one (as in the previous tale) proving himself against his brothers.

6. HALF-A-HALFLING (Nuṣṣ nṣēṣ). Narrated by a woman in her fifties from the village of ʿĒn Yabrūd, district of Ramallah.

Type 327B—The Dwarf and the Giant.

Parallels: Palestine—al-Sārīsī (1985): 189–190 "Fly, O Bran, Fly!" Sirḥān (1974): 152–159 "Half-a-Halfling." Sudan—al-Shahi and Moore 19 "Ab Daba Daba." General Arabic—A. Shah (1969): 52–56 "Small Abdul and the Ogress"; Nowak, Types 177, 179 (parallels following each). Tunisia—*Contes de Tunisie:* 121–122 "Chétiran et ses frères." Cf. Lorimer 18, 38 "Half-Boy"—both tales; Boratav 9 "Kléoghlan qui alla épouser la femme-des-braves."

Salient Motifs: B413 Helpful goat; D2072.0.2.1 Horse enchanted so that he stands still; D2165.1 Escape by flying through the air; F571.2 Sending to the older; G123 Giant ogress with breasts thrown over her shoulders; G514.1 Ogre trapped in box (cage); K550 Escape by false plea; L11.1 Seal of humiliation put by youngest brother [-in-law] on the backs of his rivals; L112.2 Very small hero; N812 Giant or ogre as helper; T550.6 Only half a son is borne by queen who ate merely half of mango [pomegranate]; T671 Adoption by suckling. Ogress who suckles hero claims him as her son.

The Sirḥān version is very close to ours, with the difference that the conflict is between first cousins rather than brothers. The last part of our tale, the adventure with the ghouleh, is sometimes narrated as a separate tale of adventure, as we see from ʿAbd al-Hādī 22 ("How

Am I to Sleep, and How Am I to Sleep?") Nowak cites parallels from Egypt, Algeria, Morocco, the *Arabian Nights,* and Turkey. The fact that Lorimer was able to collect two versions of the tale, one from each of the two communities represented in *Persian Tales,* is significant. It demonstrates the popularity of this tale in the Middle East, where the parallels cited here show a wide distribution, covering both the Mashreq and the Maghreb.

The small size of the hero could lead to some confusion in typology between AT 327B and AT700 ("Tom Thumb"), but, as Thompson explains (*Folktale:* 37), the two are separate types, with our tale resembling more closely Perrault's "Le petit Poucet" than it does "Tom Thumb." The Turkish version is a close parallel.

7. THE ORPHANS' COW (Baqrat il-yatāmā). See Tale 4.

Type 450—Little Brother and Little Sister.

Parallels: Palestine—al-Sārīsī (1980) 7 "The Orphan-Girl and the Prophet's Cow," (1985): 284–285 "The Orphans' Cow"; *TM* I 2: 70–73 "The Seven Boys Turned into Bulls"; *TM* IV 15:48–50 "Orphans' Cow." Syria—Ramaḍān: 89–92 "The Tale of Saʿdā." Egypt—Dulac 2 [no title; reprinted as No. 37 in Basset (1903)]. Algeria—Desparmet I:127–139 "L'enfant allaité par une ghoule"; Mouliéras II 27 "Les deux orphelins jumeaux." Morocco—Scelles-Millie (1970) 14 "L'orphelin élevé par les abeilles." North Africa—Scelles-Millie (1972) 10 "Les deux orphelins." General Arabic—Nowak, Type 138 (Tunisia and Haḍramaut), but not Types 177 and 188 (as listed on p. 408). Cf. Kunos: 1–11 "The Stag Prince"; Surmelian 8 "The Red Cow"; Dawkins 2 "Little Boy and Little Girl."

Salient Motifs: B355.2 Life of helpful animal demanded as cure for feigned sickness; B535.0.1 Cow as nurse cares for children; D114 Transformation: man to ungulate; D927 Magic spring; K2212.2 Treacherous sister-in-law; K2252 Treacherous maidservant; L111.4.2 Orphan heroine; P253.2 Sister faithful to her transformed brother; Q112.0.1 Kingdom as reward; R156 Brother rescues sister; S31 Cruel stepmother; S51 Cruel mother-in-law; W195 Envy.

Our version of this tale differs in both its opening and its ending from the plot outlined by Thompson for Type 450 (*Folktale:* 118). "The Orphans' Cow" does not end with the typical final episode of the substituted bride (as in several of the versions cited above), even though such an event is prepared for at the beginning. In place of that our tale substitutes jealousy on the part of the king's household, which brings about the reversal of fortune for the orphan queen. The tale also substitutes Motif B535.0.1 for Part II of the type analysis

("Kind and Unkind"). This feature is shared by all the Arabic versions of the tale.

Glancing over the ending of the tale, we note a certain uniformity in all the parallels cited. In the version recorded by Scelles-Millie (1972), the gazelle-brother calls down to his sister in the well in words that reflect the same order of thought as in our tale: "O ma soeur, ô ma soeur très chère / Voici les couteaux bien aiguisés / Les chaudrons sur le feu préparés / Les chasseurs jurent la mort de ton frère." In the Turkish version the brother's call to the sister is close to the one reported here. This version also explains the occurrence of the fish in the sister's response: a jealous slave girl pushes the orphan into a fountain in the middle of the palace garden and then takes her place as the substituted bride; in the fountain the girl is swallowed by a fish, and her response to his plea is "Here I am in the fish's belly / In my hand a golden saucer / On my foot a silver sandal / In my arms a little Padishah!"

In the Moroccan version cited above the sister is not swallowed by a fish; rather, a boa wraps itself around the girl's legs in order to protect her and her baby. The sister is thus bound and is unable to come to her brother's rescue. She describes the situation thus: "O mon frère, mon frère bien-aimé / Le boa est à mes pieds enroulé / Le fils du Roi sur mon sein reposé / Comment trouver le moyen d'échapper?"

For more discussion, see Dawkins: 8–9; and Scelles-Millie (1970: 132–133, 1972: 110–116; parallels in both).

8. SUMAC! YOU SON OF A WHORE, SUMAC! (Summāq, yā bni š-šarmūṭa, summāq!). Šāfiᶜ (see Tale 5).

Type 315A—The Cannibal Sister.

Parallels: Palestine—ᶜAbd al-Hādī 16 "The Country Is Calling for Its People"; al-Sārīsī (1985): 159–160 "The Ghouleh Sister." Syria—Ramaḍān: 178–182 "Scythe-Handed Woman." Cf. Walker and Uysal: 86–90 "Caldron-Headed Ax-Toothed Sister"; Dorson (1968) 125 "Rangtang."

Salient Motifs: B381 Thorn removed from lion's paw [helping lioness with difficult birth]. In gratitude the lion later rewards the man; B524.1.2 Dogs [lion cubs] rescue fleeing master from tree refuge; G275.2 Witch overcome by helpful dogs [lion cubs] of hero; G312.7 Ogress devours horses; G346 Devastating monster. Lays waste to the land; G550 Rescue from ogre; H1471 Watch for devastating monster. Youngest brother alone successful; K551.1 Respite from death granted until prayer is finished; N1.1 Hero makes fortune through gambling; N2 Extraordinary stakes at gambling; N2.4

Helpful animals lost in wager; R251 Flight on a tree, which ogre tries to cut down; T548.1 Child born in answer to prayer.

The only parallels listed in AT are five versions from India. Dorson, however, in his introductory note to the tale, cites other parallels from black American sources. He also notes that the fantastic names of the dogs distinguish the plot of this tale. Among those he lists are Jimmie Bingo and Jim Bolden; Take-um, Cut-Throat, and Suck-Blood; Crack-er-Bone and Smash-er-Meat; Wham, Jam, and Jenny-Mo-Wham; Bark and Berry; and Jupiter and Kerry.

The motif of the sister's ghoulishness discovered by the youngest brother serves as the opening episode in the Romanian tale "The Land Where Time Stood Still," anthologized by Idries Shah (1979: 230–232). In this tale the youngest brother's discovery that his sister is a ghouleh spurs him to leave his father's kingdom, without revealing her identity to him, in search of the land where there is neither death nor old age. After realizing his quest, he longs to see his family and returns, only to find the place of his birth has vanished. Although the two tales are obviously not parallel, it is still interesting to note that the destruction wrought by time in the Romanian tale is achieved by the ghoulish sister in ours. The Syrian and Turkish versions closely parallel ours.

9. THE GREEN BIRD (It-ṭēr li-xẓar). Fāṭme (see Tale 1).

Type 720—My Mother Slew Me, My Father Ate Me.

Parallels: Palestine—al-Sārīsī (1980) 8, (1985): 204–205 "Little Green Bird"; Schmidt-Kahle I 49 (no title; cited in Nowak, Type 314). Egypt—Dulac 1 (no title). Tunisia—Ben Ḥammādī: 207–210 "The Green Bird." Cf. Lorimer 14 "The Boy Who Became a Bulbul"; Dorson (1958) 119 "Eating the Baby."

Salient Motifs: E607.1 Bones of dead collected and buried. Return in another form directly from the grave; E613.0.1 Reincarnation of murdered child as bird; G61 Relative's flesh eaten unwittingly; N271 Murder will out; Q2 Kind and unkind; Q56 Love rewarded; Q211 Murder punished; S31 Cruel stepmother; S31.5 Girl persuades her father to marry a widow [neighbor] who has treated her kindly.

The Arabic versions cited are close parallels, our version embodying the greatest amount of detail and resembling most closely the four-part analysis in AT. We are at a loss to explain the popularity of the tale in Palestine and its almost total absence from the rest of the Arabic tradition, the only example cited by Nowak being the Schmidt-Kahle reference noted above. The fact that the tale is also found in Iran leads us to suspect wider distribution, which more collecting activity would unearth. It is curious to note that in the Arabic versions the bird is always green, whereas in the black American version green flies announce the death of the boy: "My mama kilt me / My papa ate me / My sister going bury my bones."

As Thompson notes (*Folktale:* 116), the bird's song is the most persistent part of the tradition surrounding this tale. It entered into the mainstream of literature when it was used by Goethe as Marguerite's song in Act 5 of *Faust:* "Meine Mutter, die Hur / hat mich umgebracht, / mein Schwesterlein klein / hub auf das Bein / an einem kühlen Ort; / da ward ich ein schönes Waldvögelein / fliege fort, fliege fort."

10. LITTLE NIGHTINGALE THE CRIER (Blēbl iṣ-ṣayyāḥ). Šāfiᶜ (see Tale 5).

Type 707—The Three Golden Sons.

Parallels: Palestine—ᶜAbd al-Hādī 24 "Little Nightingale the Crier," 41 "Lady Biqjāzya" (exact parallel); Littmann (1905) "Nightingale the Crier"; Schmidt and Kahle I 46 "Die ausgesetzen Zwillingskinder"; Sirḥān (1974): 148–154 "Little Nightingale the Crier." Iraq—McCarthy and Raffouli II 7 "The Nightingale"; Qaṣīr (1970) 19 "Magic Apple"; Stevens 33 "King and Three Sisters"; *TŠ* IX 9 (1978): 201–204 "Branch of Samandros's Daughter." Egypt—Artin Pacha 22 "El-Schater Mouhammed"; el-Shamy 9 "Promises of the Three Sisters"; Spitta-Bey (1883) 10 "Histoire du rossignol chanteur," 11 "Histoire d'Arabe Zandyq." Sudan—al-Shahi and Moore 4 "The Princess and Her Brother Salim." Algeria—Desparmet II: 241–264 "Ghoule secourable." North Africa (Berber)—Moulieras II 69 "Prince et princesse aux fronts d'or." General Arabic—*Supplemental Nights* (Burton) III: 491–549 "Two Sisters Who Envied Their Cadette," with variants supplied by Chauvin VII 375; Nowak, Type 174 (not 173, as listed on p. 408). Cf. Kunos: 53–73 "Golden-Haired Children"; Lorimer 10 "Jealous Sisters"; Surmelian 4 "Lad with Golden Locks." The episode of the magic bird occurs in Oestrup 6 "Trois princes et l'oiseau d'or"; see also Chauvin VI: 8, no. 273.

Salient Motifs: B131.2 Bird reveals treachery; B172.1 Magic bird petrifies those who approach; D231 Transformation: man to stone; D902 Magic rain; E1 Person comes to life; E761.4.4 Life token: ring rusts [becomes tight]; F571.2 Sending to the older; G123 Giant ogress with breasts thrown over shoulder; H1331.1.1 Quest for bird of truth; K2110.1 Calumniated wife; K2115 Animal-birth slander; K2115.2.1 Stone substituted for newly born babies; K2212 Treacherous sisters; N201 Wish for exalted husband realized; N455.4 King overhears girl's boast as to what she would do as queen. Marries her;

N812 Giant or ogre as helper; N825.1 Childless old couple adopt hero; R158 Sister rescues brother(s); S322 Children abandoned (driven forth, exposed) by hostile relative; S451 Outcast wife at last reunited with husband and children; W195 Envy.

In his note on this tale, el-Shamy remarks on the importance of the affectionate "bond between brother and sister" (p. 255). The care taken to emphasize the relationship between the sister and her brothers in fact distinguishes the Arabic versions from the others generally. Our tale goes furthest in this regard, referring explicitly to the security the sister must feel with two brothers to help her. At the end of the tale the sister brings her brothers back to life. The version given by Littmann is close to ours, duplicating it in almost every detail, except for the figure of the old crone who comes to visit Šamsiẓẓḥā, which is unique to our tale (all the others combine this figure with that of the midwife). The function of the episode involving the old crone seems to be solely to bring out the relationship of mutual love among the siblings, and to show the sister's material dependence on her brothers; she has the power to change the weather, yet she is helpless to make a simple decision involving even a trivial purchase if her brothers are not there to help her. The version recorded by el-Shamy is also close to ours, sharing some details that are absent from Littmann, as for example the sister's saving of her brothers at the end.

Aside from the details of the narrative, which vary slightly from one tale to another, the majority of tales grouped here share two important features. The first is the king's readiness to accept as a gift from Allah the animals that his wife supposedly gave birth to. In the version set down by Artin Pacha, the king loves his animal offspring to the point of madness, always taking them with him and keeping one on his right knee and the other on his left. In the Grimm tale (No. 96), it will be recalled, the king, at least on the first two occasions, stoically accepts the supposed offspring (two dogs and a cat), exclaiming, "What God does, is well done!" In the Iraqi versions of Stevens, and McCarthy and Raffouli, but not of Qaṣīr, when the king discovers his wife had borne two puppies, he becomes livid with anger and punishes her severely by burying her up to her waist and permitting passersby to throw stones at her. The motif of giving birth to a stone, incidentally, is not unusual in popular lore. Its first occurrence in the folklore of the Middle East is in the Hittite tale "The Monster Made of Stone," reconstructed by Gaster (pp. 110–124). In connection with the revival by Šamsiẓẓḥā not only of her brothers but also of what seemed like a whole creation, one is reminded of the Greek myth of Deucalion and Pyrrha (see Gaster: 124–133 for an informative discussion of this issue). It will also be recalled that Rhea, the wife of the Titan Cronus, saves the baby Zeus by presenting her husband with a stone wrapped in a blanket in place of the newborn infant.

The second feature that all the tales share is the importance accorded in them to the blood relationship between the king and his children. When he meets his children after they have grown up, the king feels mysteriously drawn to them even before he knows who they are. In the version recorded by Schmidt and Kahle, the first time the king sees his son, his soul becomes attached to him (*itʿallaqat rōḥe ʾibe*)—upon which the narrator asks parenthetically, "Is it possible that blood should turn into water?" (*ʾay hū-ddam biṣīr mayy?*).

The number of versions on record indicates that Type 707 is very popular in the Arab world, a conclusion that is confirmed by el-Shamy, who notes its current popularity in Egypt, where it is known as the story "of the sisters who said, 'If the king were to marry me I'd do such and such for him,'" adding that fourteen versions of it exist in the Egyptian Folklore Archives (pp. 254–255). Thompson supports this opinion as well, saying that "though no adequate investigation has been given to this story, it is clear that it is one of the eight or ten best known plots in the world. A cursory examination of easily available reference works shows 414 versions, an indication that a thorough search might bring to light several hundred more" (*Folktale:* 121). In the late nineteenth century Chauvin observed that the tale was popular in "the Orient" as a folktale (VII:95). This tale is also one of the most frequently anthologized tales in selections from the *Arabian Nights,* especially those designed for a younger audience.

How this tale came to be part of the *Arabian Nights* is in itself a curious story. Chauvin notes (VII:95) that the tale's Arabic text has not been found and that Galland "composed" it for inclusion in his edition of the *Mille et une nuits,* as based on an Arabic version he had heard somewhere (most likely in an Arab country). Writing in the *Supplemental Nights* (III:619), Clouston (see *Book of the Thousand Nights and a Night*) notes the popularity of the tale in the European literary tradition and confirms Chauvin's statement: "It is clear . . . that Galland neither invented the story nor borrowed it from Straparola or Madame d'Aulnois. Whence, then, did he obtain it?—that is the question. His Arabic source has not yet been discovered, but a variant of the world-wide story is at the present day (circa 1886) orally current in Egypt." Clearly, then, Galland is responsible for having entered this tale as part of the canon of the *Thousand and One Nights,* and presumably Burton included it in his edition of the *Nights* following Galland's example, basing his translation, as Chauvin notes, on a Hindustani text.

Although Thompson is undoubtedly correct in his judgment that more recent scholarship has inadequately investigated this story, nevertheless Burton, in his footnote introducing the tale, offers a considerable number of references to the European literary tradition where the tale occurs, as well as a few variants in the folk tradition. Clouston complemented Burton's analysis, offering in *Supplemental Nights* (III:617–648) a wide-ranging comparative analysis. He first notes the existence of a Babylonian analog, then proceeds to offer English translations of nine variants: Modern Arabic (Spitta-Bey, cited above), North African Qabāʾilī, Modern Greek, Albanian, Breton, German, Icelandic, Bengali, and Buddhist (Sanskrit). Clouston holds that this last version, although really only a truncation of AT 707, is the original form of the tale.

Curiously, Joseph Jacobs considers this tale to be one of the most popular folktales in Europe and includes it in his *European Folk and Fairy Tales* (1916:51–65); see his notes (pp. 233–235), where he claims that the tale is of European origin. Thompson apparently agrees with this view, for he says that the tale's "distribution would suggest European origin" (*Folktale:* 122); as el-Shamy observes, however (p. 256), this view should be "reconsidered in light of the new evidence provided by Arab, Berber, and African variants of Type 707." Significantly, Thompson does not cite any Arabic parallels for Type 707, not even the reference from the *Thousand and One Nights.*

11. THE LITTLE BIRD (Il-ʿaṣfūra z-zġīre). Fāṭme (see Tale 1).

Types 235C; 715*—Bird Has New Clothes Made; Demi-coq.

Parallels: Tunisia—Dorson (1975): 164–165 "Sparrow and King"; *Contes de Tunisie:* 14–16 "Histoire de petit oiseau au grain de blé."

Salient Motifs: B171.1.1 Demi-coq crows in king's body when the king eats him; B172 Magic bird; E168 Cooked animal comes to life; F234.1.15 Fairy in form of bird; K233.1 Bird has new clothes made: flies away without paying.

The tale of the Clever Cock is very popular in Palestine, and that of the Little Bird is a unique adaptation of it. In the former, instances of which were reported by Crowfoot (*PEQ* LXXXIII:162–164), Stephan (*JPOS* III:185–187), and Abū-Shanab in Syria (pp. 55–57), the clever cock obtains a grain of wheat, which he exchanges for a loaf of bread, which he exchanges for something bigger and better until eventually he obtains a bride. Like our tale, these also end with a ditty: "Kikkikeeki! I am the rare cock, I am the clever cock! For the grain I got a loaf, and for the loaf I got a bunch of onions, and for the onions I got a kid, and for the kid I got a calf, and for the calf I got a buffalo, and for the buffalo I got a bride" (Stephan).

The only Arabic versions resembling ours closely enough to be cited as parallels are from Tunisia, although Dorson (1975:164) cites other references from North Africa. In the versions cited here, the conflict is between two masculine wills rather than between the masculine and the feminine. In Dorson, the sparrow obtains a grain of wheat, which he uses to make a necklace and challenge the king: "What the king has I have!" He makes such a disturbance that the king orders him caught ("I am not afraid!") and his throat slit ("What a beautiful necklace!"); he is then dropped into boiling water ("What a beautiful bath!") and his feathers are plucked ("Don't tickle me so hard!"). After being eaten, the bird shouts from inside the king's belly, "What a spacious palace! What a luxurious palace!" The bird causes the king so much stomach pain that he expels him. In the Dorson version the place of emergence is left vague ("There is the sparrow breaking loose . . ."), which leads us to suspect that he emerged from the king's lower end. The other Tunisian version cited here specifies the king's mouth as the place of exit, but the text was probably altered for the sake of politeness. Once free of the king's belly, the bird continues to shout: "I found a grain of barley. I made a necklace with it. I had what the king had. The king got jealous of me. . . . What a fat king. What a round stomach on that king!" (Dorson).

12. JUMMĒZ BIN YĀZŪR, CHIEF OF THE BIRDS (Jummēz ibin Yāzūr, šēx iṭ-ṭyūr). Narrated by a woman in her sixties from Jerusalem.

Type 432—The Prince as Bird.

Parallels: Palestine—ʿAbd al-Hādī 19 "Roses and Roses Daqqūš," 44 "I Am the Doctor with the Cure"; al-Sārīsī (1985): 282–283 "Hot Pepper"; Schmidt and Kahle I 47 "Der verzauberte Jussif." Lebanon—al-Bustānī: 128–139 "Lady Rose and Hot Pepper." Syria—Ramaḍān: 50–57 "Peppercorn, Victim of Love," 169–173 "Roseblossom and Sitt el-Ḥusun." Iraq—Stevens 6 "The Crystal Ship." Arabian Peninsula—al-Juhaymān IV 17 "Little Nightingale the Crier." Sudan—Mitchnik: 93–100 "Hassan the Physician." Cf. Walker and Uysal: 104–111 "Shemsi Bani, Padishah of Pigeons"; Dawkins 15 "The Gift to the Youngest Daughter."

Salient Motifs: B614 Bird paramour; B642 Marriage to person in bird form; D641.1 Lover as bird visits mistress; D2072.0.2 Animal rendered immovable; D2072.0.3 Ship [camel caravan] held back by magic; D2072.2 Magic paralysis by curse; E113 Resuscitation by blood; H335.0.1 Bride[groom] helps suitor perform [her] tasks; H383.3 Bride test: skillful sweeping; H1129.2 Task: filling twelve bed-ticks with feathers; H1151.24 Task: stealing ogress's drum [straw tray]; H1385.5 Quest for vanished lover; K1825.1.4 Girl masks as doctor to find departed lover; K2212 Treacherous sisters; L221 Modest request: present from the journey; M205.2 Curse as punishment for broken promise; N452 Secret remedy overheard in conversation with animals (witches); S181 Wounding by trapping with sharp knives (glass); W181 Jealousy.

Despite minor variation, the Arabic tales are close parallels, conforming in narrative detail to all the episodes belonging to the type. Common motifs are D641.1 (or a variant thereof), E113, H1385.5, K2212, N452, and S181. The version from the Arabian Peninsula, however, introduces a complexity not found in any of the others. In that tale the figure of the bird-prince is ambiguous. At first he is presented more as a magic helper who can be summoned when needed than as a lover. Yet the daughter's desire for him so enrages her father that he dismisses her from the house, even though (or perhaps because) he loved her best of all his daughters. Once out of the house, the girl quickly finds a substitute father, under whose protection she is able to commune with her bird companion freely. In the end the sexual nature of the relationship is revealed when the couple become husband and wife.

The father's harsh treatment of his daughter in the tale from the Arabian Peninsula illuminates a significant feature, shared by nearly all the versions under discussion, concerning the tale's psychological structure—namely, the father's forgetting to fulfill his daughter's initial request. This forgetfulness is a symptom of the father's distress at his daughter's request, caused perhaps by jealousy and certainly (in the Arab context) by concern over family honor.

The title of the Sudanese version points to another important element common to the Arabic versions of this type: the male disguise the heroine must wear, as the traveling physician with the recipe to cure Jummēz. (Significantly, this cure, except in the Lebanese version, is obtained from the blood and hearts of two birds—presumably a male and a female dove.) In the Lebanese tale the heroine, Rose, must wear a disguise twice; the second time is as a traveling physician, but the first time, Hot Pepper does not respond to her call, and so she goes in search of him herself. After receiving her request, Hot Pepper answers in a message that says, "Explode and die, you're not going to get me!" Rose then decides to go in search of him disguised as a handsome youth, and it is in this guise that Hot Pepper (whose name is quite revealing) is first drawn to her.

Our tale has affinities with the tale of Beauty and the Beast (Type 425C) on the one hand, and with that of Cupid and Psyche on the other. The Beauty and the Beast story frequently starts out as ours does, with the youngest daughter making a strange request that only an enchanted beastlike creature can fulfill. The parallel with "Cupid and Psyche" is even closer, for the two tales share all the major narrative features, including the tasks imposed by Venus (here, Jummēz's sisters) and the help that Psyche receives from Cupid in executing them. See *The Folktale:* 102–103 for a discussion of this tale type in the European literary tradition.

13. JBĒNE. Narrated by a seventy-five-year-old woman from il-Mizraᶜa š-Šarqiyye, district of Ramallah.

Type—Motif N711.1: Prince (king) finds maiden in woods (tree) and marries her.

Parallels: Palestine—ᶜAbd al-Hādī 8 "Jbēne" (cf. 2, also called "Jbēnē"); Hanauer: 158–160 "Ijbeyneh"; al-Khalīlī (1979) 11 "Lady Jbēnē" (cf. 14 "Green Camel"); al-Sārīsī (1980) 9, (1985): 206–210 "Jbēne." Cf. Galley: 30–50 "Badr az-Zīn."

Salient Motifs: D2036 Magic homesickness; K1821.2 Disguise by painting body; L162 Lowly heroine marries prince; N711.1 (see above, under Type); R111.2.5 Girl rescued from tree; S143.2 Abandonment in tall tree; T548.1 Child born in answer to prayer; Z142 Symbolic color: white; Z143 Symbolic color: black; Z143.1 Black as a symbol of grief.

We cannot explain the popularity of this tale among Palestinians and its apparent absence from the general Arabic tradition. Perhaps the clue lies in the very simplicity of its structure, which combines two popular themes—separation and reunion, and marriage—that can be developed, separately or together, to produce a more elaborate tale. Because different features of all the Palestinian versions of "Jbēne" are brought together in "Badr az-Zīn," it is instructive to review the process by which a more elaborate story may be constructed from the nucleus that is our tale. In our version the mother is childless but in Hanauer she has seven sons and no daughters (the situation prevailing at the beginning of Tale 8 in this collection). When her wish is fulfilled, the brothers are given the wrong signal and they stay away from home, thereby forcing the sister to go in search of them—exactly as in "Badr az-Zīn." In this manner we already have the opening episodes of AT 451 (The Maiden Who Seeks Her Brothers).

In our tale the maiden dyes herself black to disguise herself as a servant, yet this function may be split such that a maidservant, who later becomes the substitute bride or sister (Galley, al-Khalīlī, al-Sārīsī), accompanies the girl on her journey. The discovery of her true identity uniformly occurs as a result of the animals' fasting in sympathy with her song (Motif H12). Discovery may lead to marriage (here, and in al-Sārīsī) or to reunion with brothers and family (Galley, al-Khalīlī). Further adventures may befall the heroine on the way back to her family (Galley, al-Sārīsī), thereby completing AT Type 451.

14. SACKCLOTH (Abū l-lababīd). Almāza (wife of Šāfiᶜ), fifty-eight, ᶜArrābe, Galilee (also Tales 18, 37; see Introduction, "The Tellers").

Type 510B—The Dress of Gold, of Silver, and of Stars (Cap o' Rushes).

Parallels: Palestine—ᶜAbd al-Hādī 34 "Little Woodling." Syria—Ramaḍān: 223–225 "Sackcloth." Iraq—Qaṣīr (1976) 15 "The King and the Ring"; Stevens 5 "Dungara Khshebyān." Sudan—Hurreiz 8 "The Son of Nimēr"; al-Shahi and Moore 20, 23 "Fatma the Beautiful," 21 "Fatma of the Anklet," 22 "Dawm-Palm Dress." Cf. Dawkins 40 "The Girl Whose Father Wanted to Marry Her"; Calvino 103 "Wooden Maria."

Salient Motifs: K521.4.1.1 Girl escapes in male disguise; K1227.1 Lover put off till girl bathes and dresses. She escapes; K1816.0.2 Girl in menial disguise at lover's court; K1836 Disguise of man in women's dress; L131 Hearth abode of unpromising hero (heroine); L162 Lowly heroine marries prince; N711.6 Prince sees maiden at ball and is enamored; R213 Escape from home; R221 Heroine's threefold flight from ball; T136.3.1 Dancing at wedding; T311.1 Flight of maiden (bridegroom) to escape marriage; T411.1 Lecherous father. Unnatural father wants to marry his daughter.

The Palestinian, Syrian, and Iraqi versions are close parallels. The fact that al-Shahi and Moore chose to include so many versions in their collection reflects the popularity of the tale among the various Nile River communities represented in the book. Both el-Shamy

(p. 197) and Hurreiz (p. 161) allude to the existence of Egyptian Nubian versions of this tale, none of which are in print.

In all the Sudanese versions, the threatened incest is with the brother rather than the father. These variants illustrate an important feature of our tale, which is presented in a muted manner (no doubt purposefully, as it touches on women's honor) at the end. The son of the sultan, we recall, makes the girl remove her sackcloth (under which she is presumably naked) and then calls his mother. In the Sudanese tales this removal does not take place so easily. There is a contest at the end of each tale (wrestling, a game of chess or of *mancala*), the stake being the removal of the loser's outer garment. The woman wins this contest three times in a row and absolves the man from his debt. It is only on the fourth try that the male is able to overcome the female and remove her outer garment.

In his synopsis of this type, Thompson observes that the heroine of this tale assumes a "peculiar disguise" (*Folktale:* 128). This observation holds true for all the Arabic versions as well. In this respect our version is the closest to Grimm 65, "Allerleirauh" (literally, "of different kinds of fur"), with even the assumed name of the heroine (Roughskin) corresponding. In the Iraqi version the dress the heroine uses for disguise is made of iron; in al-Shahi and Moore 21 it is made of wood; and in all the other Sudanese versions it is an old man's skin. Herein lies a major difference between the Arabic versions and the European ones: whereas in the former the disguise implies a change of gender, in the latter that is not necessarily the case. Correspondingly, the disguise of the hero as a woman (Motif K1321.1) is missing from the European versions. Regarding disguises, the contests that close the Sudanese tales take better advantage of the initial change of gender than our tale does, because the power implied in the (apparent) change is followed through to the end.

See al-Shahi and Moore: 50–53, where they discuss the significance of this tale in terms of the perceived tension in the society between endogamy (which, taken to an extreme, leads to incest) and marrying outside the family. See also el-Shamy (p. 197) and his observation that one woman narrator refused to tell a stranger the story of "the man who wanted to marry his daughter" because it was "disruptive of good relations and defamatory." "Is there a man," she asked, "who would marry his own daughter?" Margaret Mills touches on the question of gender change in her article "A Cinderella Variant in the Context of a Muslim Women's Ritual," in Dundes (1982): 80–92.

15. ŠAHĪN. Šāfiᶜ (see Tale 5).

Type 879 (Parts III, IV)—The Basil Maiden (The Sugar Puppet, Viola).

Parallels: Palestine—Bauer: 190–196 "ᶜAlī Zēbaq and the Merchant's Daughter"; Littmann (1905) 18 "Maryam the Bedouin Woman from Ḥijāz"; *TM* III 9:114–117 "Iš-šēx i-Nṭaf." Syria—Ramaḍān: 212–217 (two versions) "Daughter of the Fava Bean Seller." Egypt—Artin Pacha 15 "Les trois filles du marchand de fèves." Sudan—Hurreiz 13 "The Daughter of the Bean Grower." Tunisia—*Contes de Tunisie:* 169–170 "Le fils du sultan et la fille du boulanger." Algeria—Galley: 152–174 "La fille du marchand de pois chiches" (other parallels, p. 180).

Salient Motifs: F562 People of unusual residence; F721.1 Underground passages; H1556.4 Fidelity in love tested; J1251.1 Humiliated lover in repartee with disdainful mistress; J1794 Statue mistaken for living original; K1214.1.1 Importunate lover is induced to undergo series of humiliations; K1836 Disguise of man in women's dress; K1837 Disguise of woman in man's clothes; P251 Brothers; T15 Love at first sight; T55 Girl as wooer. Forthputting woman; T61 Betrothal; T131.0.1.1 Father promises that girl may wed only man of her choice; T131.1.2 Father's consent to son's (daughter's) marriage necessary; T160 Consummation of marriage; X52 Ridiculous nakedness or exposure; Z71.12 Formulistic number: forty.

Although there are some differences in Part III of the analysis for this tale ("Tricks and Countertricks"), all the versions cited have enough details in common to be considered close parallels, the closest to ours being the variant in *TM*. The versions in Bauer and Littmann share details not found in ours, whereas the Egyptian and Algerian versions share a number of details not found in any Palestinian version—viz., the imposed task of arriving walking-riding or laughing-crying. The Algerian and Tunisian versions are the only ones embodying Part II of the analysis for the Type ("Questions and Counterquestions"); all versions share Part IV ("The Sugar Puppet"). In the Bauer version the theme of the tale is expressed directly at the end, when ᶜAlī, newly married but not victorious, says to his bride, "Believe me, you are the man and I am the bride."

16. THE BRAVE LAD (Iš-šabb iš-šujāᶜ). Narrated by a ninety-five-year-old woman from the village of Rammūn, district of Ramallah.

Type 461 (Parts II, IV)—Three Hairs from the Devil's Beard.

Parallels: Egypt—el-Shamy: 274 "Saint of the Forty."

Salient Motifs: G84 Fee-fi-fo-fum. Cannibal returning home smells human flesh and makes exclamation; G334 Ogre keeps human prisoners; G500 Ogre defeated; G530.1 Help from ogre's wife; G532 Hero hidden and ogre deceived by his wife when he says he smells human blood; H1273.2 Quest for three hairs from the devil's beard; L101 Unpromising hero (male Cinderella); L161 Lowly hero marries princess; Q53 Reward for rescue; R11.1 Princess (maiden) abducted by monster (ogre); T68.1 Princess offered as prize to rescuer.

El-Shamy observes (p. 274) that this tale type has been adapted in the Arab Islamic tradition to accommodate the cycle of tales embodying etiological beliefs around the theme "Moses converses with God." In these stories, Prophet Moses, on his way to converse with God, meets different people who want to have their questions answered—viz., the hermit will never enter Paradise because he hid the extra piece of bread Allah had sent him to share with Moses, whereas the forty robbers will enter Paradise because they did share their food with the Prophet. See *The Folktale:* 140.

17. GAZELLE (Ġazāle). Narrated by Im Nabīl, sixty-five, from the village of Turmusʿayya, district of Ramallah (also Tales 19, 28, 30, 39; see Introduction, "The Tellers").

Types 552 (Parts II, III); 300 (Parts II, III); 302 (Parts I, II, III)—The Girls Who Married Animals; The Dragon Slayer; The Ogre's (Devil's) Heart in the Egg.

Parallels: Palestine—Bauer: 182–186 "Two Brothers"; al-Sārīsī (1985): 195–201 "Ninety-nine Heads." Egypt—el-Shamy: 3–14 "The Trip to Wag-el-Wag." Sudan—Hurreiz 41 "Karajōk"; al-Shahi and Moore 30 "Muhammad the Clever." Tunisia—al-ʿIrwī IV: 35–58 "Magic Ring." General Arabic—A. Shah (1969): 1–12 "The Sultan and the Four Strange Brothers-in-Law." General Arabic—Nowak, Type 82. Other (not always close) parallels are cited in Nowak: 408 for all the AT types outlined above. Cf. Kunos: 112–133 "The Wind Demon"; Dawkins 23 "Magic Brothers-in-Law"; Megas 34 "Navel of Earth."

Salient Motifs: B11.2.3.1 Seven-headed dragon; B11.7.1 Dragon controls water supply; B11.10 Sacrifice of human being to dragon; B11.11 Fight with dragon; B314 Helpful [animal] brothers-in-law; B450 Helpful birds; B873.2 Giant scorpion; C611 Forbidden chamber; D832 Magic objects acquired by acting as umpire for fighting heirs; D1254 Magic staff; D1421.0.3 Magic hair when thrown into fire summons supernatural helper; D1581 Tasks performed by use of magic object; E712.4 Soul hidden in box; E715 Separable soul kept in animal; E715.1 Separable soul kept in bird; G510.4 Hero overcomes devastating animal; G512.5 Ogre killed by burning [crushing] external soul; H945 Tasks voluntarily undertaken; H1101 Task: removing mountain (mound) in one night; H1161.6 Task: killing devastating tiger; K956 Murder by destroying external soul; K975.2 Secret of external soul learned by deception; Q53 Reward for rescue; R111.1.3 Rescue of princess (maiden) from dragon; S262 Periodic sacrifices to a monster; S263.3 Person sacrificed to water spirit to secure water supply.

Apparently, the "Animal Brothers-in-Law" tale lends itself comfortably to combination with other types. As Thompson observes (*Folktale:* 56), AT 552 is frequently combined with AT 300 or AT 302—or with both, as in our version. Judging from the Arabic tradition, it is easy to see why these three types are combined here, for they are all adventure tales with a generic hero whose name is usually "Clever Ḥasan" or "Clever Mḥammad." Although Thompson acknowledges the existence of the tale, or the combination, in Palestine (without, unfortunately, citing a reference), the combination of types that we find here is not common in the Arabic tradition. Thus the version in Bauer incorporates AT 300 with AT 301 (see Tale 3, above); that in Hurreiz combines AT 552A with AT 560 and AT 401; and that in al-Shahi and Moore belongs to AT 300 (note generic name of hero), and that in Nowak to AT 302. The Tunisian version combines AT 552 with AT 560. The version in A. Shah is an elaborate form of AT 552 alone, and the Turkish version is a sophisticated combination of AT 552 and AT 302. Curiously, the only version cited above that comes closest as a parallel to ours is the Greek tale recorded by Dawkins, who provides a set of other Greek parallels and a helpful discussion with further references (pp. 121–123).

18. LŌLABE. Almāza (see Tale 14).

Types 408; 310 (Part II); 313 (Part III)—The Three Oranges; Rapunzel; The Girl as Helper in the Hero's Flight.

Parallels: Palestine—al-Sārīsī (1980) 6, (1985): 133–136 "Daughters of the Citron." Lebanon—al-Bustānī: 140–148 "Ṯurayya, Daughter of the Ghoul." Syria—Ramaḍān: 162–166 "Daughter of the Ghoul." Iraq—Jamālī: 107–110 "Lilwa and Ḥusēn"; Qaṣīr 8 "Prince Nūr al-Zamān and Princess Fatīt al-Rummān." Egypt—el-Shamy 8 "Louliyya, Daughter of Morgān." Tunisia—*Contes de Tunisie:* 33–36 "Le petit pigeon." Cf. Lorimer 22 "The Orange and Citron Princess"; A. Shah (1975): 13–18 "Girl Who Had Seven Dīvs for Brothers"; Kunos: 12–29 "Three Orange-Peris"; Walker and

Uysal: 64–71 "Young Lord and Cucumber Girl"; Dawkins 1 "The Three Oranges"; Calvino 107 "Love of Three Pomegranates."

Salient Motifs: D150 Transformation: man to bird; D253 Transformation: man to needle; D475.4.5 Tears become jewels; D610 Repeated transformation; D672 Obstacle flight; D765.1.2 Disenchantment by removal of enchanting pin; D1611 Magic objects answer for fugitive; F848.1 Girl's long hair as ladder into tower; G84 Fee-fi-fo-fum; G263.1.5 Witch transforms man to bird; G275.3 Witch burned; H31.7.1 Recognition by ability to shed pearls for tears; J1791.6.1 Ugly woman sees beautiful woman reflected in water and thinks it herself; K1911.1.3 False bride takes true bride's place at fountain; K1911.3 Reinstatement of true bride; K2251.1 Treacherous slave-girl; M301.2.1 Enraged old woman prophesies for youth; N711.2 Hero finds maiden in (magic) castle; Q414 Punishment: burning alive.

The Arabic tradition in folk narrative obviously finds congenial some combination of episodes from the three types enumerated, for the majority of parallels cited take portions from one or more of these types and combine them much as was done in our tale. The only exceptions are the other Palestinian version and the Tunisian one, both of which belong to Type 408 alone. Thus, the Iraqi and Lebanese versions combine episodes from AT 310 and AT 313 with the opening episode from AT 408, and the Egyptian version combines them with initial and final episodes from AT 408. The proliferation reflected in the typology here can perhaps be blamed on Aarne-Thompson's *The Types of the Folktale,* which endows the tale of Rapunzel as found in Grimm (on which the analysis for Type 310 is based) with a separate type number. In his study of this tale, however, Lüthi (1976: 109–119) demonstrates, through comparison of Grimm with other European versions, that episode III of "The Girl as Helper in the Hero's Flight" (Type 313), which is not part of the Grimm "Rapunzel," is actually part of the Rapunzel *type* (310). Hence, the combination of these two types in the Arabic tradition should not be surprising, for they belong together even in the European tradition outside Grimm.

None of the Arabic versions belonging primarily to the Rapunzel type (Lebanese, Iraqi, and Egyptian) open in the same manner as Type 310, with the parents promising the child away before it is born. The fact that the opening episode of Type 408 serves to open these versions as well is understandable in view of the Arab cultural emphasis on having children, and of folk beliefs concerning vows and curses. As we see from other tales in this collection (e.g., Tales 1, 8, 40), parents, particularly mothers, will pray to have children regardless of the consequences. And when, as here, the child does come and it is a boy, his birth is interpreted as a consequence of the vow. Therefore, failure to fulfill the conditions of the vow incurs the anger of the supernatural forces, who, through the mechanism of the old woman's curse, send the spoiled son on a dangerous journey. In this manner the son's journey seems properly motivated, arising out of causes that are inherent in the tale's dramatic situation.

See el-Shamy's extensive notes on this tale (pp. 251–254), where many other parallels and references are cited. (A word of caution, however, concerning Schmidt and Kahle I 27, which he cites as a parallel but which does not belong to any of the types discussed here.)

19. THE OLD WOMAN GHOULEH. (Il-ġūle l-ᶜajūz). Im Nabīl (see Tale 17).

Type—Motif D821: Magic object received from old woman.

Parallels: Palestine—*TM* I 3:124–128 (no name).

Salient Motifs: D821 (see above, under Type); D981 Magic fruit; D1071.1 Magic beads; D1074 Magic bracelet; D1420.4 Helper summoned by calling his name; G302.3.3 Demon in form of old woman; G303.4.5 The devil's feet and legs; G312 Cannibal ogre; G420 Capture by ogre; G512 Ogre killed; K800 Killing or maiming by deception; N810 Supernatural helpers; R151 Husband rescues wife.

This tale forms part of a cycle revolving around the ghouleh figure (cf. Tales 29, 30), in which the ogress obtains what she wants through trickery and is finally overcome by the family or community. It is not surprising, in view of common assumptions concerning women's tricks, that the ghouleh should gain her ends through trickery, whereas ghouls, in tales where they play a significant part (e.g., Tales 16, 20, 28), are relatively free of deceit, relying instead on brute force to gain their ends (Tale 16). Both ghouls and ghoulehs, however, do exhibit kindness, the former adopting outcast heroines (Tales 20, 28) and the latter adopting and assisting heroes in their quests (Tales 10, 22).

With reference to our discussion of endogamy in the Introduction, it is interesting to note that in the parallel cited, the role of the ghouleh is assumed by the bridegroom's seven cousins, whom he had passed over in choosing his mate.

20. LADY TATAR (Is-sit Tatar). See Tale 3.

Type 898—The Daughter of the Sun.

Parallels: Palestine—ᶜAbd al-Hādī 64 "Daughter of the Elephant";

al-Khalīlī (1979) 8 "Her Mother the Sun, Her Father the Moon." Syria—Oestrup 3 "Fille du demon"; Lewin 4 "Tochter des Nims." Arabian Peninsula—al-Juhaymān III 14 "Daughter of the Ghoul." Egypt—Spitta-Bey (1880) 9 (no name). Cf. Calvino 74 "Daughter of the Sun."

Salient Motifs: D1030.1 Food supplied by magic; D1472.1.34 Part of human body furnishes food; D1601.9 Household articles act at command; F402.6.3 Demons live in well; G84 Fee-fi-fo-fum; H323 Suitor test: learning girl's name; J2411.3 Unsuccessful imitation of magic production of food; K2212 Treacherous sisters; L162 Lowly heroine marries prince; N774.2 Adventures from seeking (lost) domestic beast [hen]; N812 Giant or ogre as helper; T11.4.1 Love through sight of hair of unknown princess; W181 Jealousy; W195 Envy.

With Parts I ("The Virgin in the Tower") and II ("Rescued Child") of the analysis missing, each of the Arabic versions opens in its own way, but, except for the version in Lewin, they all end more or less alike, with the groom having to learn either what the bride's name is (al-Juhaymān) or how to address her (all others). All involve a ghoul as well, who acts as father figure to the girl, giving her instructions on how to deal with her husband. As for the opening episode, it does not in our version prepare the way for the ending or explain why Lady Tatar (also the name of the heroine in al-Juhaymān) should have the moon for a father and the sun for a mother. (We note in passing that the sun in Arabic is feminine in gender.) The version supplied by al-Khalīlī in synopsis form explains this matter clearly. There, a childless wife is always praying to become pregnant (an opening favored by Palestinian tellers). One day her husband brings home some milk, which she sets on the windowsill. At night the light of the moon shines on the milk, and in the morning the rays of the sun fall on it. When the woman drinks it, she becomes pregnant and gives birth to a daughter who is endowed with the magical abilities described in the tale.

21. ŠŌQAK BŌQAK! Narrated by Im Darwīš, sixty-five, from the village of ʿArrābe, Galilee (also Tale 45; see Introduction, "The Tellers").

Type—Motif T311.1: Flight of maiden (bridegroom) to escape marriage.

Parallels: Palestine—ʿAbd al-Hādī 17 "My Uncle the Gypsy" (very close parallel). Lebanon—al-Bustānī: 164–171 "O Servant, O Barbarian!" Iraq—Stevens 37 "Prince, and Daughter of Thorn-Seller." Egypt—Spitta-Bey (1880) 9 (no title).

Salient Motifs: D1273 Magic formula (charm); F721.1 Underground passages; H113 Identification by handkerchief; H1381.3.1.1 Quest for bride for king (prince); K2110 Slanders; L162 Lowly heroine marries prince; N711.3 Hero finds maiden in (magic) garden; T56.4 Beautiful woman enticed by wonderful flowers; T311.1 Flight of maiden (bridegroom) to escape marriage; W181 Jealousy; Z65.1 Red as blood, white as snow.

The Egyptian parallel cited is actually an elaborate tale combining several types (cf. Tales 20, 26); it incorporates major details from our tale but without the poetry. In that tale the maiden (who is not yet married to the prince) comes into his garden, but his gardener stands in her way. She puts a spell on him, using the same formula as in ours—"Šōqak bōqak! That which is below you / May it rise to the top!"—and he turns upside down. The prince comes later and finds his garden in disarray, sees the girl, falls in love with her, and marries her.

The striking image of the blood on the snow (Motif Z65.1) also occurs in "The Juniper Tree" (Grimm 90). When the wife cuts her finger, with the blood running on the snow, she wishes for a child "as red as blood and as white as snow." The image is adapted in our tale to convey a feeling of beauty and sexual arousal. For an extended discussion of this image, see Cosquin: 218–246.

22. CLEVER ḤASAN (Iš-šāṭir Ḥasan). Narrated by a sixty-five-year-old woman from Gaza (also Tales 32, 35).

Type 314 (Parts V, VI), combined with Type 590 (Parts II–VI)—The Youth Transformed into a Horse; The Prince and the Arm Band.

Parallels: Types 314 and 590: Syria—Ramaḍān: 204–210 "Abū Ḥajlān." Arabian Peninsula—al-Juhaymān III 22 "Little Baldhead and His Father's Wife." Tunisia—Stumme 1 "Mḥammad Belhajjāla."

Type 314: Palestine—Campbell (1954): 125–134 "Story of the Horse and Son of King"; Littmann 10 "Tree with Three Branches"; Schmidt and Kahle I 53 "Kahlköpfchen und das Wunderpferd." Iraq—Stevens 12 "Blind Sultan." Egypt—Artin Pacha 7 "Le cheval enchanté"; el-Shamy 4 "The Magic Filly." Algeria—Galley: 70–105 "Hāroun er-Rachīd"; Mouliéras I: 16–25 "Fils du sultan et chien des chrétiens," II: 391–410 "Haroun er-Rachid devient marchand du beignets." Morocco—Scelles-Millie (1970) 6 "Histoire d'Abderrahman." General Arabic—Katibah (1929): 28–129 "Clever Hasan and Talking Horse." Cf. Kunos: 74–83 "Horse-Devil and Witch"; Dawkins 39 "Prince in Disguise"; Calvino 110 "Mangy One."

Type 590: Palestine—Schmidt and Kahle I 42 "Abenteuer des verbannten Köningsohnes." Lebanon—al-Bustānī: 219–226 "The Lemon Tree Has Revived." Iraq—Qaṣīr (1976) 17 "Janjal, Jnējil, and Zēn Bin Rabāba." Egypt—Dulac 3 (no title); Spitta-Bey (1883) 8 "Histoire du prince et de son cheval."

Salient Motifs: D253 Transformation: man to needle; D1831 Magic strength resides in hair; E80 Water of life. Resuscitation by water; F571.2 Sending to the older; G123 Giant ogress with breasts thrown over her shoulders; G530.3 Help from ogre's mother; H311 Inspection test for suitors; H970 Help in performing tasks; H1212 Quest assigned because of feigned illness; H1321.1 Quest for water of life; K1818.2 Scald-head disguise; N810.2 Helper's beard and eyebrows cut. Only after hero has performed this service is help forthcoming; N812 Giant or ogre as helper; P313 Milk brotherhood. Friends bound in brotherhood through partaking of milk from the same woman; Q41 Politeness rewarded; Q41.2 Reward for cleansing loathsome person [ghoul]; S12 Cruel mother; S12.1 Treacherous mother marries ogre and plots against son; S162 Mutilation: cutting off legs (feet); T131.0.1 Princess has unrestricted choice of husband.

This complex tale is a combination of two separate types. The first, Type 314, we encounter at the story's end, where the hero, as a disguised outcast riding horses of different colors on three successive occasions, wins the princess's hand and saves her father's kingdom or cures his illness. The hero's true identity is somehow revealed, and he is reconciled with his father-in-law and admitted to his favor, usually inheriting the kingdom upon his death. With slight variation this outline is accurate for all Type 314 tales listed above. In Schmidt and Kahle 53, the hero covers his head with a she-goat's stomach, and people call him Qrēʿūn ("Little Baldy"); and in the Moroccan version he is known as *Le Teigneux* (Scald-Head—cf. the Italian title, "Mangy One"). According to the type, the hero's hair serves an important function in the story: supposedly golden, it symbolizes his uniqueness and his worth, and it is in order to hide it that he pretends to be a scald-head. In our version the hero's hair is the source of his strength (Motif D1831, Magic strength resides in hair—reminiscent of Samson and Delilah), although it is not specifically stated to be golden. The Turkish version is the only one among all those cited in which the youth is transformed into a horse. (See *Folktale:* 59–60 for a summary of this type and a discussion of its distribution.)

Type 590, as is evident from the parallels cited, is also popular in the Arabic tradition. This type usually opens with the hero becoming an outcast, or an exile, from his own society. In the Iraqi version, the young hero's exile is brought about by the father, who is terrified of his son's strength (Motif F610, Remarkably strong man). In the Egyptian version, the boy, Clever Mḥammad, is so strong that after his father's death he kills everyone in town, except his mother and a slave who eventually becomes the treacherous mother's lover. In Schmidt and Kahle 42, the potential conflict between father and son is made even more explicit: the father is told in a dream that when his wife reaches the age of seventy she will bear a son who will turn against him; when the wife does give birth, the father sends mother and son on their way. In our version, the teller glosses over the theme of exile at the beginning, but she does confirm it indirectly in the middle of the tale, when Clever Ḥasan is adopted into the family of the ghouleh, who is kinder to him than is his own mother. The motif of remarkable strength is also demonstrated without explicit reference. (See *Folktale:* 113–114 for a plot summary of this type and a discussion of its distribution.)

23. THE CRICKET (Il-xunufse). Fāṭme (see Tale 1).

Type 2023—Little Ant Finds a Penny, Buys New Clothes with It, and Sits in Her Doorway (Motif Z32.3).

Parallels: Palestine—Crowfoot *PEQ* LXXXIII: 165–157 "Little Beetle"; Stephan (two versions) *JPOS* III 4:181–184 "Little Scarabee and Her Suitors"; al-Khalīlī (1979) 4 "The Cricket And Her Mother." Syria—Ramaḍān: 191–193 "The Cricket." Iraq—McCarthy and Raffouli II 1 "Black Beetle"; Stevens 10 "The Blackbeetle Who Wished to Get Married." Cf. Lorimer 45 "The Sad Story of the Beetle, the Mouse and the Ant."

Salient Motifs: B211.1.5 Speaking cow [bull]; B211.1.6 Speaking camel; B211.2.8 Speaking mouse; B211.4 Speaking insects; B281.2.2 Wedding of mouse and cockroach [cricket]; B620 Animal suitor; J1920 Absurd searches for the lost; L112.2 Very small hero; R141 Rescue from well; R151 Husband rescues wife; T200 Married life; X142 The humor of small stature; Z32.3 (see above, under Type).

This humorous tale is very popular in Palestine, as seen in the number of parallels cited. We collected several versions of it as well, including one from Im Nabīl (to be discussed below). All the Palestinian versions are closely parallel, utilizing even the same expressions in the cricket's refrain. The Iraqi versions do not end happily: the mouse (rat) falls into a jar of honey and drowns.

This tale uses animals to represent a human situation allegorically, with metaphor and symbol expressing socially sensitive themes. Indeed, in these tales, although most bodily functions are referred to quite frankly, sexual themes are usually displaced through symbol. (Cf. Tale 21, where a thorn wounds the girl's foot, drawing blood.) The dominant metaphor in the tale deals with size, referring to both social status and sexual compatibility, and the dominant symbol is the tail, which the mouse dangles in the water to bring his wife out. In our version the teller prepares the audience for this unusual event by asking first, "What was he to do?" Of course, the concern here could be merely with politeness, as it is impolite in Arab society to turn one's back on someone else. Yet the implications of the tail dangling in the water are better understood with reference to Im Nabīl's version. When she came to this part of the tale, Im Nabīl laughed out loud; her son, who was present during the taping session, interrupted her by saying, "What my mother really means is that the mouse puts his member in the water." Seen this way, the whole episode of falling in the water could be interpreted as an oblique reference to the couple's first sexual experience, especially since it is followed by a meal and a ritual cleansing.

24. THE SEVEN LEAVENINGS (Imm is-sabiʿ xamāyir). Fāṭme (see Tale 1).
Type—Motif N825.3: Old woman as helper.
Parallels: None located.
Salient Motifs: D2072.0.3 Ship held by magic; F591 Person who never laughs; K1847.1.1 Deceptive report of birth of heir; K1923.3 Barren woman pretends to bear child. Substitutes another woman's child; K2112 Woman slandered as adulteress; M411.5 Old woman's curse (satire); N825.3 Old woman as helper; Q458.1 Daily beatings as punishment; W181 Jealousy; Z142 Symbolic color: white; Z143 Symbolic color: black.

The two parts that form this tale are in reality two different tales brought together around the personality of the old woman and the single theme of wife beating. But the similarity stops there. In the first tale the husband does not undergo a process of self-discovery and remains oblivious to the deception practiced on him. In the second part, however, the husband is made aware by the old woman that his beating of his wife is based on a wrong assumption. The tale's narrative situation takes advantage of a common process in the Palestinian tradition and elsewhere, namely, the literalization of the metaphor of black on white—or, viewed the other way around, the unfolding of the tale's narrative structure can be seen as a metaphorizing of the literal statement about the black grapes on the white platter. In either case, there is something about this process which seems not only congenial to the folktale spirit but also fundamental to folktale art, which thrives on these and other linguistic "sleights of hand."

25. THE GOLDEN ROD IN THE VALLEY OF VERMILION (Qaẓīb iḏ-Ḏahab fī Wādī l-ʿAqīq). Šāfiʿ (see Tale 5).

Types 1359; 1511 (Part I)—The Husband Outwits Adulteress and Paramour; The Faithless Queen.

Parallels: Syria—Ramaḍān: 84–88 "Lady Rose and King Pine."

Salient Motifs: B25 Man [woman]-dog; B80.2 Monster half-man [-woman], half-fish; D1163 Magic mirror; K1550.1 Husband discovers wife's adultery; K2112 Woman slandered as adulteress; Q451.4 Tongue cut off as punishment; Q451.5.1 Nose cut off as punishment for adultery; Q458.1 Daily beatings as punishment; S182 Girl fastened by hair to rafter; T230 Faithlessness in marriage; T351 Sword of chastity; T481 Adultery; W181 Jealousy.

Of all the tales in this collection, this one and "Ṡōqak Bōqak!" (Tale 21) are concerned most directly with sexuality. In Tale 21 the groom's sexual initiation was at issue, and here (as in Tale 24) the subject is irrational sexual jealousy. Both tales deal with the question of the man's sexual fears, and both are replete with sexual imagery and symbolism, either from the plant world (Tale 21) or using body parts with obvious phallic implications (hair, nose, tongue). The title itself is a direct statement of the theme of sexuality.

This tale demonstrates the narrative mastery of Šāfiʿ, who carefully creates and maintains suspense through the tale-within-a-tale, reflecting the influence of the *Thousand and One Nights* with its wealth of such elaborate narrative devices. The purpose of weaving one narrative within another, of course, is to lend a measure of realism to the merchant's tale, since part of his story concerns the tale of the Golden Rod. The two tales are organically related, crossing narrative paths when the Golden Rod steals the merchant's wife at the end. The image of the mirror is central not only to the plot but to the narrative art itself, the tale-within-a-tale being itself a mirror image of the main tale. Thus at the end the two tales are connected when the heroine disappears into the mirror and out of the first tale into the second—that is, as if out of a real-life situation into a fiction.

26. MINJAL. Fāṭme (see Tale 1).

Types 1384; 1540—The Husband Hunts Three as Stupid as His Wife; The Student from Paradise.

Parallels: Palestine—ʿAbd al-Hādī "O Ramaḍān, Take Your Provisions"; al-Sārīsī (1985): 300 "Dirdabbe"; Schmidt and Kahle II 87 "Allerlei Leichtgläubige." Syria—Abū-Shanab: 103–106 "The Seller of Names." General Arabic—Katibah: 42–53 "The Wife Who Bought Herself a New Name"; Nowak, Type 421.

Salient Motifs: H1312.1 Quest for three persons as stupid as his wife; J2093 Valuables given away or sold for a trifle; J2326 The student from Paradise; J2326.1 Foolish woman gives swindler money for her parents in heaven; J2382 How did the cow get on the pole? (A fool hides his purse on a pole on a cliff. Rascal substitutes cow dung for money. Fool interested only in how the cow could have reached the purse); K343.1 Owner sent on errand and goods stolen; K346.1 Thief guards his pursuer's horse while the latter follows a false trail. Steals the horse; M205 Breaking of bargains or promises; T298 Reconciliation of separated couple.

In *The Types* (p. 412) Aarne and Thompson observe that Type 1384 "combines with many other types"—including Type 1540. Except for Nowak, all the Arabic versions cited are closely parallel, combining only these two types and none of the others mentioned by Aarne and Thompson. Moreover, all these versions start out with the episode of selling a name, which is apparently unique to the Arabic tradition. Because the two parts of this tale are so well integrated and always occur together in this tradition, it seems redundant (and somewhat confusing) to assign it two separate type numbers. Furthermore, given that the wife in the end gets her husband to address her by her new name, and in view of the importance in the Palestinian tradition of respecting the wife's wish to be addressed in whatever manner she chooses (cf. final episode of Tale 20), it would appear that the wife in Type 1384 may not be "stupid" after all. See *Folktale:* 168–169 (where further references are cited) for a discussion of Type 1540, and p. 210 for Type 1384.

27. IM ᶜĒŠE. See Tale 4.

Type 1681B—Fool as Custodian of Home and Animals, incorporating episodes belonging to various types, such as Motifs J1835 (Type 1211) The Peasant Woman (Man) Thinks the Cow Chewing Her Cud is Mimicking Her (Him). Kills the Cow; and J1871 (Type 1291B) Filling the Cracks with Butter.

Parallels: Palestine—al-Sārīsī (1980) 11, (1985): 297–298 "ᶜĒše and Im ᶜĒše." Arabian Peninsula—al-Juhaymān IV 8 "ᶜĒše, Im ᶜĒše, and Abū ᶜĒše."

Salient Motifs: J1873 Animals or objects kept warm; J1919.5 Genitals cut off through ignorance; J2465.4 Washing the child. Fool uses boiling water and kills it.

Im ʿĒše and Abū ʿĒše represent folk types that are usually referred to as "Fools and Numskulls" (*Folktale:* 190)—and so they are presented in both parallels. The tale from the Arabian Peninsula shares most of its details with ours, except for the ending, where the fools drown themselves in a well, into which they jump to satisfy their thirst without knowing how to swim. Although the other Palestinian example shares the major motif around which our tale revolves (J2465, Washing the child), it uses different details to demonstrate the foolishness of the characters (e.g., carrying the oven door, taking unbaked dough for a gift, and killing all ʿĒše's pigeons by bathing them in boiling water).

The fool, says Thompson, "lives in a mental world of his own, and he may endow objects or animals with any qualities that suit his passing fancy" (*Folktale:* 190). While this observation does hold true for our characters, the overall effect of the tale is not necessarily comic. The tragicomic ending unifies the tale's seemingly random events, helping to weave them into a meaningful whole centering on the question of fertility.

28. CHICK EGGS (Bēẓ faqāqīs). Im Nabīl (see Tale 17).

Type 480—The Spinning-Women by the Spring. The Kind and the Unkind Girls.

Parallels: Palestine—ʿAbd al-Hādī 45 "Yā bīr, yā banābīr!"; al-Sārīsī (1985): 163–164 "Orphan Girl and Prophet's Cow," 187–188 "Two Sisters"; Schmidt and Kahle I 45 "Goldmarie und Pechmarie." Syria—Ramaḍān: 116–118 "Summer and Winter." Arabian Peninsula—al-Juhaymān I 16 "Qāṭ Qāṭ." Algeria—Desparmet II: 265–278 "Le jardin de la bonne ghoule." North Africa—Scelles-Millie (1970) 13 "Les deux jeunes servants." Cf. Lorimer 13 "Little Fātima"; Dawkins 76 "The Two Women and the Twelve Months"; Megas 39 "The Twelve Months."

Salient Motifs: D454.2 Transformation: bread to another object; D457.13 Transformation: animal dung to another object; D472.1 Transformation: food to muck; K2222 Treacherous co-wife; L55 Stepdaughter heroine; L55.1 Abused stepdaughter; N825.2 Old man helper; Q41 Politeness rewarded; Q111 Riches as reward; Q415 Punishment: being eaten by demon; S322 Children abandoned (driven forth, exposed) by hostile relative; T511.7.2 Pregnancy from eating an egg; T579.8 Signs of pregnancy; W195 Envy.

The version from Schmidt and Kahle is a close parallel, duplicating our tale almost detail for detail. In the Arabian Peninsula version, Qāṭ Qāṭ is a desert monster who rewards a poor girl lost in the desert after she shows kindness to him by answering his questions nicely (e.g., "Who am I?" "You are the king of beasts and lord of the desert, and the source of blessing as well as destruction"). A neighbor girl is curious about this wealth and, after much insistence, learns how it was obtained, except that the first girl instructs her to give negative answers to the monster's questions (e.g., "Who am I?" "You are the destructive beast and the deceitful enemy"); thus the second girl meets her doom as a result of her jealousy and curiosity. In the tale set down by Scelles-Millie, a family of ghouls living near an oasis is so large that they need human servants to carry out their daily chores. The first servant they hire is idle and curious; she does not carry out her tasks correctly and is sent home. The second servant observes all the taboos and does her job well. When the two servants are married, the first is punished and the second is rewarded.

With reference to Roberts's major study of this tale (1958), our version, as well as the others discussed, belongs to the first of two major subtypes, "Encounters en Route" (Part II of the analysis, itself based on Roberts, of the AT Type 480). The Algerian version, in contrast, combines both subtypes, "Encounters en Route" and "Following the River." According to Roberts's analysis, this combination is an anomaly, because the second subtype does not normally incorporate encounters. Cf. the analysis of Tale 43, below.

29. THE GHOULEH OF TRANS-JORDAN (Ġūlit šarq il-Urdun). Narrated by a man in his nineties from the village of ʿĒn Yabrūd, district of Ramallah.

Types 334; 956D—Household of the Witch; How the Girl Saves Herself When She Discovers a Robber Under Her Bed.

Parallels: Palestine—ʿAbd al-Hādī 13 "The Woodcutter and the Ghouleh"; Littmann 30 "The Tale of ʿAlī the Woodcutter"; Sirḥān (1974): 191–196 "Pomegranate Seeds"; *TM* II 6:122–127 "Il-maftūliyye"; *TM* IV 16:45–46 "Iʿrēje." Iraq—Stevens 7 "Old Couple and Their Goat." Algeria—Desparmet II: 123–145 "Le Mqī-dech l'ouïe-fine et son frère l'embrumé."

Salient Motifs: G11.15 Cannibal demon; G247 Witch[es] dance[s]; G512 Ogre killed; J652 Inattention to warnings.

Despite minor variation (e.g., in Sirḥān the ghouleh is the man's sister, and in Desparmet she is his maternal aunt), the essential features of this tale are fairly constant across all the parallels. The poor breadwinner in the family (peasant, woodcutter) is offered an easy living by an older woman who pretends to be his aunt, and he prefers the comfort of having his food ready-to-hand rather than having to earn it. In some versions the wife is suspicious from the very start, but the husband refuses to believe that his benefactress is a ghouleh. In all the variants cited the wife escapes unharmed, and the husband is devoured, regretting his inattention to his wife's warnings.

The Algerian version forms the introductory part of a much longer tale, belonging to an altogether different tale type having to do with the adventures of two brothers. In that version the wife and her son are rescued from the ghouleh by a jinni, who marries the wife. She bears him a son, and the rest of the tale revolves around the friendship and love of the two half-brothers for each other.

30. BEAR-CUB OF THE KITCHEN (Dibbit il-miṭbax). Im Nabīl (see Tale 17).

Type 462—The Outcast Queens and the Ogress Queen.

Parallels: Palestine—ʿAbd al-Hādī 15 "Lady Mosquito"; al-Sārīsī (1985): 240–241 "Son of Seven Mothers"; Schmidt and Kahle I 44 "Der Sohn der Blinden und die Galle des blauen Kamels im tiefen Meer." Egypt—Spitta-Bey 2 "Histoire d'ours de cuisine"; Nowak, Type 177 "Aus-der-Küche-holen." Cf. Jacobs (1969) 16 "Son of Seven Queens"; Calvino 113 "Son of Seven Queens."

Salient Motifs: D2136.2 Castle magically transported; E712.7 Soul hidden in [water] bottle; F234.2.5 Fairy in the form of a beautiful young woman; G72.2 Starving woman abandoned in cave eats newborn child; G211.5 Witch in form of an insect; H931 Tasks assigned in order to get rid of hero; H1212 Quest assigned because of feigned illness; K956 Murder by destroying external soul; K975.2 Secret of external soul learned by deception; L71 Only youngest of a group of imprisoned women refuses to eat her newborn child; S165 Mutilation: putting out eyes; S435 Cast-off wife abandoned in pit; S438 Abandoned queen blinded; S451 Outcast wife at last united with husband and children; T581.2 Child of woman abandoned in pit; T615 Supernatural growth; Z215 Hero "son of seven mothers."

Although both Schmidt and Kahle and Spitta-Bey are listed in the bibliography that opens *The Types of the Folktale,* no Arabic references are cited in the geographic distribution following the analysis for this type, where mention is made only of twenty-four Indian versions. It is also regrettable that Schmidt and Kahle, careful as they were with the colloquial text of the tales, did not obtain from their raconteurs the Arabic names of the tales they recorded. As we have already seen from previous tales (and from Spitta-Bey above), these names often co-occur. Indeed, one of the most intriguing aspects of this particular tale is its name. Bears have been extinct in Palestine for many hundreds of years, although there were still some in the forests of northern Syria until recently. It is not clear why the child's nimbleness and stealth should be compared to a bear's, particularly since in popular speech the term *bear* connotes a clumsy person.

See the notes provided by Jacobs (p. 248), where other parallels are cited, the most important being those from Lorraine (Cosquin) and Sicily (Gonzenbach). Following Cosquin, Jacobs categorically asserts that this tale is of Indian origin.

Nowak summarizes the version found in Schmidt and Kahle under her type number 189 but does not provide the AT equivalent (Type 462).

31. THE WOMAN WHOSE HANDS WERE CUT OFF (Li-mqaṭṭaᶜat id-dayyāt). Narrated by a twenty-two-year-old woman from the village of Rammūn, district of Ramallah.

Type 706—(Parts I, II, IV) The Maiden without Hands.

Parallels: Lebanon—al-Bustānī: 13–40 "Lamis, Princess of Beirut." Syria—Ramaḍān: 152–154 "Woman with Cut-Off Hands." Arabian Peninsula—al-Juhaymān I 19 "Salīm, His Wife, and His Sister."

Salient Motifs: B491.1 Helpful serpent; B511.1.2 Snake heals mutilated maiden [with magic herbs]; D958 Magic thorn; D1513 Charm removes thorn; E782.1 Hands restored; H11.1 Recognition by telling life history; K2110 Slanders; K2116.1.1.1 Innocent woman accused of eating [her] newborn children; K2155.1 Blood smeared on innocent person brings accusation of murder; K2212.2 Treacherous sister-in-law; L111.4.2 Orphan heroine; Q451.1 Hands cut off as punishment; W181 Jealousy.

The version from the Arabian Peninsula pits the sister against the wife, who is having an affair in her husband's absence. The sister discovers the affair, and to protect herself the wife feeds the sister the eggs of the *ḥummar,* a desert bird. (Compare the manner in which pregnancy takes place in Tale 28.) The sister's belly swells, and the brother abandons her in the desert. She gives birth to a little *ḥummar* bird, which feeds her and takes care of all her needs, eventually revealing the situation to her brother by alighting on his house wall and singing a little ditty. The brother follows the bird to the sister's cave in the desert, where they have a touching reunion.

In the Lebanese version, in contrast, the conflict is not between wife and sister but rather between wife and daughter. A king marries a woman who merely pretends friendship for her husband's beloved daughter. But when the wife proves unable to bear children, the king's affections shift back to the daughter and the wife becomes jealous. She then weaves a web of intrigue that leads to the cutting off of the daughter's hands and her banishment. This elaborate version includes several adventures under Part III ("The Calumniated Wife") that are missing from ours.

Nowak summarizes this Lebanese version under her Type 199, but incorrectly provides Type 707 (rather than 706) as the AT equivalent. Thompson discusses this type (*Folktale:* 120) in connection with other tales of slandered wives; see the discussion following Tale 2 above.

One element common to both this tale and another tale in this collection involving brothers and sisters (Tale 42) involves the revelation of the sister's situation through the telling of a story (Motif H11.1).

32. NʿAYYIS (Little Sleepy One). See Tale 22.

Type 425B—The Disenchanted Husband: The Witch's Tasks.

Parallels: Syria—Ramaḍān: 63–67 "The King's Son and the Jinn Woman," 144–147 "Leave Her Alone, Sandman."

Salient Motifs: D2176.3 Evil spirit exorcised; F165.6.1 Other world (fairyland) as place of sorrowful captivity; F302.3.1.3 Man is carried to fairyland by fairy and marries her; F324.3 Youth abducted by fairy; F375 Mortals as captives in fairyland; F382 Exorcising fairies; G273.1 Witch powerless when one makes the sign of the cross; H923.1 Task assigned before wife may rescue husband from supernatural power; H970 Help in performing tasks; K1847 Deception by substitution of children; L162 Lowly heroine marries prince; R47 Captivity in lower world; R152 Wife rescues husband; R152.3 Father rescues children; T670 Adoption of children.

Although the motif of fairies taking human lovers or husbands who are later disenchanted (F324.3) is common both in Palestinian and Arabic folklore and in Western folklore (see *Folktale:* 97–102, 246–253), and even though the salient motifs in this version exist in other traditions as well (as evidenced by the assignment of numbers to them), we have been unable to locate a parallel for our tale. No single available version combines the motifs listed as "Nʿayyis" does, although, taken together, the two Syrian versions form a close parallel. Indeed, the type number suggested for this tale is an approximation at best.

What is intriguing about this tale is the manner in which the disenchantment is effected. Disenchantment by means of the sign of the cross or by pronouncing an appropriate religious formula (e.g., "In the name of Allah, the Compassionate, the Merciful!") is common in both Eastern and Western folklore, but the notion of involving a surrogate bride to act out, or mimic, in the human world events supposedly taking place in fairyland as a means of disenchantment appears to be unique to this tale.

33. IM ʿAWWĀD AND THE GHOULEH (Im ʿAwwād w-il-ġūle). Narrated by a woman in her seventies from Rammūn, district of Ramallah.

Type—Motif G302.3.3: Demon in form of old woman.

Parallels: None located.

Salient Motifs: C742 Tabu: striking monster twice; G250 Recognition of witches; G302.3.3 Demon in form of old woman; G312 Cannibal ogre; G512.3 Ogre burned to death.

This tale belongs to a class of tales in which there is an encounter between a woman and a ghouleh. Two other such tales are included in this collection, Tales 19 and 29. Another tale belonging to this group but that we did not include incorporates Motifs G211.1.3 (Witch in form of cow) and B214.3 (Laughing cow). In this tale a poor woodcutter finds a cow in the wild and keeps her. One day, while the wife is milking her, the cow laughs. The wife tells her husband that she suspects the cow to be a ghouleh, but he refuses to believe her (Motif J652, Inattention to warnings). One night the wife escapes with the children, leaving the husband to be devoured by the ghouleh. In the tale of the laughing cow, "Im ʿAwwād," and Tale 29, the woman always escapes, leaving either her husband or her son to be devoured by the ghouleh. These tales all teach the importance of respecting the wife's opinion. In Tale 19, in contrast, a newlywed bride is encouraged to share her secrets with her husband from the very beginning of the marriage relationship.

34. THE MERCHANT'S DAUGHTER (Bint it-tājir). Narrated by a woman in her eighties from Gaza.

Types 327C; 328; 1122—The Devil (Witch) Carries the Hero Home in a Sack; The Boy Steals the Giant's Treasure; Ogre's Wife Killed Through Other Tricks.

Parallels: Palestine—al-Sārīsī (1985): 181–182 "Woodling." General Arabic.

Salient Motifs: F821.1.4 Wooden coat; G61 Relative's flesh eaten unwittingly; G61.2 Mother recognizes child's flesh when it is served to be eaten; G81 Unwitting marriage to cannibal; G500 Ogre defeated; G530.2 Help from ogre's daughter (or son); G550 Rescue from ogre; G610 Theft from ogre; H94 Identification by ring; K521 Escape by disguise; K527 Escape by substituting another person in place of the intended victim; K620 Escape by deceiving the guard; K1821.9 Escape by wooden covering; R11.1 Princess (maiden) abducted by monster; R111.1 Princess (maiden) rescued from captor; R169.5 Hero rescued by friend [neighbor].

As we said in our discussion of Tale 32, the motifs that constitute this tale are common in Arabic folklore, but their arrangement into the narrative pattern found here is apparently unique to the Palestinian tradition since the version recorded by al-Sārīsī is a very close parallel. The type numbers adduced are approximations at best.

In the Palestinian tale "The Shepherd's Cave" (Bauer: 212–214), a similar strategy to that here is used to summon help. A shepherd is attacked by bandits, who tie him up and slaughter some of his animals to feed themselves. He begs to be released so that he may perform for them on his musical instrument. They untie him, and he improvises a song that summons help from his sister. The motif of wearing a wooden dress for disguise (F821.1.4) appears to be fairly common in folktales. It occurs, among other places, in the Iraqi tale "Dungara Khshebyān" (Stevens 5) and the Chilean tale the "Little Stick Figure" (Pino-Saavedra 20), where the heroine puts on a wooden dress to escape from a lecherous father. In her comment on the Iraqi tale, Stevens notes that the wooden dress "seems to indicate some Dryad legend" (p. 293).

Thompson discusses this tale (*Folktale:* 37) in connection with a basic type (AT 327) that involves a whole constellation of events centering on children and an ogre (AT 327A–G). Tale 6 in this collection also belongs in this group (AT 327B) and, as we said, is one of the most popular in the country. An important feature of "The Merchant's Daughter," however, is that it bridges the gender gap: it is an adventure story belonging to a popular type, yet it involves a girl rather than a boy. There is no hint in either *The Folktale* or *The Types* that this group of tales could have heroines rather than heroes.

35. POMEGRANATE SEEDS (Ḥab Rummān). See Tale 22.

Type 894 (Parts I, III, IV)—The Ghoulish Schoolmaster and the Stone of Pity.

Parallels: Palestine—ʿAbd al-Hādī 25 "Sitt il-Yadab"; al-Sārīsī (1980) 5, (1985): 127–132 "Pure Pomegranate and Gold"; Sirḥān 3 "Sitt il-Yadab." Syria—Ramaḍān: 105–108 "Pure Pomegranate and

Gold"; Abū-Shanab: 117–123 "Pomegranate Seeds." Arabian Peninsula—al-Juhaymān II 21 "Orphan Girl and Sorcerer Schoolmaster." South Arabia—Jahn 11 (quoted in Cosquin: 114). Egypt—Artin Pacha 4 "La princesse Tag-el-Agem"; Ibrahim: 68 "Kaškōl dahab." Algeria—Desparmet I: 343–354 "La femme qui se sauva de chez un ghoul." Cf. Noy 48 "Deceived Girl and Stone of Suffering"; Dawkins 33 "Ogre Schoolmaster"; Megas 29 "Sleeping Prince." See also Cosquin: 112–121 for a discussion and further references.

Salient Motifs: D953 Magic twig; D1174 Magic box; D1208 Magic whip; D2072.0.2 Animal rendered immovable; D2072.2 Magic paralysis by curse; D2176.3 Evil spirit exorcised; G11.9 Ogre schoolmaster. Girl sees schoolmaster eat human flesh. Refuses to tell him what she saw. He persecutes her. G442.1 Ogre abducts newborn, keeping it captive for seven years; K2155.1 Blood smeared on innocent person brings accusation of murder; K2116.1.1.1 Innocent woman accused of eating her newborn children; L221 Modest request: present from the journey; M205.2 Curse as punishment for broken promise; N711.1 Prince (king) finds maiden in woods (tree) and marries her; Q64 Patience rewarded; R111.2.5 Girl rescued from tree; S451 Outcast wife at last reunited with husband and children; T210.2 Faithful husband; T298 Reconciliation of separated couple.

In the European tradition, Type 894 usually occurs in combination with the episode of the Sleeping Prince (designated as Part II in the analysis of the type), and it is in relation to this episode that Dawkins discusses his version (p. 175). In the Arabic tradition, however, the two tales are always separate (e.g., they are Nos. 3 and 4 in Artin Pacha).

Except for the ending, our version shares all its narrative details with one or another of the Arabic tales. The lost slipper and the sheikh's rhyming question are also common to the Syrian, Egyptian, and Algerian variants. The Syrian tale found in Abū-Shanab shares almost word for word the sheikh's question, including the rhyming scheme. In all these variants the girl runs away from the sheikh in horror but keeps his secret regardless of his cruelty; she then marries a personage of high degree and eventually regains her children and her status. Motifs G11.9, G261, and K2116.1, among others, are common to all these versions. Lodging with the same type of shopkeepers (with similar disastrous results) and taking shelter in a tree (Motif N711.1) occur in the Algerian version. In most variants the king loves his wife (Motif 210.1) and does not want to see her punished, although the mode of punishment does vary in degree of cruelty from one version to another (ours being the least cruel). The husband's journey (Motif L221), or something like it, is also a common theme.

The differences, however, are significant, especially in the way the ogre-sheikh is presented. Our story has him as both man and ghoul, an ambiguous figure who tortures an innocent maiden but rewards her, albeit against his will. In the elaborate Algerian version, the ambiguity in the sheikh's character is resolved at the very beginning by making him a ghoul—that is, a monster. Furthermore, the girl does not see him devouring one of her classmates, as in all the other Arabic versions, but in the embarrassing position of sitting on a donkey's head while cooking the donkey in a huge caldron. Yet his punishment for her is no less cruel than in the other tales.

In his summary of the Greek tale, Dawkins refers to the schoolmaster as a "monstrous and demoniac creature"; in the Mehri (Jahn) version, too, he is presented as a monster who kills the queen's children in front of her the moment they are born. In the Egyptian version, the girl sees her teacher, not eating a fellow schoolmate or skinning him (as in the tale from the Arabian Peninsula), but beating another girl almost to the point of death. Yet, although just as vengeful as the others, at the end of the tale he is presented as a benign figure whose purpose, he declares, was to test her patience. This detail provides a good clue about the meaning of the maiden and the sheikh's encounter: one is reminded of the tale of Job, who, like Pomegranate Seeds, is tested by the Devil acting at the behest of Divine Providence. Like Pomegranate Seeds, Job is rewarded in the end for his patience. Other than asking his fearful question, the sheikh in our tale never addresses the girl directly or attempts, as he does in the Egyptian and some other versions, to explain his actions to her. He remains an enigmatic instrument of fate throughout.

All the Palestinian variants share the same ending, following the pattern for Type 894 with its final episode of "The Stone of Patience or Pity" (Part IV of the type analysis). In every other version the persecuted wife asks her husband to bring back from his journey two objects (usually a knife and a box), which she then uses to tell her woes to. The husband, meanwhile, curious to know what these strange objects are for, stations himself outside her door and overhears her story. Our tale, in contrast, ends on more of an exorcism than a mere recitation of woes. Pomegranate Seeds' whipping of the box of myrrh with the seven switches of pomegranate wood is a dramatic enactment of her (bitter) situation, involving a magic sympathy between her name and the type of wood she uses.

36. THE WOODCUTTER (Il-ḥaṭṭāb). Fāṭme (see Tale 1).

Type 563—The Table, the Ass, and the Stick.

Parallels: Palestine—al-Sārīsī (1985): 176–177 "The Club"; Sirḥān 3 "The Wooden Bowl"; *TM* III 14:29–34 "Abū Sālim, His Wife, and His Children." South Arabia (Ḥaḍramaut)—Hein and Müller 28 "Die drei Wunderdinge." Algeria (Berber)—Basset (1903) 11 "Les deux frères, la marmite et le bâton." Morocco—Alarcón y Santón 10 "Historia del Pescador." North Africa—Scelles-Millie (1972) 8 "La petite massue," 9 "Djin el-Behari." General Arabic—Nowak, Type 216 (but not 303, for which see discussion following Tale 43, below). Cf. Noy 21 "Coffee Mill, Tray, and Stick"; Kunos: 40–52 "Mad Mehmed" (last episode).

Salient Motifs: D861.2 Magic object stolen by neighbor; D881.2 Recovery of magic object by use of magic cudgel; D1030.1 Food supplied by magic; D1401.1 Magic club (stick) beats person; D1470.1 Magic wishing-object; D1472.1.20 Magic plate supplies food and drink; D1601.5 Automatic cudgel; F402.6.3 Demons live in well; J2355.1 Fool loses magic objects by talking about them; W195 Envy.

This tale resembles the type very closely, as evidenced by the fact that most of the motifs listed above may be found in the type analysis. The great popularity in the Arabic tradition of the punishment by a magic stick motif can be seen in the number of parallels adduced (with the Nowak reference adding a version from Tunisia). Even more Arabic and other parallels may be found in the informative footnotes following each of the Scelles-Millie tales.

The Moroccan version recorded by Alarcón y Santón has an interesting twist. In this tale the hero's neighbors betray his possession of a magic lamp to the cadi, who confiscates it for his own use only to be beaten by four slaves who emerge from it. The cadi in turn presents it to the sultan, who also is beaten by the four slaves and ends up repenting his greed. The details of the version supplied by Basset (reprinted from his earlier *Nouveaux contes populaires berbères,* Paris, 1897) may be surmised from the title; there it is the richer brother who deprives the poorer one of his magic pot.

All the Palestinian versions are close parallels, and the Ḥaḍramī version is close to all these as well. In that tale a poor man is given three gifts, although by a person who is not specifically stated to be of the jinn. The first gift is a magic she-goat that gives birth to a hundred gold pieces every day (perhaps a polite version of Motif B103.1.1, Gold-producing ass. Droppings of gold). The second gift is a wooden bowl that fills with food on command. The first is stolen by the sultan's son and the second by a carpenter, with substitute objects returned to the rightful owner (as in our version). The third gift is a magic stick that beats the covetous thieves until they return the original objects. This stick is used differently in this tale, however; each thief, on seeing the stick, is curious about it and starts to play with it, but it immediately beats him into unconsciousness.

Of the two parallels recorded by Scelles-Millie, No. 8 is quite close to ours. An aging woodcutter, attempting to chop down a particular tree, disturbs its resident jinni, who sends him away with a magic semolina-grinding mill, bidding him to keep it a secret. His wife betrays their secret to the neighbors, who borrow the mill and keep it, bringing back an ordinary mill in its place. The woodcutter does not suspect the neighbors but assumes simply that the mill's effectiveness has run out. Eventually he becomes poor again and has to earn his living by chopping wood. The jinni gives him a stick, which, on being given the command "Petite massue, fais ton travail!" descends on the neighbors and beats them until they agree to return the magic mill.

Thompson notes that this tale appears in a collection of Chinese Buddhist legends as No. 468 in Edouard Chavanne's *Cinq cent contes et apologues extraits du Tripitake chinois,* vol. 3 (see *Folktale:* 72–75).

37. THE FISHERMAN (Is-sammāk). Almāza (see Tale 14).

Types 465; 1930—The Man Persecuted Because of His Beautiful Wife; Schlaraffenland.

Parallels: Types 465 and 1930: Palestine—ʿAbd al-Hādī 59 "The Turtle"; al-Sārīsī (1985): 193–194 "Holding on to Good Fortune"; Sirḥān 1 "A Tale Consisting of Lies from the Beginning to the End"; Spoer and Haddad: 167–173 "A Lie Through and Through." Egypt—Spitta-Bey (1883) 4 "Histoire du pecheur et de son fils"; el-Shamy 3 "The One Sesame Seed." Sudan—Mitchnik: 79–84 "The Fisherman and the Prince." Cf. A. Shah (1975): 62–68 "The Bead-Seller and the Jinn's Sister."

Type 465: Arabic parallels—none located (Nowak 177 and 227, as indicated in her index, p. 408, are only marginally related to this type number, if at all). Cf. Dawkins 18B "The Animal Wife"; Walker and Uysal: 55–63 "Son of the Fisherman." See Cosquin: 289–296 for a general discussion of this type, including reference (p. 293) to Armenian and other Turkish versions.

Type 1930: Palestine—al-Khalīlī 20 "A Tale of Lies from Beginning to End"; al-Sārīsī (1985): 392–393 "A Tale of Lies from Beginning to End"; Schmidt and Kahle I 33 "Eine Geschichte, die von Anfang bis zu Ende eine Lüge ist." Syria—as part of Oestrup 6 "Les trois princes et l'oiseau d'or." Iraq—Campbell (1954): 83–87 "Story of the Lie Which Could Not Be Believed." North Africa—Scelles-Millie (1972) 7 "Le mensonge le plus doux." General Arabic—Basset (1924) II 22 "Le plus menteur des trois"; Katibah (1928): 258–266 "Story That Is All Lies." See Chauvin VIII:62–63, no. 27, for references regarding unusual infants, particularly the "infant who speaks before or just after his birth." Cf. Noy 44 "The Great Lie"; Lorimer 2 "City of Nothing in the World." See Webber for a discussion of the "all lies" story in a Tunisian context. See also Schwarzbaum: 197–202 for a general discussion and further references.

Salient Motifs: D1030.1 Food supplied by magic; D1652.1.1 Inexhaustible bread; F234.2.5 Fairy in the form of a beautiful young woman; F236.3 Fairies with belts and hats; F303 Wedding of mortal and fairy; F343.7 Fairy-wife furnishes provisions; F343.13 Fairy gives mortal a child; F346.0.1 Fairy serves mortal; F885 Extraordinary field; H509.5 Test: telling skillful lie; H931.1 Prince envious of hero's wife assigns hero tasks; H1233.2.1 Quest accomplished with help of wife; J1920 Absurd searches for the lost; N831.1.1 Mysterious housekeeper is fairy mistress; T585.2 Child speaks at birth; W181 Jealousy.

In the Introduction we explored the notion of lying as a generative metaphor in the definition of the folktale form itself. The multifunctional Tale of Lies helps to establish this point more firmly. Not only is it part of a larger tale's contents, but it also, like the tale-within-a-tale in "The Golden Rod," serves as a counterpoint to the frame tale's believability. As unrealistic as the story of the fisherman may be, it seems fairly credible in comparison with the outrageous events in the Tale of Lies. This kind of imaginative depth and reflexive commentary is an important aspect of the folktale genre. This thought may be better appreciated in relation to the Tale of Lies found in Oestrup (which itself is part of a larger tale). There, two brothers on a search for the Golden Bird for their father each stand to win a magic garden if they can tell a tale that is all lies from beginning to end. "That's easy," says the eldest, and he commences: "Once there was a merchant . . ."—whereupon the owner of the garden, an exacting critic, stops him on the pretext that because merchants exist his tale could not be considered all lies. The second brother falls into the same trap ("Once there was a woman and her husband"). Therefore, telling a tale consisting of nothing but lies is not as easy as it appears, for the esthetic foundation of fiction itself is thereby called into question. Only a genuine hero, the youngest son (who tells a tale substantially similar to ours), is capable of the feat. In a thoughtful commentary on this tale, Scelles-Millie (p. 87) summarizes our point thus: "Nous avons traduit le mot 'kad'ab' litteralement par mensonge. En réalité, il s'agit plutôt d'une allégorie, d'une parabole, apparantée aux procédés littéraires des mystiques islamiques."

The Tale of the Fisherman (Type 465) does not seem to exist on its own in the Arabic tradition; it has been parasitized (so to speak) by the Tale of Lies. Told by itself, the Tale of Lies offers a good field for the inventive power of the folk imagination. Basset (1924, II: 22) locates Type 1930 in a written version (*Rawāʾiḥ al-ʿawāṭir* [Scents of perfume], Cairo, 1302H). In that version three men find a dinar and agree that it should go to the one who can tell the best lie; the first man then relates a tale that is similar to ours in some details (including the field on top of the tree, Motif F885, and the knife in the watermelon) but is not as extensive in its fictional scope. In the versions recorded by Schmidt and Kahle and by Scelles-Millie the Tale of Lies constitutes the bridewealth a prospective husband must bring to win the hand of the king's daughter.

As for Type 465, its opening episode exhibits considerable variety. In some versions the king simply sees a beautiful woman (the wife of a bead seller in the Afghani version and of a fisherman in most others) and wants her for himself. When informed that the woman is the wife of another man, the king (or prince) sets the husband impossible tasks, all of which he performs successfully with the help of his wife. The tasks assigned also vary. In the Greek tale, for example, the husband must "overlay the palace with gold outside and inside"; in the Afghani version he must provide the king with a curtain for the latticework behind the throne; and in the Egyptian version of el-Shamy he must come to the king's palace "riding-walking." In the Sudanese tale his first task is to appear before the prince both laughing and crying, and his second is to come both dressed and naked. Despite differences in detail, however, all versions coincide in essential features, especially in making the wife the savior of the husband, who, after each task assignment, invariably comes to her crying that he is about to lose his life. In each case the wife sends him to one of her relatives, either her mother or her sister, who is able to help the husband to fulfill his task and thus saves his life. For more discussion and references, see *Folktale:* 93.

38. THE LITTLE SHE-GOAT (Il-ʿanze l-iʿnēziyye). Fāṭme (see Tale 1).

Types 123; 2032—The Wolf and the Kids; The Cock's Whiskers.

Parallels: Palestine—al-Sārīsī (1980) 18, (1985): 327 "Little She-Goat"; Sirḥān 6 "Little She-Goat"; Stephan 1 "Courageous Goat,"

2, 3 "The Goat and the Ghoul." Iraq—Nowak, Type 22. Egypt—Nowak, Type 16. Tunisia—*Contes de Tunisie:* 117–118 "Hamkam et Zamzam"; Nowak, Type 16. Morocco—Nowak, Type 25.

Salient Motifs: F913 Victims rescued from swallower's belly; J144 Well-trained kid does not open door to wolf [hyena]; K971 Wolf comes in the absence of mother and eats up the kids (motif found under the type number but not in Thompson's *Motif-Index*); K1839.1 Wolf puts flour on his paws to disguise himself [nonvocal deception: cutting off the tail].

This tale's popularity among the Palestinian people can be seen from its inclusion in nearly every available collection of Palestinian folktales. It is undoubtedly popular in other parts of the Mashreq as well, including the Arabian Peninsula, but for some reason collectors have ignored it. Of the Palestinian parallels, only Stephan 2 and 3 incorporate AT 2032, but all share the she-goat's rhyming challenge at the end. In some versions the animal that loses its young is not always a she-goat, and the aggressor is not necessarily a hyena, but the general outline of the tale remains constant. See *Folktale:* 39–40.

39. THE OLD WOMAN AND HER CAT (Il-ʿajūz w-il-biss). Narrated by a woman in her late sixties from Bēt Imrīn, district of Nablus (also Tale 40).

Type 2034—The Mouse [Cat] Regains Its Tail.

Parallels: Palestine—Schmidt and Kahle II 84 "Wie der Fuchs wieder zu seinem Schwanz kam." Iraq—Stevens 2 "Goat and Old Woman." Tunisia—*Contes de Tunisie:* 77—79 "Omi Sissi et son chat." Cf. Kunos: 97–101 "One Piece of Liver"; Lorimer 30 "Sad Tale of Mouse's Tail." See Schwarzbaum: 321 for extensive references in the Jewish and world traditions.

Salient Motifs: Z41.4 The mouse [cat] regains its tail.

Like the tale of the little she-goat, this one depicts scenes from Palestinian village life, demonstrating the interdependence of various elements within the community. In the Schmidt and Kahle version, which is quite close to ours, the animal that loses its tail is a fox. In the Tunisian version an old woman buys some halvah for her daughter, the cat eats it, and she cuts off its tail; to regain it, the cat must go through a cycle similar in outline to the one here, but different in detail. Thompson notes the broad reach of this type in the popular tradition: "Not only is this [type] common all over Europe, but there are interesting analogues from all parts of Africa" (*Folktale:* 233). The Iraqi version, it must be noted, is not an exact parallel, as it belongs more accurately to Type 2030 (The Old Woman and Her

Pig), but it is close enough to exemplify the popularity of this general type of cumulative tale among the Arab peoples.

40. DUNGLET (Bʿērūn). See Tale 39.

Type 2028—The Troll (Wolf) Who Was Cut Open.

Parallels: Palestine—Hanauer: 145–146. Cf. Lorimer 8 "Nukhudū, or Master Pea"; Dorson (1958) 216 "I Eat a Barrel of Pickle."

Salient Motifs: C758.1 Monster born because of hasty wish of parents; D437.4 Transformation: excrements to person; D1002 Magic excrements; D1610.6.4 Speaking excrements; F913 Victims rescued from swallower's belly; G33 Child born as cannibal; G376 Ogre in shape of small boy; T548.1 Child born in answer to prayer; T550 Monstrous births; T556 Woman gives birth to a demon; Z33.4 The fat troll.

The fact that in this tale blind men finally kill the troll is certainly a significant contribution to the type, for it enlarges the meaning of the troll image to include the realm of illusion. The blind men are able to overcome the troll because they cannot see him, and therefore do not know the danger he represents (if indeed he even represents a danger at all). Also, because they are strangers to him, they do not share the bonds of mutual obligations that tie him to his extended family. Another feature that distinguishes both Palestinian versions from the basic type is their focus on the relationship between the child and the family. Indeed, the equation of children first with dung and then with trolls, which is not found in the type, is undoubtedly susceptible to interpretation on many levels at once. Generation itself, certainly a major theme in the culture (as discussed in the Introduction), is brought under a harsh light in this tale.

The swallowing aspect of this tale connects it with the story of Cronus, who, fearing a prophecy that his sons will destroy him, swallows them as soon as they are born. When Zeus, whom Rhea saves by presenting Cronus with a stone wrapped in a blanket in the baby's stead, later rises up and kills his father, all the swallowed children, including the stone wrapped in a blanket, emerge unharmed.

41. THE LOUSE (Il-qamle). See Tale 4.

*Type 2021**—The Louse Mourns her Spouse, the Flea.

Parallels: Palestine—al-Sārīsī (1985): 330 "The Flea." Lebanon—Katibah (1928): 24–28 "All for the Death of a Flea." Syria—Ramaḍān: 79–82 "The Louse and the Flea." Arabian Peninsula—al-Juhaymān I 4 "Mosquito and Louse." Cf. Lorimer 4 "Sūskū and Mūshū" (second half), 45 "Sad Story of Beetle, Mouse and Ant" (second half).

This tale belongs in a group of chain tales involving death, with animal actors (Types 2021–2024). All are closely related in content, with the death of an apparently insignificant member of the chain having a catastrophic effect throughout the system. The Lebanese version (Katibah), in fact, states this theme explicitly at the end: "Come along with me, Abu Mahmoud," says the goat owner, "come to the goat-pen! There you shall have a handful of jumper princes [fleas] lest the whole world go to rack and ruin for the sake of a flea" (p. 28). The particular type number for this tale in *The Types* was assigned on the basis of a single Walloon example; the list of parallels given here provides several more from the Middle East. The example from the Arabian Peninsula, although it belongs to this group, does not fit any of these type numbers because it does not involve an actual death; death is its theme, though. See Schwarzbaum: 247 for a Type 2021 parallel in the Jewish tradition.

42. THE WOMAN WHO FELL INTO THE WELL (Illī wiqᶜit fī l-bīr). See Tale 4.
Type 883C—The Boys with Extraordinary Names.
Parallels: General Arabic—Nowak, Type 338. Cf. Walker and Uysal: 215–218 "Immoral Khoja and Daughter of Aga."
Salient Motifs: H11.1 Recognition by telling life history; K2150 Innocent made to appear guilty; K2258 Treacherous peasant; R141 Rescue from well; R213 Escape from home; R215 Escape from execution; Z71.5.1 Seven brothers and one sister.

Judging from the plot summary provided by Nowak under her Type 338, the parallels she cites, except for the unusual names of the children, are apparently not exact. Similarly, the Turkish variant really belongs to AT 883A (The Innocent Slandered Maiden), but in their discussion of this tale (pp. 290–291n.11) Walker and Uysal summarize the plot of a version of AT 883C that seems to be very close to ours. The names of the children in that tale are "What Have We Become?" "What Shall We Become?" and "What Shall We Inherit?" The authors point out that both versions cited in *The Types* for AT 883C were collected in Anatolia. We have already on several occasions identified parallels between Turkish tales and ours (and in one instance—Tale 8—the Turkish version was as similar as the other Palestinian versions cited). The prevalence of close parallels between the two traditions should not be surprising, considering the prolonged cultural contact between the Turkish and Arab peoples and the Ottoman dominance over most parts of the Arab world for over four hundred years. Taking also into consideration the existence of several Arabic versions of AT 883A (cited in *The Types*), it is impossible to determine whether this general type is originally Arabic or Turkish. We may speculate, however, and with some certainty given the emphasis on fate in our tale, that it is Islamic in origin.

43. THE RICH MAN AND THE POOR MAN (Il-ġanī w-il-faqīr). Fāṭme (see Tale 1).

Type 480—The Spinning-Women by the Spring. The Kind and the Unkind Girls.

Parallels: Palestine—ʿAbd al-Hādī 62 "Pour out the Molasses," 63 "The Woman Who Gathers Wood"; Littmann (1905) 14 "The Two Brothers"; Schmidt and Kahle II 87 "Vom Tischlein deck dich!"; *TM* I 1:153–160 "The Tale of ʿAbdalla." Egypt—Katibah (1929): 52–76 "After Distress—Relief." Sudan—al-Shahi and Moore 14 "The Two Sisters." Tunisia—al-ʿIrwī IV:153–160 "Intelligence Enriches Him Who Has It"; *Contes de Tunisie:* 37–39 "La poule aux oeufs d'or." Cf. A. Shah (1969): 126–131 "The Rich Merchant, the Poor Merchant, and the Jinn."

Salient Motifs: D1454.2 Treasure falls from mouth; F92.2 Person swallowed up by earth and taken to lower world; F101 Return from lower world; H1023.13 Catching a man's [woman's] broken wind; J2401 Fatal imitation; L200 Modesty brings reward; M431.2 Curse: toads [scorpions] from mouth; Q111 Riches as reward; W195 Envy.

We have already discussed a version of this type in our analysis of Tale 28. But although this tale also clearly belongs to AT 480, by its title it could belong to a group of tales about two brothers rather than two sisters. Yet the only type acknowledged by Aarne-Thompson where two brothers, one rich and greedy, the other poor but contented, undergo a similar set of changes as in our tale is AT 676 (Open Sesame)—and indeed, there are some affinities, such as the phrase in our tale "Earth, open up and swallow me!" With ʿAbd al-Hādī 63, too, which also clearly belongs to AT 480, a connection with AT 676 exists in the episode of the piece of gold sticking to the rich neighbor's scales (see *The Types:* 238). None of the parallels with male protagonists, however, properly belong to AT 676, even though they do have affinities with it; likewise with AT 480, since by its very structure that type is about women. The parallels, then, seem to form a composite of both tales, belonging properly to neither and having no type number that accurately fits them.

Now, in these parallels, when the protagonists are male, they are always brothers, yet when the protagonists are female they are not always sisters. Schmidt and Kahle, for example, equate their tale with Grimm 36, and Nowak follows them in classifying her Type

303 as AT 563. Although this typology is not incorrect, their tale, like all the others with male protagonists, is as much about the brothers' relationship as it is about the acquisition, loss, and recovery of the magic food-providing objects. Further, some of the versions with sisters as protagonists (e.g., Egypt and Sudan) also focus more on the relationship between the sisters than on their changed fortunes (rich to poor and vice versa). Here, then, is another set of affinities that relates our tale with AT 676: the fact that by calling the tale "The Rich *Man* and the Poor *Man*," and by making the protagonists not only sisters but also sisters who are wives of two brothers thereby doubling the bonds of relationship, the teller herself understood the tale to be about kindness and unkindness among siblings—a fact which does not figure prominently in the content of AT 480.

What emerges from these deliberations is the idea that, to some extent, the act of typing is a sort of culturally determined compromise. Meaning emerges not only from the tale's structure (its type number, so to speak), but also from its content. Thus, as far as the type index is concerned, the fact that the protagonists in our tale are sisters is incidental, whereas in Palestinian and Arab culture this fact assumes an overwhelming significance. This realization does not necessarily play havoc with the type index, but it does show that types must be determined with some caution.

44. MAᶜRŪF THE SHOEMAKER (Maᶜrūf is-skāfī). Šāfiᶜ (see Tale 5).

Type 560—The Magic Ring.

Parallels: Syria—Nowak, Type 148. Egypt—Artin Pacha 21 "El-Said Aly." General Arabic—Basset (1906): 273–291, "Le roi et la bague magique" (also cited in Nowak, Type 148); *Thousand and One Nights,* "Maarouf the Cobbler" (Nights 959–972, Mardrus-Powys IV:418–446; Nights 989–1000, Burton X:1–53); Chauvin VI:81, no. 250, "Ma'rouf."

Salient Motifs: D840 Magic object found; D861.4 Magic object stolen by rival for wife; D1421.1.6 Magic ring summons genie; D1470.1.15 Magic wishing-ring; D1662.1 Magic ring works by being stroked; D2121.5 Magic journey: man carried by spirit or devil; F721.4 Underground treasure chambers; K1817.4 Disguise as merchant; L161 Lowly hero marries princess; N534.1 Stumble reveals depository of treasure; N630 Accidental acquisition of treasure or money; P453 Shoemaker; Q42 Generosity rewarded; Q83.1 Reward for wife's fidelity; Q581.0.1 Loss of life as a result of one's own treachery; R161.0.1 Hero rescued by his lady; R164 Rescue by giant; R169.5 Hero rescued by friend; T210.1 Faithful wife; W195 Envy.

This tale is an oral version of the celebrated story of Maarouf the cobbler, the last tale in the *Arabian Nights* (at least in the Burton edition). The tale seems to have enjoyed wide popularity in Europe, where it was turned into an opera in five acts (*Marouf, le savetier du Caire*) by Henri Rabaud, with substantially the same plot as here and in the *Nights*. The opera premiered in Paris in 1915, and since then it has not been entirely neglected, being occasionally performed in Europe, the United States, and South America. It therefore seems strange that the tale of Maᶜrūf is not cited at all in *The Types,* particularly considering it was available in an oral version in Artin Pacha, which Aarne and Thompson include in their bibliography, and because the plot summary provided for AT 560 accurately represents the tale. We have not seen the Littman version cited in Nowak, Type 148, but that found in Basset is more a variant than a parallel. Unlike most of the tales and legends Basset anthologized in the *Revue des traditions populaires* (Paris) over many years (of which this version is number 717, "DCCXVII"), this tale seems to have all the characteristics of an oral narrative: the hero, initially unmarried, weds the king's daughter, who turns into his worst enemy because he defeats her in battle in order to win her hand; she is made out to be a cruel and ruthless woman who will stop at nothing to destroy her husband once she acquires the ring from him. Indeed, the emphasis in this tale is so different from the story of Maᶜrūf that, despite the similarity in basic plot, it is almost a different tale altogether.

Although the Egyptian version has the name of Maᶜrūf's neighbor, ᶜAlī, for its title, it is nevertheless substantially the story of Maᶜrūf—a close parallel to our version and to that found in the *Arabian Nights*. Of course, we know that our raconteur, Šāfiᶜ, can read, even though his ability is not that of an educated person; and because his version is so close to the one found in the *Nights* (a copy of which he owns), we at first suspected that he had adapted the published story for oral narration. But when we discovered the versions in Artin Pacha and Basset, we realized that the tale is still alive in the Arabic tradition. We therefore concluded that he probably knew the oral version first and used the one in the *Arabian Nights* to polish it. As we have noted elsewhere, Šāfiᶜ's narrative style is heavily influenced by the *Arabian Nights* in all his tales.

Even if Šāfiᶜ did take the tale directly from the *Nights,* it is still interesting to observe the differences between the written and the oral versions, particularly when a masterful raconteur performs the tale, as here. In Šāfiᶜ we note a very close identification with the hero:

he obviously admires Maᶜrūf's generosity and goodness of heart. Šāfiᶜ also brings much humor to the narration, as in the episodes in which Maᶜrūf stands before the cadi or is being chased by a crowd of street urchins who call him a crazy man. Also, as we observed in the footnotes following the tale, Šāfiᶜ localizes the action in the region of the Galilee to which he belongs: the shoemaker and the peasant he describes are real characters in his village. Finally, a major difference between the two versions is Šāfiᶜ's treatment of Maᶜrūf's first wife. In the *Nights* she is a nasty, insensitive creature who derives great pleasure from tormenting her husband. She shows up in Cairo at the end of the tale and, after being well received by her husband, attempts to steal the ring and destroy him. Šāfiᶜ, in contrast, is gentle in his treatment of this woman; he even brings a touch of humor to his portrait of her. Herein lies a major distinction between the two versions: the written one tends to freeze an antifeminist posture, perhaps received from tradition, whereas in the living oral tale the image of woman changes from teller to teller and from one occasion to another.

In closing, we must note that the plot outline for this tale as provided in *The Types* is more general, and hence more suitable to our purposes, than that based on Aarne's study of the tale, which Thompson summarizes in *The Folktale* (pp. 70–71). In that version animals play a major role in obtaining the ring in the first place and later in recovering it. From Aarne's study, Thompson concludes that the tale "was made up in Asia, probably in India."

45. IM ᶜALĪ AND ABŪ ᶜALĪ. Im Darwīš (see Tale 21).

Type 1641—Dr. Know-All.

Parallels: Palestine—ᶜAbd al-Hādī 23 "Tales and Complaints"; al-Khalīlī 17 "If Not for Locust, Swallow Would Not Have Been Trapped." Lebanon—al-Bustānī: 206–213 "Lucky Numskull." Iraq—Stevens 13 "Jarāda." Egypt—Dulac 3 "Asfour et Garada" (in *Memoires de la mission archéologique en Egypte 1881–84,* cited in Oestrup: 16). Sudan—Mitchnik 1 "Destiny"; al-Shahi and Moore 57 "Jiraida" (Little Locust). General Arabic—Katibah (1928): 131–144 "Lucky Soothsayer"; Nowak, Type 467 (where, aside from al-Bustānī and Stevens, three Moroccan and one additional version from Egypt and Lebanon, respectively, are cited). Cf. Lorimer 3 "Fortune Teller"; I. Shah: 192–198 "Cobbler Who Became Astrologer" (Persian version); Jacobs (1969) 11 "Harisarman"; and Schwarzbaum: 54 for Jewish references.

Salient Motifs: F941.1 Castle sinks into earth; H911 Tasks assigned at suggestion of jealous rivals; K1955.3 Sham physician predicts the sex of unborn child; K1956.1.1 Sham wise man claims to find stolen goods by incantation [geomancy]; K1956.5 Sham wise man stays alone feigning study; K1961.1.5 Sham holy man; N611.1 Criminal accidentally detected: "that is the first"—sham wise man; N688 What is in the dish: "Poor Crab"; Q111 Riches as reward; Z71.12 Formulistic number: forty.

This version of Type 1641 is the most elaborate of those cited, constituting a sort of compendium of all the episodes found in the others as well as some that are unique to it (giving birth in the upstairs and downstairs quarters, and the incident of the sinking palace—Motif K941). In most of these versions the plot involves two or three basic incidents, such as finding a lost ring and discovering the thieves (usually forty in number) who robbed the king's treasury. The specific details are not always identical; the number of incidents and thieves in each tale, as well as the manner of discovery of the lost articles, may vary, but the "fake" astrologer always achieves fame and success at the end (except in Mitchnik, on which more below).

All the Arabic tales share two other basic features as well. The action is nearly always motivated by an ambitious wife, even though her characterization is not consistent throughout. In the Sudanese version of Mitchnik (and in the Persian one of I. Shah) she is presented as being considerably more shrewish than in our tale, where she comes across as a helpful, if somewhat insistent, mate. Hunger and anxiety about her children drive Im ʿAlī, not greed or envy as in some versions. The other shared feature lies in the importance of names. In every version except Mitchnik's, a major incident involves a pun on the hero's name—with "Swallow" and "Locust" forming the basis for the wordplay in most. The importance of the pun to the story explains why husband and wife in our tale have two names each. The raconteur is careful not to confuse their identity as individuals, whose names are Abū ʿAlī and Im ʿAlī, with the punning and somewhat humorous function their names serve in the tale. We note in passing that "Abū ʿAlī" and "Im ʿAlī" are the names of the characters in an Egyptian tale (Artin Pacha 18 "La bonne Oum-Aly") that resembles ours in intent if not in detail. There, in striving to alleviate her family's hunger, Im ʿAlī, trusting fate, moves into a mansion where she is rewarded with treasure, which, along with the mansion, becomes hers.

The title of the Sudanese version in Mitchnik, "Destiny," teaches us that more is involved in our tale than mere coincidence. In "Destiny," AT 1641 is used as part of a larger frame involving the working of fate. Destiny appears to the hero (Sheikh Ramadan) as a shining woman and grants him the powers of a diviner, which bring him wealth and fame, but she does not grant him the power of knowing when she will desert him. He must accept what is written. The tale ends tragically, as the king plunges his dagger into the heart of Sheikh Ramadan at the moment that Destiny deserts him.

In summarizing the tale (*Folktale:* 144–145), Thompson ascribes to it an Oriental origin; and Jacobs, in his notes to the tale (p. 244), cites Somadeva's *Kathā sarit sāgara* I:272–274 in the Tawney translation (Calcutta, 1880) as the source for his version.

Appendix A: Transliteration of Tale 10

Note: For a description of the system used for rendering the Palestinian dialect, see the Note on Transliteration. In the transcription of the tale, glottalization (initial hamza) has been indicated much more extensively than in the smaller bits of discourse from the dialect occurring elsewhere in the book. Because the tale was actually performed, Šāfiʿ used glottalization for emphasis (*mā ʿindhin ʾišī ġēr hal-ġazli:* "They did not have *anything* except their spinning"). To avoid confusion, a stress mark has been used where necessary to indicate an assimilated third-person singular masculine pronoun in the accusative case following a long vowel in the verb (normally indicated by final aspiration); thus, *rabbūh* ("they brought him up") becomes here *rabbū́*. (Without the accent mark, the verb *rabbū* means simply, "They brought up.")

The tale was narrated in the dialect characteristic of male speech in the upper Galilee. Thus we note that Šāfiʿ articulates the uvular voiceless stop *q*, which women in the region normally glottalize; thus Šāfiʿ says *qāl* ("he said"), whereas a woman would say *ʾāl*. This dialect differs from the Palestinian Arabic spoken in other parts of the country in that the unrounded high front vowel *i* rather than the higher midvowel *e* is used to indicate feminine endings; thus *l-ikbīri* ("the eldest one [sister]") rather than *l-ikbīre*. (Elsewhere in the book we use the midvowel to render similar instances in short bits of discourse from the dialect.) Another feature that distinguishes this dialect is the utilization of the unrounded lower high-back vowel (somewhere between *o* and *u*) to render the third-person-singular pronoun—when not following a long vowel, as in the case indicated above. To avoid proliferation of symbols, we rendered this pronoun simply as *o*, as it is articulated in other parts of the country; thus, *qāllo* ("he said to him"), *ʾibno* ("his son").

blēbl iṣ-ṣayyāḥ

—waḥdū l-lāh
—lā ʾilāha ʾilla l-lāh

kān fī hōn haṯ-ṯaliṯ banāt, ġazzālāt, mā ʿindhin ʾišī ġēr hal-ġazli. kul yōm yiġizlū wyinizlū ʿala s-sūq ybīʿūhā wyištrū ʾakil. yōm nāda l-imnādī ʾinno mamnūʿ iẓ-ẓay bil-imdīni ʿašān il-malik biddo yimtḥin ʾahil l-imdīni, mīn ṭāyʿa wmīn ʿāṣyi. dār bil-lēl il-malik uwazīro tayitfaqqadū mīn ẓāwī wmīn miš ẓāwī. haḏōl šū bidhin isāwū? mā ʿindhinniš ʾišī ġēr hal-ġazli. kul yōm waḥadi minhin tiġzil hal-ġazli tbīʿhā wyištrū fīhā ʾakiḻ, yōklū ṯ-ṯalāṯi maʿ baʿeẓhin. ʾissa šū bidhin yiʿmalū? bidhin yiġizlū wmiš mistarijyāt yiẓwū. qāmat il-bint l-ikbīri qālat, "yā rabbī yā ḥabībī ykūn il-malik māriq wyismaʿnī, wyōxiḏnī lal-farrān ibtāʿo tannī ʾākul wašbaʿ xubiz!" qāmat il-wasṭā qālat, "yā rabbī yā ḥabībī ʾinno ykūn il-malik māriq wyismaʿnī, wyōxiḏnī lal-ʿaššī llī ʿindo tannī ʾākul wašbaʿ ṭabīx!" ʾiz-zġīri qālat, "yā rabbī yā ḥabībī ykūn il-malik māriq wyismaʿnī, wyōxiḏnī laʾibno wajīb waladēn ubint, ʾasammī wāḥad Bahaʾiddīn uwāḥad ʿAladdīn, wil-bint Šamsiẓẓḥā, wil-bint ykūnhā n kānat id-dinyā tšattī wẓiḥkit, itšammis id-dinyā, win kānat imšammsi wbikyit itšattī d-dinyā!"

ʾil-malik marīq, laʾajl iṣ-ṣudaf, ʾijā simiʿhin. qallo, "wazīrī, dabbirnī!" qallo, "bidabbir il-mulk ṣāḥbo, yā malik iz-zamān." xatamū hal-xušši wrawwaḥū. ʾiṣ-ṣubiḥ, waddā ʿaskar. qallhin, "taʿālū ʿind il-malik." ʾijū hal-banāt, rāḥū: "ʾamir, yā sīdī!" qallhin, "taʿālū! ʾintū šū quṣṣitkū?" qalūlo, "yā sīdī, ʾiḥna ṯaliṯ banāt maʿinnāš ḥadā wmaʿnāš walā ʾišī llī nōklo, wint ʾamart mamnūʿ iẓ-ẓay. wšū binna niʿmal? ʾillī smiʿto, ʾaḥkenā." qallhin, "ṭayyib, taʿālū." jawwazhin. ʾil-bint l-ikbīri lal-farrān, wil-wasṭā lal-ʿaššī, wil-bint l-izġīri laʾibno.

xawāthā ṣārū yġārū minhā, kīf hī ʾaxḏat ibn il-malik uhaẓḻāk il-farrān wil-ʿaššī. ṣārū bidhin yintiqmū minhā. ḥiblit ʾawwal dōr. waqt mā qaʿdat bidhā txallif, rāḥū lad-dāyi barṭalūhā wqalūlhā, "xuḏī hāẓā jarw zġīr uḥuṭṭī taḥt uxitnā waʿṭīnā l-walad. ʾiḥnā bnistannāki bāb il-bēt, bitliffī l-walad ubitnāwlīnā yyā wbitḥuṭṭīlhā l-jarw. bas jābat, laffat hal-walad uḥaṭṭat hal-jarw taḥtīhā wqāmat nāwalthin iyyā wrijʿit.

"šū jābat kinnit dār il-malik?"

"yī! šū jābat? jābat jarw!"

rabbū hal-jarw, wiʿtazzū bīh. haẓlāk šū sāwū? rāḥū lal-walad laffū wḥattū bṣandūq uzattū bin-nahir. fī ʿalā šatt han-nahir bustān, wfī xtyār wixtyāra bhal-bustān. ṭilʿū hal-ixtyariyyi ṣ-ṣubiḥ lāqū haṣ-ṣandūq bil-may. ʾaxaḏū haṣ-ṣandūq fataḥū lāqū fī haṭ-ṭifil. malhinniš wlād. qallhā, "tānrabbī yā xtyāra balkī nifiʿnā laquddām." rabbū.

rjiʿnā lakinnit dār il-malik. ḥiblit uxrā dōr, bidhā txallif. yam bas qaᶜdat bidhā txallif rāḥū xawāthā lad-dāyi qalūlhā, "xuḏī hal-biss wlīd. xuḏí, ḥuṭṭí taḥtīha, wqaddēš biddik maṣārī bnaᶜṭīkī, wnāwlīnā l-walad." barẓo nafs il-ʾišī, bas xallafat, laffat hal-walad bhaš-šrīṭa ṭilᶜit nāwalathin iyyá ᶜal-bāb, uḥaṭṭatilhā hal-bis taḥtīhā.

"šū jābat kinnit dār il-malik?" qālū, "šū jābat? jābat bis!" haẓlāk ᶜimlū nafs il-ʾišī, ḥaṭṭú bṣandūq urāḥū ramú bin-nahir. barẓo ṭilᶜū l-ixtyariyyi llī bhal-bustān lāqū haṣ-ṣandūq. ʾaxaḏú wfataḥú, lāqū hal-walad. rabbú. ṣārū ṯnēn.

nirjaᶜ lal-ʾim. ḥiblit ubidhā tjīb uxrā marra. ʾajū xawāthā qālū lad-dāyi, "xuḏī maṣārī, wxuḏī hāẓ ḥajar huṭṭīlhā l-ḥajar willī bitxalfo nāwlīnā yyá." jābat haḏīk. ʾijit ʾaxḏat hal-bint illī xallafathā, laffathā bhaš-šrīṭa wnāwalathin iyyāhā wḥaṭṭat hal-ḥajar. ʾaxaḏūhā, rāḥū ḥaṭṭūhā bhaṣ-ṣandūq uramūhā bin-nahir.

"šū jābat kinnit dār il-malik?" qālū, "šū jābat? jābat ḥajar!" haẓāk ibn il-malik qāl, "šū! dōr jābat kalb, dōr bis, dōr ḥajar!" hajarhā. ʾil-bint barẓo laqūhā l-ixtyariyyi, waxaḏūhin rabbūhin. ṣārū šabāb, wṣārū kbār, wil-bint ṣārat ṣabiyyi. wil-bint ʾijit ᶜala manwit immhā. ʾin aštat id-dinyā wẓiḥkit itšammis id-dinyā. win šammasat ubikyit, itšattī d-dinyā. yōm hal-ixtyār māt waᶜṭāhin ṭarwto kullayāthā—hal-xušši, hal-bustān; šū ᶜindo hal-ixtyār, aᶜṭá lahal-wlād. hal-wlād qālū labaᶜeẓhin, "šū! ʾiḥna binnā nẓal qāᶜdīn hōn ibhal-bustān laḥālnā! tanrūḥ inᶜammirilnā sahli wnuqᶜud fīhā!" wēn rāḥū? rāḥū ᶜala mdīnt abūhin. ʾijū ᶜala hal-imdīni qbāl qaṣr abūhin šārū šaqfit ʾarẓ uᶜammarū qaṣir miṯil qaṣr abūhin, uḥaṭṭū ḥālhin ibhal-qaṣir uqaᶜadū. fišš ilhin ḥadā, ġēr hiyyāhin laḥālhin. whinni yrūḥū wyījū bil-balad ᶜirfūhin xalāthin. fihmū ᶜanhin xalāthin inno haḏōla l-wlād illī ramūhin. kīf bidhin yiᶜmalū? bidhin ywaddrūhin. dabbarū xtyāra ḥaṭṭat ibṣiniyyi hēk wšwayyit taqatīq urāḥat ᶜal-qaṣir uṣārat itnādī. hāy l-ixtyāra xallat ixwithā taṭilᶜū ᶜaṣ-ṣēd urāḥat taḥt hal-qaṣir uṣārat itnādī. haḏīk qāᶜdi ᶜaš-šubbāk. ʾixwithā miš hanāk, uhī bidhā tištrī min hal-ʾišī llī maᶜ l-ixtyāra. ṣārat tibkī. nizlit idmūᶜhā ᶜala ḥinnayāt l-ixtyāra jabbalathin. ʾiltaftat ᶜalēhā, qālatilhā, "yī! šū biddī ʾadᶜī ᶜalēki? lēš hēk yā ḥabībtī?" qālatilhā, "yā sittī, ʾixwtī miš hōn, wanā baᶜrif? bkīt." qālatilhā, "ṭayyib."

ʾijat, nādat ᶜalēhā. dārat laᶜindhā l-ixtyāra, qālatilhā, "yā habībtī, xuḏī haḏōl il-ḥinnayāt, ušū biddik iyyá baᶜṭīki yyá, wṣārat tiṭṭallaᶜ hēk bijnāb hal-qaṣir itfaqqid: "yī! walla yā ḥabībtī qaṣrik imlīḥ, wmā nāqṣo ʾišī ʾillā mā hū nāqṣo ġēr blēbl iṣ-ṣayyāḥ." qālatilhā, "yā sittī, mnēn blēbl iṣ-ṣayyāḥ? hāẓā mīn biddo yjībo?" qālatilhā, "bijībú ixwtik. mahinn iṣ-ṣalā ᶜan-nabī ᶜanhin! ᶜindik šabāb iṯnēn ubitqūlī mīn biddo yjīblī yyá?"

qaᶜdat hal-bint uṣārat tibkī. ġayyamat id-dinyā, arᶜadat, ṣārat haddinyā tšattī. qālū, "ʾabṣar šū ʾijā ᶜalā ʾuxtnā, šū mālhā!" rawwaḥū yurukẓū. qālūlhā, "mālik xaytā?" qālatilhin, "malīš. ʾijat ᶜindī waḥadi wqālatlī qaṣrik nāqṣo blēbl iṣ-ṣayyāḥ. biddī blēbl iṣ-ṣayyāḥ."

"yā xaytā mnēn binnā njīblik blēbl iṣ-ṣayyāḥ?" qālatilhin, "baᶜrifiš. biddī yyá ʾaḥuṭṭo bqaṣirnā." ʾijā ʾaxūhā l-ikbīr qallhā, "ṭayyib. ʾiᶜmalīlī zād uzuwwād. ʾanā biddī ʾarūḥ." bʾīdo xātim. qāl laxú llī ʾazġar minno, "ḥuṭṭ il-xātim ibʾīdak. ʾin iẓyaqq il-xātim ᶜalā ṣbaᶜak ibtilḥaqnī ṯaliṯt iyyām uṯilṯ in-nhār. ʾin mā ẓyaqqiš il-xātim ᶜalā ṣbaᶜak ibtilḥaqnīš, bakūn anā bxēr." ᶜimlitlo haz-zuwwādi wᶜaddadatlo ᶜalā hal-iḥṣān urikib umišī. mišī.

uhū māšī bhaṭ-ṭarīq, bhal-xalā, ʾijā ᶜalā hal-ġūl: "is-salām ᶜalēkum, yā ʾabūnā!" qāllo, "ᶜalēk is-salām. lōlā salāmak sabaq kalāmak, lafaṣfiṣ laḥmak qabl iᶜẓāmak! šū? wēn rāyiḥ yā sīdī?" qāllo, "rāyḥ ajīb blēbl iṣṣayyāh." qāllo, "ʾā. infid laquddām. ʾilī ʾaxū, ʾakbar minnī bšahir wawᶜa minnī bdahir. hū bidillak." nafad. mišī, ʾijā ᶜalā ṯ-ṯānī: "ʾis-salām ᶜalēk, yā ʾabūnā!" qāllo, "ᶜalēk is-salām! lōlā salāmak sabaq kalāmak, lafaṣfiṣ laḥmak qabl iᶜẓāmak! wēn rāyiḥ yā ᶜAladdīn?" qāllo, "walla rāyḥ ajīb blēbl iṣ-ṣayyāḥ." qāllo, "rūḥ yābā laquddām nitfi bitlāqī ʾuxtī. ʾin laqēthā bṭiṭḥan miliḥ wiᶜyūnhā ḥumur, bitqaddim ᶜalēhā btōkil min milḥāthā wibtirẓaᶜ min ibzāzhā. win laqēthā bṭiṭḥan sukkar itqaddimiš ᶜalēhā." qāllo, "ṭayyib." mišī. ʾijā ᶜalā hal-ġūli bṭiṭḥan miliḥ nāfši rāshā wimdallyi bzāzhā min hōn umin hōn quddāmhā, wibṭiṭḥan miliḥ. ʾijā riẓiᶜ min bizzhā l-yamīn. qālatlo, "mīn illī riẓiᶜ min bizzī l-yamīn? ṣār aᶜazz min ibnī Smāᶜīn." dār uriẓiᶜ min bizzhā š-šmāl. qālatlo, "mīn illī riẓiᶜ min bizzī š-smāl? ṣār aᶜazz min ibnī ᶜAbdirraḥmān." dār laquddāmhā wʾakal min illī ᶜammāl ibṭiṭḥano. qālatlo, "ᶜalēk alla wamān alla, wilxāyin ixūno ʾalla. šū biddak?" qāllhā, "biddī blēbl iṣ-ṣayyāḥ." qālatlo, "ʾā. hāẓā blēbl iṣ-ṣayyāḥ ṭēr fī l-bustān il-fulānī. stanna tayījū wlādī. btiġdariš inte tiṣalo."

ʾaxḏato, nafxat ᶜalḗ, ᶜimlato ʾibri wḥaṭṭato brāshā bᶜuṣbithā wqaᶜdat taʾijū wlādhā. qāmat har-rīḥ uhaz-zawābiᶜ, willā hinni wlādhā jāyīn. ʾarbᶜīn wāḥad. fīhin wāḥad izwak. ʾijū. min sēᶜit mā ʾōjahū miñ ġād: "rīḥtik ins, yammā!" qālatilhin, "lā rīḥtī ins walā ᶜindī ʾišī. ʾuquᶜdū wusuktū." ẓallū yuburmū wyqūlū "rīḥtik ins." qālatilhin, "ʾismaᶜū taqulkū! hāẓā riẓiᶜ min ibzāzī, ṣār ibnī miṯl iḥkāyitku. ʾirmū l-ʾamān kullayātku, babayyinilku yyá." qalūlhā, "ᶜalḗ ʾalla wamān alla, wil-xāyin ixūno ʾalla!" ʾaṭlaᶜatilhin iyyá. šāfú. sallamū ᶜalḗ. qaᶜadū hinni wiyyá. qālatilhin, "btiᶜirfū hāẓā šū biddo?" qālūlhā, "laʾ." qālatilhin, "hāẓā ʾaxūku, whāẓā biddo blēbl iṣ-ṣayyāḥ. mīn minku llī biddo yōxḏo." hāẓā qāl ibᶜašart iyyām, haẓāk ibyōmēn, ibyōm, ibsēᶜa. naṭṭ l-eᶜraj, qāllhā, "ʾanā bawaṣṣlo. bas turmuš ᶜēnik witfattiḥ." qālatlo, "yalla! bas dīr bālak yā ᶜAladdīn! hāẓā blēbl iṣ-ṣayyāḥ fī qafaṣ imᶜallaq bis-sajara bījī bibāt fí. biqaf ᶜalas-sajara biqūl, 'anā blēbl iṣ-ṣayyāḥ! mīn yqūl ʾanā? ʾanā blēbl iṣ-ṣayyāḥ! mīn yqūl ʾanā?' ᶜalā ṯaliṯ marrāt. ʾiḏā raddēt ᶜalḗ, bitrūḥ. wiḏā mā raddētiš ibtinjaḥ. btimisko wbitjību." qāllhā, "ṭayyib."

ḥamalo l-eᶜraj waxaḏo. ṭār fí laᶜind hal-bustān illī bījī ᶜalḗ blēbl iṣ-ṣayyāḥ. ḥaṭṭo, whū fāt ᶜal-bustān, uhaẓāk rijiᶜ. ʾijā blēbl iṣ-ṣayyāḥ, wiqif ᶜahas-sajara ṣār yqūl, "ʾanā blēbl iṣ-ṣayyāḥ! mīn yqūl ʾanā?" ʾawwal marra sakat. ṯanī marra qāllo, "ʾanā!" qāllo, "ʾinte!" nafax ᶜalḗ, qalabo ḥajar udaḥalo bqāᶜ hal-bustān.

ʾiẓyaqq il-xātim ᶜala ʾīd axú. rikib uliḥqo. barẓo miṯil mā ᶜimil ʾaxú, ᶜiml iṯ-ṯānī. ʾijā ᶜalā l-ġūli wrāḥ ᶜalā l-bustān. uhāẓā l-walad qabil ma yījī, ʾaᶜṭā l-xātim laʾuxto. rāḥ ᶜalā l-bustān. barẓo ʾijā ṭ-ṭēr: "ʾanā blēbl iṣ-ṣayyāḥ! mīn yqūl ʾanā?" ʾawwal marra wiṯ-ṯānī, maraddiš. iṯ-ṯāliṯ qāllo, "ʾanā!" qāllo, "ʾinte!" nafax ᶜalḗ wramá, miṯl axú. šū ẓal? ẓallat il-bint. il-bint iẓyaqq il-xātim ᶜalā ṣbaᶜhā. kīf bidhā tiᶜmal? qālat, "rāḥū ʾixwtī." liḥqithin. ᶜaddadat ᶜalā hal-iḥṣān, witxaffat uliḥqithin.

nafs il-ʾišī, rāḥat ᶜalā l-ġūli. qālatilhā l-ġūli, "hā! bitrūḥī ʾinti wixwtik ubiᶜūdilkūš iḏ-ḏikrā. ʾūᶜī truddī ᶜalḗ!" qālatilhā, "laʾ!" ʾaxadūhā ᶜahal-bustān ṭilᶜit ᶜahas-sajara l-bint ulabdat. ʾijā haṭ-ṭēr: "ʾanā blēbl iṣ-ṣayyāḥ! mīn yqūl ʾanā?" "ʾanā blēbl iṣ-ṣayyāḥ . . ." ẓallo yqūl tanno nṣaṭaḥ, uhaḏīk lābdi ᶜahas-sajara, maqiblitiš tiḥkī. fāt ᶜalā l-qafaṣ. yam haḏīk wara hal-qafaṣ lābdi ᶜalā has-sajara saddat hal-qafaṣ ᶜalḗ wsakkarato wḥamlato bʾīdhā. nizlit ᶜan has-sajara. qāllhā, "daxlik! xallīnī ʾaṭlaᶜ! barquslik, baġannīlik, šū llī biddik iyyá basāwīlik." qālatlo, "min qillt is-salāmi! ʾiṭliᶜlī ʾixwtī!" qāllhā, "qīmī min kōm hal-ixlund haẓāk min hat-trābāt haẓlāk uruššī ᶜal-iḥjārāt, biqūmū ʾixwtik." qāmat itrāb uraššat ᶜal-iḥjārāt qāmū xwithā. ṣārat itqīm witrušš ᶜalā hal-iḥjār kullayāthā qāmat hal-xalīqa kullayāthā wkul wāḥad rawwaḥ ᶜalā ʾahlo. whī ʾaxdat hal-qafaṣ wijat hī wixwithā ᶜalā hal-ġūli. waddaᶜū l-ġūli waxadū blēbl iṣ-ṣayyāḥ urawwaḥū.

wiṣlū dārhin, ᶜallaqū hal-qafaṣ ibhad-dār uṣarū yrūḥū ᶜaṣṣēd uyījū yuquᶜdū bhal-qahāwī. ʾin-natīji, tsāmaᶜt fīhin l-imdīni: "mnēn hal-wlād? mnēn? mnēn?" yōm iltaqū hinni wabūhin bil-qahwi bidūn mā yiᶜirfū baᶜeẓ. šū ḥabbhin uṣār yiᶜzimhin laᶜindo wyuqᶜud hū wiyyāhin! qālū la-būhin, qālūlo, "biddak titġaddā ᶜinnā. inte ṣurt ᶜāzimnā marrtēn ṯalāṯi, w'issa biddak tījī titġaddā ʿinnā, yā malik iz-zamān." qāllhin, "'ā. lēš la'." ʿimlū hal-ġadā. qāllhin blēbl iṣ-ṣayyāh, "ḥuttū maʿ il-ġadā jazar maʿ il-fawākih." ḥattū hal-ġadā, tġaddū wmā šalla ʿanhin! ukayyafū wʿuqub mā tġaddū jābū hal-fawākih ḥaṭṭūhā wḥaṭṭū ṣaḥin hal-jazar. qalūlo, "taʿāl kol yā blēbl iṣ-ṣayyāḥ!" qāllhin, "lā walla! blēbl iṣ-ṣayyāḥ mā bōkil jazar, yā 'ahil l-imdīni yā ḥamīr yā baqar! ʿumurku smiʿtū kinnit dār il-malik bitjīb kalb uqitt uḥajar!" ṣafan il-malik. qāllo, "ʿīdhā yā blēbl iṣ-ṣayyāḥ!" qāllhin, "'anā blēbl iṣ-ṣayyāḥ, mā bākul jazar. yā 'ahil l-imdīni, yā ḥamīr yā baqar! ʿumurku smiʿtu kinnit dār il-malik bitjīb kalb uqitt uḥajar!" qāllo, "šū btiḥkī yā blēbl iṣ-ṣayyāh?" qāllo, "hāẓā llī baḥkī. kinnit dār il-malik mā bitjīb kalb uqitt uḥajar. wlādak Bahā'iddīn uʿAlladdīn uŠamsiẓẓḥā hiyyāhin hadōl illī ʿindak!" rāḥ il-malik jāb id-dāyi qāllhā, "yā btiḥkīlī šū l-qiṣṣa, yā baqtaʿ rāsik!" qālatlo, "daxlak yā malik iz-zamān! 'anā mā xaṣṣnīš. kānū ybariṭlūnī xawāthā wyaʿṭūnī hadōla 'aḥuṭṭhin taḥtīha wanāwilhin l-wlād. hadōla wlādak!"

jāb id-dāyi wxawāthā iṯ-ṯintēn, ḏabaḥhin uqāl, "yā mīn iḥibb is-sulṭān yjīb ḥaṭab uqaḥfit nār!" ḥaṭṭhin ibhan-nār, ḥaraqhin udarrāhin.

uhāy iḥkāytī ḥakēthā, wʿalēku ramēthā.

Appendix B: Index of Folk Motifs

The motifs for each tale are listed in alphabetical order under the heading "Salient Motifs" in the Folkloristic Analysis. Additions or deletions adapting the wording of Thompson's *Motif-Index* to the context are indicated in square brackets.

Motif Number		Tale Number
	B. Animals	
B11.2.3.1	Seven-headed dragon	17
B11.7.1	Dragon controls water supply	17
B11.10	Sacrifice of human being to dragon	17
B11.11	Fight with dragon	17
B25	Man [woman]-dog	25
B80.2	Monster half-man [-woman], half-fish	25
B131.2	Bird reveals treachery	10
B171.1.1	Demi-coq crows in king's body when the king eats him	11
B172	Magic bird	11
B172.1	Magic bird petrifies those who approach	10
B211.1.3	Speaking horse	5
B211.1.5	Speaking cow [bull]	23
B211.1.6	Speaking camel	23
B211.2.8	Speaking mouse	23
B211.4	Speaking insects	23
B281.2.2	Wedding of mouse and cockroach [cricket]	23
B314	Helpful [animal] brothers-in-law	17

Motif Number		Tale Number
B335.2	Life of helpful animal demanded as cure for feigned sickness	7
B381	Thorn removed from lion's paw [helping lioness with birth]. In gratitude the lion later rewards the man	8
B401	Helpful horse	5
B413	Helpful goat	6
B450	Helpful birds	17
B470	Helpful fish	5
B491.1	Helpful serpent	31
B511.1.2	Snake heals mutilated maiden [with magic herbs]	31
B524.1.2	Dogs [lion cubs] rescue fleeing master from tree refuge	8
B535.0.1	Cow as nurse cares for children	7
B535.0.7	Bird as nurse for child	2
B548.2.1	Fish recovers ring from sea	5
B571	Animals perform tasks for man	5
B600	Marriage of person to animal	4
B614	Bird paramour	12
B620	Animal suitor	23
B642	Marriage to person in bird form	12
B873.2	Giant scorpion	17

C. Tabu

C611	Forbidden chamber	17
C742	Tabu: striking monster twice	3, 33
C758.1	Monster born because of hasty wish of parents	40

D. Magic

D114	Transformation: man to ungulate	7
D150	Transformation: man to bird	18
D231	Transformation: man to stone	10
D253	Transformation: man to needle	18, 22
D437.4	Transformation: excrements to person	40
D454.2	Transformation: bread to another object	28
D457.13	Transformation: animal dung to another object	28
D472.1	Transformation of food to muck	28

Motif Number		Tale Number
D1513	Charm removes thorn	31
D1581	Tasks performed by use of magic object	17
D1601.5	Automatic cudgel	36
D1601.9	Household articles act at command	20
D1601.12	Self-cutting shears	2
D1605.1	Magic thieving pot	1
D1610.6.4	Speaking excrements	40
D1611	Magic object answers for fugitive	18
D1652.1.1	Inexhaustible bread	37
D1662.1	Magic ring works by being stroked	44
D1831	Magic strength resides in hair	22
D2036	Magic homesickness	13
D2072.0.2	Animal rendered immovable	12, 35
D2072.0.2.1	Horse enchanted so that he stands still	6
D2072.0.3	Ship [and camel caravan] held back by magic	12, 24
D2072.2	Magic paralysis by curse	12, 35
D2121.5	Magic journey: man carried by spirit or devil	44
D2136.2	Castle magically transported	30
D2165.1	Escape by flying through the air	6
D2176.3	Evil spirit exorcised	32, 35

E. The Dead

E1	Person comes to life	10
E80	Water of life. Resuscitation by water	5, 22
E113	Resuscitation by blood	12
E168	Cooked animal comes to life	11
E607.1	Bones of dead collected and buried. Return in another form directly from the grave	9
E613.0.1	Reincarnation of murdered child as bird	9
E712.4	Soul hidden in box	17
E712.7	Soul hidden in [water] bottle	30
E715	Separable soul kept in animal	17
E715.1	Separable soul kept in bird	17

Motif Number		Tale Number
E761.4.4	Life token: ring rusts [becomes tight]	10
E782.1	Hands restored	31

F. Marvels

F92.2	Person swallowed up by earth and taken to lower world	43
F101	Return from lower world	43
F165.6.1	Other world (fairyland) as place of sorrowful captivity	32
F234.1.15	Fairy in form of bird	11
F234.2.5	Fairy in the form of a beautiful young woman	30, 37
F236.3	Fairies with belts and hats	37
F302.3.1.3	Man is carried to fairyland by fairy and marries her	32
F303	Wedding of mortal and fairy	37
F324.3	Youth abducted by fairy	32
F343.7	Fairy-wife furnishes provisions	37
F343.13	Fairy gives mortals a child	37
F346.0.1	Fairy serves mortal	37
F375	Mortals as captives in fairyland	32
F382	Exorcising fairies	32
F402.6.3	Demons live in well	20, 36
F562	People of unusual residence	15
F571.2	Sending to the older	6, 10, 22
F591	Person who never laughs	24
F721.1	Underground passages	15, 21
F721.4	Underground treasure chambers	44
F821.1.4	Wooden coat	34
F848.1	Girl's long hair as ladder into tower	18
F885	Extraordinary field	37
F913	Victims rescued from swallower's belly	38, 40
F941.1	Castle sinks into earth	45

G. Ogres

G11.9	Ogre schoolmaster. Girl sees schoolmaster eat human flesh. Refuses to tell him what she saw. He persecutes her	35

Motif Number		Tale Number
G11.15	Cannibal demon	29
G33	Child born as cannibal	40
G61	Relative's flesh eaten unwittingly	9, 34
G61.2	Mother recognizes child's flesh when it is served to be eaten	34
G72.2	Starving woman abandoned in cave eats newborn child	30
G81	Unwitting marriage to cannibal	34
G84	Fee-fi-fo-fum	3, 16, 18, 20
G123	Giant ogress with breasts thrown over her shoulders	6, 10, 22
G211.5	Witch in form of an insect	30
G247	Witch[es] dance[s]	29
G250	Recognition of witches	33
G263.1.5	Witch transforms man into bird	18
G273.1	Witch powerless when one makes the sign of the cross	32
G275.2	Witch overcome by helpful dogs [lion cubs] of hero	8
G275.3	Witch burned	18
G302.3.3	Demon in form of old woman	19, 33
G303.4.5	The devil's feet and legs	19
G312	Cannibal ogre	19, 33
G312.7	Ogress devours horses	8
G334	Ogre keeps human prisoners	16
G346	Devastating monster. Lays waste to the land	8
G376	Ogre in shape of small boy	40
G420	Capture by ogre	19
G442.1	Ogre abducts newborn babe, keeping it captive for seven years	35
G500	Ogre defeated	16, 34
G510.4	Hero overcomes devastating animal	17
G512	Ogre killed	19, 29
G512.3	Ogre burned to death	33
G512.5	Ogre killed by burning [crushing] external soul	17
G514.1	Ogre trapped in box (cage)	6
G530.1	Help from ogre's wife (mistress)	3, 16
G530.2	Help from ogre's daughter (or son)	34

Motif Number		Tale Number
H1151.24	Task: stealing ogress's drum [straw tray]	12
H1161.6	Task: killing devastating tiger	17
H1212	Quest assigned because of feigned illness	22, 30
H1213	Quest for remarkable bird caused by the sight of one of its feathers	5
H1233.2.1	Quest accomplished with aid of wife	37
H1273.2	Quest for three hairs from the devil's beard	16
H1312.1	Quest for three persons as stupid as his wife	26
H1321.1	Quest for water of life	5, 22
H1331.1.1	Quest for bird of truth	10
H1381.3.1.1	Quest for bride for king (prince)	21
H1385.5	Quest for vanished lover	12
H1471	Watch for devastating monster. Youngest brother alone successful	3, 8
H1556.4	Fidelity in love tested	15

J. The Wise and the Foolish

J144	Well-trained kid does not open door to wolf [hyena]	38
J652	Inattention to warnings	29
J1251.1	Humiliated lover in repartee with disdainful mistress	15
J1791.6.1	Ugly woman sees beautiful woman reflected in water and thinks it herself	18
J1794	Statue mistaken for living original	15
J1873	Animals or objects kept warm	27
J1919.5	Genitals cut off through ignorance	27
J1920	Absurd searches for the lost	23, 37
J2093	Valuables given away or sold for a trifle	26
J2326	The student from Paradise	26
J2326.1	Foolish woman gives swindler money for her parents in heaven	26
J2355.1	Fool loses magic objects by talking about them	36

K. Deceptions

Motif Number		Tale Number
K1816.0.2	Girl in menial disguise at lover's court	14
K1817.4	Disguise as merchant	44
K1818.2	Scald-head disguise	22
K1821.2	Disguise by painting body	13
K1821.9	Escape by wooden covering	34
K1825.1.4	Girl masks as doctor to find departed lover	12
K1836	Disguise of man in woman's dress	14, 15
K1837	Disguise of woman in man's clothes	15
K1839.1	Wolf puts flour on his paws to disguise himself [nonvocal deception: cutting off the tail]	38
K1847	Deception by substitution of children	32
K1847.1.1	Deceptive report of birth of heir	24
K1911.1.3	False bride takes true bride's place at fountain	18
K1911.3	Reinstatement of true bride	18
K1911.3.2	True bride takes house near husband. This eventually secures his attention	2
K1923.3	Barren woman pretends to bear child. Substitutes another woman's child	24
K1955.3	Sham physician predicts the sex of unborn child	45
K1956.1.1	Sham wise man claims to find stolen goods by incantation [geomancy]	45
K1956.5	Sham wise man stays alone feigning study	45
K1961.1.5	Sham holy man	45
K1984.5	Blind fiancée betrays self. Mistakes one object for another	4
K2110	Slanders	21, 31
K2110.1	Calumniated wife	10
K2112	Woman slandered as adulteress (prostitute)	24, 25
K2115	Animal-birth slander	10
K2115.2.1	Stone substituted for newborn babies	10

L. Reversal of Fortune

M. Ordaining the Future

Motif Number		Tale Number
M411.5	Old woman's curse (satire)	24
M431.2	Curse: toads [scorpions] from mouth	43

N. Chance and Fate

N1.1	Hero makes fortune through gambling	8
N2	Extraordinary stakes at gambling	8
N2.4	Helpful animals lost in wager	8
N201	Wish for exalted husband realized	10
N271	Murder will out	9
N365.1	Boy unwittingly commits incest with his mother	2
N452	Secret remedy overheard in conversation with animals (witches)	12
N455.4	King overhears girl's boast as to what she would do as queen. Marries her	10
N534.1	Stumble reveals depository of treasure	44
N611.1	Criminal accidentally detected: "that is the first"—sham wise man	45
N630	Accidental acquisition of treasure or money	44
N681	Husband (lover) arrives home just as wife (mistress) is to marry	3
N688	What is in the dish: "Poor Crab"	45
N711.1	Prince (king) finds maiden in woods (tree) and marries her	13, 35
N711.2	Hero finds maiden in (magic) castle	18
N711.3	Hero finds maiden in (magic) garden	21
N711.6	Prince sees maiden at ball and is enamored	14
N774.2	Adventures from seeking (lost) domestic beast [hen]	20
N810	Supernatural helpers	19
N810.2	Helper's beard and eyebrows cut. Only after hero has performed this service is help forthcoming	22

Motif Number		Tale Number
R47	Captivity in lower world	32
R111.1	Princess (maiden) rescued from captor	34
R111.1.3	Rescue of princess (maiden) from dragon	17
R111.2.1	Princess(es) rescued from lower world	3
R111.2.5	Girl rescued from tree	13, 35
R141	Rescue from well	23, 42
R151	Husband rescues wife	19, 23
R152	Wife rescues husband	32
R153.2	Father rescues children	32
R156	Brother rescues sister(s)	7
R158	Sister rescues brother(s)	10
R161.0.1	Hero rescued by his lady	44
R164	Rescue by giant	44
R169.5	Hero rescued by friend [neighbor]	34, 44
R213	Escape from home	14, 42
R215	Escape from execution	42
R221	Heroine's threefold flight from ball	14
R251	Flight on a tree, which ogre tries to cut down	8

S. Unnatural Cruelty

S12	Cruel mother	22
S12.1	Treacherous mother marries ogre and plots against son	22
S21	Cruel son	4
S22	Parricide	2
S31	Cruel stepmother	7, 9
S31.5	Girl persuades her father to marry a widow [neighbor] who has treated her kindly	9
S51	Cruel mother-in-law	2, 7
S143.2	Abandonment in tall tree	13
S162	Mutilation: cutting off legs (feet)	22
S165	Mutilation: putting out eyes	30
S181	Wounding by trapping with sharp knives (glass)	12
S182	Girl fastened by hair to rafter	25
S262	Periodic sacrifices to a monster	17
S263.3	Person sacrificed to water spirit to secure water supply	17

Motif Number		Tale Number
T556	Woman gives birth to a demon	40
T579.8	Signs of pregnancy	2, 28
T581.2	Child born of woman abandoned in pit	30
T585.2	Child speaks at birth	37
T615	Supernatural growth	30
T670	Adoption of children	10, 32
T671	Adoption by suckling. Ogress who suckles hero claims him as her son	6

W. Traits of Character

W181	Jealousy	2, 12, 20, 21, 24, 25, 31, 37
W195	Envy	5, 7, 10, 20, 28, 36, 43, 44

X. Humor

X52	Ridiculous nakedness or exposure	15
X120	Humor of bad eyesight	4
X142	The humor of small stature	23

Z. Miscellaneous

Z32.3	Little ant finds a penny, buys new clothes with it, and sits in her doorway	23
Z33.4	The fat troll (wolf)	40
Z41.4	The mouse [cat] regains its tail	39
Z65.1	Red as blood, white as snow	21
Z71.5.1	Seven brothers and one sister	42
Z71.12	Formulistic number: forty	15, 45
Z142	Symbolic color: white	13, 24
Z143	Symbolic color: black	13, 24
Z143.1	Black as a symbol of grief	13
Z215	Hero "son of seven mothers"	30

Appendix C: List of Tales by Type

Name	Type Number
1. Ṭunjur, Ṭunjur	591
2. The Woman Who Married Her Son	705
3. Precious One and Worn-out One	301
4. Šwēš, Šwēš!	1477*
5. The Golden Pail	531
6. Half-a-Halfling	327B
7. The Orphans' Cow	450
8. Sumac! You Son of a Whore, Sumac!	315A
9. The Green Bird	720
10. Little Nightingale the Crier	707
11. The Little Bird	235C*, 715
12. Jummēz Bin Yāzūr, Chief of the Birds	432
13. Jbēne	Motif N711.1
14. Sackcloth	510B
15. Šāhīn	879
16. The Brave Lad	461
17. Gazelle	552, 300, 302
18. Lōlabe	408, 310, 313
19. The Old Woman Ghouleh	Motif D821
20. Lady Tatar	898
21. Šōqak Bōqak!	Motif T311.1
22. Clever Ḥasan	314, 590
23. The Cricket	2023
24. The Seven Leavenings	Motif N825.3
25. The Golden Rod in the Valley of Vermilion	1359, 1511
26. Minjal	1384, 1540
27. Im ʿĒše	1681B
28. Chick Eggs	480
29. The Ghouleh of Trans-Jordan	334, 956D
30. Bear-Cub of the Kitchen	462
31. The Woman Whose Hands Were Cut Off	706

Name	Type Number
32. Nʿayyis (Little Sleepy One)	425B
33. Im ʿAwwād and the Ghouleh	Motif G302.3.3
34. The Merchant's Daughter	327C, 328, 1122
35. Pomegranate Seeds	894
36. The Woodcutter	563
37. The Fisherman	465, 1930
38. The Little She-Goat	123, 2032
39. The Old Woman and Her Cat	2034
40. Dunglet	2028
41. The Louse	2021*
42. The Woman Who Fell into the Well	883C
43. The Rich Man and the Poor Man	480
44. Maʿrūf the Shoemaker	560
45. Im ʿAlī and Abū ʿAlī	1641

Selected Bibliography

The majority of works listed in the Bibliography are cited in this book. Works included but not cited are restricted mostly to collections of Arabic folktales that were surveyed for parallels. The transliteration of all bibliographic references is according to the Library of Congress system of romanization, following the standard practice in this field.

Aarne, Antti, and Stith Thompson. *The Types of the Folktale: A Classification and Bibliography*. Helsinki: Suomalainen Tiedeakatemia, 1974.

ʿAbd al-Hādī, Tawaddud. *Kharārīf shaʿbīyah* (Folktales). Beirut: Dār Ibn Rushd, 1980.

Abū-Shanab, ʿĀdil. *Kān yā mā kān* (Once Upon a Time). Damascus: Ittiḥād al-Kuttāb al-ʿArab, 1972.

Alarcón y Santón, Maximiliano. *Textos arabes en dialecto vulgar de Larache*. Madrid, 1913. Published by the author.

Amīn, Aḥmad. *Qāmūs al-ʿādāt wa-al-taqālīd wa-al-taʿābīr al-Miṣrīyah* (Dictionary of Egyptian Customs, Traditions, and Expressions). Cairo: Maktab al-Nahḍah al-Miṣrīyah, 1953.

Antoun, Richard T. *Arab Village: A Social Structural Study of a Trans-Jordanian Peasant Community*. Bloomington: Indiana University Press, 1972.

ʿArnīṭah, Yusrah. *Al-funūn al-shaʿbīyah fī Filasṭīn* (Folk Arts in Palestine). Beirut: Palestine Research Center, 1968.

Artin Pacha, Yacoub. *Contes populaires inédits de la vallée du Nil*. Paris: Maisonneuve & LaRose, 1893.

al-Barghūthī, ʿAbd al-Laṭīf. *Ḥikāyāt jān min Banī Zayd* (Jinn Tales from Banī Zayd). Birzeit (West Bank): Birzeit University Press, 1979.

Basset, René. "Contes et légendes arabes, no. DCCXVII: 'Le roi et le bague magique.'" *Revue des traditions populaires* XXI (1906): 273–291.

———. *Contes populaires d'Afrique*. Paris: Librairie Orientale et Américaine, 1903.

———. *Mille et un contes, recits et légendes arabes*. 3 vols. Paris: Maisonneuve frères, 1924–1926.

Bauer, Leonhard. *Das palästinische Arabisch: Die Dialekte des Städters und des Fellachen*. Leipzig: J. C. Hinrichs, 1926.

Ben Ḥammādī, Ṣāliḥ. *Dirāsāt fī al-asāṭīr wa al-muʿtaqadāt al-ghaybīyah* (Studies in Myths and Superstitions). Tunis: Dār Bū Slāmah, 1983.

Bergsträsser, Gotthelf. *Neuaramäische Märchen und andere Texte aus Maʿlūla*. Leipzig: F. A. Brockhaus, 1915.

The Book of the Thousand Nights and a Night, with *Supplemental Nights*. Translated by Richard F. Burton. 16 vols. Denver: Carson-Harper, 1900.

The Book of the Thousand Nights and One Night. Rendered into English from the French Translation of Dr. J. C. Mardrus by Powys Mathers. 4 vols. New York: St. Martin's Press, 1972.

Boratov, Pertev Naili. *Contes turcs*. Paris: Editions Erasme, 1955.

Bushnaq, Inea, trans. and ed. *Arab Folktales*. New York: Pantheon Books, 1986.

al-Bustānī, Karam. *Ḥikāyāt lubnānīyah* (Lebanese Folktales). Beirut: Dār Ṣādir, 1961.

Calvino, Italo. *Italian Folktales*. New York: Pantheon Books, 1980.

Campbell, Charles G. *From Town and Tribe*. London: Ernest Benn, 1952.

———. *Tales from the Arab Tribes*. New York: Macmillan, 1950.

———. *Told in the Market Place*. London: Ernest Benn, 1954.

Canaan, Taufik. *Aberglaube und Volksmedizin im Lande der Bibel. Abhandlungen des Hamburgischen Kolonialinstituts* XX (1914).

———. "The Child in Palestinian Arab Superstition." *Journal of the Palestine Oriental Society* VII (1927): 159–186.

———. "The Curse in Palestinian Folklore." *Journal of the Palestine Oriental Society* XV (1935): 235–279.

———. "Dämonenglaube im Lande der Bibel." *Morgenland Darstellung aus Geschichte und Kultur des Ostens* XXI (1929): 1–63.

———. "Haunted Springs and Water Demons in Palestine." *Journal of the Palestine Oriental Society* I (1920–1921): 153–170.

———. *Mohammedan Saints and Sanctuaries in Palestine*. London: Luzac, 1927.

———. "The Palestinian Arab House." *Journal of the Palestine Oriental Society* XII (1932): 233–247; XIII (1933): 1–83.

———. "Plant-Lore in Palestinian Superstition." *Journal of the Palestine Oriental Society* VIII (1928): 129–168.

Chauvin, Victor. *Bibliographie des ouvrages arabes ou relatif aux arabes*. 12 vols. Liège: H. Vaillant-Carmanne, 1892–1922.

Cohen, Abner. *Arab Border Villages in Israel*. Manchester: University of Manchester Press, 1965.

Conder, Claude Reigner. *Tent Work in Palestine: A Record of Discovery and Adventure*. 2 vols. London: Richard Bentley, 1879.

Contes de Tunisie. Tunis: Maison Tunisienne de l'Edition, 1971.

Cosquin, Emmanuel. *Les contes indiens et l'occident*. Paris: Edouard Champion, 1922.

Crowfoot, Grace M. "Folktales of Artas." *Palestine Exploration Quarterly* LXXXIII (1951): 156–167; LXXXIV (1952): 15–22.

Crowfoot, Grace, and Louise Baldensperger. *From Cedar to Hyssop: A Study in the Folklore of Plants in Palestine*. London: Sheldon, 1932.

Dalman, Gustaf. *Arbeit und Sitte in Palästina*. 7 vols. Gütersloh, Ger.: Bertelsmann, 1928–1942.

———. *Palästinischer Diwan: Als Beitrag zur Volkskunde Palästinas*. Leipzig: J. C. Hinrichs, 1901.

Dawkins, R. M. *Modern Greek Folktales*. Oxford: Clarendon Press, 1953.

Desparmet, J. *Contes populaires sur les ogres recueillis à Blida*. 2 vols. Paris: Ernest Leroux, 1909–1910.

Donaldson, Bess Allen. *The Wild Rue: A Study of Muhammadan Magic and Folklore in Iran*. London: Luzac, 1938.

Dorson, Richard, ed. *American Negro Folktales*. New York: Fawcett World Library, 1968.

———. *Folktales Told Around the World*. Chicago: University of Chicago Press, 1975.

Dulac, H. M. "Contes arabes en dialecte de la Haute-Egypt." *Journal asiatique*. 8th ser. V (1885): 5–38.

Dundes, Alan, ed. *Cinderella: A Folklore Casebook*. New York: Garland Publishing, 1982.

———. *Interpreting Folklore*. Bloomington: Indiana University Press, 1980.

Dwyer, Daisy Hilse. *Images and Self-Images: Male and Female in Morocco*. New York: Columbia University Press, 1978.

Einsler, Lydia. "Das böse Auge." *Zeitschrift des deutschen Palästina-Vereins*. XII (1889): 200–222.

Fernea, Elizabeth, ed. *Women and the Family in the Middle East*. Austin: University of Texas Press, 1985.

Fischer, Wolfdietrich, and Otto Jastrow. *Handbuch der arabischen Dialekte*. Wiesbaden: Otto Harrassowitz, 1980.

Galley, Micheline, ed. *"Badr az-zīn" et six contes algériens*. Paris: Armand Colin, 1971.

Gaster, Theodore H. *The Oldest Stories in the World*. Boston: Beacon Press, 1958.

Granqvist, Hilma. *Birth and Childhood Among the Arabs: Studies in a Muhammadan Village in Palestine*. Helsinki: Söderström, 1947.

———. *Child Problems Among the Arabs: Studies in a Muhammadan Village in Palestine*. Helsinki: Söderström, 1950.

———. *Marriage Conditions in a Palestinian Village*. 2 vols. Helsinki: Akademische Buchhandlung, 1931, 1935.

———. *Muslim Death and Burial: Arab Customs and Traditions Studied in a Village in Jordan*. Helsinki: Societas Scientiarium Fennica, 1947.

Grant, Elihu. *The People of Palestine*. Philadelphia: J. B. Lippincott, 1921.

Grimm, Jakob L. K., and Wilhelm Grimm. *Grimm's Household Tales*. Translated and edited by Margaret Hunt. 2 vols. London: G. Bell & Sons, 1884.

Hanauer, J. E. *Folklore of the Holy Land: Moslem, Christian and Jewish*. London: Sheldon, 1935.

———. *Tales Told in Palestine*. Edited by H. G. Mitchell. Cincinnati: Jennings & Graham, 1904.

Hein, Wilhelm, and David Müller. *Südarabische Expedition*. Vol. 9: *Mehri- und Hadrami-Texte*. Vienna: A. Hölder, 1909.

Howard, C. G., ed. *Shuwa Arabic Stories*. Oxford: Oxford University Press, 1921.

Hurreiz, Sayyid. *Jaᶜāliyyīn Folktales*. Bloomington: Indiana University Press, 1977.

Ibrahim, Nabīlah. *Qaṣaṣunā al-shaᶜbī min al-rūmānsīyah ilā al-wāqᶜīyah* (Our Folk Narrative from Romanticism to Realism). Beirut: Dār al-ᶜAwdah, 1974.

al-ᶜIrwī, ᶜAbd al-ᶜAzīz. *Hikāyāt al-ᶜIrwī* (The Tales of al-ᶜIrwī). Vol. 4. Tunis: Al-Dār al-Tunusīyah li-l-Nashr, 1978.

Jacobs, Joseph. *European Folk and Fairy Tales*. New York: G. P. Putnam's Sons, 1916.

———. *Indian Fairy Tales*. New York: Dover, 1969.

Jäger, Karl. *Das Bauernhaus in Palästina: Mit Rücksicht auf das biblische Wohnhaus untersucht und dargestellt*. Göttingen: Vandenhoeck & Ruprecht, 1912.

Jahn, Alfred. *Südarabische Expedition*. Vol. 3: *Die Mehri-Sprache in Südarabien*. Vienna: A. Hölder, 1902.

Jamali, Sarah Powell. *Folktales from the City of the Golden Dome*. Beirut: Khayats, 1965.

Jaussen, Antonin. "Le cheikh Saᶜad ad-Din et les *djinn* à Naplouse." *Journal of the Palestine Oriental Society* III (1923): 145–157.

———. *Coutumes des Arabes au pays de Moab*. Paris: Victor Lecoffre–J. Gabalda, 1903.

———. *Coutumes palestiniennes I: Naplouse et son district*. Paris: Paul Geuthner, 1927. (Only Volume I appeared.)

al-Jawharī, Muḥammad. *ᶜIlm al-fūlklūr* (The Science of Folklore). 2 vols. Cairo: Dār al-Maᶜārif, 1975, 1980.

al-Juhaymān, ᶜAbd al-Karīm. *Asāṭīr shaᶜbīyah min qalb Jazīrat al-ᶜArab* (Folk Legends from the Heart of the Arabian Peninsula). 4 vols. Beirut: Dār al-Thaqāfah, 1967–1970.

Kanaana, Sharif, et al. *Al-malābis al-shaᶜbīyah al-filasṭīnīyah* (Palestinian Folk Costume). Al-Bīrah (West Bank): Jamᶜiyyat Inᶜāsh al-Usrah, 1982.

———. "Al-ṭābūn" (The Ṭābūn). *Al-turāth wa-al-mujtamaᶜ* IV (1980–1982) 13:104–107; 14:106–108; 15:80–84; 16:47–51.

Katibah, Habib. *Arabian Romances and Folktales.* New York: Charles Scribner, 1929.

———. *Other Arabian Nights.* New York: Charles Scribner, 1928.

al-Khalīlī, ᶜAlī. *Al-baṭal al-filasṭīnī fī al-ḥikāyah al-shaᶜbīyah* (The Hero in the Palestinian Folktale). Jerusalem: Muʾassasat Ibn Rushd, 1979.

———. *Al-turāth al-filasṭīnī wa-al-ṭabaqāt* (Palestinian Folklore and Social Classes). Beirut: Dār al-Ādāb, 1977.

Kunos, Ignácz. *Turkish Fairy Tales.* Translated by R. Nisbet Bain. New York: Dover Publications, 1969.

Leach, Edmund R. "Magical Hair." *Journal of the Royal Anthropological Institute.* LXXXVIII (1958): 147–164.

Lewin, Bernhard. *Arabische Texte im Dialekt von Hama.* Wiesbaden, 1966.

Littmann, Enno. *Arabische Beduinenerzählungen.* Strassburg: Karl J. Trübner, 1908.

———. *Modern Arabic Tales.* Leiden: E. J. Brill, 1905.

Löhr, Max. *Vulgärarabische Dialekt von Jerusalem.* Giessen: Alfred Töpelmann, 1905.

Lorimer, D. L. R., and E. O. Lorimer. *Persian Tales: Written Down for the First Time in the Original Kermānī and Bakhtiāri.* London: Macmillan, 1919.

Lutfiyya, Abdullah M. *Baytīn, a Jordanian Village: A Study of Social Institutions and Social Change in a Folk Society.* The Hague: Mouton, 1966.

Lüthi, Max. *Once Upon a Time: On the Nature of Fairy Tales.* Translated by Lee Chadeyne and Paul Gottwald. Bloomington: Indiana University Press, 1976.

McCarthy, Richard J., and F. Raffouli. *Spoken Arabic of Baghdad.* 2 vols. Beirut: Librairie Orientale, 1965.

MacDonald, Jan. "Palestinian Dress." *Palestine Exploration Quarterly* LXXXIII (1951): 55–75.

Maspero, Gaston. *Popular Stories of Ancient Egypt.* New York: G. P. Putnam's Sons, 1915.

Megas, Georgios A., ed. *Folktales of Greece.* Chicago: University of Chicago Press, 1970.

Mills, Margaret. "A Cinderella Variant in the Context of a Muslim Women's Ritual." In *Cinderella: A Folklore Casebook,* edited by Alan Dundes, 180–192. New York: Garland Publishing, 1982.

Mitchnik, Helen. *Egyptian and Sudanese Folktales.* Oxford: Oxford University Press, 1978.

Mouliéras, Auguste. *Légendes et contes merveilleux de la Grand Kabylie.* Translated by Camille Lacoste. 2 vols. Paris: Imprimerie National, 1965.

Namikawa, Banri. *Taiyō no somaru mon'yō: Paresuchina no minzoku ishō* (Costumes Dyed by the Sun: Palestinian Arab National Costumes). Tokyo: Bunka Shuppankyoku, 1982.

Newton, Frances E. *Fifty Years in Palestine.* Wrotham, Eng.: Coldharbour Press, 1948.

Nowak, Ursula. *Beiträge zur Typologie des arabischen Volksmärchen.* Freiburg im Breisgau, 1969.

Noy, Dov, ed. *Folktales of Israel.* Translated by Gene Baharav. Chicago: University of Chicago Press, 1963.

Oestrup, J. *Contes de Damas.* Leiden: E. J. Brill, 1897.

Pino-Saavedra, Yolando, ed. *Folktales of Chile.* Translated by Rockwell Gray. Chicago: University of Chicago Press, 1967.

Qaṣīr, Amīn. *Al-ḥikāyah wa-al-insān* (The Tale and the Human Being). Baghdad: Wazārat al-Iʿlām, 1970.

———. *Ḥikāyāt wa-falsafah* (Tales and a Philosophy). Baghdad: Wazārat al-Iʿlām, 1976.

Ramaḍān, Muḥammad Khālid. *Ḥikāyāt shaʿbīyah min al-Zabadānī* (Folktales from Zabadānī). Damascus [?]: N.p., 1977 [?]

Rhodokanakis, Nikolaus. *Südarabische Expedition.* Vol. 8: *Vulgärarabische Dialekt im Dofār (Ẓfār).* Vienna: A. Hölder, 1908.

Roberts, Warren E. *The Tale of the Kind and the Unkind Girls.* Berlin: De Gruyter, 1958.

Rogers, Mary Eliza. *Domestic Life in Palestine.* Cincinnati: Poe & Hitchcock, 1865.

Saarisalo, Aapeli. "Topographical Researches in Galilee." *Journal of the Palestine Oriental Society* IX (1929): 27–40.

al-Sārīsī, ʿUmar A. *Al-ḥikāyah al-shaʿbīyah fī al-mujtamaʿ al-filasṭīnī: Dirāsah wa-nuṣūṣ* (The Folktale in Palestinian Society: A Study with Texts). Beirut: Al-Muʾassasah al-ʿArabīyah li-l-Dirāsat wa-al-Nashr, 1980.

———. *Al-ḥikāyah al-shaʿbīyah fī al-mujtamaʿ al-filasṭīnī: Al-nuṣūṣ* (The Folktale in Palestinian Society: The Texts). Amman: Dār al-Karmel, 1985.

Scelles-Millie, J. *Contes arabes du Maghreb.* Paris: Maisonneuve & LaRose, 1970.

———. *Contes mysterieux d'Afrique du Nord.* Paris: Maisonneuve & LaRose, 1972.

———. *Traditions algériennes.* Paris: Maisonneuve & LaRose, 1979.

Schmidt, Hans, and Paul Kahle. *Volkserzählungen aus Palästina.* 2 vols. Göttingen: Vandenhoeck & Ruprecht, 1918, 1930.

Schwarzbaum, Haim. *Studies in Jewish and World Folklore.* Berlin: De Gruyter, 1968.

Shah, Amina. *Arabian Fairy Tales.* London: Frederick Muller, 1969.

———. *Folktales of Central Asia*. London: Octagon Press, 1975.

Shah, Idries. *World Tales*. New York: Harcourt Brace Jovanovich, 1979.

al-Shahi, Ahmed, and F. C. T. Moore. *Wisdom from the Nile: A Collection of Folk-Stories from Northern and Central Sudan*. Oxford: Clarendon Press, 1978.

el-Shamy, Hasan M. *Folktales of Egypt*. Chicago: University of Chicago Press, 1980.

Sirḥān, Nimr. *Al-ḥikāyah al-shaᶜbīyah al-filasṭīnīyah* (The Palestinian Folktale). Beirut: Al-Muʾassasah al-ᶜArabīyah li-l-Dirāsāt wa-al-Nashr, 1974.

———. *Mawsūᶜat al-fūlklūr al-filasṭīnī* (Encyclopedia of Palestinian Folklore). Amman, 1977–1981. Published by the author.

Spitta-Bey, Wilhelm (Guillaume). *Contes arabes modernes*. Leiden: E. J. Brill, 1833.

———. *Grammatik des arabischen Vulgärdialektes von Aegypten*. Leipzig: J. C. Hinrichs, 1880.

Spoer, Hans, and E. Nasrallah Haddad. *Manual of Spoken Palestinian Arabic for Self-Instruction*. Jerusalem: Syrisches Waisenhaus, 1909.

Stephan, Stephan H. "Animals in Palestinian Folklore." *Journal of the Palestine Oriental Society* V (1925): 92–155; VIII (1928): 65–112.

———. "Palestinian Animal Stories and Fables." *Journal of the Palestine Oriental Society* III (1923): 167–190.

———. "Studies in Palestinian Custom and Folklore III: Modern Palestinian Parallels to the *Song of Songs*." *Journal of the Palestine Oriental Society* II (1922): 199–278.

———. "Studies in Palestinian Folklore and Custom: The Number Forty." *Journal of the Palestine Oriental Society* VIII (1928): 214–222.

Stevens, E. S. *Folktales of 'Iraq, Set Down and Translated from the Vernacular*. Oxford: Oxford University Press, 1931.

Stillman, Yedida Kalfon. *Palestinian Costume and Jewelry*. Albuquerque: University of New Mexico Press, 1979.

Stumme, Hans. *Tunisische märchen und gedichte*. Leipzig: J. C. Hinrichs, 1893. (2 vols. in 1)

Surmelian, Leon. *Apples of Immortality: Folktales of Armenia*. London: Allen & Unwin, 1968.

Thompson, Stith. *The Folktale*. Berkeley and Los Angeles: University of California Press, 1977.

———. *Motif-Index of Folk-Literature*. 6 vols. Bloomington: Indiana University Press, 1955–1958.

Al-turāth al-shaᶜbī (Folk Heritage). Baghdad, 1969–.

Al-turāth wa-al-mujtamaᶜ (Heritage and Society). Al-Bīrah (West Bank), 1974–.

Walker, Warren, and Ahmet E. Uysal. *Tales Alive in Turkey*. Cambridge, Mass.: Harvard University Press, 1966.

Webber, Sabra. "Women's Folk Narrative and Social Change." In *Women and the Family in the Middle East,* edited by Elizabeth Fernea, 310–316. Austin: University of Texas Press, 1985.

Westermarck, Edward. *Ritual and Belief in Morocco.* 2 vols. New Hyde Park, N.Y.: University Books, 1968.

Zagloul, Ahmed, and Zane Zagloul. *The Black Prince and Other Folktales.* New York: Doubleday, 1971.

Footnote Index

References are to tale number followed by footnote number, with a brief subject identification.

Designer: Laurie Anderson
Compositor: G&S Typesetters, Inc.
Text: 10/13 Bembo
Display: Weiss Italic
Printer: Maple-Vail Book Mfg. Group
Binder: Maple-Vail Book Mfg. Group